RIGOS PRIMER SERIES

MULTISTATE PERFORMANCE

2018 EDITION

Table of Contents

Chapter	Subject	Page
1	**Introduction and Success on the MPT**	1-1
2	**Persuasive Briefs**	
	Text	2-17
	Working Through a Sample Question and Answer	2-24
	Practice Question 1	2-61
	Grading Guide / Sample Answer to Practice Question 1	2-91
	Practice Question 2	2-97
	Grading Guide / Sample Answer to Practice Question 2	2-127
3	**Objective Memoranda**	
	Text	3-135
	Working Through a Sample Question and Answer	3-140
	Practice Question 1	3-173
	Grading Guide / Sample Answer to Practice Question 1	3-199
	Practice Question 2	3-205
	Grading Guide / Sample Answer to Practice Question 2	3-231
4	**Office Tasks**	
	Text	4-239
	Working Through a Sample Question and Answer	4-244
	Practice Question 1	4-279
	Grading Guide / Sample Answer to Practice Question 1	4-297
	Practice Question 2	4-301
	Grading Guide / Sample Answer to Practice Question 2	4-323
5	**Litigation Tasks**	
	Text	5-331
	Working Through a Sample Question and Answer	5-336
	Practice Question	5-371
	Grading Guide / Sample Answer to Practice Question	5-393
6	**Professional Responsibility Material**	6-397
	Index	

Course 5329. Copyright 2018 by Rigos UBE Review Series – MPT.

PREFACE

Welcome to the 2018 Rigos Primer Series UBE Uniform Bar Exam books. Thank you for purchasing our Multistate Performance Test (MPT) textbook. This is all you need to pass the United States MPT administered by the National Conference of Bar Examiners (NCBE). Please begin by carefully reading the introductory chapter. It contains valuable information about the MPT exam and insights into the question characteristics of the tasks. The chapter also serves as your tasks planning session and road map for successfully passing the MPT.

EDITORIAL DIRECTION

James J. Rigos is an Attorney-CPA, a graduate of Boston University Law School, and Editor-in-Chief of the creating team of this Primer Series Review Series. He has written and lectured for professional associations and Bar and CPA exam review programs for 40 years. Mr. Rigos is a national Director and former Officer of the American Academy of Attorney-CPAs and chairs their national ethics and dual practice committee. The author also publishes a series of other CLE and CPE courses focusing on professional ethics. Professors Maretta Ward, Jean Rocklin, and Matt Conrad contributed significant editorial assistance in the development of this MPT review material.

ACKNOWLEDGEMENTS

This work product was substantially enriched because of the encouragement and editorial involvement of many thoughtful individuals. Laura Colberg, Matt Conrad, Tracy Duany, Drew Foerster, Lisa Goldoftas, Leah Golshani, Michelle Johnson, Steve Johnson, Rachel Levine, Gina Lowe, Carolyn Plant, Aaron Rocke, Joanna Roth, Tom Smith, Kevin Stemp, Jason Stonefeld, Sidney Tribe, and Tracy Wood made significant drafting contributions. Law school Professors Janet Ainsworth, Jim Bond, Mark Chinen, David DeWolf, Sam Donaldson, Christian Halliburton, Gregory Hicks, Lisa Kelly, Tom Lininger, Peter Nicolas, John Parry, Elizabeth Porter, Chris Rigos, and Karl Tegland made important suggestions on substantive improvements and reviewed portions of the UBE textbooks. A special thanks to our past students for their many suggestions of substantive improvement and creative new learning aids. Their recommendations and successes are a part of every page of this Rigos Primer Series UBE Offerings.

TRADEMARK PROTECTION

The mark Magic Memory Outlines® and Make Your Own Exam® is a registered trademark owned by Rigos Professional Education Programs, Ltd., 2018.

COPYRIGHT PROTECTION

All textual coverage, acronyms – mnemonics, prior exam distributions, practice task questions and answers in this course are copyrighted as to substantive and compilation originality. Library of Congress registered. Unauthorized mechanical, digital, or electronic reproduction, transcription, or republication is a violation of federal law. Parties wanting to make approved use of this material should contact Jim Rigos prior to such use and receive written permission: 310 Sander Building, 4105 East Madison St., Seattle, WA 98112; Telephone (206) 624-0716, Fax (206) 624-0731, e-mail rigos@rigos.net. This MPT Review is part of the Primer Series family of professional education and ethics courses published and licensed by Rigos. These courses are distributed through Lexis-Nexis, various universities, law schools, and professional associations. Go to www.Rigos.net for additional information.

RIGOS PRIMER SERIES REVIEW
OTHER RELATED UBE COURSES

If you **liked** this UBE Performance Test (MPT) course, you **will love** our other Multistate 2018 Series publications and home study programs. Included are:

1. UNIFORM MBE OBJECTIVE MULTIPLE-CHOICE EXAM – 2 Volumes
Volume 1 – Contracts, Torts, and Property - www.createspace.com/7369335
Volume 2 – Evidence, Constitutional Law, Criminal Law and Procedure, and Federal Civil Procedure - www.createspace.com/7369381

- Succinct explanations of the **most frequently tested MBE black letter law** principles **without overwhelming you** with unnecessary concepts or depth.
- **Hundreds of acronyms, tips, and solution approaches** help you easily memorize elements covering frequently asked legal concepts.
- **"Magic Memory Outline"®** software available to assist you in synthesizing and summarizing the law in your own words.
- **Question Maps** relate the text subject being studied to related UBE practice Questions.
- **Learning questions with complete answer rationales** within each chapter **help reinforce learning the law as you go**, so that when you reach the more difficult practice questions, you are more confident.
- More than **1,500 multiple-choice exam questions** provide extensive MBE-style practice, as well as full answer rationales.
- **Mock 3-hour/100-question practice MBE-patterned exam set** allows you to simulate and test yourself in an actual MBE experience.
- **"MBE Secret Weapon"** proprietary technique provides subject focus, maximum MBE working exam efficiency, less time stress, and more correct answers.
- The **"Make Your Own Exam"** available on downloaded software allows you to randomly select varying topic questions.

2. UNIFORM MEE SUBJECTIVE ESSAY EXAM – www.createspace.com/7369424

- Prior UBE question **distribution charts** identify the **most frequently tested essay** subjects rules. The text is very concise and focused, containing only the breadth and depth of information you need to answer the unique MEE essays.
- **Hundreds of acronyms-mnemonics and MEE tips** to assist you in memorizing frequently tested legal elements and perfecting your essay checklist approach.
- **Five essay questions per subject** with **summarized pointer grading guides** and **full model answers** for all NCBE MEE subjects, the six MBE subjects, and professional responsibility.
- **Magic Memory Outline Software**, essay answer grading, and suggested substance content and **presentation improvements** available in our optional full service course.

3. UNIFORM MPRE ETHICS EXAM – www.createspace.com/7373521

- **Concise and focused** explanations of the **most frequently tested** MPRE subjects.
- **"Tips and Traps" section** helps familiarize you with typical distracters used by the examiners to confuse the MPRE exam-takers.
- **Over 350** practice **multiple-choice questions** with full answer **rationales**.
- **Advice on the best approach, time scheduling, and format** for answering the MPRE questions helps increase your abilities to analyze answer choices.
- **Simulated exam questions** categorized by topic in our **question map** with **full answer rationales** help to gauge your progress.

DESIRE MORE HANDS-ON GUIDANCE IN PERFECTING YOUR MPT SKILLS?

UPGRADE TO OUR *FULL SERVICE* MPT WRITING COURSE

You can upgrade to our *full service* 2018 MPT course. It includes detailed grading feedback and advice on how you can improve your bar exam task answers. All graders passed their bar exam with Rigos and scored high. Included are:

- Three full 90-minute MPT questions containing typical task memorandum, library, and file.

- Realistic competitive grades and feedback on your task work product, including a detailed grading guide, and a preferable sample model answer.

- Included are specific tips and suggestions covering opportunities to improve your organization and presentation skills.

- We provide you the opportunity to consider the grader's advice, make corrections, and resubmit your improved task answer for a second review.

- By incorporating our suggestions you concentrate on correcting your omissions and adding grader appeal. This is the technique that improves a good task answer and improves your own editorial skills while creating your full-set of model task answers.

- Email and/or telephone access one-on-one grader discussion sessions, which are scheduled after the student has completed at least two task questions. At this point we have sufficient information to further coach you on improving your individual task writing style, analytical skills, and presentation style.

Register at http://www.rigos.net/content.asp?ID=122.

PRACTICE MAKES PERFECT AND RIGOS MAKES PRACTICE EASY

RIGOS PRIMER SERIES UBE REVIEW

MULTISTATE PERFORMANCE TEST (MPT) REVIEW

CHAPTER 1

INTRODUCTION AND SUCCESS ON THE UBE's MPT

Introduction and Table of Contents

I. **INTRODUCTION** 1-3
    A. Summary of Introduction Chapter Orientation
    B. Uniform Bar Exam (UBE) Component
    C. Focused, Positive Mental Attitude
    D. MPT Exam Details
        1. When Is the MPT Given?
        2. Where Is the MPT Required?
        3. Presentation and Type Size
    E. Typed Versus Handwritten Answers

II. **MPT MYTHS, RUMORS, AND FACTS** 1-5
    A. Myth #1: The MBE Is the Only Key to Passing to the Bar Exam
    B. Myth #2: MPT Scores Are Not Important
    C. Myth #3: It Is Impossible to Prepare for the MPT
    D. Myth #4: No Approach Works for Every MPT Question

III. **QUESTION DETAILS** 1-5
    A. Question Source
    B. Grading System
        1. Scoring
        2. Combining the Score With Other Bar Exam Parts
    C. Skills Tested
        1. Description
        2. The Bottom Line
        3. Practice the MPT Skills
    D. Structure of an MPT Question
        1. File
        2. Library
    E. Table of Contents
    F. Other Things to Know About the MPT
        1. Jurisdiction
        2. Citations

IV. **TYPES OF MPT QUESTIONS** 1-8
    A. Persuasive Briefs
    B. Objective Memoranda
    C. Other "Office Tasks"
    D. Other "Litigation Tasks"
    E. Combined Questions
    F. Unusual Task?

  G. Professional Responsibility Issues
    1. February, 2017
    2. July, 2014
    3. February, 2013
    4. July, 2011
    5. July, 2010

V. **MPT QUESTION CHARACTERISTICS**   1-10
  A. Strategies to Avoid Pitfalls
    1. "Red Herrings" and "Seductive Distracters"
    2. "Persuasive Memoranda"
  B. Rigos MPT Approach
    1. Organization Necessary
    2. Reading Tips
    3. Time Management
    4. Writing Style and Format

VI. **RECOMMENDED MPT PREPARATION PROGRAM**   1-12
  A. Substantial Effort Necessary
    1. Disassemble Book
    2. You Must Work Questions
    3. Time Commitment
    4. 90-Minute Time Blocks
  B. Five Element Success Program
    1. Seamless Process
    2. Chapter-by-Chapter Approach
    3. Detailed Study
    4. Work the Chapter's Practice Questions
    5. Answer Critiques

VII. **EXAM SITE TIPS**   1-14
  A. Be Punctual
    1. Consider a Convenient Hotel
    2. Arrive Early
    3. Improve Morning Performance
  B. What to Bring with You
    1. Admission Card and Identification
    2. Exam Aids
    3. Comfort and Practicality
    4. Snacks
  C. Focus Only on the MPT
    1. Preserve Your Mental Energy
    2. Concentrate on the Task
  D. Be Confident
    1. Relax
    2. Exam and Poise
    3. Contemplate the Moment
  E. Go the Distance

VIII. **CONCLUSION**   1-15

IX. **PRIOR MPT EXAM QUESTION DISTRIBUTION CHART**   1-16

RIGOS PRIMER SERIES UBE REVIEW

MULTISTATE PERFORMANCE TEST (MPT) REVIEW

CHAPTER 1

SUCCESS ON THE MPT

I. INTRODUCTION

Welcome. This introduction is an overview of the 2017 edition of our Multistate Performance Test (MPT) Review Course required in 38 states which tests fundamental lawyering skills. It describes our recommended organized MPT preparation program. You should follow this advice and our MEE writing style suggestions at MEE page 1-14 to ensure that you score high on the MPT portion of the bar exam. The planning information in this chapter is important. You should study it thoroughly prior to beginning your review program.

A. Summary of Introduction Chapter Orientation

1. Learning the Process: This text contains everything you need to score high on the Performance tasks. Mastering our presented resource analysis process is critical.

2. Resources: Every assigned task has three resource components: the assignment, a file, and a library. If possible, take the MPT book apart to assist your analysis.

3. Four Analytical Categories: We distribute all the past NCBE Performance question tasks into four different categories. This is helpful for analytical and approach purposes.

4. Practice Makes Perfect: Every bar exam candidate completed performance question style essays in law school writing classes, so prior experience is not any guarantee. You need to do much more than read our editor's resource analysis and "model" answers. To do well on the MPT you must actually practice the Rigos Performance question techniques.

B. Uniform Bar Exam (UBE)

This manual is one of our Uniform Bar Exam (UBE) Series. The full UBE has now been adopted by a majority of states and 37 states require the MPT. Successfully passing the UBE allows a candidate to be admitted in any or all these "Uniform" states. In jurisdictions using the UBE, the full bar exam usually consists of three independent segments: two 90-minute MPT writing tasks; the 200-item multiple-choice Multistate Bar Exam (MBE); and six 30-minute essays on the Multistate Essay Exam (MEE). These exams are all created by the National Conference of Bar Examiners (NCBE). We offer review manuals for all these exams, as well as the Multistate Professional Responsibility Exam (MPRE), which you preferably passed during your third year of law school.

C. Focused, Positive Mental Attitude

What the mind can conceive, dedicated hard work can achieve. You must believe you can and will pass the bar exam and become a successful attorney.

1. Join the Winning Team: Your goal of passing the MPT portion of the bar exam at the first sitting is very attainable with this course. The Rigos Primer Series courses have more than 100,000 professional alumni who used our structured programs to pass their professional entrance and ethics exams.

2. Success-Focused Program: Exam confidence is the result of a well-organized and well-executed preparation program. Students following the complete Rigos Primer Series UBE "seamless process" are geared for bar exam success.

D. MPT Exam Details

The MPT is a lawyering skill-testing product of the NCBE that is administered in more than three quarters of the states (including all the UBE jurisdictions). MPT questions are designed to present a simulated law office work assignment that a new lawyer might be asked to complete as an associate in a typical firm. Unlike other bar exam components, the MPT is generally not intended to test knowledge of substantive law.

1. When Is the MPT Given? The jurisdictions using the MPT schedule this exam as a part of the overall comprehensive bar exam. Candidates usually take the MPT portion on the Tuesday before the last Wednesday in February or July.

2. Where Is the MPT Required? The MPT is now required in 38 jurisdictions, including the District of Columbia, Guam, and the Northern Mariana Islands. The list grows every year. The NCBE currently creates two MPT questions for each exam. Each jurisdiction decides how many and which MPT questions to administer to their candidates. UBE states must offer both tasks.

3. Presentation and Type Size: Both this Rigos Bar Review Series text and most of the materials in MPT question packets are printed in 12-point Times New Roman type.

E. Typed Versus Handwritten Answers

1. Check Whether Laptops Are Allowed: In most jurisdictions, you may elect to type your answers on your laptop using approved software that disables all other programs, including spell-check, on your laptop while you are using it. A few states still require handwritten answers; check with your local bar admission authority. You will likely have to pre-register to type your answers and there may be an additional charge for software. Typists must comply with deadlines for downloading the approved software and uploading answers after the exam. Typists are usually placed in a separate room from handwriters.

2. Decide Whether to Type or Handwrite: You should choose the method that is most comfortable to you and will least interfere with your thought process during the exam.

a. Laptop Considerations: Many authorities believe typed answers score higher than sloppy cursive handwritten answers. Usually more words can be put down in less time, resulting in additional time to think and organize. Typing can minimize finger/hand cramps if you are ergonomically conscious. Some states allow spell check and cut-and-paste functions. A few limit the character spaces.

b. Handwriting Considerations: Some people are more comfortable writing performance tasks by hand. Computers and software can malfunction, causing you to lose time that you will not be allowed to make up. Typed mistakes and spelling errors are often more noticeable than such shortcomings expressed in handwritten answer form. There is usually a software surcharge imposed on typers. Get several black ink, easy flowing pens. Make a conscious effort to write legibly, because presentation skills may be considered. Relax your fingers, and don't over-grip your pen or press hard.

c. Practice in Your Chosen Format: Typed answers are almost invariably easier to read. Some say typing makes good answers seem better and poor answers seem worse. All things being equal, most candidates opt to use their laptops. Turn off your spell-check feature. Bring pens in case you need to handwrite due to a computer failure.

II. MPT MYTHS, RUMORS, AND FACTS

Candidates risk being misled by rumors that the MPT is not as important as the essays or MBE. Some bar review courses may claim that passing the bar exam is primarily dependent upon your MBE score. To the contrary, a commitment to master all portions of the bar exam will improve your confidence and dramatically increase your likelihood of passing.

A. Myth #1: The MBE Is the Only Key to Passing the Bar Exam

In some jurisdictions, the MPT carries less weight than the MBE or essays. A few states may even disregard the rest of a candidate's exam if she achieves a very high MBE score. However, all components of the bar exam are important, so it is unwise to gamble that your MBE score will be high enough to qualify for an automatic "pass" or that your scores on the essays and MBE will offset a low MPT score. You should treat the MPT with respect and prepare with the diligence it deserves.

B. Myth #2: MPT Scores Are Not Important

Although every state may assign their own weight to the MPT, the score you earn is still significant to your overall performance. For example, New York used to administer only one MPT question, so 10% of the total score consists of your MPT effort. Given that state's notoriously low bar pass rate, it would be unwise not to prepare adequately for the MPT. Each performance question is usually valued the same as three essays and for serious students the MPT may be the easiest part of the UBE to pick up extra points. The difference between passing and failing may come down to just a few subjective points and your presentation skills.

C. Myth #3: It Is Impossible to Prepare for the MPT

To excel on the MPT, you need to understand the skills required, resources provided, and see the big picture. Think of this exam as an extension of your own school's first and second year research writing courses. Remember that the MPT is a standardized test, much as is the MEE. Thus, the same set of skills is important on all the MPT questions, and you may use the same basic organizational approach. If you prepare adequately, you will know what the graders want to see in your written work product. You need to learn what to look for in the File and the Library (see *infra* on page 1-7), and how to organize and plan your answers.

D. Myth #4: No Approach Works for Every MPT Question

All MPT problem-solving questions, regardless of the task assigned, are somewhat predictable at least as to organization and form. Common strategies for problem-solving success (and common pitfalls) are applicable to most MPT questions. By learning common strategies, you will increase the effectiveness of your problem-solving approach and reduce your stress.

III. QUESTION DETAILS

According to the NCBE, each MPT task is the type of assignment (in both quantity and quality) that a "beginning lawyer" in a law firm "should be able to accomplish satisfactorily." Think of this part of the bar exam as the law firm quality control entrance standard.

A. Question Source

A drafting committee of the NCBE creates and develops each MPT question. Each question is reviewed by outside experts and the admission authorities in jurisdictions that administer the MPT before the final draft is approved for publication. This ensures high standards of consistency in question quality and a uniformity in requirement scope.

B. Grading System

1. Scoring: Each jurisdiction handles the actual grading of their own candidates' answers. The NCBE provides graders guides, called "Point Sheets," which itemize issue points raised by the task and possible satisfactory approaches. Usually the graders use a 0 to 6 point scale, going down from 6 (very good comprehension), 5 (fairly complete understanding), 4 (good answer with a fair understanding), 3 (adequate but a little below average with limited understanding), 2 (below average and significantly flawed), and 1 (among the worst). A 3.0 to 3.5 average is usually a pass. Horrendous spelling errors are damaging.

2. Combining the Score With Other Bar Exam Parts: Each jurisdiction decides how to combine MPT scores with other tests given as part of its overall bar exam.

a. State Rules Vary: Most states combine the MPT and scores from other portions of the bar exam using their own formulas and weights. Some states use two 90-minute MPT questions, while others only include one task. This process also allows a state to adjust a score. This may be necessary either because of a grading irregularity or to account for local variations in the difficulty or applicability of the MPT questions.

b. Check Your Jurisdiction: For details of the passing and part combination details in your jurisdiction, check with your individual state bar. Go to http://www.ncbex.org/bar-admissions/ for a listing of state-by-state bar exam information.

C. Skills Tested

1. Description: According to the NCBE, the MPT is intended to test the candidate's ability to perform the following:

a. Analyze Facts: MPT questions contain factual settings which you will need to sift through to find the useful fact determinates that relate to the desired outcome. Some information may not be relevant or may contain "seductive distracters" that could lead you astray. You might be asked to identify additional facts that would be helpful in resolving the problem and/or suggest an investigatory or discovery plan to obtain those facts.

b. Analyze Sources of Law: MPT questions present statutes and applicable case precedent as interpreted by a court. As with the facts given, some legal authority is less important or persuasive than others. Some of their information provided may also be largely redundant, irrelevant, or inconsequential.

c. Apply the Law to the Facts to Solve a Client's Problem: Clients seek a lawyer's advice because they have a legal problem that needs to be resolved. Problem-solving skills start with factual analysis and applicable legal issue-spotting. The relevant facts must be applied to the controlling law. Consider preparing an inventory planning sheet. This helps you develop the optimum action plan to create the required written work product that will resolve the problem. These steps involve fundamental lawyering skills.

d. Communicate in Writing: The graders expect you to "know your audience." For example, a letter to a layperson calls for a less formal and sophisticated tone than a letter addressed to a senior law firm partner. If writing to a layperson, such as a firm client, you will need to explain legal concepts in a manner understandable to a non-lawyer. A document prepared for filing or presentation in court usually calls for more formal tone. Regardless of the audience, you should always write in a clear, concise, organized, and professional manner. Your work product should look as if it was created by an attorney.

e. Work Under Time Pressure: Students who have worked in a law office may actually be at a disadvantage on the MPT. In the real-world practice of law, it is very unlikely that you would be asked to perform the necessary research, organize, and draft a final legal document in only a relatively short 90 minutes. Remember that all the law you need is contained within the closed world of the MPT question booklet. Also keep in mind that the graders understand the time pressure; they do not expect you to write an answer that is polished and error-free. Still your performance task answers must be your best effort.

f. Spot and Handle Ethics Issues: Some MPT questions require you to recognize and address ethical dilemmas. If a question contains a lawyer's ethical quandary, you may be told explicitly what the issues are. Ethical issues may also be implicitly at issue. Resolving the substantive task and exploring any ethical consequences will be your main objectives. Look for the words "lawyer" and/or "attorney" in the fact pattern for a potential application of the ABA Model Rules of Professional Conduct (RPC). See chapter 6 *infra* at page 397.

2. The Bottom Line: The MPT, for the most part, evaluates your written analytical legal reasoning and presentation skills. This includes applying the relevant legal rule or standard to the facts and discussing whether the facts meet the rule requirements. You must identify the issues, locate the relevant controlling authority, and organize your planned presentation.

3. Practice the MPT Skills Tested: To become proficient at and comfortable with the skills tested on the MPT requires practice. Merely reading old questions is not enough.

D. Structure of an MPT Question

Each MPT question packet will provide two resources: a File and a Library.

1. File:

a. Task Memorandum: The first document in the File is usually a memorandum from a supervising attorney or judge assigning the task you are to complete. This memorandum is the most important part of the question packet, as it provides the requirements or "call of the question." Your answer must be directly responsive to the assignment.

> **MPT Tip:** Your answer must be focused on the specific task directions. Spend the time to prepare an inventory planning sheet and be sure your approach is directly responsive.

b. Pointer Memorandum: The File may contain a second "pointer" memorandum providing instructions as to the preferred form of answer presentation. An example is an imaginary law firm's standard format for preparing a last will and testament.

c. Other Materials: The File also contains factual information relevant to your task. Examples include letters, notes from an interview with the client, a private investigator's report, the transcript of a deposition, a draft of a contract or court pleading. These examples are by no means exhaustive, since emails and newspaper articles have been included.

2. Library: The Library contains all of the law you need to perform the task; do not go beyond what is presented for legal authority. There is usually a statute and two or three case opinions given. Note that the Library may include authority that is not directly relevant, but may contain helpful information. For instance, a statute may list the elements of a rule or category classification requirements in a clear and concise presentation.

> **MPT Tip:** The NCBE has apparently reserved the right to ask an MPT question that contains no Library. Statistics through the 2016 exams show that they have not yet done so.

E. Table of Contents

The NCBE does not include a table of contents of the materials in the File or Library. In the Rigos Bar Review Series, we have created such tables of contents to help you get organized and become familiar with the typical content of a question. However, you will not have this learning aid during the actual exam.

F. Other Things to Know About the MPT

1. Jurisdiction: Questions are typically set in a fictitious state, Franklin, located in the fictitious federal 15th Circuit with imaginary laws and facts. Other fictitious jurisdictions that occasionally appear in MPT questions are the states of Olympia and Columbia, both of which are always foreign states, also in the 15th Circuit.

a. Franklin State Courts: Franklin state has three court levels: District Courts (trial courts), Courts of Appeal (mid-level appellate courts), and a Supreme Court (Franklin's highest appellate court).

b. Precedent: Materials in the Library may be authoritative and binding precedent, such as Franklin cases, 15th Circuit cases, U.S. Supreme Court cases, the United States Code, or the Code of Federal Regulations. Statutes from Franklin or other jurisdictions may also be provided. Other authority may be merely persuasive, including law from other jurisdictions and secondary authority such as a treatise excerpt, model statutes or codes.

> **MPT Tip:** Legal authority from another state – including Olympia or Columbia – or, less frequently, a federal Circuit other than the 15th, will never be directly binding authority. If, however, no other relevant authority is given, the authority presented may be quite persuasive.

2. Citations: If your task calls for citation to legal authority, your citations should be simple and direct. For case law, you may simply state the name of one of the parties. The MPT is not a test of how well you know the technical *ALWD* or *Bluebook* rules.

IV. TYPES OF MPT QUESTIONS

We have broken down MPT questions into four possible task categories: 1) persuasive briefs; 2) objective memoranda; 3) other "office tasks"; and 4) other "litigation tasks." The MPT Distribution Chart at the end of this chapter on page 1-16 sets forth the general type of task contained in every MPT question given from July 2004 to February 2017 and illustrates their relative frequency. Refer to page 1-16 as you read the four task sections below.

A. Persuasive Briefs

An assignment to write a persuasive brief is one of the two most common MPT tasks. One-third of all MPT questions require the task to be a persuasive document. The questions often describe the document with another term, such as a "memorandum of points and authorities," "argument section of trial brief," or "appellate brief" that directs you to produce a persuasive document. Here you need to adopt the mindset of an advocate since you will be preparing an argumentative document that sometimes will be filed in court. Avoid equivocal, incomplete, or two-handed analysis that leads to no firm conclusion.

> **MPT Tip:** A persuasive brief question often contains a second "pointer" memorandum in the File that sets forth the expected form of your brief. This form usually includes point headings that apply the applicable rules of law to the facts of your case. An answer consisting of mere facts, a legal rule by itself, or a simple legal conclusion will not be sufficient.

B. Objective Memoranda

This is the other most common MPT task; approximately one-third of all MPT questions ask the candidate to write an objective memorandum. These questions call for a more balanced pro and con analysis than a persuasive brief, but you still need to reach a focused conclusion. In an objective memoranda assignment, your supervising attorney or judge is relying on you to provide an authoritative and neutral memorandum of authority. Note that these questions occasionally also ask you to perform a secondary task that is persuasive in nature, such as how our law firm can best defend against adverse precedent.

C. Other "Office Tasks"

Roughly 20% of all MPT questions require completion of an "office task." These could be persuasive (*e.g.*, drafting a demand letter to opposing counsel) or objective (*e.g.*, drafting an opinion letter for a client of the law firm). To answer these questions, it is important to know your target audience. If you are writing to a layperson, your work product should be understandable to a person without legal training. You should always write in a professional, lawyerly fashion, while remaining clear and concise.

D. Other "Litigation Tasks"

Other litigation tasks currently are the least common types of MPT questions and offered only two or three times. This type of MPT task will likely be persuasive in nature – *e.g.*, preparing a closing argument. In some instances it might call for a relatively neutral tone, such as drafting a set of discovery interrogatories or preparing a case planning memorandum.

E. Combined Questions

Many MPT questions include both main and secondary tasks. One MPT question involved drafting a will in accordance with the client's wishes, including disinheriting a son and vesting control of the family business in a daughter. The task also required explaining the reasoning and method used to accomplish the result.

F. Unusual Task?

The NCBE has historically tended to stick with persuasive briefs, objective memoranda, and letters. If a task strikes you as unusual, don't panic. Take a deep breath or two, and read the task memorandum carefully to understand what you are being asked to do. Remember, the MPT task is one that would be appropriate for a newly admitted lawyer to perform in practice.

G. Professional Responsibility Issues

Professional responsibility (PR) issues are directly tested on the MPT. PR issues may also be embedded in the task's facts. See *infra* at 397. Recent PR testing includes:

1. February 2017: The assignment was to prepare an internal analysis of three potential conflicts of interest that could disqualify the opposing law firm.

2. July 2014: The task requirement was to draft a law firm opinion letter containing a provision specifying any client disagreement was to be resolved by arbitration.

3. February 2013: The task requirement was to draft an ethical opinion letter regarding fees due a prior discharged lawyer in an unusual contingent fee engagement.

4. July 2011: The task requirement was to prepare an ethical prosecution memorandum against a lawyer for aggressive internet advertising and solicitation.

5. July 2010: The task requirement was to prepare a motion to quash a subpoena *duces tecum* served on a lawyer to testify in a trial and produce records.

V. MPT QUESTION CHARACTERISTICS

A. Strategies to Avoid Pitfalls

1. "Red Herrings" and "Seductive Distracters": Both the File and Library may contain extraneous, redundant, and misleading facts or law. Be sure to identify these distracters so they do not waste your time, confuse, or mislead you. Don't let them guide you away from performing your exact assigned task.

2. "Persuasive Memoranda": A common MPT twist is to thinly disguise what is essentially a persuasive brief task by changing the form to that of a memorandum. For example, a supervising attorney may ask you to write a memorandum that sets forth the best persuasive arguments for your client to make in a matter.

B. Rigos MPT Approach

As noted, you will only have 90 minutes to complete each MPT question. You need to make the most of this limited time. Work the easiest question first.

1. Organization Necessary: Approach the question in an organized manner and write efficiently. Failure to master these skills can be fatal. The following three areas of advice will assist you.

2. Reading Tips: The objective is to read as efficiently as possible. Scan everything quickly to get a general sense of the task and content of the file and library pages.

a. Read Quickly, but Accurately: Make an effort to read accurately while using as little time as possible. Focus and comprehension are particularly critical when reading the Library because you are looking for the applicable rules of controlling statutes and cases.

b. The MPT is an "Open-Book" Exam: The File and Library can be referenced at any time. You can always come back to reread something you missed or did not fully understand the first time through. Don't get bogged down – if necessary, move on and return to the problematic portion later.

c. Multiple Reads: The NCBE and most authorities suggest you gradually build your understanding of the facts (File) and controlling law (Library). Multiple reads tend to accomplish this well. Build your resource inventory and plan your answer approach.

d. Use Your Highlighter (if Permitted) or Pen Sparingly: Don't slow down your reading by extensively marking up the question task memorandum or Library material. Be very selective; no points are given for highlighting and notations.

> **MPT Tip:** Rigos has added summaries in the practice questions to create organization and reinforce a suggested recommended approach.

3. Time Management: Carefully manage your time as you proceed through the question. The NCBE suggests spending about 45 minutes preparing to write your answer and about 45 minutes to actually write it out. Some authorities suggest only 35 or 40 minutes in research and planning preparation. As you review the resources provided, take an inventory and jot down notes on scratch paper or a blank page of the test booklet. Using this overall guide, we recommend you allocate your functional time approximately as follows:

Function	**Suggested Time**
a. Instructions to exam task	
b. Task Memorandum (First Read)	3 minutes
c. File (First Read)	5 minutes
d. Task Memorandum (Second Read)	2 minutes
e. Library	14 minutes
f. Task Memorandum (Third Read)	1 minute
g. File (Second Read)	5 minutes (slightly more if needed)
h. Blueprint / Outline of Your Answer	10 minutes
i. Write, re-read, and Proof Your Answer	50 minutes
TOTAL	90 minutes

a. Instructions: Spend only a few seconds reading the instructions. After completing the practice questions in this text, the standard instructions will be familiar to you. Quickly scan your MPT exam questions to make sure that nothing has changed or is unusual.

b. Task Memorandum (First Read): The task memorandum is the most important document in the File, because it provides the requirements or "call of the question." You must be directly responsive to the instructions. We suggest reading the memorandum three times while you develop your analysis and resource inventory.

c. File (First Read): For the next 5 minutes, skim through the rest of the File and quickly jot down notes on your File inventory sheet. Identify each party, who they are (doctor, defendant, lawyer, etc.), and each material transactional event (someone being injured, money changing hands, etc.). At this point, think about only the facts and move on. You are not looking for rules in the File, only factual issue spotting, so your subsequent reading of the Library is more focused and effective. Now that you understand the facts, begin to highlight and/or underline favored wording.

d. Task Memorandum (Second Read): Carefully read the task memorandum a second time to see if you missed anything important now that you understand the facts. Begin to highlight and/or underline important wording.

e. Library: The Library is much longer than the File and thus takes more time to get through. Spend about 15 minutes reading the Library and take inventory notes on the table of contents page. These suggestions should help you get through it quickly.

(1) Statutes: If the Library contains statutes, just skim them the first time through. Don't read a statute thoroughly until after you know whether the call of the question or any case in the Library requires you to construe that statute. If a reported case interprets a statute, keep in mind that the case, and not the statute, will be more authoritative.

(2) Cases: You generally are searching for legal rules, which usually take the form of a legal test of an issue consisting of required elements. Your task answer should usually refer to all the cases given. Weave them in and keep focused on the basic facts, as your answer may need to distinguish the result reached in at least one of the cases.

f. Task Memorandum (Third Read): Review the task memorandum for a third time just after you have studied the Library material. This will ensure the details in every given resource are helpful to the assigned task or "call of the question." Remember, the task memorandum is your road map to guide you through the assigned task.

g. File (Second Read): After reading the task memorandum a third time, carefully skim the rest of the File again to find those facts that are relevant to the legal issues you have identified. We suggest spending about 5 minutes doing this, although you may need a few more minutes if your File is especially long or complicated (*e.g.*, contains lengthy transcripts). Look for facts that are germane to the elements of a legal rule. Make brief notes that assign each rule of law to a set of facts. By now, you should begin seeing the big picture.

h. Blueprint / Outline of Your Answer: Just as building a house begins with an architectural blueprint, you should create a brief outline to plan and organize your answer. This phase should take approximately 10 to 15 minutes. Jot down the issues on scratch paper, referring back to the task memorandum as necessary. Then for each issue, assign a rule of law – usually from a controlling statute or case on your resource inventory. Finally, make quick, abbreviated notes about the facts applicable to each element of the legal rules.

i. Write and Proof the Answer: Spend the next 45 to 55 minutes writing your answer from the blueprint / outline you prepared. Your time allocation will depend on the task at hand. Do not prepare a summary or use abbreviations in your answer unless specifically so directed. Quoting salient key wording from cases or statutes may be helpful. Leave enough time to proof your answer. Spelling errors are very damaging and computer spell check is not allowed. Reading your final work product backward word-by-word will help.

4. Writing Style and Format: Good writing characteristics, which we cover in detail in our Rigos UBE Multistate Essay Exam (MEE) Review, all apply to the MPT. Overall, focus on creating a clear and well organized presentation of compelling legal arguments.

a. Structure of Answer: Your answer should start by identifying the parties. Summarize the task assigned. Give your answer an attractive visual structure and organization by using headings and appropriate listings of topic and subtopic detail. Short sentences and paragraphs help. Planning these subparts of your analysis is very important. You do not want to repeat yourself and the sequence of your answer should flow logically.

b. IRAC Format: The four answer components of Issue, Rule, Analysis, and Conclusion are somewhat helpful on the MPT. The majority of your sentences in any analysis should center around a "because" or "consequently." Some students prefer to begin with a combined conclusion/issue and repeat the conclusion after the analysis of the applicable rule-fact situation presented. While this modified CIRAC is acceptable, the quality of your analysis is always the most important part of your answer. If you have difficulty completing a task in the 90-minute time limitation, stay with the standard "pure" IRAC format.

VI. RECOMMENDED MPT PREPARATION PROGRAM

A. Substantial Effort Necessary

Make the commitment to put in the hours and effort to achieve a MPT high score.

1. Disassemble Book: Consider carefully taking this book apart at the perforation, a few pages at a time. 3-hole punch the pages and place everything in a three-ring binder. This will help you to study more efficiently and save you from having to flip between portions of the book. When you do practice questions, spread out the task memorandum, File, and Library for easy reference. This advantage of spreading out the resources may not be available on the actual MPT, but it will help you here to practice building your approach skills.

2. You Must Work Questions: Aim to complete all the Rigos questions before you sit for the MPT. You may download, at no charge, the MPT information booklet that contains past MPT questions along with their "Point Sheet" grading guides; see http://www.ncbex.org/study-aids/. This website also allows you to purchase printed copies and electronic downloads of recent questions with "official answers."

3. Time Commitment: The total necessary preparation time depends largely on your legal work experience and how efficient you are in learning the particulars of the MPT.

a. Time Variables: Our successful MPT students average at least five hours per chapter studying the text and working through the sample question and answer. Students with legal work experience generally need less preparation, although they still need to become proficient at working within the artificially short amount of time given to complete MPT tasks. Conversely, a student with little or no legal work experience could need more preparation time. Some law schools and many bar associations have practice courses for 3Ls and newly admitted lawyers. If available, these can be quite helpful.

b. Do It Right: It is a mistake to underestimate the necessary effort required to pass the MPT portion of the exam. This is a very competitive exercise and you must practice to gain the necessary MPT skills. The prudent approach is to aim for a healthy margin of safety.

c. Strive for a Defensive Score: Bar exam graders required to defend a low score of less than 3 out of 6 they gave typically cite one or more of four deficiency justifications. First, the answer is poorly organized. Second, some important issues were not identified. Third, the quality of analysis was inadequate. Fourth, too many spelling errors.

4. 90-Minute Time Blocks: Get used to working tasks in 90-minute solid blocks of time. The NCBE allows this exam time for each task, and you need to be able to concentrate and complete the task within this time frame without interruption. You may need to start with shorter blocks of time and work on increasing your time without breaks to the full 90 minutes.

B. Five Element Success Program

The Rigos MPT Review is most effective in a structured learning environment.

1. Seamless Process: A multi-step approach works best because you are exposed to the question nuances from many different viewpoints. The result is a complete preparation program and a seamless process that leaves nothing to chance. This total integrated preparation effort is more effective than the sum of the individual parts.

2. Chapter-by-Chapter Approach: The most efficient approach is to master one of our four functional chapters in each learning session, allocating at least 3-5 hours per chapter. You need to read carefully, learn the material and approach, and review the sample question. When beginning a new chapter, it is helpful to quickly scan the chapter's topic coverage before digging into the details. We cover only what is tested on the MPT.

3. Detailed Study: Study the chapter's text slowly and carefully. Pay particular attention to the MPT Tips that point out common pitfalls, distracters, and technique suggestions. Be sure to read and understand the "Working Through a Sample Question" section in each chapter. Editors' summaries are integrated into the File and Library sections to help you learn the recommended solution approach. Spend sufficient time on sample questions to become comfortable with the structure of each particular type of assignment.

4. Work the Chapter's Practice Questions: Next, work the practice questions at the end of the chapter. The editors' summaries of the File and Library are not given for the practice questions, but you may want to prepare your own. Start by spending 2 hours on a question. As you practice more questions, gradually reduce your time to 90 minutes.

5. Answer Critiques: After each practice question, we have provided a sample grading guide with a list of key factual and legal points. Use the grading guides to evaluate their answer coverage as compared with yours as to organization and content. Also compare and contrast your issue-by-issue analysis with the model answer. Consider this as a learning opportunity and go back to the File and Library to identify your weaknesses so you can improve. Some serious students redo their first attempt to create a "model answer."

> **MPT Tip:** The number 1 reason students do not pass the MPT is because they did not practice. Merely reading this book is only the first step. You must work our practice questions to pass.

VII. EXAM SITE TIPS

A. Be Punctual

1. Consider a Convenient Hotel: Consider a hotel within walking distance from the exam site to avoid all problems and stresses of traveling to the exam site. If possible scout out the site prior to the day of the exam.

2. Arrive Early: Don't be rushed on the morning of the exam. Plan to arrive at the exam site significantly before the scheduled starting time. If traffic is bad or your car breaks down, you won't get extra time on the exam (if you are even allowed to sit for it at all). Check in at the registrar's desk. Look over the facilities and restroom locations.

3. Improve Morning Performance: If you are usually a late riser, practice getting up early every morning for a week before the exam. First thing in the morning, review a few varied types of questions to get into the test-taking intense mental routine as you start the day.

B. What to Bring With You

1. Admission Card and Identification: Bring to the exam site the written instructions and any admission documents provided by the state bar testing authority. Also bring two pieces of backup identification bearing your signature and photo, preferably a driver's license or passport.

2. Exam Aids: Take an accurate analog watch or small clock to both morning and afternoon exams. Mini-computers, digital watches, cell phones, Blackberry handhelds, and iPod devices are not usually allowed in the exam room. Bring your laptop with the downloaded software if you will be typing. Whether you plan on typing or handwriting the exam, bring at least three pens with you. Your pens and any other permissible items must usually be contained in a transparent plastic bag when you bring them into the exam room.

3. Comfort and Practicality: Dress comfortably in the clothes that make you feel the best. Layered clothing is recommended, as it allows you to compensate for an excessively hot or cold testing room. Some candidates who are easily distracted bring earplugs. If you are going to use earplugs in the actual exam, get used to wearing them while you are practicing.

4. Snacks: Food and beverages are not usually allowed in the exam room but there may be a local exception. Do not consume a large meal or a massive amount of liquid just before the exam; restroom breaks cost you valuable exam time and break your task concentration. Eat foods that provide energy and are easy to digest (raisins, peanuts, apples, oranges, bananas, energy bars), but do not give you a letdown or make you feel tired.

C. Focus Only on the MPT

1. Preserve Your Mental Energy: Get a full night's sleep the night before the exam. Take at least one short stretch break per exam set. Fight to keep mentally sharp and intense for the task's full 90-minute session. If you find your mental intensity weakening toward the end, pause, close your eyes, and take four deep breaths.

2. Concentrate on the Task: Imagine you and the exam question are in a glass box. During the 90 minutes in each MPT session, only think about making your best effort on this exam. Personal problems should be left outside the exam room. Don't daydream or allow your thoughts to wander. Stay focused on your task at hand.

D. Be Confident

1. Relax: Consciously attempt to relax; deep, slow breathing will facilitate this mental state. Don't listen to the pre-exam chatter of nervous candidates. You do not want their test anxiety to affect you; this distraction could confuse and drain you. It is better not to talk to anyone. If the other candidates are bothering you, take a little walk away.

2. Exam and Poise: Get psyched up to make the MPT (and the rest of the bar exam) your finest intellectual effort. Approach the exam with mental confidence and poise. Think of the MPT as a game that you are going to win. Don't get discouraged by a question that appears difficult. Think of it as an opportunity to use your keenly developed MPT analytical skills. Work quickly without sacrificing accuracy. Many of your competitors have not followed a thorough "seamless process" review program and are there "on a wing and a prayer." Rigos Primer Series Bar Review candidates are there to pass.

3. Contemplate the Moment: Just before the examiner says, "Start your exam," contemplate the moment. Close your eyes and picture the bar admission ceremony in which you will be sworn in. Every lawyer has been there. This is our professional rite of passage and you will only do it once. Prepare yourself mentally to go for every grading point, and make a commitment not to leave the session early. Come off the blocks strong, focused, and determined. The most important race of your professional life has just begun.

E. Go the Distance

Fight to the end of the MPT session and do not leave any part of either task incomplete. The difference between a passing and failing score on the bar exam can get down to one or two points. Leaving any exam session early assumes your answer is perfect. Perfection is not possible on the performance exam, so use all the time available to improve your answers.

Re-read your answers thoroughly with a view toward avoiding the four most common MPT mistakes: (1) poor organization; (2) missing important issues; (3) inadequate quality of analysis, particularly on the most important issues; and (4) numerous spelling mistakes. Proofread and read your answer backward to spot and correct any spelling errors. Finally, consider the overall presentation of your task answer, especially the last portion of the document. Leave the grader with a positive last impression.

VIII. CONCLUSION

The MPT portion of the UBE is very passable the first time. Our seamless preparation program works well for those candidates willing to work hard at it. Remember, there is simply no short cut to organizing and following a complete preparation program. Test yourself by working our questions. We suggest you create a schedule that works for your schedule and stick with it.

After you get your results, please take the time to fill out the User Survey at the end of this book. It will help us to improve our course for students following you, and we may publish your ideas and thoughts. Good luck on the MPT and in your legal career.

James J. Rigos, Editor-in-Chief
Rigos UBE Review Series
January 1, 2018

IX. PRIOR MBE-MPT SECTION EXAM QUESTION DISTRIBUTION CHART

	Persuasive Brief	Objective Memorandum	Opinion Letter	Demand Letter	Will	Interrogatories	Closing Argument	Draft Document
Feb 2017		X[1]						X[2]
July 2016	X[3]	X[4]						
Feb 2016	X[5]			X[6]				
July 2015		X[7]	X[8]					
Feb 2015	X[9]	X[10]						
July 2014	X[11]	X[12]						
Feb 2014	X[13]			X[14]				
July 2013	X[15]							X[16]
Feb 2013	X[17]	X[18]						
July 2012	X[19]	X[20]						
Feb 2012	X[21]		X[22]					
July 2011	X[23]	X[24]						
Feb 2011	X[25]	X[26]						
July 2010	X[27]	X[28]						
Feb 2010	X[29]				X[30]			
July 2009	X	X[31]						
Feb 2009	X	X[32]						
July 2008		X						X
Feb 2008		X X						
July 2007	X	X						
Feb 2007		X			X			
July 2006	X	X						
Feb 2006	X	X						

---

[1] 2/2017. Prepare an objective memorandum covering if law firm conflicts of interest demand disqualification.
[2] 2/2017. Draft findings of fact and conclusions of law in a guardianship appointment.
[3] 7/2016. Draft a persuasive tax court brief highlighting arguments to support a tax deduction for costs of a home operated business.
[4] 7/2016. Prepare an objective memorandum advising a tenant of her options with regard to numerous problems in her rental house.
[5] 2/2016. Prepare an objective memorandum advising a landlord whether a handyman is legally an independent contractor or employee.
[6] 2/2016. Draft a demand letter to opposing counsel for civil assault and battery, and a memo of the compensatory and punitive damages.
[7] 7/2015. Draft client memorandum of the legal strength of their claim and recommend acceptance of the defendant's offer of settlement.
[8] 7/2015. Draft an opinion letter for the partner's signature covering client's right to dispute a bank's credit card unauthorized charges.
[9] 2/2015. Draft an objection memorandum identifying inverse condemnation recovery theories applicable to a rezone application denial.
[10] 2/2015. Draft a response to a government complaint that our client, a hospital, disclosed confidential patient information.
[11] 7/2014. Prepare a persuasive brief in support of an employee's appeal of denial of the right to leave under FMLA..
[12] 7/2014. Prepare an objective memorandum if a law firm's contract may require clients to submit fee disputes to binding arbitration.
[13] 2/2014. Prepare a persuasive brief for submission to the Immigration Authority on behalf of client married to U.S. citizen.
[14] 2/2014. Draft memorandum of potential liability for employees' use of internet involving social media and recommend relevant changes.
[15] 7/2013. Prepare the argument section in support of defendant's motion for summary judgment.
[16] 7/2013. Redraft the recording contract of a successful musical band and explain the proposed changes.
[17] 2/2013. Draft ethical opinion letter regarding fees due a discharged prior lawyer in a contingency fee matter.
[18] 2/2013. Prepare brief to transfer minor guardianship proceedings from civil to Indian tribal court.
[19] 7/2012. Prepare the argument section of a brief in support of preliminary injunction in a nuisance claim.
[20] 7/2012. Prepare a bench memorandum addressing hearsay issues and oral statements in custodial interrogation.
[21] 2/2012. Prepare a legislative persuasive brief supporting new law benefitting the client's royalties.
[22] 2/2012. Draft client letter explaining statute of limitations legal status and the consequences.
[23] 7/2011. Prepare ethical prosecution memorandum in inquiry against lawyer for wrongful internet solicitation.
[24] 7/2011. Research memorandum and draft arbitration clause for inclusion in corporate client sales contract.
[25] 2/2011. Memorandum for senior partner regarding marital invalidation and draft related closing arguments.
[26] 2/2010. Draft an objective memorandum analyzing whether a condemnation action is preempted by a federal statute.
[27] 7/2010. Draft two motions for evidence suppression based upon wrongful stop and investigation activities by police.
[28] 7/2010. Prepare Early Dispute Resolution (EDR) draft document arguing contributory negligence defense.
[29] 2/2010. Prepare the arguments supporting motions to suppress drug evidence on basis the search was conducted illegally.
[30] 2/2010. Prepare initial draft of a settlement brief containing analysis of both the strengths and weaknesses of the client's case.
[31] 7/2009. Draft an objective memorandum defending a tabloid newspaper's right to use an athlete's picture for commercial purposes.
[32] 2/2009. Prepare an objective memorandum evaluating the merits of a motion to disqualify a law firm on the basis they inadvertently received a letter from the opposing law firm that allegedly violated the attorney-client privilege.

RIGOS UNIFORM BAR EXAM (UBE) REVIEW SERIES

MULTISTATE PERFORMANCE TEST (MPT) REVIEW

CHAPTER 2

PERSUASIVE BRIEFS

Table of Contents

I. INTRODUCTION	2-19
A. Approach	
1. Objective	
2. Unfavorable Facts or Law	
B. Common Disguise	
II. STRUCTURE OF THE QUESTION	2-19
A. File	
1. Task Memorandum	
a. Supporting Brief	
b. Viable Claim	
c. Don't Stray from Requirements	
d. Point Sheets Control	
2. "Pointer" Memorandum	
a. Portions of the Brief to Write	
b. Point Headings	
3. Other Materials	
B. Library	
1. Content	
2. Stay Within the Library	
III. AN APPROACH TO ANSWERING THE QUESTION	2-21
A. Planning Your Answer	
B. Format of Answer	
1. Time Allocation	
2. Good Point Headings	
3. Use Numerous Headings	
4. Heading Combining Facts and Law	
a. Example of an Insufficient Point Heading (Here, a Pure Rule of Law)	
b. Example of Better Point Heading (Here, a Legal Conclusion)	
c. Example of a Good Point Heading (Combining the Facts with the Law)	
C. Statement of Facts	
1. Relevance	
2. Harmful Facts	
a. Active Voice	
b. Passive Voice	
3. Wording Opportunities	
D. Applying Case Law	

        1. General Approach
        2. Do Not Ignore Unfavorable Case Law
           a. Precedential Value of Case Law
           b. Conflicting Case Law
               (1) Analogize and Distinguish as Appropriate
               (2) Recent Authority Usually Trumps Older Authority
               (3) Older Authority May Still Be Controlling
               (4) Different Facts
    E. Applying Statutory Law (Including Administrative Regulations)
        1. Conflicting Authority
        2. Focused Application
    F. Applying Other Sources of Law
    G. Secondary Authority
    H. Anticipating Opposing Counsel's Arguments
        1. Bad
        2. Good

IV. WORKING THROUGH A SAMPLE QUESTION:
    PROPERTY CLERK v. GRINNELL   2-25
    A. Overview Table of Contents Instructions File
    B. The Task Memorandum
        1. Objective
        2. Negative Instruction
    C. The Pointer Memorandum
        1. Instructions
        2. Negative Instructions
    C. Statement of Facts
    D. Argument
    E. Work Through Other Practice Questions   2-59

V. PRACTICE QUESTION 1:
    PEOPLE v. WILS   2-61
    A. File   2-65
    B. Library   2-81

VI. EDITORS' PREPARED GRADING GUIDE FOR
     PRACTICE QUESTION 1: *PEOPLE v. WILS*   2-91

VII. SAMPLE ANSWER TO PRACTICE QUESTION 1: *PEOPLE v. WILS*   2-93

VIII. PRACTICE QUESTION 2:
    MORALES et al. v. PARSONS   2-97
    A. File   2-101
    B. Library   2-109

IX. EDITORS' PREPARED GRADING GUIDE FOR
     PRACTICE QUESTION 2:
     MORALES et al. v. PARSONS   2-127

X. SAMPLE ANSWER TO PRACTICE QUESTION 2:
    MORALES et al. v. PARSONS   2-129

RIGOS UNIFORM BAR EXAM (UBE) REVIEW SERIES

MULTISTATE PERFORMANCE TEST (MPT) REVIEW

CHAPTER 2

PERSUASIVE BRIEFS

I. INTRODUCTION

The task of writing a persuasive brief is one of the two most common types of MPT assignments. The MPT may refer to this document as a "memorandum of points and authorities" or simply a "memorandum"; other titles have also been used such as arguments in support of a motion to suppress on the July 2010 exam or a "leave behind" legislative document on February 2012. A persuasive brief may be accompanied by other requirements, such as on February 2011 that also asked for a related trial closing argument.

A. Approach

Regardless of the name assigned to the function, you must adopt the mindset of an advocate and argue your client's position when completing this task.

1. Objective: Your goal is to persuade the court to reach a decision favorable to your client.

2. Unfavorable Facts or Law: Although you cannot misstate or ignore unfavorable facts and legal authority, you should try to identify and distinguish them. Overall, present them in the light most favorable to your client's side of the dispute. See *infra* for examples.

B. Common Disguise

A common MPT twist is to disguise what is essentially a persuasive brief assignment by changing the form of the assignment to that of a memorandum. For example, a supervising attorney may ask you to write a memorandum that sets forth the best arguments for your client's position. You should complete these tasks using the same general strategy you would apply to a traditional persuasive brief question.

II. STRUCTURE OF THE QUESTION

The materials in the question packet will include at least three resources: Instructions, a File, and a Library. Separate your book and lay out these three separate sections on your desk for working convenience as you tackle our practice questions.

A. File

The File for the task is usually much longer than the Library. You can expect to find the following in the File:

1. Task Memorandum: The first document in the File provides you with the question requirements, or "call of the question." The format is an instructive memorandum from a supervising attorney assigning your task.

a. Supporting Brief: The task memorandum generally will ask you to write a brief in support of a client's position. This may be limited to a relatively minor motion or a portion of a brief in support of a larger important motion, such as one for summary judgment. In the latter case, the task memorandum will probably tell you which issues to address and which issues to exclude.

b. Viable Claim: The task may also ask whether a potential client has a viable cause of action. This involves an analysis of the law presented in the Library.

c. Don't Stray from Requirements: It is crucial that you complete only the task assigned. Be very alert for an instruction that either requires or excludes some defined aspects of a task. Follow the directions even if contrary to logic.

> **MPT Tip:** You must follow the instructions exactly. Departing from the directions is guaranteed to result in a poor score, as it suggests an inability to follow simple directions.

d. Point Sheets Control: The grading is tightly structured. The grader will find it difficult to give your answer a good score if you haven't covered the topics contained on the Point Sheet.

2. "Pointer" Memorandum: If you are explicitly asked to write a persuasive brief, the second item in the File will often, but not always, be a "pointer" memorandum setting forth content guidelines. You will probably be asked to write the "Argument" section of the brief, with point headings for each issue.

a. Portions of the Brief to Write: In addition to the "Argument" section, the instructions should indicate whether or not you should include a "Statement of Facts." It is unlikely, although possible, you could be specifically told to prepare additional portions of the brief. For example, you might be asked to write a short statement of the court's subject matter jurisdiction over the case.

b. Point Headings: If you receive a pointer memorandum, you can expect instructions to write point headings that combine the facts with the law. See *infra* for more information on this type of requirement.

> **MPT Tip:** As is the case with the task memorandum, failure to follow the instructions in the pointer memorandum will not impress the grader and may seriously hurt your score.

3. Other Materials: As discussed in the first chapter of this book, you can expect to find other materials in the File. Examples include a party or witness written affidavit, notes taken during an interview with a client, a transcript/video recording of a deposition, or oral statement summary from a critical witness.

B. Library

1. Content: The Library will contain all the law necessary to complete your designated task. It will be much longer than the File.

2. Stay Within the Library: Do not go beyond the materials in the Library and cite other "real-world" legal authority. You could, however, earn a few points by including a brief description of an issue raised by a well-known legal principle, such as ambiguity in a contract being construed against the drafter.

MPT Tip: Not everything in the File or Library will be critical, compelling, or even relevant. The materials may even contain "red herrings" and "seductive distracters" that have the potential to mislead you into writing an answer that is not directly responsive. Be selective.

III. AN APPROACH TO ANSWERING THE QUESTION

A. Planning Your Answer

We covered task answer planning involving multiple steps which will help you make a good answer a great answer on page 1-11.

B. Format of Answer

1. Time Allocation: The structured time spent here is important. See page 1-11 *supra* for recommended allocation.

2. Good Point Headings: If the File contains a pointer memorandum, it will include instructions on how to write good point headings that combine the facts with the law. Further, it will probably state that you should create a separate point heading for each issue. Even if you are not given instructions as to form, starting each section with a point heading.

3. Use Numerous Headings: Visual organization creates a grader's good first impression. Unless directed to the contrary, use a three section task approach of:

INTRODUCTION
DISCUSSION and/or ANALYSIS
CONCLUSION

The introduction and conclusion sections are usually presented in one undivided paragraph. The main discussion or analysis section should be subdivided by the major issues and/or points. Try I, II, III IV, or A, B, C, D for appropriate subdivisions.

4. Heading Combining Facts and Law: Do not merely state a rule of law or legal conclusion in the task assignment. The following are examples illustrating insufficient, better, and good point headings:

a. Example of Insufficient Point Heading – Pure Rule of Law Without Conclusion: A DRIVER APPROACHING A GREEN TRAFFIC LIGHT HAS NO AFFIRMATIVE DUTY TO LOOK BOTH WAYS BEFORE PROCEEDING THROUGH THE INTERSECTION.

b. Example of Better Point Heading – Legal Conclusion: DRIVER HOGAN HAD NO DUTY AND THEREFORE WAS NOT CONTRIBUTORILY NEGLIGENT AS A MATTER OF LAW.

This direct conclusion makes it easy for the grader to get their focus.

c. Example of Good Point Heading Combining the Facts with the Law: AS A MATTER OF LAW, MR. HOGAN WAS NOT CONTRIBUTORILY NEGLIGENT, BECAUSE IT IS UNDISPUTED THAT THE TRAFFIC LIGHT WAS GREEN WHEN HE ENTERED THE INTERSECTION AND A DRIVER HAS NO ABSOLUTE INQUIRY DUTY TO LOOK BOTH WAYS BEFORE PROCEEDING.

The above is also an useful point heading because it features the law and salient facts. Detailed paragraphs will follow to analyze the factual and legal conclusion of no duty.

C. Statement of Facts

If you are asked to write a statement of facts, you will need to examine the File and Library to determine which facts are important to the task at hand. The challenge is to determine which facts to include and which to omit.

1. Relevance: Summarize those facts that are relevant and helpful to the position favoring your client.

2. Harmful Facts: Do not simply exclude relevant facts that are harmful, but present them in a light that is favorable to your client. The examiners want to see how well you mitigate the damage. Consider "burying" the detrimental facts in the middle of a paragraph or sentence or writing in a passive voice to de-emphasize these facts. Compare:

a. Active Voice: "The Franklin City Police cited Mr. Larner at his nightclub on grounds that he violated Franklin's 'noise pollution' statute, Franklin City Environmental Code § 3.18.78."

b. Passive Voice: "Mr. Larner was cited by two Franklin City Police officers who alleged a violation of Franklin's 'noise pollution' statute, Franklin City Environmental Code § 3.18.78, by operating his nightclub."

Notice that the violation of the above statute by Mr. Larner has less emphasis when stated in the passive voice.

3. Wording Opportunities: Skillful use of facts may help. In reporting and summarizing the situation presented, it may be possible to emphasize or de-emphasize background facts to support your position.

a. Example 1: If the facts state that the defendant was arrested and taken into custody, the prosecution may state that "the accused was arrested by the police," while the defense might state that "the suspect was taken into custody by the authorities."

b. Example 2: Another example is a traffic fender-bender incident described by the plaintiff as a "collision" as opposed to a mere "accident" characterization advanced by the defendant. The former wording suggests reckless behavior while the latter descriptive characterization suggests mere fortuity.

D. Applying Case Law

1. General Approach: The "IRAC" (Issue, Rule, Analysis, and Conclusion) answer components you used on law school exams will generally serve you well here. However, unlike many law school exams, you are writing a persuasive brief. Most law school exams require an objective discussion of a legal problem.

2. Do Not Ignore Unfavorable Case Law: If the Library contains case law that is unfavorable to your client, you still must address it as best you can. The graders will assess your handling of the law. If possible, distinguish the facts or reasoning of the problematic authority that is negative in your case.

a. Precedential Value of Case Law: Remember, only cases from Franklin courts, the 15th Circuit, or the U.S. Supreme Court are binding. A favorable binding case will make it simple for you to raise and dismiss an unfavorable non-binding case.

b. Conflicting Case Law: You might find in the Library multiple Franklin Court of Appeal decisions, seemingly in conflict, from different divisions of the same court.

(1) Analogize and Distinguish as Appropriate: One way to handle this problem is to analogize your case to the favorable decision and distinguish it from the unfavorable decision.

(2) Recent Authority Usually Trumps Older Authority: Another tactic is to consider the dates of the cases. If one decision was handed down after the other and the second decision is more favorable to your client, you might suggest that the judge who wrote the later decision was likely aware of the previous decision and therefore intended to change the controlling law.

(3) Older Authority May Still Be Controlling: Conversely, if the previous decision is more favorable, note whether the more recent decision specifically overruled or even mentioned the prior decision. If the later decision neither mentions nor expressly overrules the prior decision, the older case remains at least arguably in part good law.

(4) Different Facts: Are there significant factual differences? If so, it may serve to distinguish the holding.

E. Applying Statutory Law (Including Administrative Regulations)

Most of what has been presented above about case law also applies to the analysis and application of statutory law and administrative regulations.

1. Conflicting Authority: It is unlikely you will come across an actual conflict between controlling statutes. More likely, you will encounter a statute or administrative regulation that provides specific protection for a particular wrong.

2. Focused Application: General statutory or constitutional provisions are unusual. In this situation, there is no actual conflict, unless something else in the File suggests that the statute is void or not applicable to the situation at issue.

F. Applying Other Sources of Law

The Library may contain other sources of law, such as court rules governing evidence or legal professional responsibility ethical standards. If so, the task memorandum will probably indicate that you need to resolve an evidentiary or ethical issue. Be sure any rule you use is appropriate for the situation.

> **MPT Tip:** If the Library contains court rules, some of them are likely irrelevant. Be careful not to let such rules waste your time by leading you astray.

G. Secondary Authority

Your Library may contain some secondary authority, such as an excerpt from a treatise or law review journal article.

1. Legal Issue Environment: Usually this material is included to help you understand the detailed law underlying the legal issues.

2. Answer Structure Approach: The secondary authority may also be intended to assist you by providing a structure or form for your answer. In the latter case, the task memorandum may explicitly tell you to follow the treatise's suggested form. Incorporate any relevant suggestions or approaches that you feel are helpful.

H. Anticipating Opposing Counsel's Arguments

Try to anticipate arguments the other side is likely to make. Frame your answer to preemptively attack them. But in doing so, you do not want to make opposing counsel's argument, only to diffuse the import of their critical argument. Compare two alternatives of a statute of limitations issue:

1. Bad: Opposing counsel may argue that this lawsuit is still timely because the statute of limitations was tolled by the "discovery rule" adopted in the *Ahern* case, and the Plaintiff could not have been expected to discover the physician's mistake until....

2. Better: This lawsuit is untimely under the applicable statute of limitations. The "discovery rule" set forth in *Ahern* is inapplicable in this case because the Plaintiff knew or should have known of the physician's mistake almost immediately. Within one week after the surgery....

> **MPT Tip:** Some authorities assert examiners pay special attention to your approach in overcoming negative factual factors and legal authorities.

IV. WORKING THROUGH A SAMPLE QUESTION:

PROPERTY CLERK v. GRINNELL

Here, we will apply the above text in this chapter to a practice MPT question, *Property Clerk v. Grinnell*. The table of contents begins on the next page.

PROPERTY CLERK v. GRINNELL

TABLE OF CONTENTS

Documents Provided for Task — **Page**

- Instructions — 2-27
- File — 2-29
  - Task Instruction Memorandum — 2-30
  - Brief Guideline Memorandum — 2-31
  - (Editors' Summary of the Task Memorandum and the Pointer Memorandum) — 2-32
  - Trial Transcript — 2-33
  - Record of Arrest and Disposition — 2-38
- Library — 2-39
  - Selected Provisions of *The Franklin Civil Forfeiture Act* — 2-40
  - *Bennis v. Michigan* — 2-42
  - *U.S. v. Metzger* — 2-45
  - (Editors' Summary of Key Facts) — 2-52
- Sample Answer, Part 1 — 2-53
  - (Editors' Summary of Legal Authority) — 2-54
  - Sample Answer, Part 2 — 2-55
- Working Other Practice Questions — 2-59

PROPERTY CLERK v. GRINNELL

INSTRUCTIONS

1. You will have 90 minutes to complete this session of the examination. This performance test is designed to evaluate your ability to handle a select number of legal authorities in the context of a factual problem involving a client.

2. The problem is set in the fictional State of Franklin, one of the United States, located in the fictional Fifteenth Circuit. Franklin has District Courts (trial courts), Courts of Appeal (mid-level appellate courts), and a Supreme Court (Franklin's highest appellate court).

3. You will have two sets of materials with which to work: a File and a Library.

4. The File contains factual materials about your case. The first document is a memorandum containing the instructions for the tasks that you are to complete.

5. The Library contains the legal authorities needed to complete the tasks. The case reports may be real, modified, or written solely for the purpose of this performance test. If the cases appear familiar to you, do not assume that they are precisely the same as you have read before. Read each thoroughly, as if it were new to you. You should assume that cases were decided in the jurisdictions and on the dates shown. In citing cases from the Library, you may use abbreviations and omit page citations.

6. Your response must be written in the answer book provided. You should concentrate on the materials provided, but you should also bring to bear on the problem your general knowledge of the law. What you have learned in law school and elsewhere provides the general background for analyzing the problem; the File and Library provide the specific materials with which you must work.

7. Although there are no restrictions on how you apportion your time, you should probably allocate at least 45 minutes to reading and organizing before you begin writing your response. You may make notes anywhere in the test materials, but may not tear out pages from this booklet.

8. Your response will be graded on its compliance with instructions and on its content, thoroughness, and organization.

File

Property Clerk

v.

Grinnell

1. Fact Memorandum — 2-30
2. Brief Guideline Memorandum — 2-31
3. Editors' Summary — 2-32
4. Trial Transcript — 2-33

City of Madison, Franklin
Office of the City Attorney

TASK INSTRUCTION MEMORANDUM

To: Applicant
From: Deena Wright, City Attorney
Re: Property Clerk v. Paul and Sarah Grinnell
Date: July 29, 20X3

On April 29, 20X3, Paul Grinnell was arrested for the crime of driving under the influence of alcohol ("DUI") in the city of Madison, Franklin. His blood alcohol level was .08 percent, which was above the legal limit. Paul Grinnell pleaded guilty to the charges two weeks ago. The issue now is the fact that the Grinnells' vehicle was seized at the time of Paul Grinnell's arrest. Sixty days ago, both Paul and his wife Sarah Grinnell were served a summons and complaint indicating that the Property Clerk was seeking the forfeiture of their vehicle, and giving them 10 days to answer. After the answer was filed, a hearing was scheduled. That hearing was today.

All our lawyers must adhere to high ethical standards, but as you know, I have recently implemented a "Zero Tolerance on Drinking and Driving" initiative. I instructed the Madison Police Department to seize and initiate forfeiture actions on vehicles being driven by drivers who are arrested for drunk driving violations. The forfeiture statute has been on the books for many years, but has never been used in the DUI context until this case.

Following the hearing, the Grinnells' counsel sought to dismiss the action claiming the forfeiture statute violated the Eighth Amendment as applied to Paul Grinnell, and separately argued that: 1) Sarah Grinnell's interest should not be forfeited under § 311-2 of the statute; and 2) such a forfeiture would violate the Due Process Clause of the Fourteenth Amendment. The court gave the parties until tomorrow to brief these issues.

Please write a memorandum of points and authorities using the city's guidelines (attached) concerning Sarah Grinnell's § 311-2 and Due Process arguments.

City of Madison, Franklin
Office of the City Attorney

BRIEF GUIDELINE POINTER MEMORANDUM

To: All Deputy City Attorneys
From: Executive Committee
Re: Persuasive Brief Guidelines

To clarify the expectations of the City Attorney's Office and to provide guidance to Deputies, all persuasive briefs, including Briefs in Support of Motions (also called Memoranda of Points and Authorities), whether directed to an appellate court, trial court, arbitration panel, or administrative officer, shall conform to the following guidelines.

All briefs shall include a Statement of Facts. Select carefully the facts that are pertinent to the legal arguments. The facts must be stated accurately, although emphasis is not improper. The aim of the Statement of Facts is to persuade the tribunal that the facts so stated support our position.

The City Attorney's Office follows the practice of writing carefully crafted subject headings which illustrate the arguments they cover. The argument heading should succinctly summarize the reasons the tribunal should take the position you are advocating. A heading should be a specific application of a rule of law to the facts of the case and not a bald legal or factual conclusion or a statement of an abstract principle. For example, IMPROPER: FRANKLIN HAS PERSONAL JURISDICTION. PROPER: DEFENDANT'S RADIO BROADCASTS INTO FRANKLIN CONSTITUTE MINIMUM CONTACTS SUFFICIENT TO ESTABLISH PERSONAL JURISDICTION.

The body of each argument should analyze applicable legal authority and persuasively argue how the facts and law support our position. Authority supportive of our position should be emphasized, but contrary authority should generally be cited and addressed in the argument. Do not reserve arguments for reply or supplemental briefs.

The Deputy should not prepare a table of contents, a table of cases, a summary of argument, or the index. These will be prepared, where required, after the draft is approved.

EDITORS' APPROACH AND RESOURCES PROVIDED SUMMARY

A. The Task Memorandum

1. Requirements: The task memorandum here provides you with a clear "call of the question," as well as all the basic facts you need. You are a Deputy City Attorney working on a case involving the forfeiture of a car, which was illegally driven by an intoxicated driver.

2. Argumentative Focus: Your task is to draft a brief to persuade the court to reject the argument by the driver's spouse that the forfeiture statute protects her interest in the family car from seizure. Furthermore, you are also instructed to argue against the spouse's position that a forfeiture would violate her Fourteenth Amendment Due Process Clause rights. Your answer must address both of these issues; otherwise, you will not have fully answered the question.

2. Requirement Exclusions: Note that you are explicitly told not to address the driver's Eighth Amendment claim. Also note that the driver has already pled guilty to driving under the influence ("DUI"), so you need not consider or address whether the driver actually violated the DUI statute.

B. The Pointer Memorandum

1. Brief Form: The pointer memorandum regarding the proper form for a brief sets forth what you need to do: write a statement of facts and write an argument with point headings. Note the instructions on how to write your point headings, which are similar to those discussed previously in this text.

2. Advocacy Rule: You are also reminded that while you must present the facts and the law accurately, you should do so in a manner that supports the city's position.

3. Negative Instructions: Finally, you are told what portions of the brief not to write (table of contents, summary of argument, etc.).

We will now examine the rest of the File and the Library.

TRIAL TRANSCRIPT

CLERK: Calling the matter of Property Clerk versus Paul Grinnell and Sarah Grinnell for trial.

DEENA WRIGHT (WRIGHT): City Attorney Deena Wright appearing for plaintiff Property Clerk.

THOMAS SCHWAB (SCHWAB): Tom Schwab appearing for defendants Paul and Sarah Grinnell.

COURT: You may proceed, Ms. Wright.

WRIGHT: Thank you, your honor. We will be brief. The plaintiff asks that the judgment of conviction in *People v. Paul Grinnell* be marked as Plaintiff's Exhibit 1 and be admitted.

COURT: Any objection?

SCHWAB: No objection.

COURT: Plaintiff's 1 is received into evidence.

WRIGHT: Counsel for defendants and I have stipulated to the following facts: The car which is the subject of this forfeiture, a 20X0 Honda Civic, is registered in Franklin, and the title is in the names of Paul Grinnell and Sarah Grinnell; that at the time of his arrest for drunk driving, Paul Grinnell was driving the 20X0 Honda Civic; and that Paul Grinnell pleaded guilty to an offense for which he could have been fined $1,000.

SCHWAB: We agree to the stipulated facts, your honor.

WRIGHT: We believe that Exhibit 1 and the stipulated facts establish a *prima facie* case for forfeiture, and therefore, the plaintiff rests.

COURT: Mr. Schwab, you may call any witnesses.

SCHWAB: Thanks. I call Paul Grinnell.

[The witness is sworn and identified.]

DIRECT EXAMINATION BY SCHWAB

Q: Please describe your activities on the evening on which you were arrested for the DUI.

PAUL GRINNELL (A): About three months ago, I stayed late at work to finish rearranging my store. I work as an assistant manager at Kroll-Mart. We just expanded the floor space of my store, and another assistant manager and I had to stay late moving stuff around. At about 10:00 p.m. we finished and decided to have a drink to sort of celebrate. That was my mistake. I hadn't eaten anything much since lunch, and I was pretty tired. I only had a couple of beers. I know, it probably sounds like every DUI you've ever heard about – but really, I didn't think I was drunk. Anyway, we both got into our cars at around 11 p.m. to head home. It takes me about a half-hour to drive home from where I was. About twenty minutes after getting on the road, I got pulled over by a Madison Police Department patrol car. The officer said that my car was weaving. He did a breathalyzer on me. It measured .08. He arrested me, and took me to the police station.

Q: What happened at the police station?

A: I was booked – fingerprints, mug shot, jail cell and one phone call. It was a nightmare.

Q: Was this the first time?

A: Yes, I had never been arrested for anything before. And I've only had one speeding ticket my entire life. I had to call my wife to come down to the station to bail me out.

Q: Now I'd like to turn to the seizure of your car. What happened?

A: My car got impounded. The officer told me that the Madison Police Department was instructed to seize vehicles involved in DUI's. Then we got this summons and complaint. It says that my car could be forfeited to the city because of this.

Q: What's your wife's name?

A: Sarah.

Q: How many cars do you own?

A: We only have the one car.

Q: And the car's owned and registered in both of your names?

A: Yes.

Q: And do both of you work outside of the home?

A: Yes, I work downtown, and Sarah works in Greenfield, about 15 miles away.

Q: How do you manage with only one car?

A: Sarah takes public transportation when I have to stay late. Otherwise, we carpool. She drops me off and picks me up. So as of right now, since the car's been impounded, I have an hour-long commute by bus each way. Sarah's is about an hour-and-a-half each way.

Q: What kind of car was impounded?

A: It's a three-year-old Honda.

Q: What's its approximate value?

A: About $15,000, I'd say.

Q: Is it paid off?

A: Yes, we actually got it as a gift from Sarah's parents. There's no way we could've afforded the car on our own. We had about $5,000 saved up a couple of years ago, and we looked around for used cars, but we couldn't find anything reliable and safe at that price. We've tried to qualify for loans, but we don't make enough money. We also had a baby two years ago, so now we don't even have any savings.

Q: Tell me more about your financial situation.

A: Well, I make about $24,000 a year. Sarah makes about $18,000. I don't know how much longer Sarah will be able to hang onto her job. She's been late to work the last week or so because the buses are always late. Luckily, Sarah's mom has been able to take care of the baby for us, but that's going to change. That's another reason we need our car back. Starting in a couple of months, we have to put Cammie, our daughter, in daycare. We won't be able to manage that without a car.

Q: How much drinking do you do?

A: I hardly ever drink at all. Once a month, maybe a beer or two. That's it.

Q: Well, thank you, Mr. Grinnell. That's all I have for now.

CROSS-EXAMINATION BY WRIGHT

Q: Just a few questions, your honor. Mr. Grinnell, was your car insured, as required by law?

A: Yes.

Q: How much did that cost?

A: About $1,200 a year.

Q: You must have had the car serviced periodically – oil changes, lube jobs, new tires, etc.?

A: Yes, but not very often.

Q: Still, you must have spent a couple of hundred dollars a year on the car?

A: Probably.

Q: And we all know how expensive gas is. Mr. Grinnell, did you ever calculate whether public transportation was in fact cheaper than driving?

A: No, because it wasn't convenient.

Q: Nothing further, your honor.

SCHWAB: Your honor, I have no redirect. I now call Sarah Grinnell.

[The witness is sworn and identified.]

DIRECT EXAMINATION BY SCHWAB

Q: Ms. Grinnell, are you a co-defendant in this forfeiture action?

SARAH GRINNELL (A): Yes, they're trying to take our only car.

Q: And are you a co-owner of the vehicle in question?

A: I am. Actually, my parents gave the car to the two of us. We can't afford to buy another one.

Q: You are employed?

A: Yes. I'm a receptionist in a medical service office but I only get paid about $18,000 a year.

Q: And you have a child?

A: Yes. Cammie, our daughter, is two.

Q: If you lost this car would your family be affected?

A: Oh my goodness, it would be terrible. Paul and I work in different directions. Usually, one of us drops off the other and then picks up after work. Public transportation isn't very good and it takes so long. It's been terrible since they seized the car. I've been late to work several times and I'm worried about getting fired. And then there's Cammie. I don't know what's going to happen to her.

Q: What about Cammie?

A: Well, my mother has been taking care of her but she's not that well. We have to place Cammie in daycare soon but I don't know how we'd get her there. And then we have to worry about pick-up. What will we do if she gets sick and they call us to take her home or to the doctor?

Q: OK. Let me ask you about Paul. Is he in the habit of drinking?

A: Oh no, almost never. Maybe once a month, on the weekend, and usually just at home or at a friend's house.

Q: Have you ever known him to drink and drive?

A: Never.

Q: So on the evening in question did you have any inkling that Paul would be driving in a legally intoxicated state?

A: No, none at all.

Q: Nothing further, your honor.

COURT: All right. Your witness, Ms. Wright.

CROSS-EXAMINATION BY WRIGHT

Q: Thank you, your honor. Ms. Grinnell, your husband called you from work the day he was arrested, correct?

A: Yes. He called around 4:30 to see if I could get a ride home.

Q: And he told you he'd be working late that night, didn't he?

A: Yes. They were finishing up a big rearrangement of the store. He said he wouldn't be done until about 10 o'clock.

Q: He also told you that he and his co-worker would go out to celebrate the conclusion of this job?

A: Well, he said they'd probably stop for something afterward. He mentioned that he hadn't had any lunch and he wouldn't have time to get any dinner.

Q: And he told you they would stop at the Roadhouse Bar and Grill?

A: Yes.

Q: And you knew he was pretty tired because he had been working so hard, right?

A: Yes, he had been working long hours.

Q: I have nothing further.

SCHWAB: No more questions.

* * *END OF TRIAL* * *

State of Franklin

Record of Arrest and Disposition

NAME

Grinnell, Paul

OFFENSE

DUI

DATE OF OFFENSE

April 29, 20X3

DISPOSITION

Guilty plea;

Misdemeanor;

$500 fine;

90-day license restriction;

DUI school

DATE OF DISPOSITION

July 18, 20X3

PLAINTIFF'S EXHIBIT 1

Library

Property Clerk

v.

Grinnell

1. Selected Provisions of the
   Franklin Civil Forfeiture Act   2-40
2. *Bennis v. Michigan*   2-42
3. *U.S. v. Metzger*   2-45

SELECTED PROVISIONS OF THE FRANKLIN CIVIL FORFEITURE ACT

§ 310. Definitions

In this article:

1. "Property" means and includes: real property, personal property, money, negotiable instruments, securities, or any thing of value or any interest in a thing of value.

2. "Proceeds of a crime" means any property obtained through the commission of a crime defined herein, and includes any appreciation in value of such property.

3. "Substituted proceeds of a crime" means any property obtained by the sale or exchange of proceeds of a crime, and any gain realized by such sale or exchange.

4. "Instrumentality of a crime" means any property, including vehicles, other than real property and any buildings, fixtures, appurtenances, and improvements thereon, whose use contributes directly and materially to the commission of a crime defined in subdivision six hereof.

5. "Real property instrumentality of a crime" means an interest in real property the use of which contributes directly and materially to the commission of a specified felony offense.

6. "Crime" means violation of any penal code section, whether charged as a misdemeanor or felony.

7. "Defendant" means a person against whom a forfeiture action is commenced and includes a "criminal defendant" and a "non-criminal defendant."

8. "Criminal defendant" means a person accused of a crime defined herein. For purposes of this article, a person has criminal liability when (a) he has been convicted of a crime, or (b) the Property Clerk proves by clear and convincing evidence that such person has committed a crime.

9. "Non-criminal defendant" means a person, other than a criminal defendant, who possesses an interest in the proceeds of a crime, the substituted proceeds of a crime or an instrumentality of a crime.

10. "Property Clerk" means all persons appointed or elected by counties or cities to maintain custody of property subject to forfeiture and to initiate and prosecute forfeiture actions.

§ 311 Procedures

1. A civil action may be commenced by the Property Clerk against a criminal defendant or non-criminal defendant to forfeit the property which constitutes the proceeds of a crime, the substituted proceeds of a crime, an instrumentality of a crime or the real property instrumentality of a crime, or to recover a money judgment in an amount equivalent in value to the property which constitutes the proceeds of a crime, the substituted proceeds of a crime, an instrumentality of a crime, or the real property instrumentality of a crime. Any action under this article must be commenced within five years of the commission of the crime and shall be civil, remedial in nature, and shall not be deemed to be a penalty or criminal forfeiture for any purpose.

2. No property shall be forfeited under this section if, and to the extent that, the property is held by an owner who did not know of, or consent to, the act or omission constituting the crime.

3. In a forfeiture action commenced by the Property Clerk against a criminal defendant or a non-criminal defendant, the burden shall be upon the Property Clerk to prove by a preponderance of the evidence the facts necessary to establish a claim for forfeiture.

4. An action for forfeiture shall be commenced by service pursuant to this chapter of a summons with notice or summons and verified complaint. No person shall forfeit any right, title, or interest in any property who is not a defendant in the action.

BENNIS v. MICHIGAN

United States Supreme Court (1996)

Petitioner Tina Bennis ("Bennis") was a joint owner, with her husband, John, of an automobile in which her husband engaged in sexual activity with a prostitute. A Michigan court ordered the automobile forfeited as a public nuisance, with no offset for her interest, notwithstanding her lack of knowledge of her husband's activity. We granted certiorari in order to determine whether Michigan's abatement scheme has deprived petitioner of her interest in the forfeited car without due process, in violation of the Fourteenth Amendment. We affirm.

Detroit police arrested John after observing him engaged in a sexual act with a prostitute in the automobile while it was parked on a Detroit city street. John was convicted of gross indecency. The State then sued both Bennis and her husband, John, to have the car declared a public nuisance and abated as such under Michigan's forfeiture law.

Bennis defended against the abatement of her interest in the car on the ground that, when she entrusted her husband to use the car, she did not know that he would use it to violate Michigan's indecency law. The Wayne County Circuit Court rejected this argument, declared the car a public nuisance, and ordered the car's abatement. In reaching this disposition, the trial court judge recognized the remedial discretion he had under Michigan's case law. He took into account the couple's ownership of "another automobile," so they would not be left "without transportation." He also mentioned his authority to order the payment of one-half of the sale proceeds, after the deduction of costs, to "the innocent co-title holder." He declined to order such a division of sale proceeds in this case because of the age and value of the car (an 11-year-old Pontiac sedan recently purchased by John and Tina Bennis for $600); he commented in this regard: "There's practically nothing left minus costs in a situation such as this."

The gravamen of Bennis' due process claim is not that she was denied notice or an opportunity to contest the abatement of her car; she was accorded both. Rather, she claims she was entitled to contest the abatement by showing she did not know her husband would use it to violate Michigan's indecency law. But a long and unbroken line of cases holds that an owner's interest in property may be forfeited by reason of the use to which the property is put even though the owner did not know that it was to be put to such use.

In *Calero-Toledo v. Pearson Yacht Leasing Co.* (1974), the most recent decision on point, this Court concluded that "the innocence of the owner of property subject to forfeiture has almost uniformly been rejected as a defense." Petitioner is in the same position as the various owners involved in the forfeiture cases beginning with the earliest in 1827. She did not know that her car would be used in an illegal activity that would subject it to forfeiture. But under these cases the Due Process Clause of the Fourteenth Amendment does not protect her interest against forfeiture by the government.

Petitioner relies on a passage from *Calero-Toledo*, that "it would be difficult to reject the constitutional claim of . . . an owner who proved not only that he was uninvolved in and unaware of the wrongful activity, but also that he had done all that reasonably could be expected to prevent the proscribed use of his property." But she concedes that this comment was *obiter dictum*, and "it is to the holdings of our cases, rather than their *dicta*, that we must attend." And the *holding* of *Calero-Toledo* on this point was that the interest of a yacht rental company in one of its leased yachts could be forfeited because of its use for transportation of controlled substances, even though the company was "in no way involved in the criminal enterprise carried on by [the] lessee" and "had no knowledge that its property was being used in connection with or in violation of [Puerto Rican Law]." Petitioner has made no showing beyond that here.

In *Altman v. U. S.* (1993), this Court held that because "forfeiture serves, at least in part, to punish the owner," forfeiture proceedings are subject to the limitations of the Eighth Amendment's prohibition against excessive fines. There was no occasion in that case to deal with the validity of the "innocent-owner defense," other than to point out that if a forfeiture statute allows such a defense, the defense is additional evidence that the statute itself is "punitive" in motive. In this case, however, Michigan's Supreme Court emphasized with respect to the forfeiture proceeding at issue: "It is not contested that this is an equitable action," in which the trial judge has discretion to consider "alternatives [to] abating the entire interest in the vehicle."

In any event, for the reasons pointed out in *Calero-Toledo*, forfeiture also serves a deterrent purpose distinct from any punitive purpose. Forfeiture of property prevents illegal uses "both by preventing further illicit use of the [property] and by imposing an economic penalty, thereby rendering illegal behavior unprofitable." This deterrent mechanism is hardly unique to forfeiture. For instance, because Michigan also deters dangerous driving by making a motor vehicle owner liable for the negligent operation of the vehicle by a driver who had the owner's consent to use it, petitioner was also potentially liable for her husband's use of the car in violation of Michigan negligence law. The law thus builds a secondary defense against a forbidden use and precludes evasions by dispensing with the necessity of judicial inquiry as to collusion between the wrongdoer and the alleged innocent owner.

We conclude today, as we concluded 75 years ago, that the cases authorizing actions of the kind at issue are "too firmly fixed in the punitive and remedial jurisprudence of the country to be now displaced." The State here sought to deter illegal activity that contributes to neighborhood deterioration and unsafe streets. The Bennis automobile, it is conceded, facilitated and was used in criminal activity. Both the trial court and the Michigan Supreme Court followed our longstanding practice, and the judgment of the Supreme Court of Michigan is therefore affirmed.

U.S. v. METZGER

United States Court of Appeals, 2d Circuit (1995)

Marcia Metzger ("Metzger"), the owner of property in Pembroke, New York (the "property"), appeals from a judgment entered in the United States District Court of New York following a bench trial ordering the forfeiture of the defendant property to the United States pursuant to the Controlled Substances Act ("CSA"), as a result of the use of the property by her son Mark Metzger ("Mark") to grow marijuana. On appeal, Metzger contends principally (1) that the district court erred in rejecting her defense that she was an innocent owner, and (2) that the forfeiture violated the Excessive Fines Clause of the Eighth Amendment. For the reasons below, we reject her contentions and affirm the decision of the district court.

The land in question, an 85-acre parcel in Pembroke, New York, was purchased by Mark Metzger in January 1985 for $26,000 cash; most of that money was supplied by his mother, Marcia Metzger. In December 1986, Mark conveyed the property to Marcia Metzger for one dollar. Between 1986 and 1990, a house was constructed on the land at an estimated cost of $40,000. The property is not Marcia Metzger's primary residence; she lives some 10-15 miles away in Depew, New York.

In August 1990, law enforcement agents conducted a consensual search of the property. They found a total of 1,362 marijuana plants growing on and around the farm, 845 of them on the property itself. Mark told the agents he kept some of his marijuana on the adjacent property "because he did not want to get caught with marijuana on his property." Inside a barn located near the house, 183 harvested marijuana plants were found drying along the wall.

Inside the house, the agents found in Mark's bedroom a loaded revolver in a dresser drawer. A film canister containing marijuana seeds was found on top of a second dresser, and an electronic seed separator was found in the closet. In a cupboard accessible from both the kitchen and the dining room, a small cellophane bag containing marijuana was discovered, and inside a hutch in the dining room several packages of cigarette rolling paper and a silver marijuana pipe were found.

Mark was convicted in state court, after a plea of guilty, of criminal possession of marijuana. The United States commenced this action in the district court seeking forfeiture of the defendant property pursuant to the CSA. Marcia Metzger filed a claim to the property and contended that the property was not subject to forfeiture because she owned it and was innocent of any wrongdoing. She also contended that a forfeiture of the property would violate the Excessive Fines Clause of the Eighth Amendment.

The district court held a six-day bench trial and heard testimony from Metzger and law enforcement agents. One agent testified that Mark had been arrested in 1980 for growing marijuana while living in Metzger's residence. In connection with that arrest, officers executed a search warrant at Metzger's home; in her garage, they found 1,000 containers of marijuana seeds; in her basement, they found marijuana plants, packaging material, and plant lights. In Mark's bedroom in Metzger's home, they found in plain view, marijuana, marijuana packaging material, scales, photographs of Mark standing next to tall marijuana plants, and books on growing marijuana. Another agent testified during the search of the property at issue here, Marcia Metzger told him "that she was aware that Mark had a problem with marijuana, that he had been arrested several years prior for growing marijuana at her house, and she told me that she built the farm so that Mark would have a place to do his farming."

As to the property at issue here, Metzger testified that she visited the farm once a week to cook, clean, and do her son's laundry, but that she did not have knowledge of her son's marijuana farming. Although admitting that she had gone into cabinets and drawers where the police later discovered marijuana, drug paraphernalia, and a handgun, she testified that she did not see those items.

The district court denied Metzger's claim. Crediting the testimony of the law enforcement officers, the court expressly found that Metzger's testimony was not wholly credible. The court concluded that the defendant property was forfeitable, finding that the property had been used to facilitate a narcotics felony, and that Metzger was not an innocent owner because it was too implausible to accept she lacked knowledge of the illegality. The district court also rejected Metzger's excessive-fines contention, stating that "this is not a case where a small amount of drugs was found in a discrete part of the defendant property on one single occasion. To the contrary, Mark used the entirety of the defendant property to further his advanced drug enterprise."

On appeal, Metzger argues that the district court erred in rejecting her innocent-owner defense and her Eighth Amendment excessiveness contention. We reject both arguments.

A. The Innocent-Owner Defense

The CSA provides that a parcel of real property that has been used to commit or to facilitate the commission of a narcotics felony is forfeitable to the United States, unless the owner can establish a degree of innocence:

> "no property shall be forfeited under this paragraph to the extent of an interest of an owner, by reason of any act or omission established by that owner to have been committed or omitted without the knowledge or consent of that owner."

Matters of knowledge and willful avoidance of knowledge are questions of fact, and the district court's findings as to those facts may not be set aside unless they are clearly erroneous. Assessment of the credibility of witnesses is peculiarly within the province of the trier of fact and is entitled to considerable deference.

A total of 1,362 marijuana plants were found growing on and around the property, 845 of them on the property itself. In addition, the house was used to store seeds, guns and marijuana; the barn/greenhouse was used to dry and strip the plants, as well as house the pots in which the marijuana grew; larger plants were transported across the defendant property and through a path to several marijuana fields; and guard dogs kept watch over the marijuana fields.

The trial court's finding that Metzger's testimony that she never saw Mark's substantial marijuana crop was not credible was supported by the magnitude of Mark's marijuana growing operation on the property, with some large plants growing within 80 feet of the house, and by Metzger's own testimony that in cleaning and putting away laundry on the defendant property, she had gone into cabinets and drawers where the police later discovered marijuana and drug paraphernalia. The court's finding that Metzger either knew or deliberately avoided knowing of the unlawful use of the defendant property in 1990 was also supported by the testimony of law enforcement agents, which the court expressly found credible, as to Mark's 1980 arrest for growing marijuana and the items seized at that time from Metzger's house, and as to Metzger's statement at the time of the search of the defendant property that she had been aware of the previous arrest and of Mark's problem with marijuana.

In light of the record and the credibility assessments made by the trial court, we cannot conclude that there is clear error in the court's findings that Metzger either knew of or deliberately closed her eyes to the fact that her son was growing marijuana on the property. Accordingly, we uphold the finding that Metzger was not an innocent owner.

B. The "Excessive Fines" Clause

The Eighth Amendment provides that "excessive bail shall not be required, nor excessive fines imposed, nor cruel and unusual punishments inflicted." In *Altman v. U.S.* (1993) the Supreme Court ruled that an *in rem* civil forfeiture under the CSA constitutes punishment and, as such, is subject to the limitations of the Excessive Fines Clause of the Eighth Amendment. The *Altman* Court declined, however, to delineate the factors that should inform a determination of whether a given civil forfeiture is constitutionally excessive.

We adopt the instrumentality principle and now undertake to state the appropriate standard to be applied in conducting an excessiveness analysis under the Eighth Amendment for *in rem* forfeitures. To do this, we begin by looking more closely at the historical justification for forfeiture and the effect that a forfeiture has on the property's owner.

In rem forfeitures were historically grounded on the fiction that the property itself was considered the "offender" and accordingly, the innocence of an owner was not a defense. Nonetheless, a forfeiture of property effects punishment on its owner. This appears more clearly so when, as provided in the Controlled Substances Act, the forfeiture law provides an innocent owner defense, implying that some owner culpability is being punished by the Act's forfeiture provisions. Since, however, the property itself is the object of the action, and not its value, the value of the property is irrelevant to whether it is forfeitable. The question is not how much the confiscated property is worth, but whether the confiscated property has a close enough relationship to the offense. Any analysis under the Eighth Amendment into excessiveness thus must go to whether the property was an instrumentality of the offense.

It is apparent that Congress, in providing for civil forfeiture of property involved in drug offenses for which punishment exceeds one year, did not intend to punish or fine by a particular amount or value; instead, it intended to punish by forfeiting property of whatever value which was tainted by the offense. Accordingly, the constitutional limitation on the government's action must be applied to the degree and the extent of the taint, and not to the value of the property or the gravity of the offense.

The question of excessiveness is thus tied to the "guilt of the property" or the extent to which the property was involved in the offense, and not its value. This point can be illustrated by comparing two hypotheticals. Forfeiture of a $14 million yacht, specially outfitted with high-powered motors, radar, and secret compartments for the sole purpose of transporting drugs from a foreign country into the United States, would probably offend no one's sense of excessiveness, even though the property has such a high value. On the other hand, forfeiture of a row house, which is owned by an elderly woman and which shelters her children and grandchildren, upon discovery of a trace amount of cocaine in a grandson's room, might arguably be found to be excessive, even though the house has a relatively low value of $30,000.

In both the above hypotheticals, the intuitive excessiveness analysis centers on the relationship between the property and the offense – the more incidental or fortuitous the involvement of the property in the offense, the stronger the argument that its forfeiture is excessive. When measuring the strength or extent of the property's relationship to the offense, *i.e.*, its instrumentality in the offense, we would look at whether the property's role was supportive, important, or even necessary to the success of the illegal activity. We would also inquire into whether the use of the property was deliberate or planned, as distinguished from incidental or fortuitous. We would note whether the property was used once or repeatedly, whether a small portion was used, and whether the property was put to other uses and the extent of those uses.

While our aim under this instrumentality test for determining excessiveness is directed at discovering the property's role in the offense, we are also mindful that the punishment effected by a forfeiture is imposed on the owner. Thus, while the extent of the owner's culpability may be of minor relevance to the question of whether a forfeiture can properly be imposed, it becomes more relevant when determining whether the "fine" is excessive. Thus, where the owner's involvement in the offense is only incidental, as opposed to extensive – *e.g.*, where he is simply aware of the offense but not a perpetrator or conspirator – this fact will weigh on the excessiveness side of the scales.

Finally, we note that since the property in kind is at stake, and not its value, a judgment of forfeiture is largely an all-or-nothing situation, and an inquiry into excessiveness can determine only on which side of the line the facts place the property. We might very well say that it would be an excessive fine to forfeit a building in which an isolated drug sale happens to occur, but that it would not be excessive to forfeit a building that acted solely as a drug emporium for packaging, selling, distributing, and using drugs. However, a concern about excessiveness may be tempered by the pragmatic possibility of separating offensive property from property not implicated, when the offending property is readily separable.

For these reasons, we now hold, in determining excessiveness of an *in rem* forfeiture under the Eighth Amendment, that a court must apply a three-part instrumentality test that considers (1) the nexus between the offense and the property and the extent of the property's role in the offense, (2) the role and culpability of the owner, and (3) the possibility of separating offending property that can readily be separated from the remainder. In measuring the strength and extent of the nexus between the property and the offense, a court may take into account the following factors: (1) whether the use of the property in the offense was deliberate and planned or merely incidental and fortuitous; (2) whether the property was important to the success of the illegal activity; (3) the time during which the property was illegally used and the spatial extent of its use; (4) whether its illegal use was an isolated event or had been repeated; and (5) whether the purpose of acquiring, maintaining or using the property was to carry out the offense. No one factor is dispositive, but to sustain a forfeiture against an Eighth Amendment challenge, the court must be able to conclude, under the totality of circumstances, that the property was a substantial and meaningful instrumentality in the commission of the offense, or would have been, had the offensive conduct been carried out as intended.

Addressing first the nexus between the property and the offense, Metzger's property served as the *situs* for a significant marijuana operation comprising cultivation, storage and processing. While it would appear that the farm had some purposes other than serving as an instrument of drug

activity, the property nevertheless was an important, if not necessary, instrument for the drug activity, in providing a secluded location.

On the extent of the use of the property for illegal activities, evidence showed not only the large number of plants growing on the property, but also that the use permeated to the barn and the house.

Considering the second part of the test, the role and culpability of Metzger, it can hardly be argued that she was not culpable. Though she was not prosecuted for or convicted of any offense, the court's findings plainly indicated that she had a significant degree of culpability in the criminal use of the property. The court found that Metzger "would have to have been blind not to have been aware of her son's marijuana activities, or would have to have consciously and purposefully ignored signs of such activities." The trial court determined that her testimony that she was not aware was "simply not credible." Those findings are amply supported not only by the evidence of Metzger's frequent visits to the property, the proximity of numerous plants to the house, and her forays into cabinets and drawers where marijuana and drug paraphernalia were found, but also by the evidence relating to Mark's previous arrest for growing

marijuana while living in Metzger's own residence. Just prior to that arrest, the officers had found 1,000 containers of seeds in her garage, marijuana plants growing under strong lights in her basement, and in plain view in Mark's room in her home, marijuana, marijuana packaging material, scales, photographs of Mark standing next to tall marijuana plants, and books on growing marijuana. Admittedly aware of Mark's involvement in growing marijuana, she proceeded to buy him a farm.

Finally, while Metzger has urged that we mitigate the punishment that the forfeiture will impose on her by forfeiting only the areas of the 85-acres where the cultivation occurred, she has provided no evidence that this area is on a separately platted property that could be readily separated. In the absence of such evidence, and in light of the ample evidence in support of forfeiture, the entire 85-acre property, as identified in the warrant for its seizure, may be forfeited.

Judgment affirmed.

EDITORS' SUMMARY OF KEY FACTS

C. Statement of Facts

All of the facts you need to complete this task are contained within the Trial Transcript. Two important points are to:

1. Resist the Temptation to Sympathize with the Defendants: In completing this task, you need to persuade the court to adopt the city's position. The facts, as set forth in the Trial Transcript, indicate that Paul and Sarah Grinnell are relatively sympathetic defendants. Seizing their family's only car may seem excessively heavy-handed, especially in light of their work and family childcare situations. Nonetheless, you must put your emotions aside and be a strong advocate for the city. This is one of the MPT assignments that demands you take positions many soon-to-be lawyers would often consider unpleasant and unfair.

2. Emphasize Key Favorable Facts: The facts set forth in the Trial Transcript are not terribly favorable to the city with respect to Sarah's "innocent-owner defense" under § 311-2. According to her undisputed testimony, she had no actual knowledge and little constructive knowledge that Paul would drink and drive on the night of his arrest.

3. Create Complicity: Thus, you must emphasize all the facts suggesting that Sarah should have known that Paul might illegally drink and drive. This would include arguing her knowledge that Paul had an empty stomach and would be going to an establishment named "Roadhouse Bar and Grill."

4. Paul's Involvement Important: Additionally, discussing facts concerning Paul's activities and arrest are helpful for two reasons: 1) they tell the story of how this civil forfeiture action came to be; and 2) they create a more negative impression of Sarah, simply by virtue of her being Paul's spouse and a co-defendant in this civil action.

5. Sample Statement of Facts: With the above in mind, your Statement of Facts might look like the example on the next page.

STATEMENT OF FACTS

One night three months ago, Paul Grinnell stayed late at his job at Kroll-Mart to complete a task with a co-worker. They celebrated by becoming intoxicated.

At the time he commenced drinking, Mr. Grinnell knew that he was "extremely tired," and moreover that he was drinking on an empty stomach because he had not eaten lunch. Nonetheless, he drank what he describes as "a couple of beers." Intoxicated, he got into his car to go home. En route, at about 11:20 that evening, a patrol car pulled him over for weaving across the road. His blood alcohol level was measured at 0.08, which is above the legal limit for a charge of driving under the influence of alcohol ("DUI"). He was thus charged with DUI and pleaded guilty. DUI carries a potential fine of $1,000.

Pursuant to this charge, the car that the defendant drove to commit his crime, a 2000 Honda Civic, was seized and impounded. The vehicle is registered in Franklin, and title is in the name of Paul Grinnell and Sarah Grinnell, his wife.

Although Ms. Grinnell was not in the car at the time of the crime, she was aware of the circumstances that led to its perpetration. She received a phone call from Paul at 4:30 that afternoon. Paul told her that he and his co-worker would finish their task at 10:00 that night. He also told her that they planned to celebrate by stopping at the Roadhouse Bar and Grill. In addition, Paul informed Sarah that he had not eaten any lunch. Sarah knew that he was extremely tired, because he had been working so hard. Thus she was aware of all of the elements that led to Paul's inebriation. She knew, moreover, that he planned to drive home afterwards. Nevertheless, Sarah did nothing to persuade or otherwise prevent Paul from unrestricted alcohol drinking which directly led to her spouse then committing DUI. Her inaction occurred despite the high risk that her husband would become intoxicated at the Roadhouse Bar and Grill and then committing DUI.

EDITORS' SUMMARY OF LEGAL AUTHORITY

D. Argument

After drafting your statement of facts, you will need to write your Argument. To do so, you must weave the facts and the law together, as well as create the point headings required by the pointer memorandum.

1. The Due Process Claim: You need to briefly address Sarah's claim under the Fourteenth Amendment Due Process Clause. As it has little merit in light of *Bennis v. Michigan*, it can be addressed relatively quickly.

2. The Section 311-2 Claim: Most of your argument should be devoted to attacking Sarah's "innocent-owner defense" under § 311-2. To do this, you should analogize your case to *U.S. v. Metzger* as much as possible. While a large marijuana-production operation is quite different from a DUI conviction stemming from a couple of beers, *Metzger* is the best case in support of your argument for two reasons. First, it explains the innocent-owner defense and its limits. Second, the trial court there found that Marcia Metzger knew or should have known that her son was operating a marijuana enterprise; similarly, you want to argue that Sarah knew or should have known it was likely that Paul would drink and drive.

> **MPT Tip:** Some experts would reverse the above two points under the theory one should not start with the opponent's position. Others would argue that it is preferable to first diminish the opposing position rather than deal with it later where it might undercut your best arguments.

3. Red Herrings: Beware of the discussion of the Eighth Amendment in both *Bennis* and *Metzger*. Sarah has not raised any Eight Amendment claim, and furthermore, you were instructed not to address Paul's Eighth Amendment argument. Also, while § 311-2 is crucial to your answer, most other provisions of the Franklin Civil Forfeiture Act provided in the Library give essentially no assistance.

4. Ethical Issues: While you have been assigned this role, the extremely aggressive position demanded by the City Attorney is very close to violating a Prosecutor's required minimum higher standard of advocacy. The City Attorney's new elevated policy of "zero tolerance" borders on oppressive, and this attack on a relatively innocent family may be too zealous. An associate in a law firm or Deputy Prosecutor may not engage in unethical zealous attacks for political purposes, even if so directed by a supervisory lawyer. See RPC 3.8. Still, the model answer does not contain this disclosure that would perhaps be appropriate if this task was an objective memorandum as opposed to a one-sided argumentative brief.

5. Sample Argument: With the above in mind, your Argument might look like the example on the next page.

INTRODUCTION

The issue here is whether Sarah Grinnell is an "innocent owner," and thus would be allowed to keep her interest in a drunkenly-operated vehicle taken under the applicable forfeiture statute. The negative conclusion is compelling that she should not receive this benefit because arguably she was not an innocent owner under a reasonable interpretation of the statute as guided by the controlling case authority in Metzger.

DISCUSSION

(1) SARAH GRINNELL HAS NO CONSTITUTIONAL CLAIM UNDER A LONG LINE OF SUPREME COURT JURISPRUDENCE THAT REJECTS FOURTEENTH AMENDMENT DUE PROCESS CLAIMS BY THOSE CLAIMING TO BE "INNOCENT OWNERS."

Before addressing the specifics of Section 311-2, it is useful to realize that Sarah Grinnell, unlike her husband, does not even have a potential constitutional claim against the forfeiture. In Bennis v. Michigan, the Supreme Court refused to protect a wife against the abatement of her interest in a car, even though she was not aware of the fact that her husband had used it to sleep with a prostitute. Despite her claims of ignorance and innocence, Ms. Bennis' interest in the car was abated. The Supreme Court rejected her Fourteenth Amendment Due Process Claim and justified its decision by pointing out that the self-proclaimed innocence of the owner of property subject to forfeiture has almost uniformly been rejected as a defense. See also Calero-Toledo, in which a self-proclaimed innocent owner of a yacht had his property interest abated due to a crime in which the owner was in no way involved.

The application of these holdings from the High Court to this case is clear. Even if Ms. Grinnell were an innocent owner, she would have no constitutional right to demand the restitution of her interest. Her claim must fail because of her complicity. She must, therefore, rely entirely on the defense mechanism of Section 311-2 of the Franklin Forfeiture Statute.

(2) SARAH GRINNELL IS NOT AN INNOCENT OWNER UNDER SECTION 311-2 OF THE FORFEITURE STATUTE BECAUSE HER IGNORANCE OF THE CRIME AMOUNTED TO WILLFUL IGNORANCE.

In the absence of a legitimate constitutional claim, Sarah Grinnell must rely on the statutory defense of Section 311-2 of the Forfeiture Statute. That section reads, in relevant part, that property shall not be forfeited to the extent that it is owned by an owner who <u>did not know of or consent to</u> the crime (emphasis added). Sarah will argue she is an innocent owner under the statute whose interest should be preserved because she was not in the car at the time of the offense. She will further argue that she did not expressly consent to Paul's driving under the influence of alcohol.

This conception of innocence, however, is here too narrow to be persuasive. While <u>Altman</u> held that the trial judge has discretion to consider "alternatives to abating the entire interest in the vehicle" (<u>see Bennis</u>), it is also clear under that same decision that forfeiture statutes are both punitive and prophylactic. Indeed, the city has a strong incentive in punishing not only the perpetrators of DUI, but also those who know that a DUI offense is about to occur, are in a position to prevent it, yet fail to act. The city thus has a strong preventative interest in punishing the "willfully ignorant" such as Sarah Grinnell.

This was the approach taken by the Second Circuit in <u>U.S. v. Metzger</u>. In that opinion, Marcia Metzger's land was seized for her son's drug violations on that land. She claimed innocence, alleging that she had no knowledge of his illegal use of the land, and invoked a statutory defense substantively identical to Section 311-2. The court rejected her arguments, because it agreed with the district court that her ignorance was willful. Metzger made frequent visits to the property, where her son had planted multiple marijuana plants in close proximity to the house. She forayed into cabinets where he kept his drug paraphernalia. She also knew of her son's previous arrests for drug possession, and even admitted on a prior occasion that she knew he had a marijuana problem. The <u>Metzger</u> majority thus held that blinding oneself to the clear truth, or high probability of an infraction, does not qualify as "innocence" or "lack of knowledge."

The same can be said here of Sarah Grinnell. Before her husband committed the crime of DUI, he called her from work. He told her that he would be using the car that evening to get home after an alcoholic celebration with his co-worker. He further revealed that he would be drinking on an empty stomach, and Ms. Grinnell knew that her husband had been extremely tired from working so hard for long hours. Nonetheless, she did not encourage him to take a taxi or not to drink, and she made no offer to have a friend pick him up. Ms. Grinnell may not have been in the car during the accident, but her failure to object to her husband's plans to drink with an empty stomach was a silent concurrence to a clear likelihood of DUI. This rendered her complicit to the DUI perpetration. Thus, she cannot be said to have suffered a forfeiture as an owner who "did not know of" or "consent to" the crime. Under the standard articulated by Metzger, Ms. Grinnell was as culpable as her husband.

Any distinction between Metzger and Grinnell based upon the difference between the continuing and systematic nature of Mark Metzger's criminal activities and his mother's knowledge thereof, is not controlling here. Similarly the reportedly uncharacteristic nature of Mr. Grinnell's overindulgence in alcohol is unimportant because in both cases the law was broken using the instrumentality at issue here.

(3) FORFEITURE OF THE ENTIRE AUTOMOBILE IS NOT EXCESSIVE BECAUSE THE ENTIRE VEHICLE WAS INVOLVED IN THE DUI OFFENSE; FURTHERMORE, THERE IS NO PRACTICABLE WAY TO DIVIDE IT INTO PORTIONS.

Dicta in the Metzger decision states that forfeiture of an entire asset may be "excessive" when one owner's involvement is merely incidental, as opposed to extensive. This includes situations where that owner is simply aware of the offense, but is not a perpetrator or conspirator. One might rely on this authority to claim that the forfeiture of the entire car is "excessive" under the standard articulated in Metzger's *dicta*.

Yet this argument ignores the equally important qualifying *dicta* later in that same opinion. The court went on to say that this concern about excessiveness may be tempered by the pragmatic possibility of separating offensive property from non-implicated property.

As discussed above, the Grinnells' car, in its entirety, was used in committing the crime. Unlike a piece of land, it practically cannot be broken up, separated, or sold in pieces. Therefore, the means to temper such theoretical "excessiveness" is impossible, and the entire automobile should be seized.

CONCLUSION

SARAH GRINNELL IS NOT ENTITLED TO A DEFENSE UNDER SECTION 311-2 BECAUSE HER IGNORANCE WAS WILLFUL.

The city's penal interest in punishing drunk driving extends not only to the perpetrators of that crime, but also to those who learn of its imminent perpetration yet do nothing to stop it. Sarah Grinnell was effectively advised by her husband that there was a high likelihood that he would drive under the influence of alcohol, and she said or did nothing to dissuade him. Therefore, she does not qualify as a "nonconsenting," "unknowing," or "innocent" party under the language of Section 311 of the Franklin Forfeiture Statute.

OPTIONAL ETHICAL ARGUMENT

Prosecutors are ethically restrained in that they must not bring a case unless they have "credible evidence" on each and every element required for the offense. RPC 3.8 This negative proposition – that willfulness equals a lack of knowledge – gets very close to violating this standard. Sarah Grinnell would argue that they could simply take her husband's name off the automobile title and that it was her separate property as a gift from her mother, so much more than her speculative knowledge of the future is necessary to foreclose her interest. But there are other prosecutor's arguments presented, so the totality of the case is not likely frivolous.

E. Working Other Practice Questions

1. Begin Testing Yourself: Now that you've examined a typical persuasive brief MPT question and answer, you should complete the following two practice questions on your own. Afterwards, compare your persuasive brief with the sample grading guide and answer provided.

> **MPT Tip:** One of the major mistakes students make in preparing for the MPT exam is to eliminate self-testing. It is too easy to read the Library and File and then refer to the answer and say to yourself "yep, that's how I would have done it." You need to gain experience in actually creating the task answer.

2. Learning-Testing Conditions: You should create your own conditions as close to those of the MPT bar exam as possible. This would mean you should allocate a minimum of a full 90-minute time block for the question. You will have to work up to this time limit and to start perhaps allow yourself a full 120 minutes.

3. Concentration Objective: Ideally, you should complete the answer without taking a break. Again, you may have to work up to this. Concentration during your writing time is critical. Turn off all phones and do not answer email during this testing period.

4. Grading Your Answer: After you have completed the task, use our grading guides to objectively evaluate your answer coverage. Also, you should compare your answers with the sample answers provided for substance, organization, form, and overall presentation. Don't be discouraged if your answer is missing something important or if it contains a significant mistake. Use this as a learning opportunity to figure out how and why you went wrong so you can improve your future MPT performance.

5. Re-Write Helpful: Many candidates find correcting and supplementing their first answer helpful. If you typed your answer this is quite easy, but even if your answer was in long hand, it may be worth doing. Add to your first answer any omissions you feel are important. Redoing your answer allows you to create a persuasive brief "model answer" to refer back to later. This self correction effort also reduces the chance you will repeat similar errors on other persuasive briefs.

> **MPT Tip:** Some students find it too difficult to actually spend the full 90 minute time creating their own complete answer to the questions before looking at our Editor's Summary and Sample Answer. If that temptation applies to you, you may not get the task creation practice you need to pass the MPT. Consider enrolling in our supplemental personal MPT Writing Program Service described in the foreword information just before the introductory chapter 1.

V. PRACTICE QUESTION 1:

PEOPLE v. WILS

TABLE OF CONTENTS

Documents Provided for Task	**Page**
Instructions	2-63
File	2-65
Task Memorandum	2-66
Pointer Memorandum	2-67
Excerpts from Trial Transcript	2-69
Jury Instructions	2-78
Library	2-81
Selected Constitutional and Statutory Provisions	2-82
People v. Brown	2-83
People v. Cutler	2-85
People v. Alvarado	2-88
Editors' Prepared Grading Guide	2-91
Sample Answer	2-93

PEOPLE v. WILS

INSTRUCTIONS

1. You will have 90 minutes to complete this session of the examination. This performance test is designed to evaluate your ability to handle a select number of legal authorities in the context of a factual problem involving a client.

2. The problem is set in the fictional State of Franklin, one of the United States, located in the fictional Fifteenth Circuit. Franklin has District Courts (trial courts), Courts of Appeal (mid-level appellate courts), and a Supreme Court (Franklin's highest appellate court).

3. You will have two sets of materials with which to work: a File and a Library.

4. The File contains factual materials about your case. The first document is a memorandum containing the instructions for the tasks that you are to complete.

5. The Library contains the legal authorities needed to complete the tasks. The case reports may be real, modified, or written solely for the purpose of this performance test. If the cases appear familiar to you, do not assume that they are precisely the same as you have read before. Read each thoroughly, as if it were new to you. You should assume that cases were decided in the jurisdictions and on the dates shown. In citing cases from the Library, you may use abbreviations and omit page citations.

6. Your response must be written in the answer book provided. You should concentrate on the materials provided, but you should also bring to bear on the problem your general knowledge of the law. What you have learned in law school and elsewhere provides the general background for analyzing the problem; the File and Library provide the specific materials with which you must work.

7. Although there are no restrictions on how you apportion your time, you should probably allocate at least 45 minutes to reading and organizing before you begin writing your response. You may make notes anywhere in the test materials, but may not tear out pages from this booklet.

8. Your response will be graded on its compliance with instructions and on its content, thoroughness, and organization.

File

People

v.

Wils

1. Public Defender Memorandum   2-66
2. Opening Appellate Briefs Memorandum   2-67
3. Excerpts From Trial Transcript   2-69
4. Jury Instructions   2-78

OFFICE OF THE STATE PUBLIC DEFENDER
STATE OF FRANKLIN

MEMORANDUM TASK ASSIGNMENT

To: Applicant

From: Susan Sola, Supervising Deputy State Public Defender

Date: July 29, 20X3

Subject: *People v. Wils*, Franklin Court of Appeal No. 1610201

Our office has recently been appointed by the Franklin Court of Appeal to represent Thomas Wils, an indigent Ruritanian émigré, on his appeal from a judgment of the Franklin District Court convicting him on a jury's verdict of burglary and robbery. I believe that Wils' only potentially meritorious claims of error on appeal are that the trial court: (1) refused to instruct the jury on a *bona fide* belief in a claim or right to another's personal property relating to burglary; and (2) refused to instruct the jury on a *bona fide* belief in a claim or right to another's personal property relating to robbery.

Please draft for my approval only the following section of an opening appellate brief: an argument demonstrating, for each of the two claims of error identified above, that the trial court erred and that its error requires reversal of the judgment.

I shall draft the remaining sections of the brief in due course. In performing each of these tasks, please follow the office guidelines set out in the memorandum on the drafting of opening appellate briefs.

OFFICE OF THE STATE PUBLIC DEFENDER
STATE OF FRANKLIN

MEMORANDUM GUIDELINES

To: Deputy State Public Defenders

From: Beth Jay, State Public Defender

Date: April 5, 20X0

Subject: The Drafting of Opening Appellate Briefs

All opening appellate briefs must conform to the following guidelines:

1) All opening appellate briefs must include the following sections: a table of contents; a table of cases; a summary of argument; a statement of the jurisdictional basis of the appeal; a procedural history; a statement of facts; an argument comprising one or more claims of error; and a conclusion.

2) The *statement of facts* must contain the facts that support our client's claims of error and must also take into account the facts that may be used to support the People's opposition. It must deal with all such facts in a persuasive manner, reasonably and fairly attempting to show the greater importance of the ones that weigh in our client's favor and the lesser importance of the ones that weigh in the People's favor. Above all, it must tell a compelling story in narrative form and not merely recapitulate each witness's testimony.

3) The *argument* must analyze the applicable law and bring it to bear on the facts in each claim of error, urging that the law and facts support our client's position. It need not attempt to foreclose each and every response that the People may put forth in their brief, but should anticipate their strongest attacks on our client's weakest points, both legal and factual.

4) Your brief must display a *subject* heading summarizing each claim of error and the outcome that it requires. The subject heading must express the application of the law to the facts, and not a statement of an abstract principle or a bare conclusion. For example, do *not* write: "The Trial Court Erroneously Instructed the Jury on Defense of Others." *Do* write: "By Failing to State That Defendant Was Entitled to Defend Strangers as Well as Members of His Family, the Trial Court Erroneously Instructed the Jury on Defense of Others."

EXCERPTS FROM TRIAL TRANSCRIPT

BY DEPUTY DISTRICT ATTORNEY JAMES LEIBSON

Q: What is your name, sir?

A: Arno Pir.

Q: Where were you born?

A: Ruritania.

Q: When did you come to this country?

A: More than 50 years ago, as a child. My parents fled as refugees.

Q: Where do you live?

A: I live with my wife at 2211 Blake Street in New Hope.

Q: What do you do for a living?

A: I'm a wine merchant.

Q: Do you know the defendant, Thomas Wils?

A: Yes, I did, I do.

Q: Can you identify him?

A: Yes, he's the young man at the far table, in the dark suit and tie.

THE COURT

Let the record reflect that the witness has identified the defendant. Proceed.

BY MR. LEIBSON

Q: When did you meet him?

A: I welcomed him to New Hope two or three years ago; I was the Secretary of the Ruritanian-American Freedom League.

Q: What is the Ruritanian-American Freedom League?

A: It is an organization dedicated to obtaining freedom for our homeland, which has long been dominated by its neighbor Caledon.

Q: You said you met him two or three years ago?

A: Yes, he had fled from Ruritania and had just received political asylum.

Q: Did he come to live with you?

A: Yes, with my wife Vivian and me.

Q: How was that?

A: He was alone in a new country, and Vivian and I had never had any children.

Q: You invited him to live with you?

A: Yes.

Q: Did you have an arrangement?

A: What do you mean?

Q: For instance, did he have to pay you rent?

A: No, no, no, of course not. We provided him with room and board, and I think my wife would give him some spending money.

Q: Did he have to repay you?

A: Not at all. All he had to do were some odd jobs around the house, jobs Vivian wanted me to do but I didn't get around to.

Q: Did you agree to pay him for any of his work?

A: No, absolutely not. I provided him with room and board.

Q: Did you agree to give him anything for his work?

A: No, I didn't, but I think Vivian did.

Q: If you know, what?

A: I think Vivian promised him an old car that I no longer used, a Fiat Spider, if he finished some work in the garage.

Q: How much was it worth?

A: Maybe $2,000.

Q: Did you end up giving it to him?

A: No.

Q: Why?

A: I believe he wanted it before he finished the work, Vivian refused, they got into an argument, and she threw him out.

Q: Did she consult you?

A: Consult? Vivian is not a person who consults.

Q: When did she throw him out?

A: I think in April of 20X2, or maybe May.

Q: Did you hear from him afterwards?

A: I was hanging up on him before long.

Q: If you would, please go back in thought to July 3, 20X2.

A: OK.

Q: Do you remember what happened that day?

A: Yes, Thomas came by my shop.

Q: Did he look like he looks today?

A: No, he was very thin and dirty and smelly.

Q: Did he say anything to you?

A: Yes, he said he wanted the Fiat. He demanded it.

Q: What did you do?

A: I tried to get rid of him as quickly and quietly as I could. I had lots of regular customers in the shop, getting ready for the Fourth of July.

Q: What did you do?

A: I told him I didn't have the car; it was at home. I also told him I didn't have the title documents; Vivian probably kept them in her purse.

Q: Did he leave?

A: No, he kept demanding the car.

Q: What happened next?

A: I told him I was leaving on a business trip later that day, and I would return on July 20th or 21st, and I would give him the car and the papers at that time.

Q: Did he leave then?

A: Yes, he did.

Q: Did you go off on your business trip later that day?

A: I did.

Q: And you returned –

A: On July 5th, right after the incident.

Q: Subsequently, did you receive any bills for credit cards issued to you and your wife?

A: Yes, I did.

Q: Did you notice any charges that were not made by you or your wife?

A: Yes, I did.

Q: What were they?

A: An airline ticket to New York on our Bank of Franklin card, and motel bills, restaurant bills, clothing, I think, jewelry, and such things on our Franklin Federal Savings and Loan card.

Q: Do you remember the amounts?

A: Roughly, I believe, $1,200 for the ticket, almost $2,000 for jewelry, maybe about $800 for the rest.

Q: What was the first date for these charges?

A: July 5th.

Q: And the last?

A: July 31st.

Q: You didn't notify the issuers of these credit cards of their loss before the 31st?

A: No, I'm embarrassed. Vivian and I had so many credit cards I didn't realize these were missing until the bills arrived.

* * *

BY DEPUTY DISTRICT ATTORNEY JAMES LEIBSON

Q: Ma'am, what is your name?

A: Vivian Pir.

Q: Where were you born?

A: Ruritania.

Q: When did you come to this country?

A: Almost 50 years ago.

Q: Did you come with your parents?

A: Yes, we escaped; I was 8.

Q: Where do you live?

A: In New Hope.

Q: What do you do for a living?

A: I'm a certified public accountant.

Q: Are you married?

A: Yes, to Arno Pir.

Q: Do you know Thomas Wils, the defendant here?

A: I do.

Q: Can you identify him?

A: Yes, he's at that table, in the navy blue suit and cobalt tie.

THE COURT

Let the record reflect that Mrs. Pir has identified the defendant. Proceed.

BY MR. LEIBSON

Q: When did you meet him?

A: About two or three years ago, when I was President of the Ruritanian-American Freedom League.

Q: Did you meet him here in New Hope?

A: Yes, I did. He had recently escaped from Ruritania.

Q: At some point, did he come to live with you and your husband?

A: Yes, he did.

Q: Did you and your husband invite him?

A: Arno did; I was hesitant.

Q: Why?

A: Well, we never had any children, and Thomas was an adolescent.

Q: Did you and your husband have an arrangement with the defendant?

A: We agreed to provide him with room and board, and he agreed to do construction work, including remodeling the garage.

Q: Did you pay him any money?

A: No; I think he got some from other Ruritanian-Americans; he would do odd jobs.

Q: Why didn't you pay him?

A: We provided all that he needed. And I wanted him to get on his own two feet, go to college, or at least get a real job.

Q: Did he want to do that?

A: No.

Q: How did you know?

A: He would say, again and again, that he wanted to enjoy life, and that he didn't want to be a "working stiff."

Q: Did you agree to give him anything for his work?

A: I agreed to give him an old car that Arno no longer used, but not in exchange for work.

Q: For what?

A: I told him I would give it to him for transportation if he went to college.

Q: Did he ever go to college?

A: No.

Q: Did he ever ask you for the car?

A: Yes, he demanded it. He said he needed to sell it for money; his odd jobs were drying up. I could understand why, with his attitude.

Q: Did you have an argument with him in April or May of 20X2?

A: Late in April.

Q: Can you describe it?

A: Yes, it was heated but short. He demanded the car and I refused and threw him out.

Q: Did you hear from him afterwards?

A: I didn't; Arno did.

Q: Do you remember what happened on July 5, 20X2?

A: Yes.

Q: Was Arno in town?

A: No, he was away on a business trip.

Q: What did you do on that morning?

A: About 9 or 9:30, I went to the dentist.

Q: When did you return home?

A: Sometime before noon.

Q: Did you see anything unusual when you entered your house?

A: No, not when I entered, but when I got near the kitchen.

Q: What did you see?

A: The kitchen was in disarray. Then I saw Thomas stuffing food into his mouth.

Q: Were you startled?

A: Yes, I screamed and demanded that he get out immediately or I'd call the police.

Q: Did he go?

A: No, he demanded the car, and started at me.

Q: What did you do?

A: I grabbed for a broom or mop to protect myself.

Q: What did he do then?

A: He punched me hard in my shoulder, pulled my purse from my arm, and started rummaging through it.

Q: Did he say anything?

A: Yes, he hollered, "If you won't give me the papers for the car, then I'll take what I can get."

Q: What did you do?

A: I was stunned that he would actually punch me; when I came to my senses, he had turned to run out of the house; I tried to chase him, but he got away.

* * *

BY DEPUTY PUBLIC DEFENDER THEODORE STROLL

Q: What is your name, please?

A: Thomas Wils.

Q: How old are you?

A: Almost 21.

Q: Where were you born?

A: Ruritania.

Q: You learned English there?

A: Yes, I started studying it in elementary school.

Q: When did you leave?

A: I didn't leave; I escaped, about three years ago. Ruritania is a police state.

Q: When did you arrive in this country?

A: The same year. I landed in New York, and then came to New Hope. I received political asylum.

Q: Were you welcomed by the Ruritanian-American community?

A: Yes, at first.

Q: And by Arno and Vivian Pir?

A: Yes, Arno was the President of the Ruritanian-American Freedom League, and Vivian was the Secretary. They invited me to live with them – in a way.

Q: What do you mean?

A: They offered me room and board if I helped around the house.

Q: You accepted?

A: Yes, but I didn't know –

Q: Let me interrupt, what was your arrangement?

A: I was supposed to do handyman work, but Vivian made me turn the garage into a guest house with a bathroom and kitchen.

Q: Did they pay you anything?

A: No, just room and board; Vivian bought me cigarettes and things like that, and sometimes she gave me a few dollars to rent a video.

Q: How old were you?

A: About 19.

Q: Did you try to change your arrangement?

A: Yes, I told Vivian I would not finish the work in the garage unless she paid me.

Q: Did she agree?

A: She promised to give me an old car that Arno didn't use anymore, a Fiat, so that I could sell it.

Q: How much was it worth?

A: I don't know, maybe $4,000.

Q: You didn't want it to drive?

A: No, I'm afraid to drive; I black out sometimes. The Secret Police in Ruritania beat me.

Q: Did you finish the work?

A: Yes, I did.

Q: What happened then?

A: I asked for the Fiat. She said no, told me to leave, and threw me out.

Q: Did you go?

A: Yes.

Q: When was that?

A: In April of 20X2.

Q: Where did you go?

A: To stay with Ruritanian friends in New Hope.

Q: Did you settle with anyone in particular?

A: No, I went from one to another, until they all turned me away.

Q: Do you know why they did that?

A: Vivian told them all I was a bum, used drugs, got drunk; I overheard her saying that once.

Q: What happened then?

A: I had to live on the streets and beg for food; it was worse than Ruritania.

Q: How long did you do that?

A: More than two months.

Q: Do you remember what you did on July 3, 20X2?

A: Yes, I went to Arno's store – he has a liquor store – and I asked for the Fiat.

Q: What happened?

A: He said he didn't have the ownership papers, Vivian did, and she had them either in her purse or somewhere in the house. He said that he was going away on a business trip later that day, and would give them to me when he got back in two weeks.

Q: Do you remember what you did on July 5, 20X2?

A: Yes, I went to Arno and Vivian's house to get the Fiat and the ownership papers.

Q: You got into the house?

A: Yes.

Q: How?

A: When I lived there, I put in a new lock in the kitchen door. I knew how to take it out.

Q: Was Vivian home?

A: No. I had waited for her to leave.

Q: Did she return?

A: Yes, about 45 minutes after I got there. I sat in the kitchen and waited for her. After a while, I made myself a sandwich out of some liverwurst I found in the refrigerator. I was starving. I hadn't eaten for days.

Q: What happened?

A: She came in the front door, walked into the kitchen, and when she saw me she started to scream and then to curse, and she told me to get out before she called the police.

Q: Did you leave?

A: No, I asked for the Fiat.

Q: Did she give it to you?

A: No, she threatened to hit me with a broom.

Q: What did you do?

A: I pushed her shoulder and took her purse from her arm; I opened the purse and looked for the ownership papers.

Q: Did you punch her in the shoulder?

A: No, that's a lie, I just pushed her shoulder.

Q: Did you find the ownership papers?

A: No, I saw some credit cards and a silver mirror and a cellular phone, and just took them instead. I figured if they wouldn't give me the car I had worked for and earned, I'd take what I could get.

Q: What happened next?

A: I ran away. She chased me, but I was faster.

Q: What did you do with the mirror and the phone?

A: I pawned them.

Q: For how much?

A: Maybe $5 for the mirror and $10 for the phone.

Q: What about the credit cards?

A: I used them to go to New York and live there awhile. I ran up about $4,000 worth of credit card debt. That's what the Fiat was worth, and so I guess I got even with them.

Q: Did you stay with any Ruritanian-American friends in New York?

A: I thought they were friends, but Vivian poisoned their minds, and they turned me in to the police.

Q: You were arrested?

A: Yes, on July 31st.

* * *

IN THE DISTRICT COURT OF THE STATE OF FRANKLIN

COUNTY OF LAKEPORT

THE PEOPLE,	)	1020161
Plaintiff,	)	
	)	JURY INSTRUCTIONS
v.	)	
	)	GIVEN
THOMAS WILS,	)	
Defendant.	)	

* * *

Defendant is accused in Count 1 of the Indictment with having committed the crime of burglary.

In order to prove such crime, the People must prove each of the following elements, and must do so beyond a reasonable doubt:

1. Defendant entered a house, apartment, or other building;

2. Defendant entered such house, apartment, or other building without consent; and

3. Defendant entered such house, apartment, or other building with the intent to commit larceny.

* * *

Defendant is accused in Count 2 of the Indictment with having committed the crime of robbery.

In order to prove such crime, the People must prove each of the following elements, and must do so beyond a reasonable doubt:

1. Defendant took personal property;

2. The personal property belonged to another;

3. Defendant took such personal property from the person or immediate presence of the other;

4. Defendant took such personal property without the consent of the other;

5. Defendant took such personal property by using force against the other or by causing the other to fear; and

6. Defendant took such personal property with the intent to commit larceny.

* * *

Larceny is the taking of the personal property of another, without his consent, with the intent to steal.

* * *

Dated: October 30, 20X2.

/s/ Patricia C. Sheehan
Judge of the District Court

Library

People

v.

Wils

1.	Constitutional and Statutory Provisions	2-82
2.	*People v. Brown*	2-83
3.	*People v. Cutler*	2-85
4.	*People v. Alvarado*	2-88

SELECTED CONSTITUTIONAL AND STATUTORY PROVISIONS

Section 13 of Article VI of the Franklin Constitution. Harmless Error.

No judgment shall be reversed, in any case, on the ground of any error of any kind, unless, after an examination of the entire case, including the evidence, the court shall be of the opinion that the error complained of has resulted in a miscarriage of justice.

*

Section 211 of the Franklin Penal Code. The Crime of Robbery.

Robbery is the larcenous taking of the personal property of another, from his person or immediate presence, and without his consent, accomplished by means of force or fear.

*

Section 459 of the Franklin Penal Code. The Crime of Burglary.

Every person who, without consent, enters any house, apartment, or other building, with intent to commit larceny, is guilty of burglary.

*

Section *484 of the Franklin Penal Code.* The Crime of Larceny.

Larceny is the taking of the personal property of another, without his consent, with the intent to steal.

*

Section 602 of the Franklin Penal Code. The Crime of Trespass.

Every person who, without consent, enters any house, apartment, or other building is guilty of trespass.

PEOPLE v. BROWN

Franklin Court of Appeal (1957)

Defendant was convicted in the district court of the crime of burglary, which had been alleged in the indictment to have been committed by entering a certain house with intent to commit larceny involving the taking of a certain bicycle. The entry was conceded, as was the taking. Defendant now appeals.

Defendant was a youth of 18 years of age, and, for a few days immediately prior to the taking of the bicycle, was staying at the home of one Ralph Yount, working for his room and board. He took the stand as a witness, and testified: "I took the bicycle to get even with George, and of course I didn't intend to keep it. I just wanted to get even with him. He was throwing oranges at me in the evening, and he would not stop when I told him to, and it made me mad, and I left Yount's house Saturday morning. I thought I would go back and take George's bike. Instead of getting hold of his, I got Frank's, but I intended to take it back Sunday night; but before I got it back they caught me. I took it down by the grove, and put it on the ground, and covered it with brush, and crawled in, and Frank came and hauled off the brush and said: 'What are you doing here?' Then I told him that I covered myself up in the brush so that they could

not find me until evening, until I could take it back. I did not want them to find me. I expected to remain there during the day, and not go back until evening."

Upon the foregoing statement of facts, the district court gave the jury the following instruction: "I think it is not necessary to say very much to you in this case. I may say, generally, that I think counsel for the defense here stated to you in this argument very fairly the principles of law governing this case, *except in one particular*. In defining to you the crime of larceny, he says it is essential that the taking must be 'larcenous.' That is true: The taking must be with the intent to deprive the owner. But counsel adds the conclusion that you must find that the taker intended to deprive him *permanently*. I do not think that is the law. I think in this case, for example, if the defendant took this bicycle, we will say for the purpose of enabling him to get away, and then left it, and intended to do nothing else except to help himself get away, it would be larceny, just as much as though he intended to keep it forever."

This trial court instruction was erroneous, and demands a reversal of the judgment as a miscarriage of justice under section 13 of Article VI of the Franklin Constitution. Section 459 of the Franklin Penal Code states: "Every person who, without consent, enters any house, apartment, or other building, with intent to commit larceny, is guilty of burglary." If defendant's story is true, he is not guilty of larceny in taking the bicycle and hence is not guilty of burglary; yet, under the instruction, the words from his own mouth convicted him. The court told the jury that larceny might have been committed, even though it was only the intent of the party taking the property to deprive the owner of it *temporarily*. We think the case authorities form an unbroken line to the effect that the larcenous intent must be to deprive the owner of the property *permanently*. While the larcenous intent of the party taking need not necessarily be an intent to convert the property to his own use, still it must in all cases be an intent to permanently deprive the owner thereof.

For the foregoing reasons, it is ordered that the judgment below be reversed.

PEOPLE v. CUTLER

Franklin Court of Appeal (1967)

Defendant was charged with the robbery of Joseph H. Anderson. A jury convicted him of the offense. The district court sentenced him to a term of imprisonment of six years. We reverse.

At trial, Anderson testified as follows. He operated a catering service in Lakeport. On the evening of May 18, 1965, the doorbell of his home rang shortly before midnight. He stepped out onto the porch. Defendant approached and demanded to be repaid a prior debt. Anderson then said I do not have any money now but I offer to pay double the amount of the money if you wait a month and defendant again said no, telling Anderson he needed his money and wished only to be paid. After some conversation, he pulled out a gun. Anderson attempted to seize the weapon.

At this point, Anderson agreed to pay him. He started to remove his wallet from his back pocket to get the money. He apparently changed his mind and returned to discuss his earlier marijuana proposal. Defendant persisted in his refusal, and Anderson again started to remove his wallet. Stopping suddenly, Anderson knocked the gun out of defendant's hand. Defendant then snatched Anderson's wallet from his back pocket and fled.

At trial, Defendant testified that he met Anderson several weeks before the incident and that Anderson employed him on one occasion to do some catering work. Anderson did not pay him for the work and, when defendant requested payment, Anderson asked him to wait a few days. On the evening of May 18th, he went to Anderson's home to obtain payment. While the two were discussing the debt on the porch, Anderson proposed giving him some marijuana instead of cash, and defendant said no. He then moved his hand to his waistband and pulled out a knife. Defendant had armed himself before going to Anderson's home because he had heard stories about Anderson's brutality; when he saw a knife in Anderson's hand, he brought out his gun to defend himself. Anderson then knocked the weapon out of defendant's hand. Taking advantage of the opportunity that presented itself in the struggle, defendant snatched Anderson's wallet and fled. Defendant did not intend to rob Anderson when he went to the house, but intended only to recover money owed to him.

Over defendant's objection, the prosecutor argued to the jury, "If you think a man owes you a hundred dollars, or fifty dollars, or five dollars, or a dollar, and you go over with a gun to try to get his money, it's robbery." And, "If you go to a man's home, and merely because he's supposed to owe you some money, take money from him at gunpoint, you have robbed him." Again objecting to further argument by the prosecutor that a robbery was committed even if defendant believed Anderson owed him money, defendant suggested that a necessary element of larceny, the intent to steal, was requisite to robbery, but was overruled by the court.

Defendant's objection was well taken. Under Section 211 of the Franklin Penal Code, "[r]obbery is the larcenous taking of the personal property of another, from his person or immediate presence, and without his consent, accomplished by means of force or fear." An essential element of robbery is the larcenous intent that accompanies the taking. Since robbery is but larceny aggravated by the use of force or fear to accomplish the taking of personal property from the person or immediate presence of the other, the larcenous intent requisite to robbery is the intent requisite to larceny. The taking of property is not larceny in the absence of an intent to steal, *i.e.*, an intent to deprive its owner of it permanently.

Although an intent to steal may ordinarily be inferred when one person takes the property of another, particularly if he takes it by force, proof of the existence of a state of mind incompatible with an intent to steal precludes a finding of either larceny or robbery. It has long been the rule in this state, and generally throughout the country, that a *bona fide* belief, even though mistakenly held, one has a right or claim to the property negates larcenous intent. A belief that the property taken belongs to the taker, or that he has a right or claim thereto, is sufficient to preclude larcenous intent. Larcenous intent exists only if the actor intends to take the property of another without believing in good faith that he has a right or claim to it.

Defendant testified that, in going to Anderson's home, "my sole intention was to try to get my money, and that was all." The jury was properly instructed that if the intent to take the money from Anderson did not arise until after defendant brought out his gun, there was no robbery. Since the jury returned a verdict of robbery, it believed defendant intended to take money from Anderson by force before he went for his gun. Accordingly, defendant's only defense to robbery was the existence of an honest belief that he was entitled to the money. The trial court's approval of the prosecutor's argument that no such defense exists was erroneous.

It removed completely from the consideration of the jury a material issue raised by substantial evidence. It precluded any finding that intent to steal was absent. It thereby caused a miscarriage of justice within the meaning of Article VI, Section 13 of the Franklin Constitution, and requires reversal.

PEOPLE v. ALVARADO

Franklin Court of Appeal (1982)

Defendant Rita Ann Alvarado was charged with burglary. Following a jury trial in the district court, she was convicted and sentenced to four years in prison. She appeals.

This case arises from a dispute between defendant, a user of heroin, and Julian Habecker, a dealer in the substance. On the morning of May 6, 1979, defendant gained entry into Habecker's house. No one was present. Defendant claimed to have bought some fake heroin from Habecker a day or two earlier. Rummaging about, defendant proceeded from room to room, taking several hundred dollars, some heroin, several phonograph records, and a few posters that had been tacked to the walls. She then left. She later boasted of her exploit to fellow heroin users, who subsequently informed on her and caused her arrest.

This was primarily a case that featured recalcitrant prosecution witnesses. The defense essentially relied on the absence of direct proof and on the untrustworthiness of the prosecution's witnesses. But there was evidence, albeit self-serving and ambiguous, that defendant was motivated by a desire to have retribution for Habecker's sale of bogus heroin. Defendant used this evidence as a basis for arguing the theory that she was not guilty because she took only the property she had given Habecker for the "drugs."

Defendant contends that the evidence is not sufficient to support her conviction for burglary. Under Franklin law, evidence is sufficient to support a conviction for a particular crime if a rational trier of fact, viewing such evidence in the light most favorable to the People, could find the defendant guilty of all of that crime's elements beyond a reasonable doubt.

Section 459 of the Franklin Penal Code states: "Every person who, without consent, enters any house, apartment, or other building, with intent to commit larceny, is guilty of burglary." It effectively defines "intent to commit larceny" as a required element.

Defendant's claim focuses on the asserted insufficiency of the evidence for the element of intent to commit larceny. Her theory rests upon the observation there was no proof the property she took was not previously hers, which she recovered because Habecker cheated her.

Under *People v. Cutler* (Frank. Ct. App. 1967), it is an established principle that a *bona fide* belief in a right or claim to the property taken, even if mistaken, negates the element of intent to commit larceny because it negates the intent to steal.

With specific reference to this case, we can identify three rational inferences from the evidence. One is that defendant intended to, and did, retrieve only the property she had given for the bogus heroin. Another is that she intended to, and did, merely take items for the general purpose of economic gain. But by far the most reasonable inference is that she intended to, and did, take what she took to "settle the score," and was not especially concerned with obtaining the *exact* amount of money and *exact* property she had given; rather, she meant to obtain whatever money and property were conveniently available, in retribution for the fraudulent drug deal. We note, for example, that she took some *heroin*. Reason does not suggest she had given Habecker heroin as some or the entire purchase price for other heroin.

The inference of intent to commit larceny is reasonable and credible. Any rational trier of fact could surely have drawn it and concluded beyond a reasonable doubt that defendant intended to steal. The other elements of the crime are essentially conceded and are well supported by the evidence. There was sufficient evidence to support the conviction.

The judgment below is affirmed.

VI. EDITORS' PREPARED GRADING GUIDE FOR PRACTICE QUESTION 1: *PEOPLE v. WILS*

Our editors have prepared a substantive grading guide outline to help you evaluate your answer. We have approached this from the perspective of the model answer structure typically used by a bar exam grader. After you complete a draft answer, compare and contrast it with the sample answer that follows this grading guide. If you missed key issues in your analysis, consider updating and perfecting your answer.

___ Trial court erred in refusing to instruct jury that a *bona fide* belief of claim to property negates intent necessary for burglary

    ___ Elements of burglary, including intent to commit larceny (Penal Code § 459)

    ___ *Brown*: Jury verdict reversed because trial court failed to instruct jury on intent

    ___ *Alvarado* and *Cutler*: *Bona fide* belief of claim to property ownership negates intent to commit larceny

    ___ *Alvarado* distinguishable because court found claim of *bona fide* belief to be implausible

    ___ Here, uncontradicted testimony is that the car was promised to Thomas and that he believed he was entitled to the car

    ___ If error results in "miscarriage of justice," appellate court should overturn judgment (Franklin Constitution, Article VI, Section 13)

___ Trial court erred in refusing to instruct jury that *bona fide* belief of claim to property negates intent necessary for robbery

    ___ Robbery is the "larcenous taking of the personal property of another" (Penal Code § 211)

    ___ *Cutler*: Robbery requires intent to steal at time of robbery

    ___ *Cutler* is analogous; defendant was trying to collect a debt

    ___ Another "miscarriage of justice" requiring reversal (Franklin Constitution, Article VI, Section 13)

VII. SAMPLE ANSWER TO PRACTICE QUESTION 1:

PEOPLE v. WILS

ARGUMENT

A. THE TRIAL COURT COMMITTED ERROR RESULTING IN A MISCARRIAGE OF JUSTICE BECAUSE IT FAILED TO INSTRUCT THE JURY THAT A *BONA FIDE* BELIEF OF CLAIM TO PROPERTY NEGATES THE INTENT TO STEAL IN A BURGLARY CASE AND, AS A RESULT, THE JURY WAS UNABLE TO CONSIDER OVERWHELMING EVIDENCE THAT WOULD HAVE NEGATED DEFENDANT'S INTENT TO COMMIT LARCENY.

The elements for a claim of burglary in the State of Franklin require that the defendant enter a house, without consent, with the intent to commit larceny. Section 459 of the Franklin Penal Code; People v. Alvarado (Franklin Ct. App. 1982); People v. Brown (Franklin Ct. App. 1957). The issue here is whether the trial court's failure to give an instruction that would have negated an element of larceny constitutes manifest injustice requiring the defendant's conviction to be overturned.

In Brown, the Court of Appeals overturned a jury verdict on the ground of an erroneous instruction on the elements of burglary. The court found that the jury instruction failed to properly set forth the intent element of the claim of larceny. In that case, the necessary element required to convict defendant that was missing from the jury instruction was the intent to deprive the defendant of his or her property permanently. Since the crime of burglary requires a larceny, the judge was required to instruct the jury on the elements of larceny as well. The appellate court ruled that the trial court was in error in refusing to allow the defendant to introduce this particular instruction and, accordingly, vacated the verdict of the trial court.

Although the element of larceny missing in the present case is not the intent to deprive permanently, the principle stated in Brown is completely applicable. Here, the jury was instructed only that defendant enter a house, without consent, with the intent to commit larceny. The District Court refused defendant's proffered instruction that a *bona fide* belief on the part of the taker of a right or claim to the property negates the intent to steal.

The law is settled that "a *bona fide* belief in a right or claim to the property taken, even if mistaken, negates the element of intent to commit larceny because it negates the intent to steal." People v. Cutler (Franklin Ct. App. 1967); cited in People v. Alvarado (Franklin Ct. App. 1982). In other words, showing a *bona fide* belief in the ownership or right to the property negates a necessary element of larceny, intent.

Although the court in Alvarado held that the defendant's actions in that particular case did not demonstrate a *bona fide* belief in the right to the property under a burglary conviction, the facts are easily distinguishable from the case here. In the Alvarado decision, the defendant entered the residence of an individual with whom she did a drug deal, allegedly to exact payment because the drugs she bought were "fake." Defendant rummaged through the house, taking more heroin, some money, posters, and other items. The trial court found the defendant's evidence of a claim of *bona fide* right completely implausible, because the defendant would not have paid someone heroin in order to obtain heroin.

Here, by contrast, at the time Thomas entered the house of the Pirs, he had the intent merely to collect on the car that had actually been promised to him and that he actually believed was his. Vivian, the witness who most contradicts Thomas' testimony, admitted herself that she had "agreed to give" the car to Thomas. Whether consideration was paid for the car or not is irrelevant with respect to whether Thomas had a *bona fide* belief in his entitlement. None of the parties has disputed his *bona fide* belief in his entitlement to the car, and the record is replete with evidence that he believed that the car was his as a matter of right.

Under the holding of Brown, because the trial court's failure (in fact, the court refused) to instruct the jury on a necessary element of larceny in a burglary case that a *bona fide* belief of entitlement would negate intent, the court committed reversible error.

Under Section 13 of Article VI of the Franklin Constitution, where the error complained of has resulted in a miscarriage of justice, the appellate court should overturn the judgment. Here, but for the failure to include the jury instruction, the jury would have been free to consider the *bona fides* of defendant's belief in his entitlement to the car. Since the record is so replete with evidence of the *bona fides* of his belief, the error was clearly a miscarriage of justice and the conviction should be reversed.

B. THE TRIAL COURT ALSO CAUSED A MISCARRIAGE OF JUSTICE BY FAILING TO INSTRUCT THE JURY THAT A *BONA FIDE* BELIEF OF CLAIM TO PROPERTY NEGATES THE INTENT TO STEAL IN A ROBBERY CASE, THEREBY PREVENTING THE JURY FROM CONSIDERING COMPELLING EVIDENCE THAT WOULD HAVE NEGATED DEFENDANT'S INTENT TO COMMIT LARCENY.

The State of Franklin defines robbery, in relevant part, as a "larcenous taking of the personal property of another." Franklin Penal Code Section 211. The courts have construed this to require that in order to convict someone of robbery, a person must have the necessary intent to steal at the time of the robbery. Cutler.

The facts of Cutler are controlling here. Cutler involved a defendant who went to another's house, claiming that he only went there to collect a debt which he believed was owed to him. On facts that were hotly disputed, a scuffle ensued, pursuant to which the defendant obtained possession of the victim's wallet, which the defendant then claimed was sufficient to extinguish the debt. The defendant ended the encounter by running away with the wallet of the victim. The trial court excluded an instruction to the jury proffered by defendant that "a necessary element of larceny, the intent to steal, was requisite to robbery." Cutler. This court overruled the trial court's exclusion of that instruction, finding that "[a]n essential element of robbery is the larcenous intent that accompanies the taking." Id. Refusing to allow the jury to consider evidence of defendant's *bona fide* belief that the debt was owed to him was prejudicial error. Such a finding would have negated intent, which is a required element of a robbery charge.

In the present case, the defendant's *bona fide* belief that the property was his is even stronger than it was in Cutler. In Cutler, the victim completely denied that the debt was even due. Here, one of the defendants has, in fact, admitted that the car was going to be given to defendant. In addition, defendant was looking in victim's purse, exactly the place he was told he could find the title to the car. Therefore, even though defendant took property other than the title to the car, it is manifestly evident, not even disputed, that defendant lacked the intent to steal when he allegedly committed the burglary and when he allegedly committed the robbery.

The fact that defendant allegedly punched the victim is also immaterial, since it does not help to show felonious intent. Whomever's story is to be believed, the victim was clearly either defending himself or at least responding to hostility of the other party.

CONCLUSION

Because the defendant lacked the required intent to steal, it was manifest injustice to exclude the jury instruction with respect to both the burglary charge and robbery charge. Therefore, the conviction should be reversed.

VIII. PRACTICE QUESTION 2:

MORALES et al. v. PARSONS

TABLE OF CONTENTS

Documents Presented for Task	**Page**
Instructions	2-99
File	2-101
Task Instruction Memorandum	2-102
Memorandum from T.C. Gutierrez, Investigator	2-107
Excerpts from Interview of Emilio Cruz	2-109
Parsons Strawberry Farm Camp Rules and Regulations	2-112
Library	2-113
Griggs v. Barnes Construction Company	2-114
Esteban Raul Lucas v. Murai Farms, Inc.	2-117
Esteban Raul Lucas v. Perry C. Pollock	2-123
Editors' Prepared Grading Guide	2-127
Sample Answer	2-129

MORALES et al. v. PARSONS

INSTRUCTIONS

1. You will have 90 minutes to complete this session of the examination. This performance test is designed to evaluate your ability to handle a select number of legal authorities in the context of a factual problem involving a client.

2. The problem is set in the fictional State of Franklin, one of the United States, located in the fictional Fifteenth Circuit. Franklin has District Courts (trial courts), Courts of Appeal (mid-level appellate courts), and a Supreme Court (Franklin's highest appellate court).

3. You will have two sets of materials with which to work: a File and a Library.

4. The File contains factual materials about your case. The first document is a memorandum containing the instructions for the tasks that you are to complete.

5. The Library contains the legal authorities needed to complete the tasks. The case reports may be real, modified, or written solely for the purpose of this performance test. If the cases appear familiar to you, do not assume that they are precisely the same as you have read before. Read each thoroughly, as if it were new to you. You should assume that cases were decided in the jurisdictions and on the dates shown. In citing cases from the Library, you may use abbreviations and omit page citations.

6. Your response must be written in the answer book provided. You should concentrate on the materials provided, but you should also bring to bear on the problem your general knowledge of the law. What you have learned in law school and elsewhere provides the general background for analyzing the problem; the File and Library provide the specific materials with which you must work.

7. Although there are no restrictions on how you apportion your time, you should probably allocate at least 45 minutes to reading and organizing before you begin writing your response. You may make notes anywhere in the test materials, but may not tear out pages from this booklet.

8. Your response will be graded on its compliance with instructions and on its content, thoroughness, and organization.

File

Morales et al.

v.

Parsons

1. Task Assignment Memorandum	2-102
2. Excerpts From Interview of Juan Morales	2-103
3. Memorandum to Jane Kimmel	2-107
4. Excerpts From Interview of Emilio Cruz	2-109
5. Parsons Strawberry Farm Camp Rules and Regulations	2-112

Law Offices of
BROWN, MARRERO & MILAN
1101 Rose Parkway
Garden City, Franklin

TASK ASSIGNMENT MEMORANDUM

TO: Applicant
FROM: Jane Kimmel
RE: *Morales and Vargas v. Parsons*
DATE: July 29, 20X3

I need your help on a case we are considering filing against a strawberry grower in Washoe County, arising out of a fire in a farm worker encampment on his property. Our potential clients are Juan Morales, a farm worker who was badly burned, and the family of one of his co-workers, Alberto Vargas, who was killed. The clients were interviewed about a week ago, and since then our investigator has been out to the scene of the fire and I have interviewed a prospective witness.

It looks like a sympathetic case to take to a jury, but I'm not sure we have a basis for the landowner's liability under Franklin law. As you'll see from the cases I've pulled together, the Court of Appeals ruled against the plaintiffs in a pair of cases with quite similar facts a few years ago.

Please draft a memorandum with an analysis and discussion section that identifies and presents as strongly as possible the arguments that the landowner owed a duty of care to our clients.

EXCERPTS FROM INTERVIEW OF JUAN MORALES

* * * * *

MS. KIMMEL (Q): Mr. Morales, let's talk about the night of the fire. Tell me how it happened.

MR. MORALES (A): No one knows for sure. I was told the fire started in Alberto Vargas' tent. He was doing something in his tent, maybe mending a shirt he had torn that day. I went to bed around nine, and the next thing I knew people were yelling and trying to get out, and the flames were all around me.

Q: Was Mr. Vargas the only one who was killed?

A: Yes.

Q: What do you think might have caused the fire?

A: I think probably his lamp got knocked over, and something like paper caught fire. He had a lot of flammable things in his tent, like cardboard boxes and magazines.

Q: What kind of lamp did he have?

A: It was an oil lamp, like most of us used. It had a glass cover, with oil in the bottom, and a wick that you light with a match. These lamps are not as bright as the kind of lamp that uses kerosene, that you pump up. But they are a lot easier to use, and cheaper. If one of them tips over, though, the oil spills everywhere, and can start a fire.

Q: Did the camp have electricity?

A: No.

Q: Was water available to fight the fire?

A: There was a shower, and a faucet where you could get water. But there was no hose, and the fire was too big to use buckets, or the cooking pots that were around.

Q: You said the flames were all around you when you woke up. How did you get out?

A: I'm not sure. I know I stood up, and saw the whole wall around the tent door was on fire, and I guess I went through it. When I got outside, with my clothes on fire, I fell to the ground and my friends threw a blanket on me to put out the flames. Then they pulled me away, to a safe place.

Q: Were these canvas tents?

A: They weren't really tents like you would buy at the store. They were more like shacks, really. Mine was made of cardboard boxes flattened out and taped together. It had sheets of plastic on the outside, in case it rained.

Q: You said earlier that Mr. Vargas' tent was right next to yours. Was it made of the same kinds of materials?

A: Yes, about the same. Most of us had a piece of plywood or a tarp for a floor, and then we just made walls of whatever we could find around the place. The owner of the farm, Mr. Parsons, let us use old boards, cardboard, whatever he didn't want. Some people had tarps that they set up like a regular tent, but they had to find a stake or a pole or something to tie them to. There weren't any big trees where the camp was, just scrub oak and bushes.

Q: Were the shacks or tents close together?

A: Yes, very close. Somebody would make a frame with stakes, and then on each side of them people would use their neighbor's frame as part of their own frame, to attach whatever they were going to use for walls – cardboard or plastic or whatever. The shacks were in rows or groups like that. They were very close together.

Q: Approximately how many of these dwellings were there in the camp?

A: I don't know for sure. There were about fifty of us living there, and some tents housed two or three people in the same space. So there were maybe 30 or 35 tents.

Q: Was there only one water faucet and one shower for the whole camp?

A: Yes. Before, we didn't even have that. Two years ago we had to carry water from the farm, and wash ourselves from a bucket. Last year Mr. Parsons paid for pipe and let us hook up to the irrigation system and run a water line to the camp.

Q: So it seems that Mr. Parsons provided some materials and services for the camp, but not a lot. What else did he provide?

A: I don't know everything he did when the camp was first built. This was only my third year working there. But since I've been there, it was mainly the water line, and letting us use scrap materials to build the houses. For example, the plastic on the outside of my house was from the rolls we use between the rows of strawberries to keep weeds from growing. He knew we were using that and didn't charge us for it or anything. And he provided two portable toilets, and had this truck come around to empty them.

Q: Was there a way to get mail, or use a telephone?

A: Mail, yes. There was a separate mailbox out by the road for employees. To make a telephone call, it was necessary to go into town and use the pay phone. People who had been working there for a long time could give the foreman's telephone number to their families, for emergencies. He would come over to the camp and tell people to call home. But that was just for some people, and for emergencies. There wasn't really a way for the rest of us to receive telephone calls. But since we were only there part of the year, it worked out.

Q: So except for some minimal services, it seems Mr. Parsons left you workers pretty much on your own in setting up and running the camp.

A: Setting up, maybe so. But he didn't really let us run it. He had rules about who could live there, who could even visit.

Q: What rules?

A: For example, only workers could live there. No wives or families or anyone else. Women couldn't even come there.

Q: Would he actually check to see who was there?

A: Not Mr. Parsons himself, but the foreman, Rudy Mendoza, did. He came around a few times a week, checking on things. And the road to the camp went right by his house, so if anybody came in a car, he came right out.

Q: And he would actually turn people away? Say, "You can't go in there," or something like that?

A: For sure, lots of times. He might let some friends from another farm visit for a few hours, but even then he'd check up to see if people were drinking too much, and make them leave if they were.

Q: So they even regulated how much you could drink?

A: They tried to, sure. They didn't actually search people's shacks or anything, but if Rudy thought someone was getting drunk, he would confiscate his liquor. It didn't come up much, except on Saturday nights. Most Sundays, we didn't have to work, so people would stay up late and talk, play cards, have a few beers. The other days, we had to get up early, so we went to bed pretty early.

Q: Was the night of the fire a Saturday?

A: No, a Tuesday. It was quiet that night. Almost everyone had gone to bed early.

Q: You said that families weren't allowed to live in the camp. Wasn't that a real hardship for some people, if they had families in the area?

A: Well, yes and no. If they could, people would like to be with their families, but it's hard to find work. Even if their family was living in Franklin, they might be twenty miles away, or fifty miles away – who can say? Nobody has a car to drive back and forth, so if they let you live where you're working, you take it. And if your family lives far away, or you're single, why spend money on a place to live? You have that much more to send home.

Q: Were there any workers at the farm during the time you were there who didn't live at the camp?

A: Field workers, no. People would come in to work on the irrigation system or operate machines that we didn't have on the farm, things like that. But the day-to-day workers all lived there.

Q: I guess what I'm trying to get at is whether you were required to live there. Would it have been possible to live somewhere else and simply come there to work every day?

A: Possible? Maybe. If you could get to work by six in the morning and go home at the end of the day, I think it would have been okay with Mr. Parsons and Rudy. But there was no cheap place to live anywhere around there, so, really, no one could do it. If you worked there, you lived there.

Q: You said this was only your third year working at the Parsons farm. Can you think of anyone who has worked there longer, who would be able to tell us more about how the camp was set up, how long it's been there and so forth?

A: Yes. Two of my friends said they will help us, and they have worked there many years. One of them can be reached through his brother, who lives near here. The other one we can reach by sending a letter, but it will take more time.

Q: That's fine. We'll start with the one who lives close by. At this point, as I said, we're just gathering information to decide whether we have a good enough case to take to court. If we file a lawsuit, we'll have plenty of time to track down the other witnesses.

Law Offices of
BROWN, MARRERO & MILAN
1101 Rose Parkway
Garden City, Franklin

MEMORANDUM

TO: Jane Kimmel
FROM: T.C. Gutierrez, Investigator
RE: Visit to Parsons Farms
DATE: February 21, 20X3

As you suggested, I parked beyond a curve in the road about a quarter mile away from the entrance to the farm, and approached on foot. Just before I reached the entrance, a beat-up panel truck drove through the gate, passed the house next to the entrance, and turned onto the dirt track leading over to the ravine on the left, where I knew the workers' camp was located. It turned out to be the regular lunch wagon – a vendor of some sort who comes in and sells food to the workers at lunchtime every day. I just followed it down to the camp, and if the foreman saw me, he probably thought I was after a sandwich. Anyway, I wasn't challenged, and I was able to hang out for almost an hour, talking to some of the workers and looking the place over. I took some pictures, and will get those to you as soon as they are developed.

The client guessed right. The camp has been completely rebuilt, if you can call it that, since the fire. The ravine is the only place that makes sense for that kind of camp, because it's one of the few places on the farm with any shade. That's why the workers go back there for lunch. At this point there are two rows of flimsy shacks or makeshift tents along the sides of the ravine, with another cluster of shacks off by itself a little farther up. The road is only passable up to the edge of the camp, and that's where the lunch wagon pulled up, and where they put the portable toilets and the dumpster for garbage.

Anyway, you'll see from the pictures that we really are talking about cardboard shacks. Some of them have an old piece of plywood for one wall, and there's some corrugated metal or plastic here and there, but the basic building materials are plastic tarps and flattened-out cardboard. You can see that a fire would spread through the place in no time. I was able to get a photo that shows where the water faucet and shower are located in relation to the shacks, and another that shows they are just 3/4-inch pipe, nothing heavy-duty or adequate for fire protection. The faucet itself is threaded, so someone could have attached a garden hose, if there had been one, but even now there is no hose in sight. Also, there is still no electricity. I was unsure how to try to document that. My shots of the camp will show there are no overhead lines, and I also have a couple of shots of kerosene lanterns hanging over the shower and cooking area.

As I said, I talked with some of the current workers, but I didn't try to get much information about the fire from them. They were pretty wary of me, even though I told some of them that I was working for a law firm that was looking into the possibility of filing a lawsuit for the people who were injured or killed. One guy actually told me he couldn't talk to me then, but could meet me in town sometime if I wanted, and told me how to set that up. If this goes further, I'll be happy to follow up with him.

I also went to the County Recorder's Office and checked the records on Parsons Farm. Parsons is the owner of record, and the property description includes the area where the camp is located. I ordered a copy of these documents.

EXCERPTS FROM INTERVIEW OF EMILIO CRUZ

* * * * *

MS. KIMMEL (Q): Mr. Cruz, thank you for agreeing to let me tape record our conversation. It really is the best way to make sure I have an accurate record of what you tell me, and it also speeds things up. Could you just restate, for the record, that the taping is fine with you?

MR. CRUZ (A): Sure. I have no problem with it. I already told Juan I would do whatever it takes to help him.

Q: I know you did, and I know he appreciates it. Now, as I told you, the main thing I want to discuss with you is how the camp came to be set up, and how it was run. I understand you've worked off and on at the Parsons farm for many years?

A: Yes, I first started working there about twelve years ago. I worked over in Gaston Valley for a couple of years, but the rest of the time I was at Parsons.

Q: Were you there when the camp was first set up?

A: Yes, that was about eight years ago.

Q: And how did that come about? I mean, where were you workers living before that, and why did you move to the Parsons farm?

A: Well, we were living in different places, over near Wiltsville, about 25 or 30 miles from the Parsons Farm. At that time we worked for a labor contractor named Sanchez. He had a couple of trucks that he would load up at his place at five in the morning, and they would drive us over to Parsons' place. But the trucks were always breaking down, you know? And then Sanchez was taking his cut. I think Parsons just wanted to eliminate the middleman, keep more of the profits for himself.

Q: So it was Parsons' idea to set up a camp at his farm?

A: I don't know if it was him or Rudy. It was Rudy who talked to us at the lunch break one day, asked us if we wanted to set up a camp at Parsons' farm, just stay there and work for them directly, every year.

Q: And the workers thought that was a good idea?

A: Sure, who wouldn't? We had to get up an hour earlier, because of the truck ride, and most of us were living in the camp at Sanchez' place, and he charged plenty of rent, which he just deducted from our pay. So we could work the same hours for Parsons at the same pay, but save money and have more time for ourselves. And I don't know if you've ever ridden in the back of a truck with 15 or 20 other people, but that's a hard way to go back and forth to work, too. The shape those trucks were in, it felt like we were risking our lives, every time.

Q: I can see why the move made sense. So you never had to pay rent at the Parsons place?

A: No. What would they charge for?

Q: Believe me, I'm not saying they should have charged you rent, I just need to know whether they did or not. I understand you left Parsons Farm after the fire?

A: Yes. I'm lucky. I have family nearby, and I've always been able to find work.

Q: Can you tell me how the camp was first constructed?

A: Well, as I said, it was in the middle of the season, eight years ago. We moved over there on a Sunday, after we got paid that Saturday night. Mr. Parsons sent his own trucks over to pick us up with our stuff, and I think he paid Sanchez what he owed him under their contract. I'm not sure about that part. Anyway, we got over there and spent the rest of Sunday rigging up a place to sleep. Rudy took some of us into town to buy stuff we needed, like flashlights and plastic tarps, duct tape, things like that.

Q: What did you do for food?

A: Most of us had been doing our own cooking at Sanchez' place, because there was electricity there, and hot plates to cook on. So we brought over whatever food we had, and bought more in town. But we were eating out of cans that Sunday and for a few days after that. By the middle of the week Rudy got Roberto Moya, who was already selling us food at lunchtime, to bring it in at night as well. Later on we got a couple of camp stoves and fixed up a fireplace with a grill over it, but a lot of people just bought from Moya.

Q: So the foreman, Rudy Mendoza, arranged for food to be brought in?

A: I think Moya was his brother-in-law or something. It's not like we had a choice. Toward the end of the week Moya would let us buy on credit, you know? And then Rudy would take what we owed him out of our pay. So they definitely had some kind of arrangement.

Q: Do you think they were cheating you?

A: No, the food was okay, and it was pretty reasonable. I just mean that Rudy made sure that Moya didn't have any competition.

Q: And is Moya the person who still sells food to the workers every day?

A: Yes.

Q: Let's go back to the building of the camp, those first few days. Did Mr. Parsons or Rudy provide any of the materials?

A: Oh, sure. They had piled some things they thought we could use at the campsite, and there were other locations on the farm where there were stacks of old boxes, boards, things like that,

that they let us use. Like there was an old henhouse on the property that wasn't being used anymore, and we took the roof from that, and some of the boards that were in good shape.

Q: Did they provide any tools you needed?

A: Yes, they let us use all the different tools. Just hand tools, you know, like hammers and shovels, things like that. There was no way to use power tools.

Q: Did they provide garbage cans and latrines from the beginning?

A: It took awhile before they had that dumpster brought in, and had a regular garbage pick-up. But the latrines, yes. They were set up before we got there.

Q: Is there anything else like that that you can think of that shows they were preparing to have you move in there?

A: Maybe the water. Like I said, we didn't get water piped to the site until last year, but before that they installed a valve on the irrigation line that ran closest to the camp, so we could get water there and carry it to the camp. They gave us the buckets, and a couple of big coolers for drinking water to keep at the camp.

Q: I know there was no telephone. What about the mail? Did they put in the mailbox right away?

A: No, I don't think they expected us to get mail, or something. It was a year or two before we had our own mailbox.

Q: Can you think of anything else they provided? If not that first year, in the years since?

A: The water line to the camp, the shower. They would save old tarps for us, things like that. All the strawberries we could eat, especially if they were too ripe to ship. And we could take anything they were throwing away. We got some dishes and stuff that way.

Q: So they didn't do that much to help. But Juan said they also didn't leave you alone, that they had a lot to say about who could live in the camp, or even who could come there, how late they could stay and so forth. Do you agree on that?

A: Oh, yeah. Lots of rules. Every year they gave everybody a copy. I brought you one.

Q: Thanks, this could come in handy. And I take it that Rudy was the main enforcer? That he actually checked up on who was there, stopped people coming in, things like that?

A: Yeah, anybody coming in had to pass his house, and he was right out there. No women. One time a nurse from the health clinic in town came out to give a guy some tests results, and she couldn't even get in. It was their private property.

* * * * *

PARSONS STRAWBERRY FARM

CAMP RULES AND REGULATIONS

* NO ONE IS PERMITTED TO LIVE ON THESE PREMISES WITHOUT THE EXPRESS PERMISSION OF THE OWNER OR HIS AGENT.

* NO OVERNIGHT VISITORS. OTHER VISITORS PERMITTED AT SOLE DISCRETION OF OWNER OR HIS AGENT.

* NO PETS OF ANY KIND.

* PLACE ALL TRASH IN DESIGNATED RECEPTACLES.

* SMOKING PERMITTED OUTSIDE OF DWELLINGS ONLY.

* NO ALCOHOLIC BEVERAGES.

* NO FIREARMS.

* NO LOUD MUSIC, TALKING, OR OTHER LOUD NOISE AFTER 10 PM, SATURDAYS EXCEPTED (MIDNIGHT SATURDAYS).

* COOKING TO BE DONE IN DESIGNATED AREAS ONLY.

* USE LATRINE AND KEEP IT CLEAN.

Library

Morales et al.

v.

Parsons

1. *Griggs v. Barnes Construction Company*   2-114
2. *Esteban Raul Lucas v. Murai Farms Inc.*   2-117
3. *Esteban Raul Lucas v. Perry C. Pollock*   2-123

GRIGGS v. BARNES CONSTRUCTION COMPANY
Franklin Court of Appeals (1992)

On December 7, 1988, Russell Griggs was electrocuted while working in a construction yard when a cable he was holding touched an overhead high voltage line. At the time of the accident, Griggs was working for Barnes Construction, a sole proprietorship owned by J.D. Barnes. Barnes Construction was engaged in several building projects in and around the town of Goose Creek in Adams County. Materials and equipment for these projects were stored in Barnes' "job yard" in Goose Creek. On the day in question, Griggs and another Barnes Construction employee, Clinton Morrow, were working in the job yard stacking timber. Morrow was operating a boom truck, and Griggs was assisting him by attaching the boom cable to bundles of timber. As Morrow was maneuvering the boom, he looked into the bright sunlight, which caused him to swing the boom into an overhead 12,000-volt power line. Unfortunately, Griggs was holding the boom cable at that very moment. The cable conducted the electricity into Griggs' body, causing his death by electrocution.

Griggs' widow and children filed suit against Barnes for wrongful death, alleging that, as a landowner, Barnes owed a general duty of due care to persons coming on his land, including employees, to protect them from the hazard presented by the high voltage lines. The trial court granted defendant's motion for summary judgment on the ground that defendant did not owe a duty of due care to the decedent, and plaintiffs appealed.

Under the common law, a landowner's duty of due care to a person coming onto his land turned on whether the person was classified as a trespasser, licensee or invitee. In *Rowland v. Christian* (1968), our Supreme Court repudiated this classification system and substituted the basic approach of foreseeability of injury to others. The court held that the proper test to be applied to the liability of the possessor of land is whether in the management of his property he has acted as a reasonable man in view of the probability of injury to others. In regard to those working on the land, the landowner who induces or knowingly permits a workman to enter the land for performance of duties mutually beneficial to both parties, is required to use reasonable care to protect the workman by supplying him with a reasonably safe place in which to work. Whether a "duty" exists in a particular case is a question of law. "Duty" is merely a conclusory expression used when the sum total of policy considerations lead a court to say that the particular plaintiff is entitled to protection.

Generally, if a danger is so obvious that a person could reasonably be expected to see it, the condition itself serves as a warning, and the landowner is under no further duty to remedy or warn of the condition. However, this is not true in all cases. It is foreseeable that even an obvious danger may cause injury, if the practical necessity of encountering the danger, when weighed against the apparent risk involved, is such that under the circumstances, a person might choose to encounter the danger. The foreseeability of injury, in turn, when considered along with various other policy considerations such as the extent of the burden to the defendant and consequences to the community of imposing a duty to remedy such danger may lead to the legal conclusion that the defendant owed a duty of due care to the person injured.

Plaintiffs argued in their opposition to the motion for summary judgment that Barnes should have taken steps to prevent the injury because he knew that the high voltage lines ran across his property and also knew that the boom truck was being stored and operated on the property. Consequently, plaintiffs contend that, viewing the evidence in the light most favorable to plaintiffs, Barnes should have reasonably foreseen that the boom might come into contact with the high voltage lines while the truck was being operated on the premises.

The most important policy consideration in determining whether a duty exists is the foreseeability of the harm. Viewing the evidence in the light most favorable to plaintiffs, as we must, we believe the harm – electrocution caused by the boom coming into contact with overhead power lines – was reasonably foreseeable by Barnes. In our view, the practical necessity of encountering the danger (*i.e.*, the necessity of using the boom truck to move materials), when weighed against the apparent risk involved (electrocution by contact with electrical wires), is such that under the circumstances, a person might (and in fact did) choose to encounter the danger. We stress, however, that we find the injury "foreseeable" only as it pertains to a general duty of care. A court's task in determining "duty" is not to decide whether a particular plaintiff's injury was reasonably foreseeable in light of a particular defendant's conduct, but rather to evaluate more generally whether the category of negligent conduct at issue is sufficiently likely to result in the kind of harm experienced that liability may appropriately be imposed on the negligent. Thus, the fact finder is still free to find that the particular plaintiff's injury (*i.e.*, Griggs' electrocution) was not foreseeable in light of this particular defendant's conduct.

In addition to foreseeability, a court should consider the following factors in determining whether a duty of due care exists: (1) the degree of certainty that the plaintiff suffered injury; (2) the proximity between the defendant's conduct and the injury suffered; (3) the moral blame attached to the defendant's conduct; (4) the policy of preventing future harm; (5) the extent of the burden to the defendant and consequences to the community of imposing a duty to exercise care with resulting liability for breach; and (6) the availability of insurance for the risk involved.

Here, the considerations numbered (1), (4), (5), and (6) militate in favor of imposing a duty in this case. The plaintiff clearly suffered injury; there is a strong policy of preventing future harm such as that which occurred here; the defendant could have easily discharged his burden by having the power lines insulated, or by specifically prohibiting the use of boom trucks or cranes in the area underneath them; and the risk here is likely covered by a standard liability policy. In short, the sum total of policy considerations lead us to say that Barnes, as a landowner, had a general duty to use due care to protect people coming onto his land from the obvious electrocution hazard on the property. Whether or not Barnes breached that duty with respect to Griggs is an issue of fact that should be left to the fact finder to decide.

Consequently, we reverse the summary judgment.

ESTEBAN RAUL LUCAS v. MURAI FARMS, INC.
Franklin Court of Appeals (1997)

Plaintiffs appeal from summary judgments granted in favor of defendants George T. R. Murai Farms, Inc. and Ramon Navarro, doing business as Chiquito Navarro Ranch. Plaintiffs Esteban Raul Lucas and Jorge Reyes (plaintiffs Guadalupe Reyes and Mario Garcia Reyes's decedent) (collectively plaintiffs) were migrant farm workers employed by Navarro at the time a fire occurred in temporary migrant farm worker housing located on property adjacent to that of Murai and Navarro. Lucas was gravely injured in the fire and Reyes was killed. Plaintiffs sued Murai and Navarro for damages for personal injuries, on theories of premises liability and negligence *per se*.

On October 22, 1987, when the fire occurred, Lucas and Reyes were undocumented Mexican nationals, working as migrant farm laborers and residing in an encampment known as the cancha, located along a creekbed on undeveloped land that was adjacent to the ranches owned by Murai and Navarro. As was their custom, Lucas, Reyes, and several co-workers built a living structure in the cancha from parts of wooden pallets, tomato stakes, cardboard, irrigation plastic, and twine, all taken from trash dump areas on the Murai and Navarro ranches.

According to his deposition, Lucas believed that the property on which he was living belonged to Murai. However, it was actually undeveloped land owned by defendant Perry Pollock. Lucas never obtained anyone's permission to live on the Pollock property and was never told to stay there by any authorities on the ranches where he worked. He did not rent a more standard dwelling because of his fear of immigration authorities, because he was sending a substantial portion of his wages home to Mexico, and because he wanted to live near his employment and his friends.

At the time of the fire, Lucas and Reyes had been working for Navarro for approximately two weeks. On the night of the fire, Lucas went into the sleeping structure about 10 p.m. to go to sleep, while Reyes remained outside reading by the light of a candle. Both drank some beer that evening. Lucas does not know how the fire started. He woke up in the hospital with serious burn injuries and learned that Reyes had died in the fire.

At the time of the fire, nonparty George Hruby, owner of Ranch-Industrial Patrol Company (RIPCO), had contracted with Murai and Navarro to provide security services to the farms. Hruby's contract did not include performing services outside the borders of either the Murai ranch or the Navarro ranch. Hruby was not told by any Murai or Navarro employees to patrol any areas outside the ranch property, such as the cancha area. However, Hruby's business provided basic police protection for the farm laborers who lived in the labor camp, since Hruby felt that no other police or border patrol agencies were ensuring the safety of the workers. RIPCO's activities in the cancha included prohibiting drinking and prostitution in the labor camp, restricting access to the camp, and expelling union organizers. RIPCO former employees signed declarations stating that their instructions regarding the cancha property and the methods used to patrol it came from Hruby, rather than anyone at Murai or Navarro.

At several points in the life of the labor camp, trash from the camp blew over onto Murai and Navarro property, and foremen employed by Murai and Navarro made the workers pick up trash in their camp. In building the shelter, Lucas used materials from trash heaps on the Murai farm, and Reyes used plastic from Navarro's farm. Navarro forbade workers to take discarded materials of any kind from the ranch, including plastic. General Manager Mark Murai prohibited anyone from taking materials from the ranch as well. Murai provided some services and amenities to workers living in the cancha, such as allowing them to use water and toilet facilities on the Murai ranch, allowing them to receive mail there, and allowing caterers and vendors access to Murai land to provide services to camp inhabitants.

Approximately a year after the fire, plaintiffs filed this action for damages for personal injuries, alleging there was a duty on the part of Murai and Navarro to provide adequate and safe housing for Lucas and decedent, as well as a duty to make safe the conditions on the cancha property or to warn plaintiffs of the dangerous conditions created by the flammable structures. After extensive discovery, Murai and Navarro each filed motions for summary judgment. At the hearing on these motions, the trial court found as a matter of law that neither Murai nor Navarro had a duty to provide housing to Lucas and plaintiffs' decedent, to ensure that the cancha was safe and habitable, or to warn Lucas and Reyes of risks involved in living in the camp. The court noted that Murai was not an employer of plaintiffs, and neither defendant had any legal authority to eject the workers from the Pollock property. The court further noted there were no triable issues of fact regarding negligence *per se*, as none of the statutes or ordinances relied upon applied to Murai or Navarro, who did not own or control the subject property.

Plaintiffs' main contention on appeal is that Murai and Navarro were not entitled to summary judgment because they did not completely establish an absence of control on their part over the area where the fire occurred, the cancha. They contend that triable factual issues remain as to the nature and extent of these defendants' control over the adjacent plot of land where the cancha was located. Plaintiffs also argue that alleged statutory violations occurred leading to liability on these defendants' parts under the Employee Housing Act.

Turning to the main issue of the extent of Murai's and Navarro's control over the cancha property, plaintiffs' theory is that the activities of Hruby's security service, RIPCO, constituted control over the premises such that the duty of a possessor of premises must be imposed upon the ranch owners. Plaintiffs also pursue an alternative theory that Murai and Navarro, as agents for each other, through the activities of their foremen, encouraged the workers to live at the cancha by providing services, amenities, and security at the premises, and controlling access to them, such that the ranch owners undertook a measure of obligation that would justify a court in imposing upon Murai and Navarro as a matter of law a duty to make the premises safe or to warn of dangers.

In support of their assertion that Murai and Navarro had a duty based upon their control of adjacent land, plaintiffs rely upon *Southland Corp. v. District Court* (Franklin Court of Appeals, 1988), where the court concluded that there were triable issues of fact concerning whether a store owner, which had an easement over adjacent land and allowed its customers to park on the land in order to gain access to the store, had a sufficient degree of control over that land, on which the plaintiff was criminally assaulted, in order to justify the imposition of a duty on the store owner to keep the premises safe for users of the property. The court noted that although the critical issue for imposition of a duty is control over premises, the concept of control as developed in case law has been somewhat elastic and the exercise of control is not necessarily confined to those premises that are owned or possessed by the defendant. A number of circumstances led to the Court of Appeals' conclusion that triable issues remained over the extent of the store owner's control over the adjacent lot, so as to legally permit the imposition of a duty to those customers using the lot, such as regular use of the adjacent lot for parking, authorization in the store lease for such parking, knowledge on the part of the store owner of the customers' regular use of the lot, and significant commercial benefit from the use of the lot.

In this case, plaintiffs rely upon several factors to support their assertion that Murai and Navarro had an adequate degree of control over the adjacent property where the cancha was located in order to support the imposition upon them of a duty of care and/or to warn of danger. First, Lucas claims that RIPCO was an agent of Murai and Navarro inasmuch as RIPCO's security activities at the cancha, such as banning alcohol and prostitutes, showed control over the entire premises. Murai, however, made a showing that it did not instruct RIPCO to patrol the camp. Navarro made a showing that he did not know about the existence of the camp until after the fire, and his contract with RIPCO also did not cover off-premises areas. It thus does not appear that any actions of Murai or Navarro, as principals, were relied upon by Lucas and Jorge Reyes to create the impression that RIPCO was the agent for the ranchers for purposes of ensuring overall camp safety. Although a principal is liable for the torts of an agent under the doctrine of *respondeat superior*, for this liability to be imposed on the innocent principal, the agent's tort must have been committed during the course and scope of his employment. We conclude that as a matter of law, the type and extent of activities that RIPCO engaged in at the cancha were not enough to constitute control of the cancha property for purposes of imposing a duty on Murai and Navarro.

Secondly, plaintiffs rely upon the activities of Murai and Navarro employees, such as the foremen at the farms, to make a showing of some degree of control over the cancha property. For instance, Murai and Navarro foremen instructed workers living at the camp to pick up trash, and allegedly permitted scrap materials to be taken from Murai and Navarro dumps for use in building the wood and plastic shelters. By their activities in allowing the workers to use water and toilet facilities on Murai property, and allowing the workers to receive mail at the Murai address, it is alleged that these employers encouraged the labor camp environment to exist, and gained an economic benefit from it, so as to justify the imposition of a duty to make the premises safe or to warn of dangers.

A number of considerations lead us to reject plaintiffs' argument that a duty existed here as a matter of law. First, a duty to exercise ordinary care not to injure another will arise out of a voluntarily assumed relationship only if public policy dictates that such a duty should be imposed. Whether in a specific case the defendant will be held liable to a third person not in privity as a matter of public policy involves the balancing of various factors, among which are the extent to which the transaction was intended to affect the plaintiff, the foreseeability of harm to him, the degree of certainty that the plaintiff suffered injury, the closeness of the connection between the defendant's conduct and the injury suffered, the moral blame attached to the defendant's conduct, and the policy of preventing future harm.

The facts here showed that both Murai and Navarro ranch owners and managers made an effort to prohibit workers from using building materials from the ranch scrap heaps, Navarro in particular because he believed the plastic used for fumigation of crops was poisonous. Even though Murai and Navarro foremen apparently did not prevent the workers from taking such scrap materials from the ranch, the factors outlining the public policy for whether to impose a duty of care based on such activities indicate that no such duty should be imposed. In particular, foreseeability of this type of harm is questionable, and the necessary closeness of connection between defendants' conduct and the injury is missing, since it was the use of an open-flame candle in the shelter (over which use these defendants had no control) that caused the injury.

The law of premises liability does not extend so far as to hold a landowner liable merely because its property exists next to adjoining dangerous property and it took no action to influence or affect the condition of such adjoining property. The activities of Lucas and the plaintiffs' decedent in building the shelters and using lighted candles in them must be distinguished in kind from the activities of the customers who used the dangerous adjacent parking lot in Southland Corp., *supra*. Lucas and Jorge Reyes were not business patrons of their employers, and no third party criminal acts were inflicted upon plaintiffs for which the ranch owners should be held responsible. Instead, plaintiffs knew of the danger of using fire in the temporary structures, but did so anyway.

Although a possessor of land must exercise reasonable care to make the premises safe or to warn regarding dangerous conditions or activities the possessor knows of or could readily discover, there is no obligation to protect the invitee against dangers which are known to him, or which are so apparent that he may reasonably be expected to discover them and be fully able to watch for himself.

An owner of property is not an ensurer of safety, but must use reasonable care to keep the premises in a reasonably safe condition and must give warning of latent or concealed perils. The danger of the structures at the cancha was obvious and was not in any sense latent or concealed, especially to those persons who built the structures and used them. Consequently, we see no basis for the imposition of a duty on the ranch owners to warn of dangers inherent in the use of the structures just off their premises, nor any duty to make those structures safe for the inhabitants.

Because of the conclusions reached above, that no duty of care or duty to warn may be imposed on Murai and Navarro towards plaintiffs, we find it unnecessary to discuss the statutory claims directed toward the employers as alleged owners and controllers of property.

The judgments are affirmed.

ESTEBAN RAUL LUCAS v. PERRY C. POLLOCK
Franklin Court of Appeals (1997)

This is the second of two cases decided today arising out of a fire in temporary migrant farm worker housing constructed on defendant Perry Pollock's land, in which plaintiff Esteban Raul Lucas was gravely injured and plaintiffs Guadalupe Reyes and Mario Garcia Reyes's decedent, Jorge Reyes, was killed. In granting Pollock's motion for summary judgment, the trial court found Pollock had breached no landowner's duties sounding in negligence that were owed to plaintiffs, and was not liable for damages. Plaintiffs appealed.

The farm where Lucas and Reyes were working at the time of the fire was located adjacent to Pollock's property, which was undeveloped and not used for any purpose, including farming. Pollock acquired this land in 1975 after he foreclosed on a trust deed, was holding it solely for investment purposes, and at the time of the accident was trying to sell it, using the services of real estate agent James Daley. Pollock never gave anyone permission to enter onto or live on his property, and he testified in his deposition he was unaware that anyone was present there at the time of the fire. He did admit to having seen that a fence was down on the northern edge of the property, and tire tracks indicating that vehicles might have entered at some time in the past. The area on Pollock's property where the migrant encampments were made was hidden deep within a gully and was obscured by thick underbrush. The shelters were invisible and inaccessible from the single paved road in the area, or from the southern portion of the adjoining ranch, where Lucas and Reyes worked. The owners of that farm denied that they had ever seen shelters near the Pollock property. Pollock never discussed his property with anyone who worked for the adjoining farms.

Approximately a year after the fire, Lucas and Reyes's survivors filed their complaint for personal injury and wrongful death against Pollock and the owners of the farms adjacent to his land, one of whom had employed the plaintiffs. As against Pollock, the cause of action was for premises liability.

After discovery had been conducted, Pollock filed his motion for summary judgment, arguing that he owed no legal duty of care to the plaintiffs and had acted reasonably in the management of his property in view of the probability of injuries to others, even trespassers. Plaintiffs' opposition focused upon allegations of Pollock's actual knowledge of conditions on the property, or imputed knowledge on the basis of his real estate agent's familiarity with the property resulting from his appraisal and attempts to sell it.

Regarding their claims of Pollock's actual knowledge, plaintiffs argue that a defendant's actual knowledge may be shown, not only by direct evidence, but also by circumstantial evidence. Hence, his denial of such knowledge will not, *per se*, prevent liability. They also argue that landowners may be held liable for failure to correct within a reasonable time such defects in the property as would have been revealed by a reasonable inspection. From all of these rules, plaintiffs argue, a triable issue of fact is created as to the existence of knowledge on the part of Pollock, impliedly creating a duty to make safe his land from the dangerous conditions which caused the fire. They argue that a landowner is responsible not only for the result of his willful acts, but also for an injury occasioned to another by his want of ordinary care or skill in the management of his property. On the issue of Pollock's constructive knowledge, plaintiffs argue that Pollock's real estate agent, Daley, was under a duty to inform Pollock of matters in connection with the agency which would affect the marketability or value of Pollock's real property. The presence of a migrant farm worker encampment is argued to be such a matter affecting the value of real property.

We find several defects with plaintiffs' reasoning. First, although the evidence showed Pollock had designated Daley as his agent in the proposed sale of the property, the scope of that agency created duties in Daley only to Pollock as the principal and to prospective purchasers of the property. Plaintiffs have made no showing that third party trespassers or bystanders on the property were entitled to any particular duties arising out of that agency, which was created for a limited purpose.

Here, the injured plaintiffs had no dealings with Pollock either directly or through Daley. In opposition to Pollock's motion, plaintiffs were able to raise only speculation and suggestions that Pollock "must have known" about the existence of the encampments.

However, such evidence is not sufficient to justify an inference of actual knowledge, nor is the same equivocal evidence as to Daley sufficient to support an inference of constructive knowledge on Pollock's part. Moreover, the evidence on which the plaintiffs rely to show notice of the presence of the encampment (*i.e.*, Pollock's knowledge that an alternative access route to the property had apparently been developed and his admission after the fire in a letter to the police department that farm workers lived on the property, along with Daley's familiarity with the property) does not as a matter of law establish that Pollock, as landowner, had a duty to these plaintiffs to make the premises reasonably safe for the purposes for which they were used. A landlord should not be held liable for injuries from conditions over which he has no control. Manifestly, Pollock had no control over the existence of hazards in the migrant farm workers' encampment, which he had not authorized to be built, and the dangers of which all the evidence showed he lacked actual or constructive knowledge.

In conclusion, even if we assume that Pollock had actual or constructive knowledge of the presence of migrant encampments upon his property, we are unable to conclude as a matter of law from such evidence (if any) that a duty existed on Pollock's part to take steps to correct or prevent the particular dangers which led to plaintiffs' injuries in this case, specifically the danger of fire in the temporary structures. Pollock's status as landowner did not create in him a duty to ensure the well-being of these third parties upon his property, nor any duty to protect them from their own activities, nor any duty to police an area in which he was conducting no activity whatsoever. Nor did the actual condition of Pollock's land in its undeveloped state, or his management of it, contribute to or cause the accident which injured the plaintiffs. The issue presented by this motion for summary judgment is whether any knowledge on Pollock's part, if shown, created a duty on the theory that his conduct was unreasonable in light of any such knowledge. The trial court's grant of summary judgment correctly resolved that issue.

The judgment is affirmed.

IX. EDITORS' PREPARED GRADING GUIDE

FOR PRACTICE QUESTION 2:

MORALES et al. v. PARSONS

Our editors have prepared a substantive grading guide outline to help you evaluate your answer. We have approached this from the perspective of the model answer structure typically used by a bar exam grader. After you complete a draft answer, compare and contrast it with the sample answer that follows this grading guide. If you missed key issues in your analysis consider updating your answer.

__ Persuasive document in memorandum format

__ Premises liability
   __ *Griggs*: Duty factors
     __ Foreseeability
     __ Certainty that P suffered harm
     __ Proximity between D's conduct and injury
     __ Moral blame
     __ Policy of preventing future harm
     __ Burden to D and consequences to community
     __ Availability of insurance
   __ *Lucas I*: Possessor of land must exercise reasonable care
     __ "Critical issue" is control over premises
     __ *Lucas I* distinguishable
       __ Ds did not own land and had no authority to eject Ps
       __ One D employed other residents, but not Ps
       __ Both Ds did not permit employees to scavenge materials that could be used for makeshift, unsafe housing
       __ Here, D actively encouraged scavenging of unsafe building materials
       __ Ps were subject to fewer rules and restrictions
       __ Camp had lesser security
       __ Ps were provided with fewer amenities on the camp site
   __ *Lucas II* distinguishable
     __ Ps had no dealings with landowner D
     __ Insufficient evidence that D had knowledge of camp's existence or dangers

X. SAMPLE ANSWER TO PRACTICE QUESTION 2:

MORALES et al. v. PARSONS

MEMORANDUM

TO: Jane Kimmel
FROM: Applicant
RE: Morales and Vargas v. Parsons
DATE: July 29, 20X3

Statement of Facts

Juan Morales was injured and Alberto Vargas was killed when, apparently, an oil lamp used to illuminate their shacks made of cardboard, plastic and other refuse was knocked over and ignited the shanties in which they lived. The camp is situated on a parcel of land owned by their employer, Parsons Strawberry Farm, whose owner, Parsons, encouraged the formation of the camp in order to reduce expenses and have a labor pool located nearby.

At the time of the fire, the camp's residents had limited access to water (one faucet and one shower), no electricity and no gas. The entire camp consisted of approximately 30 to 35 "tents" built one next to the other in two distinct sections of Parsons' land.

Issue Presented

May Vargas' family and Morales recover damages against Parsons under a theory of premises liability?

Short Answer

Yes. Both Morales and Vargas' family may proceed against Parsons under a theory of premises liability. The case law holding contrary is not on point and is distinguishable based primarily on the facts that Parsons owned the land where the camp was located and actively facilitated the camp's creation and exerted control over its operation.

Discussion

Under Franklin law the question of whether or not Parsons owed a duty to the residents of his labor camp requires the court to weigh and consider seven factors: 1) the foreseeability of harm to the plaintiff; 2) the degree of certainty that the plaintiff suffered injury; 3) the proximity between the defendant's conduct and the injury suffered; 4) the moral blame attached to the defendant's conduct; 5) the policy of preventing future harm; 6) the extent of the burden to the defendant and consequences to the community of imposing a duty to exercise care with resulting liability for breach; and 7) the availability of insurance for the risk involved. Griggs.

Morales and Vargas' Family May Recover Under the Theory of Premises Liability Because Parsons Owned the Camp, Exercised Comprehensive Control over the Grounds, and Effectively Required His Employees to Live There

"A possessor of land must exercise reasonable care to make the premises safe or to warn regarding dangerous conditions or activities the possessor knows of or could readily discover." Lucas I. In Lucas I, the plaintiffs were migrant farm workers residing in a camp just off the premises of two farmers. As is the case here, one plaintiff was severely injured and another plaintiff died as a result of a candle setting fire to a shanty comprised of highly flammable material. The surviving plaintiff and the deceased plaintiff's family were suing for recovery based on both premises liability and negligence *per se*. In regards to the premises liability theory, the court concluded that the employers owed no duty to the workers who resided on an adjacent piece of property.

"[T]he critical issue for imposition of a duty is control over the premises." Lucas I (citing Southland Corp). Generally, a party may not recover for injuries when a dangerous condition on the land is so obvious that the victim can reasonably be expected to see it. Franklin courts have held that such an "obvious" danger excuses the landowner from any further duty to remedy or warn of the condition. Griggs (employee killed by electrocution when cable he was holding on to came in contact with a high voltage, uninsulated power line). However, "[i]t is foreseeable that even an obvious danger may cause injury, if the practical necessity of encountering the danger, when weighed against apparent risk involved, is such that under the circumstances, a person might choose to encounter the danger." Griggs. Under such conditions, public policy may require courts to impose a duty on the defendant to exercise due care towards the foreseeably injured person. Griggs.

Here, the danger of fire in the camp should have been obvious to anyone. Highly flammable cardboard and plastics were used to shelter workers who used dangerous and unstable oil lamps as their primary, if not sole, method of illumination. As noted by Morales himself, though easier and cheaper than kerosene lamps, if one of the oil lamps tips over, the oil spills everywhere, and can start a fire. The question was not if a fire would have occurred at Parsons' labor camp, but when.

As an obvious danger, normally the landowner's duty in this case would have been discharged under the Lucas I and Griggs analysis. However, the court in Griggs noted an applicable exception to this general rule. When the practical necessity of encountering the danger is weighed against the apparent risks involved, and under the circumstances a reasonable person would choose to encounter the risk, then public policy requires the imposition of a duty on the landowner to exercise due care towards the foreseeable injured person.

Here, the plaintiffs were farm workers who had little or no choice but to reside on the property in order to secure their employment. The risks of living in a tinderbox were obvious, but these workers weighed their options and had little recourse but to accept the accommodations as they were. Even though residence in the camp was not technically required by either Parsons or Mendoza, there were no affordable accommodations available within a reasonable distance. In practice, all the farm workers resided in the camp because they had no alternative available. Thus, the fact that the danger was obvious should not preclude the imposition of a duty on Parsons.

Lucas I can easily be distinguished on its facts, the main difference being that the plaintiffs in that case resided on a parcel of land that did not belong to either defendant. "The court [in Lucas I] noted that Murai [defendant] was not an employer of the plaintiffs, and neither defendant had any legal authority to eject the workers from the . . . property." Lucas I. Unbeknownst to the Lucas I plaintiffs, the camp was located on the premises of a third party and not their employers. In addition, the employers, Murai and Navarro, had policies forbidding the scavenging of materials by the migrant workers from their property in order to erect shanties.

In this case, Parsons actively encouraged the practice of scavenging highly flammable material to construct shanties and the camp was situated on his land where he possessed legal authority to eject the tenants. Thus, Parsons has a greater degree of inducement and resulting culpability than either of the defendants in Lucas I.

In addition, the Lucas I plaintiffs were asserting that liability should attach to the defendants because of their agent's assertion of authority over the camp in order to ensure overall camp security and safety. Though the agent of the defendants in Lucas I did impose security measures over the camp, such as banning alcohol and prostitutes, the agent was acting without the express or implied authority to do so. Neither defendant instructed the security agency to patrol and monitor the camp. The Lucas I court thus concluded that, as a matter of law, the type of activities the security agent engaged in were not enough to constitute control of the camp property for purposes of imposing a duty on the defendants.

Again, the land in question in this case belongs to the employer, and the agent he employed to monitor camp safety, foreman Rudy Mendoza, engaged in actions sufficient to establish Parsons' control over the labor camp. As the Parsons Strawberry Farm Camp Rules and Regulations, distributed and enforced by Mendoza, indicate, the laborers at Parsons were subject to tighter scrutiny than the plaintiffs in Lucas I. They were denied any female visitors, and other visitors were allowed at the sole discretion of the foreman or Parsons himself. They also restricted pets, smoking, alcohol, firearms, and imposed a curfew. In addition, they connected a water line to run a shower and for cooking, and Parsons provided two portable toilets for the men to use which he had maintained and emptied on a regular basis.

In addition, Mendoza, through an agreement with his own family member, imposed a virtual monopoly on the farm workers' access to food for both lunch and dinner. Thus, it is clear that the legal conclusions in Lucas I are not applicable to a situation where the owner/employer exerts this degree of authority or control over the workers' lives and property.

In Lucas II, decided the same day, the Court of Appeals for Franklin affirmed the dismissal of the case solely against the landowner. The court noted that the injured plaintiffs had no dealings with the landowner, Pollack, either directly or indirectly through his real estate agent, Daley. The plaintiffs were unable to show that the owner had any knowledge of the presence of the camp on his property. Due to that camp's relative isolation and hidden features, the court refused to impose a duty on the landowner merely for failing to exercise ordinary care or skill in the management of his property. The landowner in that case did not reside on the land, received the land when he foreclosed on a trust deed, and at the time of the fire in Lucas II was looking for someone to purchase the property. The Lucas II court concluded that Pollack had no control over the existence of hazards in the migrant farm workers' encampment, he had not authorized its construction, and he lacked either actual or constructive knowledge of the camp's dangers.

Parsons is in exactly the opposite position. He exerted complete control over the camp in which Morales and Vargas resided. He not only authorized but assisted in the camp's construction and he had actual knowledge of the camp's inherent dangers because he supplied the materials that the workers used to build their "homes." The holding in Lucas II is thus inapplicable to Morales and Vargas' case against Parsons because Parsons' behavior is much more culpable then either the defendants in Lucas I or Lucas II.

Conclusion

All of the factors noted above for imposing liability on Parsons for the injuries sustained by the plaintiffs in this case are present. The harm to the plaintiffs was eminently foreseeable. There can be no doubt that the plaintiffs suffered a certain injury. The defendant's conduct is the actual and proximate cause of the plaintiffs' injury. Parsons encouraged and facilitated the camp's operation to save expenses and "cut out the middle man" he was paying to import his needed labor supply daily. He provided the flammable and substandard materials the workers scavenged from his farm in order to piece together shanties one on top of the other. He knew or had reason to know of or possibly provided the oil lamps the workers were using to light their hovels. Thus his conduct borders on recklessness beyond mere negligence.

The court should therefore conclude that Parsons owed a duty to his farm workers under the theory of premises liability.

RIGOS UNIFORM BAR EXAM (UBE) REVIEW SERIES

MULTISTATE PERFORMANCE TEST (MPT) REVIEW

CHAPTER 3

OBJECTIVE MEMORANDA

Table of Contents

I.	**INTRODUCTION**	3-137
	A. Position of Neutrality	
	B. Objective of Task	
	C. Previous Advice	
II.	**STRUCTURE OF THE QUESTION**	3-137
	A. Similarities to a Persuasive Brief	
	1. Task Memorandum	
	a. Civil Case	
	b. Criminal Case	
	2. Other Materials	
	3. Library	
	B. Important Differences from a Persuasive Brief	
	1. Ethical Issues	
	2. Format Not Specified	
	3. Beginning Heading	
	4. Memorandum Body Headings	
III.	**ANSWERING THE QUESTION**	3-139
	A. Planning Your Answer	
	B. Balanced Analysis	
	1. Objectivity	
	2. One-sided Presentation	
	C. IRAC Format	
	1. Memorandum Format	
	2. Analyzing Unfavorable Case Law	
	a. Factual Differences	
	b. Precedential Value	
	c. No Way Around It?	
	3. Statutes and Court Rules	
	4. Modified CIRAC Format	
	D. Close Calls	
	E. You Need to Reach a Conclusion	
IV.	**WORKING THROUGH A SAMPLE QUESTION:** *ADAIR v. OLDFIELD*	3-140
	A. Table of Contents	3-141
	B. Instructions	3-143
	C. File	3-145

	D. Library	3-159
	E. Editors' Summary	3-167
	F. Sample Answer	3-168
	G. Practice Questions	3-172
V.	**PRACTICE QUESTION 1:** *IN RE RYAN COX*	**3-173**
	Instructions	3-175
	File	3-177
	Task Memorandum	3-178
	Excerpts of Interview with Ryan Cox	3-179
	Memorandum re Phone Conversations with Emily and Adam Cox	3-184
	Installment Contract	3-185
	Letter Dated May 2, 20X3, from Opposing Counsel to Adam Cox	3-188
	Letter Dated July 3, 20X3, from Opposing Counsel to Adam Cox	3-189
	Library	3-191
	Cavallaro v. Stratford Homes, Inc.	3-192
	Binninger v. Hutchinson	3-194
	Tanner v. Fulk	3-196
	Editors' Prepared Grading Guide	3-199
	Sample Answer	3-201
VI.	**EDITORS' PREPARED GRADING GUIDE FOR PRACTICE QUESTION 1:** *IN RE RYAN COX*	**3-199**
VII.	**SAMPLE ANSWER TO PRACTICE QUESTION 1:** *IN RE RYAN COX*	**3-201**
VIII.	**PRACTICE QUESTION 2:** *U.S. v. ALEJANDRO CRUZ*	**3-205**
	Instructions	3-207
	File	3-209
	Task Memorandum	3-210
	Transcript of Alejandro Cruz Interview	3-211
	Letter from Office of Foreign Assets Control to Alejandro Cruz	3-215
	Customs and Border Protection Report	3-217
	Library	3-221
	Selected Provisions of the Trading with the Enemy Act	3-222
	United States v. Frade	3-224
	United States. v. Macko	3-227
	Editors' Prepared Grading Guide	3-231
	Sample Answer	3-233
IX.	**EDITORS' PREPARED GRADING GUIDE FOR PRACTICE QUESTION 2:** *U.S. v. ALEJANDRO CRUZ*	**3-231**
X.	**SAMPLE ANSWER TO PRACTICE QUESTION 2:** *U.S. v. ALEJANDRO CRUZ*	**3-233**

RIGOS UNIFORM BAR EXAM (UBE) REVIEW SERIES

MULTISTATE PERFORMANCE TEST (MPT) REVIEW

CHAPTER 3

OBJECTIVE MEMORANDA

I. INTRODUCTION

An objective memorandum is the second of the two most common types of MPT tasks. Chances are excellent that if you do not get a persuasive brief question, you will receive an objective memorandum task. If your jurisdiction's bar exam includes two MPT questions, it is likely you will receive each type of assignment. For these reasons, you need to be equally proficient in answering both objective and persuasive MPT questions.

A. Position of Neutrality

When answering such a question, you need to take the position of a neutral evaluator providing objective, candid advice. Look for requirements to "analyze," "discuss," or "evaluate" or "assess the merits of the claim/defense." This impartiality is to be distinguished from the role of an advocate, which favors and supports only one side of the dispute

B. Objective of Task

Your goal is to inform your supervising attorney (and/or your law firm client) of the objective strengths and weaknesses of various issues in their claim. The Library usually includes a controlling statute and cases interpreting some provision of the statute.

C. Previous Advice

The previous chapter's writing information and suggestions *supra* at 2-19 to 2-24 is particularly applicable in a task requiring creation of an objective memoranda. Some students quickly review these six pages at this point.

II. STRUCTURE OF THE QUESTION

The structure of an objective memorandum question is usually similar to that of a persuasive brief task.

A. Similarities to a Persuasive Brief

The question packet will contain, in addition to the instructions, a File and a Library. Separate your book pages and lay out these three resources for working convenience.

    1. Task Memorandum: The first item in the File will be a memorandum from the supervising attorney assigning your task. This memorandum provides the requirements or "call of the question." As with a persuasive brief task, be alert for an instruction telling you not to do something; *e.g.*, do not analyze one of the legal issues presented by the case.

a. Civil Case: If the client is the plaintiff, the gist of the question is whether she has the ingredients required to pursue a legal viable claim. If a potential or actual defendant in a civil case, your assignment will likely be to determine whether the plaintiff has a viable cause of action and/or if the client has any affirmative defenses.

b. Criminal Case: If your question involves the application of criminal law and you represent the prosecution, the question will probably revolve around whether a suspect or defendant meets the legal requirement of any crimes. If, on the other hand, you are counsel for a criminal defendant, your task likely will be to determine whether all the elements necessary to convict your client exist and/or whether he has any viable defenses.

2. Other Materials: The File may include documents in addition to the task memorandum. Examples are a transcript of an interview with the client or a witness, a deposition transcript, a police report, or a key piece of evidence.

3. Library Contents: As with every MPT question, all of the law necessary to write a satisfactory objective memorandum will be contained in the Library. But again, it will usually be much longer than the File and should be given more of your analysis time. A good rule of thumb is not to go beyond the Library authority provided, except perhaps for a very brief discussion of a relevant and well-known legal principle.

> **MPT Tip:** Remember that some materials in the File and/or Library will be unnecessary. Beware of red herrings that could waste your time and lead you astray.

B. Important Differences from a Persuasive Brief

There are key differences between the structure of the advocate's persuasive brief and a balanced, objective expression of position.

1. Ethical Issues: In the advocacy brief tasks, CR11 violations or RPC 3.1 unethical acts are not usually an issue, at least if they occurred on your side of the dispute. Where you are in a more objective role, such issues may be addressed.

2. Format Not Specified: The detailed form your objective memorandum answer should take is sometimes addressed in the MPT file, but also may not be specified. This does not mean your answer form is unimportant, only that no official guidance may not be given. Below we discuss how to determine the various sections in your memorandum.

3. Beginning Heading: Begin with a simple memorandum greeting such as:

MEMORANDUM OF LAW

TO: Supervising Attorney
FROM: Associate
RE: Christopher Client
DATE: July 29, 20X3

4. Memorandum Body Headings: Visual organization creates a grader's positive first impression. Unless otherwise instructed in the task, many authorities advise using three centered and capitalized content headings such as:

INTRODUCTION
DISCUSSION and/or ANALYSIS
CONCLUSION

The introduction and conclusion sections usually are a relatively short undivided paragraph. The main discussion or analysis section should be subdivided by major issues and/or points. Try I, II, III IV, or A, B, C, D for appropriate subdivisions.

III. ANSWERING THE QUESTION

Your job is to provide objective advice to your supervising attorney and/or client, not to persuade a judge. Regardless of the more balanced approach required for an objective memorandum, you will still need to reach a legal conclusion of the likely outcome.

> **MPT Tip:** Do not write your name on the memorandum, only your candidate number. Bar exam candidates' answers are graded anonymously with tight security measures to prevent graders from knowing the name of the applicant. Anonymous grading helps ensure fairness in the scoring process.

A. Planning Your Answer

All the planning steps and time allocation system we learned in persuasive briefs apply to objective memoranda.

B. Balanced Analysis

Your analysis in an objective memorandum should be more balanced than would be found in a persuasive brief.

1. Objectivity: The shading of facts techniques we learned in the Persuasive Brief chapter does not usually apply in creating an Objective Memorandum task. Resist the temptation to please the supervising attorney or client by making something seem more favorable than it really is.

2. One-sided Presentation: The facts given in some questions weigh quite heavily in one direction. Do not be afraid to be the bearer of bad news if that represents reality. A lawyer sometimes has to tell clients what they do not want to hear.

C. IRAC Format

The "IRAC" (Issue, Rule, Analysis, Conclusion) approach that you learned in law school is generally a good format for addressing each issue in your objective memorandum.

1. Memorandum Format: The discussion section will likely contain numerous sections, each containing a separate heading. Often this breakdown is based on the legal elements the Franklin courts have held controlling in their prior opinions such as whether a marriage complied with the Franklin Family Code interpretations. Planning the subparts of your analysis is very important. You do not want to repeat the same rule of law or relevant facts, and the sequence should flow logically.

2. Analyzing Unfavorable Case Law: When completing an objective memorandum task, unfavorable case law presents somewhat less of a challenge than it does in the context of a persuasive brief question. You don't necessarily need to downplay or argue around it. If a case in the Library is harmful to your client's case, you can, and should, address it in an appropriate manner.

a. Factual Differences: Look for key differences between the facts of the case in the Library and those of your case.

b. Precedential Value: The only binding cases are those handed down by Franklin state courts, the fictional federal 15th Circuit, or the U.S. Supreme Court.

c. No Way Around It?: Sometimes a proper analysis will lead only to an unfavorable conclusion. If you find yourself in such a situation, remember that you need to remain objective and be candid. Do not sugar-coat bad news. The senior partner or client wants a balanced and accurate position to decide in how best to proceed. Some NCBE questions seem more one-sided than others. Clients sometimes need to hear what they don't want to hear. Try to put the unpleasant news in as acceptable a way as possible.

> **MPT Tip:** Look for negative facts and/or law in both the File and Library. Seek and you will usually find. This information must be objectively disclosed in your memorandum

3. Statutes and Court Rules: If your Library contains multiple statutes (including administrative regulations) or court rules, chances are good that some of them are unnecessary. As always, beware of red herrings.

4. Modified CIRAC Format: Some students prefer to begin with a combined issue/conclusion statement and repeat the conclusion after the analysis. While this modified IRAC approach is perfectly acceptable, the most important part of your answer is the analysis (see *infra*). Students who find it difficult to complete objective memoranda tasks within the 90-minute testing period may benefit from using a "pure" IRAC format to avoid unnecessary and time-consuming repetition.

D. Close Calls

You may find yourself faced with an issue that has no clear answer or is dependent on facts not provided. If so, do not worry about whether your conclusion is the "right" one. The grader will be looking at the quality of your analysis and whether your conclusion logically flows from that analysis.

E. You Need to Reach a Conclusion

In any event, you must provide a final conclusion. An analysis by itself is not sufficient. If your memorandum has no conclusion, you have not completed the ultimate task of answering the questions posed to you by your supervising attorney.

IV. WORKING THROUGH A SAMPLE QUESTION:

ADAIR v. OLDFIELD

We will now take a look at a sample question, *Adair v. Oldfield*. The table of contents for the materials begins on the next page.

ADAIR v. OLDFIELD

TABLE OF CONTENTS

| **Documents Provided for Task** | **Page** |

Instructions — 3-143

File — 3-145

    Task Memorandum — 3-146

    (Editors' Summary of Task Memorandum) — 3-147

    Excerpts from the Deposition of William Oldfield — 3-148

    Excerpts from the Deposition of Greg Adair — 3-153

    Release of Liability — 3-157

Library — 3-159

    Buchan v. United States Cycling Federation — 3-160

    Leon v. Family Fitness Center — 3-164

(Editors' Summary of Key Facts and Legal Authority) — 3-167

Sample Answer — 3-168

ADAIR v. OLDFIELD

INSTRUCTIONS

1. You will have 90 minutes to complete this session of the examination. This performance test is designed to evaluate your ability to handle a select number of legal authorities in the context of a factual problem involving a client.

2. The problem is set in the fictional State of Franklin, one of the United States, located in the fictional Fifteenth Circuit. Franklin has District Courts (trial courts), Courts of Appeal (mid-level appellate courts), and a Supreme Court (Franklin's highest appellate court).

3. You will have two sets of materials with which to work: a File and a Library.

4. The File contains factual materials about your case. The first document is a memorandum containing the instructions for the tasks that you are to complete.

5. The Library contains the legal authorities needed to complete the tasks. The case reports may be real, modified, or written solely for the purpose of this performance test. If the cases appear familiar to you, do not assume that they are precisely the same as you have read before. Read each thoroughly, as if it were new to you. You should assume that cases were decided in the jurisdictions and on the dates shown. In citing cases from the Library, you may use abbreviations and omit page citations.

6. Your response must be written in the answer book provided. You should concentrate on the materials provided, but you should also bring to bear on the problem your general knowledge of the law. What you have learned in law school and elsewhere provides the general background for analyzing the problem; the File and Library provide the specific materials with which you must work.

7. Although there are no restrictions on how you apportion your time, you should probably allocate at least 45 minutes to reading and organizing before you begin writing your response. You may make notes anywhere in the test materials, but may not tear out pages from this booklet.

8. Your response will be graded on its compliance with instructions and on its content, thoroughness, and organization.

File

Adair

v.

Oldfield

1. Memorandum to Applicant — 3-146
2. Editors' Summary — 3-147
3. Excerpts from the Deposition of William Oldfield — 3-148
4. Excerpts from the Deposition of Greg Adair — 3-153
5. Release of Liability Form — 3-157

Law Office of G. Craig

TASK MEMORANDUM ASSIGNMENT

TO: Applicant
FROM: Gary Craig
DATE: July 29, 20X3

SUBJECT: *Adair v. Oldfield*

Greg Adair was seriously injured in a rock climbing fall at a weekly climbing session that was loosely operated by our client, William Oldfield. Adair has sued Oldfield for damages based on negligence. Discovery has been completed. As I prepare for settlement or trial, I must decide whether a defense of express and/or implied assumption of risk is likely to prove successful.

This is my question. The issue of express assumption of risk turns on the enforceability of the Release of Liability signed by Adair. Please write a memorandum that evaluates the likelihood of Adair prevailing based on the law and the facts in the materials.

I have another associate researching the implied assumption of risk defense, so please do not concern yourself with that issue.

EDITORS' SUMMARY OF THE TASK MEMORANDUM

A. Call of the Question

Here, the task memorandum provides you with a clear "call of the question," as well as the basic facts. You are an associate attorney helping with the defense of a personal injury claim brought against our client, who "loosely operated" rock-climbing sessions. The injury apparently occurred during a climbing session at the client's facility.

B. Express Assumption of Risk

Your task is to draft an objective memorandum to assist your supervising attorney in evaluating the viability of an express assumption of the risk defense. This term was contained within our client's contract with the climbers. Ultimately this issue will be quite important in the decision whether to go to trial or settle the matter.

C. Implied Assumption of Risk

Note that although implied assumption of the risk is another possible defense, you have been specifically told not to address that issue.

We will now continue with the rest of the File and the Library.

EXCERPTS FROM THE DEPOSITION OF WILLIAM OLDFIELD

EXAMINATION BY MS. SALISBURY, COUNSEL FOR PLAINTIFF:

* * *

Q. Let's turn to the Wednesday climbing at Handley Rock. How did you organize those sessions?

A. I didn't. When I started climbing, a group of friends would meet at Handley Rock. On summer nights and some weekends we'd get together to climb, practice, and teach ourselves how to climb. Eventually, we got into the habit of meeting on Wednesday nights, and many climbers just showed up. Since I lived nearby, I'd bring over half a dozen ropes and other gear and kind of rig the ropes for the others. That kind of explains what developed over 20 years. No one ever sat down and said, "Let's meet one night a week and put Bill in charge."

Q. But you were responsible for equipment and setting things up?

A. But I didn't direct what went on. I didn't say who could or couldn't climb or what they could do. If someone showed up who wanted to learn, someone would help him. You know, show him how to tie into the rope, probably direct him to the easiest climbs, and talk him up the rock. I wouldn't call it formal instruction.

Q. You did that as well, helping beginners, correct?

A. Yes, that includes me as well. Sometimes a person would see us climbing and ask to try it, but most beginners would show up with a friend who was a climber or had done some climbing. So I'd say it was more common for folks to show up with someone who was responsible for them.

Q. But if a beginner was there, then you or someone would take care of him?

A. Someone would usually help him get started, yes.

Q. Was there anyone else who would always show up on Wednesday nights?

A. The people changed over the years.

Q. Over all the years, you've been the one who's been there consistently?

A. I've been the most consistent, yes. That's one way to put it.

Q. You were there when Greg Adair first showed up, correct?

A. Probably. I remember he started coming out the summer before the accident. He usually came with two friends, his girlfriend and another guy. Greg seemed to be the leader of their little group. He was the one really hooked on climbing, pushing the other two to try harder climbs, and asking for help on climbs, always interested in where to go to climb. He was there often and was eager to learn.

Q. Mr. Oldfield, would you please explain how the ropes were set up at Handley Rock?

A. Most of what we do at Handley Rock is what climbers call "top roping," climbing with a rope holding you from above, so that if you fall, the rope will hold you and prevent a long fall. You do that by placing an anchor above the rock you want to climb, at the top of the "route." That anchor might be a sling, that's a piece of nylon rope, around a tree or a boulder. At Handley Rock, since we've been climbing there a long time, we've placed permanent anchors at the top of most of the routes that we climb. We drill a hole into the rock, then hammer in a bolt, usually a 3/8 to 5/8 inch piece of metal driven into the hole with a metal hanger to which you can connect the rope. Some anchors have 2 or 3 bolts. We usually don't trust just one. But more recently we've drilled and placed big construction eyebolts, 3/4 inch by 6 inches. You could haul a tank up with one of those.

Q. Then you run the rope through the bolts or eyebolt?

A. That's not done. A rope should always run through a carabiner, usually 2 of them, if it's an anchor.

Q. What's a carabiner?

A. Metal, usually aluminum, snaplinks. They're oval with a spring-loaded gate that snaps open and shut. Think of a solid safety pin, around three inches in length but without a sharp point. You open the gate, and clip the carabiner to the bolt. Release the gate, and it snaps shut. Then you take the rope, open the carabiner gate again, place the rope in the same carabiner and let it snap shut. The carabiner in effect acts as a pulley. You have the rope connected to the anchor bolt through the carabiner, but the rope can run free, since it's not actually tied to a bolt. Now, a climber can tie into one end of the rope, the rope goes up to the anchor, through the carabiners, and down again to where another climber is holding or securing the rope; we call it "belaying." As the climber ascends the rock, the climber who's belaying – we usually say the "belayer" – takes in the rope so there's never any slack in the rope. If the climber falls, the belayer holds the rope fast, and the climber shouldn't fall more than a foot or two, depending on how much slack is out, how quickly the belayer reacts, and the stretch of the rope. It shouldn't be much. That way climbers can safely practice or learn.

Q. What happens when the climber reaches the top?

A. Depends. If there's a walkoff, meaning an easy way to descend, a climber could untie and walk down, or the climber could be lowered by his belayer. You just lean back, putting all your weight on the rope, and the belayer slowly lets the rope out and the climber literally backs down the route he went up, but under the control of the belayer.

Q. Is that difficult?

A. No. You are trusting the anchor and your belayer because you're not holding on to the rock with your hands and feet as when you were climbing up. But I guess because it's easier, and we're all basically lazy, lowering is the most common way to descend. You can walk off every route at Handley Rock, but almost everybody just gets lowered. You top-out, look down to be sure your belayer's paying attention, shout "Lower me," lean back, and you're back on the ground in 10 seconds.

Q. What do you remember of the night of Greg Adair's accident, July 22nd?

A. Not much, at least before the accident. I came home from work, grabbed the ropes, and set up some on the Left Face and Main Wall. Then a group of climbers wanted to try a hard variation on another rock we call The Diagonal. It's about 50 yards south of the main climbing area, and I was there with them, when we heard the shouts from the Left Face area. We ran up there, and found Greg. It was immediately clear that he was seriously injured.

Q. What did you do?

A. Someone had already gone for help, and the rest of us did what we could to relieve the pressure on the obvious fracture of, I guess it was, his right leg, until the paramedics arrived.

Q. Where was Greg?

A. At the base of the Left Overhang route.

Q. Had you set up the rope on Left Overhang that day?

A. Yes.

Q. What do you remember about how you did that?

A. Nothing in particular.

Q. Do you remember clipping the rope to the anchor at the top of Left Overhang on July 22nd?

A. I can't say that I have a specific recollection. It's something I've done a hundred times. I can't recall anything different that night.

Q. Then you can't say that you connected the rope to the anchor on Left Overhang that night?

A. Not specifically. You develop habits or I should say practices. The Left Overhang anchor is one of those big eyebolts I told you about, 3/4 inch by 6 inches; it's never coming out. I'd clip a couple of carabiners to the eyebolt. Find the mid-rope mark on the rope, open one carabiner at a time, and clip the rope to the carabiner. Coil each end of the rope and toss them over the overhang. I can't say I remember doing exactly that on July 22nd, but that's exactly how I've done it for 20 years on each route there. And of course, if I hadn't anchored the rope, the whole rope would have gone down when I tossed the ends.

Q. Mr. Oldfield, if you anchored the rope, then how did it become unclipped when Greg was climbing?

A. I don't know. I set it up correctly, I'm sure of that, but what happened after that I don't know. I know others climbed the route before Greg's fall, and were lowered without any problem. The rope must have been anchored. Someone, somehow, unclipped it.

Q. Who unclipped the rope?

A. I don't know.

Q. Just to make clear what we may be assuming is understood: The rope and carabiners on Left Overhang on July 22nd were yours?

A. Yes.

Q. You set up the rope and carabiners?

A. Yes.

Q. When you found Greg at the foot of Left Overhang, the rope and carabiners that were there were the same ones that you had set up?

A. Yes.

Q. Do you claim that anyone else was in charge at Handley Rock on July 22nd?

A. No.

Q. And despite your role as the owner of the equipment and the one who set it up, you don't have an explanation for what happened?

A. I'm at a loss. I just don't know.

Q. Mr. Oldfield, at some time you started to ask climbers at Handley Rock to sign a form called a Release of Liability?

A. Yes.

Q. Why did you do it?

A. Well, one of the climbers was a lawyer, and he kept telling me that I should do it. Then he brought me a form he prepared and said I should make copies and ask climbers to sign.

Q. Why did he say you needed to do it?

A. We'd heard of climbing accidents involving mountain clubs, like the Sierrans, that ruined the mountain clubs financially and caused them to cease all climbing instruction.

Q. And you then made people sign the Release of Liability?

A. Asked them, that's all. When new people came out, I'd give them the form and ask them if they didn't mind signing. I couldn't make people sign. It was a favor to me.

Q. What did you say was the purpose or intent of the form?

A. That it was to prevent our climbing sessions from getting involved in litigation.

Q. Did you explain what the form said?

A. Only as I did just now.

Q. How did you get them to sign?

A. I'd usually give it to newcomers. Ask them to please read it over and sign. Then I'd come back when I remembered it, and pick them up.

Q. What happened if someone refused?

A. It never happened. But a lot of people just didn't sign. I didn't ask friends or old timers, just newcomers. If someone was climbing when I brought the forms, I couldn't ask. And many times I'd forget to pick up signed forms. Sometimes people would come to find me afterwards to give me their forms. Frankly it was pretty hit-or-miss.

Q. Did Greg Adair sign one?

A. Yes.

Q. Do you remember if he read it first?

A. Actually I don't remember. I spent some time going through the box where I kept the signed forms to find Greg's. That's the only reason that I know he signed one.

Q. So you can't say that he read it first?

A. Well, as I said, I'd give people the form, so they could read it, and pick them up afterwards. I don't remember anyone just grabbing one and signing. I think I'd remember that.

Q. Nothing further. Thank you, Mr. Oldfield. Any questions, Mr. Craig?

BY MR. CRAIG: No questions.

EXCERPTS FROM THE DEPOSITION OF GREG ADAIR

EXAMINATION BY MR. CRAIG, COUNSEL FOR DEFENDANT:

* * *

Q. Mr. Adair, would you provide your best recollection of what happened on July 20, 2006, the night of the accident?

A. I'll try. It was a Wednesday night, and I decided to go to Handley Rock to climb. I usually went with my girlfriend, Andrea, but she couldn't make it that night. I couldn't get my friend Russ to go. I hadn't been climbing in almost a month, and we were going climbing that weekend. I wanted a climbing session before the weekend. Also, we were going to a new area called Jailhouse Rock, and I wanted to get some route information from some of the others who'd been there. Anyway, I decided to go to Handley Rock without a partner. I guess I got there around 7 o'clock, and, after putting on my harness and shoes, walked down to the base of the Left Face area. It has some good moderate warm-up routes. I started climbing with a couple of guys who were there, trading off climbing and belaying with them. After doing those routes we moved over to do Left Overhang, since there was a rope on that route as well, and Left Overhang is one of the test pieces at Handley Rock. I hadn't been able to do it until that year, and it was one of the climbs I wanted to do in preparation for the weekend. Some of the others had already climbed Left Overhang, and we were talking. Well, I was asking them about Jailhouse Rock, and I guess I wasn't hurrying. I wanted to be rested for Left Overhang. Finally I roped up and started up. And that is all I remember. My next recollection is of intense pain, almost all over my body, but really excruciating in my right leg and left ankle. It turned out both were broken, and I was lying on the ground. I didn't know how I'd gotten there, and all I was conscious of was pain like I'd never known. I guess I wasn't thinking of what had happened.

Q. So between starting up and then lying on the ground you have no recollection at all of what had happened?

A. None. It's amnesia, I guess. But the pain… I'll never forget that.

Q. Well, how far up the route do you remember going?

A. I don't remember going up at all. I just remember saying to Joel, who was the one belaying me, "Got me?" and starting up. That's it. Then I was writhing and screaming on the ground. I remember people being around me asking, "What happened, what happened?"

Q. What did you respond?

A. You mean while I was lying there screaming? I don't know. I don't think I could have said anything. I didn't know, and I couldn't think of anything except how much I hurt. I'd never felt anything like that.

Q. OK. Did you learn subsequently what happened?

A. I was told that the rope had not been anchored by Bill Oldfield, and when Joel went to lower me, I fell from the top of the Left Overhang to the base, the full length of the route.

Q. Who told you that?

BY MS. SALISBURY, COUNSEL FOR PLAINTIFF:

You can answer as to what anyone else told you, since it may lead to discoverable information. However, you shouldn't mention anything that you learned from me; that would be covered by the attorney-client privilege.

A. That's what I was told by the other climbers who were at the scene. They came to see me at the hospital.

BY MR. CRAIG:

Q. That was Joel and the others you were climbing with? What did they tell you?

A. Joel Samuels and Mike Griffith. They said that I cruised the climb and pulled over the overhang. I shouted or said something, probably jazzed or pumped that I'd been able to do it without falling or hanging on the rope. Then, the moment that I leaned back to be lowered, I fell straight down next to them on the ground. The carabiners that should have been clipped to the anchor were still attached to the rope, and lying there on the ground. Obviously they hadn't been attached to the anchor as we'd assumed. We'd been climbing Left Overhang without any real top rope anchor. They were as angry as I was. We were all hugely upset. We'd trusted that Bill had set up the anchor, and he hadn't. One of us could have been killed, and my life will never be the same – crippled, fused ankle, and all.

Q. Did they say that Bill Oldfield had not set the anchor properly?

A. It was obvious to all of us. None of us would have climbed a route as stout as Left Overhang without a top rope properly anchored. At Handley Rock we trusted that there was a top-rope anchor. What if one of us had just flamed out on the climb, and just wanted to rest and hang on the rope, counting on the anchor and the rope to hold him there? None of us bargained on putting our lives on the line by climbing without an anchor on a practice climb.

Q. But if, as you say, you would not have attempted the climb if you'd known the risk, then why didn't you check the anchor? It'd have been easy to go around to the top of Left Overhang and check before you climbed it, correct?

A. That wasn't my responsibility. Bill Oldfield was the one responsible for the anchors. He and others, I guess, drilled and placed the bolts. I started going to Handley Rock because it was supervised. You could go there to learn from experienced climbers like Bill. You didn't even need to own a rope or gear. Well, just your own harness and shoes. Bill provided everything else, and they'd teach you how to tie in, belay other climbers, do basic climbing movements, like how to climb a crack or a chimney or get over an overhang. And you'd learn about all the other techniques and equipment you'd eventually need to climb real mountains, but mostly you got to practice and improve by attempting and repeating progressively harder and harder climbs with the help of better climbers and with the safety of a top rope.

Q. By the time of the accident weren't you one of the better climbers, since you were doing harder climbs like Left Overhang?

A. I wasn't a beginner and was just starting to get on the tougher climbs, but I still went to Handley Rock to learn from Bill and the other good climbers. I'd only done a couple of trips to do real climbs in the mountains. No one at Handley Rock would have considered me one of the experienced climbers. No way. Not with the others there.

Q. What had you done, doing real climbs as you say?

A. Well, the first year I was learning to climb, after going to Handley Rock for most of the summer, Andrea, Russ, and I went to a climbing area near Lake Tahoe called Lover's Leap. We went there twice that fall, and did most of the easy and a few moderate climbs. Then, the next year, about a month before the accident, we went to Yosemite for the Memorial Day weekend.

Q. What did you climb there?

A. Let's see. First we did one called the Nutcracker. Then the next day we tried one of the classics, Royal Arches, but didn't top out till after dark, got lost trying to find the descent route, and spent the night out. Not a very good start to our climbing, but others have said that it also happened to them on their first attempt of Royal Arches. So we didn't feel too bad about it.

Q. Andrea and Russ, they had started climbing with you?

A. Yes.

Q. Had they climbed more than you?

A. Probably less.

Q. On your trips to the mountains for real climbs, there were no instructors or supervision, correct?

A. No one else but us three.

Q. You wouldn't have been doing those real climbs on your own if you hadn't thought it was safe, correct?

A. I guess so. Yeah.

Q. You believed you were qualified to climb without instructors or supervisors, correct?

A. The climbs we were doing, pretty moderate ones, yes.

Q. Mr. Adair, may I show you a document entitled "Release of Liability," and ask you whether you recognize the signature?

A. It's mine.

Q. (DIRECTED TO COURT REPORTER): Will you please mark this as Defendant's 1?

Q. Do you recall signing the document?

A. Kind of.

Q. Under what circumstances did you sign the document?

A. It was at Handley Rock. Bill would come around sometimes with the forms, and ask each of us to sign.

Q. What was your understanding of what you were signing?

A. That it was necessary to protect Bill, so he wouldn't have to get insurance or something like that.

Q. Didn't you read it?

A. Bill just came up to a group of us, and asked us to sign. Since I was going to sign it anyway, I didn't really read it. It didn't make any difference to me what it said.

Q. You had a chance to read the Release of Liability, but didn't because you didn't think it made any difference?

A. Right.

Q. Did Bill say that if you didn't sign you couldn't climb at Handley Rock?

A. No. All I remember is that Bill asked us to sign.

Q. What was your understanding of what would happen if you didn't sign?

A. I don't know. It didn't come up.

Q. Did anyone say, "Sign or you can't climb," or "We won't help you," or "You can't use the ropes, unless you sign?"

A. I never heard that.

* * *

RELEASE OF LIABILITY FORM

I understand that rock climbing is an inherently dangerous activity and can result in injury or death. I waive and release all participants in rock climbing at Handley Rock from all liability and claims of damages for my injury or death which is the result of rock climbing at Handley Rock. I intend this release of liability to include Bill Oldfield and all other participants in rock climbing activities at Handley Rock.

By this release of liability, I understand that I am giving up the right ever to sue Bill Oldfield or any other participants in rock climbing activities at Handley Rock. I intend this release of liability to include all liability for my injury or death, **EVEN IF CAUSED BY THE NEGLIGENCE OF BILL OLDFIELD OR ANY OTHER PARTICIPANT.** I understand that this means that I cannot sue for injury or death resulting from falls or falling rock or resulting from defective equipment, ropes, or bolts, or resulting from improper or careless instruction, advice, or supervision.

I further understand that the risks from climbing are varied and difficult to anticipate. I intend this release of liability to include **ALL RISKS AND CAUSES OF INJURY OR DEATH**, even if the risk or cause of injury or death is not specifically identified in this release or anticipated by me at the time I sign this release.

I ACCEPT AND TAKE FULL RESPONSIBILITY FOR ALL RISKS ASSOCIATED WITH ROCK CLIMBING AT HANDLEY ROCK. I give this release of liability freely in exchange for the benefits that I may receive from my participation in rock climbing at Handley Rock.

/s/ Greg Adair
Dated: July 7, 20X0

Library

Adair v. Oldfield

1. *Buchan v. United States Cycling Federation*   3-160
2. *Leon v. Family Fitness Center*   3-164

BUCHAN v. UNITED STATES CYCLING FEDERATION
Franklin Court of Appeal, 1991

This is an appeal by defendant United States Cycling Federation (the Federation) from the judgment of the District Court in favor of plaintiff Barbara Buchan.

As will appear, the dispositive issue involves express assumption of risk.

Buchan had been a top-level athlete all her life. Her goals, at the time of her injury, were to represent the United States in the Cycling World Championship in 1982 and in the Summer Olympics in 1984. The Federation is the governing body in the United States for the Olympic sport of cycling and is the sanctioning body of the races.

Buchan was injured in one of the trial races to select the team for the 1982 World Championship, over which the Federation had total control. In races prior to the trials, the Federation segregated races according to ability, because of the substantially higher risk of mixing novices with elite racers. At the trials, however, it admitted some novices, at first not even disclosing to the racers that it was doing so. In an initial trial race, as a tight pack of racers sped downhill reaching a speed of 30 miles per hour, a novice named Pieper, not accustomed to and frightened by large packs of riders, lost control, hit the rider in front of her, and caused a chain reaction of fallen riders. The elite riders, including Buchan, unsuccessfully but repeatedly protested the inclusion of novices. At the next trial race, when once again a pack of riders descended downhill, reaching 50 miles per hour, Pieper lost control, struck another racer's back wheel, and caused an immediate chain reaction, spilling numerous riders, this time with tragic consequences. Buchan landed squarely on her head and sustained a catastrophic injury to her brain.

The Federation required every applicant for a license to race to sign an application form containing a "Release of Liability," which provided in relevant part: "I acknowledge that cycling is an inherently dangerous sport in which I participate at my own risk. In consideration of the agreement of the United States Cycling Federation to issue an amateur license to me, I hereby waive, release, and forever discharge the United States Cycling Federation, its employees, agents, members, sponsors, promoters, and affiliates whosoever from any and all liability, claim, loss, cost or expense arising from or attributable in any legal way to any action or omission to act, negligent or otherwise, of any such person or organization in connection with sponsorship, organization, or execution of any bicycle racing or sporting event, including travel to and from such event, in which I may participate as a rider, team member, or spectator. To the best of my knowledge I have no physical condition that would interfere with my ability to participate in or attend any such event or would endanger my health hereby."

Buchan signed the agreement. She testified she was given no opportunity to negotiate the terms of the release. The evidence at trial showed the Federation had no procedure whereby a racer could, for an additional fee, purchase insurance against the Federation's negligence.

The trial court denied the Federation's motion for summary judgment and the case proceeded to trial. At trial, several racers and coaches testified that crashes and falls are common; that ninety percent of the riders get broken collarbones; that riders shouldn't race unless they are willing to accept the risks; and that good bicycle riders are involved in crashes, which are a part of the sport. Buchan herself acknowledged that in 75 percent of bicycle races there are crashes involving the falling down of multiple riders. Buchan had two prior racing falls.

The Federation appeals the jury verdict awarding Buchan $1,152,000. We find it unnecessary to address all of the contentions raised by the Federation since we believe that the trial court erred in denying the Federation's motion for summary judgment and its motion for directed verdict in that the release signed by Buchan, under which she expressly assumed all risks inherent in bicycle racing, effectively barred her action.

In *Tunkl v. Regents* (Frank. Supreme Ct. 1963), the Franklin Supreme Court held that a release of liability may be effective only if it does not involve the "public interest." The court said that those factors that bear on the public interest focus on whether the party seeking exculpation is engaged in performing service of great importance and practical necessity to the public, and whether such party possesses a decisive advantage of bargaining strength against any member thereof.

Applying the "public interest" test, the Courts of Appeal have enforced releases of liability signed by racecar drivers, participants in whitewater rafting, dirt bike racers, and skydivers.

Nevertheless, the trial court concluded that the present case represents a situation in which the public interest and publicly conferred power provide the Federation an insurmountable advantage in bargaining strength against any athlete seeking to participate in amateur bicycle racing at the world-class level. Further, a cyclist who wants to participate in Olympic or other international competition can only do so through the Federation. Once a racer like Buchan entered the World Trials she came under the control of the Federation, subject to the risk of its negligence, and that she had no choice over whom she would race against, and the decision as to who would be allowed to race was at the complete discretion of the Federation.

Despite the trial court's impressive analysis of Olympic and world-class racing, we conclude on this appeal that there is no public interest in bicycle racing. This is so regardless of the level of competition or the motive of the participants. We conclude that the concept of "public interest" has no applicability to sports and recreational activities. No public policy opposes private, voluntary transactions in which one party, for a consideration, agrees to shoulder a risk that the law would otherwise have placed upon the other party.

Measured against the public interest in situations where releases of liability have been rejected, such as hospitalization, escrow transactions, banking, and the operation of common carriers, bicycle racing is not one of great importance to the public. There is no compelling public interest in facilitating sponsorship and organization of the leisure activity of bicycle racing for public participation. The number of participants is relatively small. Also, the risks involved in administering such an event certainly do not have the same potential substantial impact on the public as the risks involved in hospitalization, escrow transactions, banking, and the operation of common carriers. The service certainly cannot be termed one that is a matter of practical necessity to the public.

Buchan argues that, at least as to her, this race was of great importance, a practical necessity, and was part of her overall goal to eventually participate in the 1984 Olympics. She uses this fact to distinguish herself from what she describes as the "Sunday cyclist." However, we know of no case that has ever intimated, much less held, that great importance and practical necessity to the public are to be measured from the perspective of a single member.

To be effective, a release of liability need not achieve perfection but suffices if it clearly expresses an intent on the part of the releasor not to hold the released party liable for the consequences of its own negligence. We have no difficulty in concluding that the release here passes muster.

In cases arising from hazardous recreational pursuits, to permit released claims to be brought to trial defeats the purpose for which releases of liability are requested and given, regardless of which party ultimately wins the verdict. Defense costs are devastating. Unless courts are willing to dismiss such actions without trial, many popular and lawful recreational activities are destined for extinction.

Reversed.

LEON v. FAMILY FITNESS CENTER
Franklin Court of Appeal, 1998

Carlos Leon appeals a summary judgment entered in favor of Family Fitness Center (Family Fitness) in his negligence action for personal injuries sustained when a bench collapsed beneath him while using a sauna in its facilities. The trial court concluded that there was no triable issue of material fact regarding whether a purported release of liability he signed was legally adequate to exculpate Family Fitness from the consequences of its own negligence. We conclude otherwise.

Leon signed a Family Fitness "Club Membership Agreement (Retail Installment Contract)" in June 1993. The document is a legal-length single sheet of paper covered with writing front and back. The front page is divided into two columns, with the right-hand column containing blanks for insertion of financial and "Federal Truth in Lending" data plus approximately 76 lines of text of varying sizes, some highlighted with bold print. The left-hand column contains approximately 90 lines of text undifferentiated as to size, with no highlighting and no paragraph headings or any other indication of its contents. The back contains approximately 90 lines of text. The purported release of liability is located at the bottom of the left-hand column of the front page, and states the following:

> Member is aware that participation in a sport or physical exercise may result in accidents or injury, and assumes the risk connected with the participation in a sport or exercise and represents that he is in good health and suffers from no physical impairment that would limit his use of Family Fitness facilities. Member acknowledges that Family Fitness has not and will not render any medical services including medical diagnosis of his physical condition. Member specifically agrees that Family Fitness, its officers, employees, and agents shall not be liable for any claim, demand, or cause of action of any kind whatsoever for, or on account of injury or death resulting from or related to his use of the facilities or participation in any sport, exercise or activity within or without the premises, and agrees to hold Family Fitness harmless from same.

Summary judgment is proper only where there is no triable issue of material fact and the moving party is entitled to judgment as a matter of law.

A release of liability is not enforceable if it is not easily readable. Furthermore, the important operative language should be placed in a position that compels notice and must be distinguished from other sections of the document. A layperson should not be required to muddle through complex language to know that he is relinquishing valuable legal rights. A release is unenforceable if not distinguished from other sections, if printed in the same typeface as the remainder of the document, and if not likely to attract attention because it is placed in the middle of a document. In other words, a release must not be buried in a lengthy document, hidden among other verbiage, or so encumbered with other provisions as to be difficult to find.

To be effective, a release of liability by a releasor purporting to exculpate a released party from the conscquences of its own negligence must clearly express such intent. At the very threshold, it must clearly notify the releasor of its effect.

Here, the purported release of liability, although a separate paragraph, is in undifferentiated type located in the middle of a document. Although some other portions are printed in bold and in enlarged print, the purported release itself is not prefaced by a heading to alert the reader that it is exculpatory, contains no bold lettering, and is in the same smaller font size as is most of the document. No physical characteristic distinguishes the purported release from the remainder of the document. The document itself is titled "Club Membership Agreement (Retail Installment Contract)," giving no notice to the reader that it includes a release of liability. Of particular relevance is the fact there is no language to alert a releasor that he was thereby exculpating Family Fitness from the consequences of its own negligence. Where such exculpation is involved, the release must contain words clearly to that effect.

The purported release of liability begins with language that participation in a sport or physical exercise may result in accidents or injury, and that the purported releasor assumes the risk connected with the participation in such. The purported release is followed by a statement in bold, capital letters: **"MODERATION IS THE KEY TO A SUCCESSFUL FITNESS PROGRAM AND ALSO THE KEY TO PREVENTING INJURIES."** Family Fitness placed the purported release between these statements, which deal strictly with the risks inherent in an exercise or sports program without any mention that it insulated itself from the consequences of its own negligence.

Where a participant in an activity has released another from liability for the consequences of the other's own negligence, the law imposes no requirement for the participant to have a specific knowledge of the particular risk that resulted in the damages. Not every possible specific act of negligence must be spelled out or discussed. Where a release of liability for the consequences of negligence is given, it applies to any such negligent act, whatever it may have been. It is only necessary that the act of negligence that results in consequences to the releasor be reasonably related to the object or purpose for which the release is given.

Here, Family Fitness's negligence was not reasonably related to the object or purpose for which the purported release of liability was given, that is, injuries resulting from participating in sports or exercise rather than from merely reclining on its furniture. The object and purpose of the purported release that Leon signed was to allow him to engage in fitness activities within the Family Fitness facilities. However, it was not this type of activity that led to his injury. Leon allegedly was lying on a fixed, non-movable, permanent bench in the sauna room. Injuries resulting during the proper use of the bench would no more be expected to be covered by the purported release than those caused by the ceiling falling on his head or from a pratfall caused by a collapsing office chair. These incidents have no relation to an individual's participation in a health club's fitness regimen.

Reading the entire document leads to the inescapable conclusion that the purported release of liability does not clearly set forth to an ordinary layperson, such as Leon, that the intent and effect of the document is to exculpate Family Fitness from any and all of the consequences of its own negligence.

The judgment is reversed.

EDITORS' SUMMARY

Below we have summarized your resources and tried to focus the analysis.

A. The Facts

1. Challenge: Your main challenge is to read and sort through the deposition transcripts to find the facts that matter; *e.g.*, those related to the injury release and the circumstances under which it was executed.

2. Issue: While the transcripts contain much information regarding rock climbing in general and the specifics of the accident, it is an example of a distracter; that information is generally unnecessary to resolve the legal issue of whether William Oldfield has a viable express assumption of the risk defense, not implied. The facts from the transcripts, relating to the Release of Liability provision, along with the Release Form itself, are the facts necessary to complete this task.

B. The Law

Both the *Buchan* and *Leon* cases are helpful and necessary to answer the question.

1. Threshold Test: *Buchan* sets forth a threshold test to determine whether a release is effective; *i.e.*, it must not involve the "public interest." Thus, it must be argued that rock climbing does not meet this standard. Furthermore, you can (and should) analogize the facts of your case to those in *Buchan*.

2. Content Requirements: As for *Leon*, it sets forth additional procedural bargaining requirements that must be analyzed to determine whether a liability release is valid. You should distinguish the facts in *Leon* from those in your case by focusing on the differences between the release in *Leon* and the release in your case.

C. Sample Answer

On the next page is an example of a good answer to the question posed by the supervising attorney.

MEMORANDUM

To: Gary Craig
From: Associate
Re: Express Assumption of Risk - Adair v. Oldfield
Date: July 29, 20X3

INTRODUCTION

Whether our defense of express assumption of risk will prevail against Adair's claim of negligence will turn on the enforceability of the Release of Liability form signed by Adair. If the release is effective, then Adair will have been deemed to assume the risks set forth in the release. In order to be effective, a release must meet several requirements, which I have outlined below. I believe that the release given to Adair by Oldfield satisfies these requirements. Therefore, our defense of express assumption of risk will likely be successful and Adair will not prevail.

DISCUSSION

A. THE RELEASE DID NOT INVOLVE THE PUBLIC INTEREST, BECAUSE ROCK CLIMBING IS A PURELY RECREATIONAL ACTIVITY AND THERE WAS NO DISPARITY IN BARGAINING POWER

A release of liability is effective only if it does not involve the public interest. Buchan v. U.S. Cycling Foundation. This public interest assessment turns on two factors. First, does the activity involve the public interest when the party seeking exculpation is engaged in performing service of great importance and practical necessity to the public? Second, does the party seeking exculpation have a decisive advantage in bargaining strength over the plaintiff?

As to the first factor, Oldfield was not engaged in performing a service of great public importance. He was simply the leader of a loosely organized rock climbing association. Generally, sports and recreational events are not considered to constitute matters of great public importance. <u>Buchan</u>. Releases of liability for injury have been upheld in similar activities such as driving racecars, white water rafting, bicycle racing, and skydiving. Rock climbing is a recreational activity analogous to these activities and, therefore, also would not be considered to be a service of great public importance.

As to the second factor, Oldfield did not have a decisive advantage in bargaining strength over Adair. According to Adair's deposition, Oldfield did not force Adair to sign the release of liability. He admitted that nobody told him that if he did not sign the release, he would not be allowed to participate in the rock climbing activities of the group. The deposition of Oldfield confirms that he did not force participants in the group to sign the releases, but merely requested that they do so. Therefore, Adair's signing of the release form was totally voluntary. He was not pressured to do so, and his signing the release was not the result of any disparity in bargaining power.

In conclusion, the release signed by Adair did not involve the public interest. Therefore, the release is not unenforceable on this ground.

B. THE TECHNICAL REQUIREMENTS FOR A WRITTEN RELEASE WERE MET BECAUSE THE RELEASE WAS EASILY READABLE, CONTAINED OPERATIVE LANGUAGE THAT WAS CONSPICUOUS AND CLEARLY DISTINGUISHED FROM THE REST OF THE DOCUMENT, AND CLEARLY EXPRESSED THE INTENT TO ABSOLVE OLDFIELD OF LIABILITY FOR HIS OWN NEGLIGENCE

To be effective, the release of liability need not be perfect. Instead, it need only clearly express an intent on the part of the releaser not to hold the released party liable for the consequences of his own negligence. <u>Buchan</u>. To allow claims arising from hazardous recreational pursuits when valid releases have been signed would defeat the very purpose of having participants sign the releases; thus, courts are willing to enforce them, as previously mentioned.

To be effective, the release must meet several technical requirements. The court in <u>Leon v. Family Fitness Center</u> provided a thorough analysis of the requirements of an enforceable release. First, a release will not be enforceable unless it is easily readable. The release given to Adair satisfied this requirement. It was written in normal font and contained on a single sheet of paper. It was not excessive in length, and was clearly identified as a release of liability. Adair had ample time to review the release. Although Adair said he did not actually read the release, this should not matter because he did sign it voluntarily. The release was clear as to its terms, and Adair signed it.

Second, operative language of the release should be conspicuous and prominently distinguished from other language. The release signed by Adair satisfies this requirement. The particularly important provisions of the release are written in bold, capital letters. These provisions include the ones stating that Adair releases Oldfield from liability for injuries caused by the negligence of Oldfield or another participant, that the release applies to all risks and causes of injury or death, and that the signer of the release accepts full responsibility for all risks associated with rock climbing.

Third, a release that intends to release a party from the consequences of his own negligence must clearly express such an intent. Here, the release does state it releases Oldfield from any injuries his own negligence may cause to the participants who sign the release. This provision is clearly presented in bold, capital letters. Therefore, this requirement seems satisfied.

In <u>Leon</u>, the court found that the release of liability signed by the plaintiff was not enforceable. However, that release is readily distinguishable from the one signed by Adair. First, the release in <u>Leon</u> was only one part of a larger contract. Here, the release was a freestanding document. Second, the release in <u>Leon</u> was written in text undifferentiated as to size, with no paragraphs or highlighting, and thus not conspicuous. In contrast, the release signed by Adair contained distinct paragraphs and contained bolded portions.

In conclusion, the release signed by Adair met all of the technical requirements necessary in order for a release of liability to be considered valid.

C. THE HARM SUFFERED WAS REASONABLY RELATED TO THE PURPOSE OF THE RELEASE BECAUSE ADAIR WAS UNQUESTIONABLY INJURED WHILE ROCK CLIMBING

To be effective, the release is not required to spell out every possible act of negligence that it purports to cover. Instead, as long as the harm suffered is "reasonably related" to the release, the document need only contain a clear general release from all negligence. Leon. The release signed by Adair did just that. Adair was climbing at Handley Rock when an anchoring clip came undone, likely due to negligence on the part of somebody. Negligence is exactly the type of liability the release, which explicitly dealt with injury or death as a result of rock climbing at Handley Rock, was intended to guard against.

CONCLUSION

In conclusion, based on the controlling case law in Franklin and the facts of the present case, the release of liability signed by Adair will likely be enforceable. Our express assumption of the risk defense will most likely be successful. While this does not preclude a lawsuit, of course, it is unlikely that Adair will ultimately prevail against our client, William Oldfield.

E. Working Practice Questions

1. Begin Testing Yourself: Now that you've examined a typical objective memorandum MPT question and answer, you should complete the following two practice questions on your own. Afterwards, compare your memorandum with the sample grading guide and answer provided.

> **MPT Tip:** One of the major mistakes students make in preparing for the MPT exam is to eliminate self-testing. It is too easy to read the Library and File and then refer to the answer and say to yourself "yep, that's how I would have done it." You need to gain experience in actually creating the task answer.

2. Learning-Testing Conditions: You should create your own conditions as close to those of the MPT bar exam as possible. This would mean you should allocate a minimum of a full 90-minute time block for the question. You will have to work up to this time limit and to start perhaps allow yourself a full 120 minutes.

3. Concentration Objective: Ideally, you should complete the answer without taking a break. Again, you may have to work up to this. Concentration during your writing time is critical. Turn off all phones and do not answer email during this testing period.

4. Grading Your Answer: After you have completed the task, use our grading guides to objectively evaluate your answer coverage. Also, you should compare your answers with the sample answers provided for substance, organization, form and overall presentation. Don't be discouraged if your answer is missing something important or if it contains a significant mistake. Use this as a learning opportunity to figure out how and why you went wrong so you can improve your future MPT performance.

5. Re-Write Helpful: Many candidates find correcting and supplementing their first answer helpful. If you typed your answer this is quite easy, but even if your answer was in long hand it may be worth doing. Add to your first answer any omissions you feel are important. Redoing your answer allows you to create an objective memorandum "model answer" to refer back to later. This self-correction also reduces the chance you will repeat similar errors on other objective memoranda.

> **MPT Tip:** Some students find it too difficult to actually spend the full 90 minute time creating their own complete answer to the questions before looking at our Editor's Summary and Sample Answer. If that temptation applies to you, you may not get the task creation practice you need to pass the MPT. Consider enrolling in our supplemental personal MPT Writing Program Service described in the foreword information just before the introductory chapter 1.

V. PRACTICE QUESTION 1:

IN RE RYAN COX

TABLE OF CONTENTS

Documents Provided for Task   Page

Instructions	3-175
File	3-177
Task Memorandum	3-178
Excerpts of Interview with Ryan Cox	3-179
Memorandum re: Phone Conversations with Emily and Adam Cox	3-184
Installment Contract	3-185
Letter Dated May 2, 20X3, from Opposing Counsel to Adam Cox	3-188
Letter Dated July 3, 20X3, from Opposing Counsel to Adam Cox	3-189
Library	3-191
Cavallaro v. Stratford Homes, Inc.	3-192
Binninger v. Hutchinson	3-194
Tanner v. Fulk	3-196
Editors' Prepared Grading Guide	3-199
Sample Answer	3-201

IN RE RYAN COX

INSTRUCTIONS

1. You will have 90 minutes to complete this session of the examination. This performance test is designed to evaluate your ability to handle a select number of legal authorities in the context of a factual problem involving a client.

2. The problem is set in the fictional State of Franklin, one of the United States, located in the fictional Fifteenth Circuit. Franklin has District Courts (trial courts), Courts of Appeal (mid-level appellate courts), and a Supreme Court (Franklin's highest appellate court).

3. You will have two sets of materials with which to work: a File and a Library.

4. The File contains factual materials about your case. The first document is a memorandum containing the instructions for the tasks that you are to complete.

5. The Library contains the legal authorities needed to complete the tasks. The case reports may be real, modified, or written solely for the purpose of this performance test. If the cases appear familiar to you, do not assume that they are precisely the same as you have read before. Read each thoroughly, as if it were new to you. You should assume that cases were decided in the jurisdictions and on the dates shown. In citing cases from the Library, you may use abbreviations and omit page citations.

6. Your response must be written in the answer book provided. You should concentrate on the materials provided, but you should also bring to bear on the problem your general knowledge of the law. What you have learned in law school and elsewhere provides the general background for analyzing the problem; the File and Library provide the specific materials with which you must work.

7. Although there are no restrictions on how you apportion your time, you should probably allocate at least 45 minutes to reading and organizing before you begin writing your response. You may make notes anywhere in the test materials, but may not tear out pages from this booklet.

8. Your response will be graded on its compliance with instructions and on its content, thoroughness, and organization.

File

In re Ryan Cox

1.	Memorandum to Applicant	3-178
2.	Excerpts of Interview with Ryan Cox	3-179
3.	Memorandum to Cox File	3-184
4.	Installment Contract	3-185
5.	Letter to Adam F. Cox, May 2, 20x3	3-188
6.	Letter to Adam F. Cox, July 3, 20x3	3-189

Dillard & Savim

Attorneys at Law

345 College Street

Shermer, Franklin

TASK ASSIGNMENT MEMORANDUM

To: Applicant
From: Logan Dillard
Re: *In re Ryan Cox*
Date: July 29, 20X3

We have been retained by Ryan Cox to represent him in the sale of a piece of real property. The purchaser has backed out of the deal and is threatening to bring suit to recover the money that has already been paid. The property is in the name of Mr. Cox's son, Adam, as is the contract for sale. Adam has informed me that he considers his father the true owner of the property and will, therefore, do whatever he must to accomplish whatever his father desires.

I've conducted the initial client interview and have done some research. Before I speak to the opposing attorney I will need to speak to Mr. Cox again and counsel him concerning his options. Therefore, please write me a memorandum in which you analyze the enforceability of the land installment contract.

EXCERPTS OF INTERVIEW WITH RYAN COX
* * * * *

LOGAN DILLARD (Q): Why don't you start at the beginning and tell me what happened?

RYAN COX (A): Well, I guess it started when my wife, Ruth, died two years ago. We had been living in our house in Franklin during the winter months, then going to Columbia during the summer to be near our older daughter, Sarah.

Q: Do you own a house in Columbia?

A: No. We would take our motor home and live in it.

Q: Okay, so what happened with the death of Ruth?

A: The kids started to talk to me about selling the place in Franklin. They were afraid I couldn't take care of myself; something might happen and I couldn't get help.

Q: Anything in particular?

A: Well, I've had a couple of heart attacks and I've got diabetes; so I guess they had a point.

Q: So, what happened?

A: My younger daughter, Emily, works with some people, Nicky and Marsha Belmont, who live in Franklin during the winter. They work a carnival, the county fair route during the summer. Well, anyway, my daughter, not Sarah, but Emily, who lives here in Franklin, says the Belmonts might be interested in buying the house, but they don't have the money up front and besides which, they can't get a bank to lend them the money because of the kind of work they do, you know, seasonal, self-employed. And besides which, I'm not sure I want to leave. I mean it's not just the house. I've got this big pole barn there that has all of my tools in it. Where would I put them in Columbia, much less how much would it cost to ship them there? So I don't think anything about it.

Q: You must have a lot of tools.

A: Yes. I'm a carpenter. Used to build houses. Since I was 60, though, what with the heart disease and all I had to stop. But I kept the tools and do the odd repair jobs there at the house. You know, a merry-go-round needs a new floor, a popcorn wagon needs fixing, they bring it over and I do the work.

Q: Does that keep you busy?

A: Yes, and at my age, there aren't a lot of options.

Q: How old are you?

A: 75.

Q: So then what happens?

A: Couple of months later Emily comes back and says, "Hey Dad, this couple says they really like you and they don't mind the idea that you could maybe sell them the house, but keep the motor home on the property and also use the pole barn for as long as you like." Well, this sounds kind of interesting, I don't really need that much space, but there's still the problem that they don't have the money. My daughter says, "Hey, why don't you just take payments from them? You can use the income anyway. All you would do with the money is put it in the bank. You can be the bank."

Q: So did you agree to do that?

A: Not right away. I wasn't so sure, but I got to talking to this guy at the Showman's Club, that's where I go on Friday nights, a bunch of the carnival people go there. Well anyway he says he has lots of property and sometimes he sells it through what he called a land installment contract. He said if you get a big enough down payment there really is no risk. So I start thinking about it. This guy then says he would be happy to show me the contract he uses, even modify it to meet my house sale.

Q: Did he do that?

A: Yes. I've got it here.

Q: Good. Let me see it. I'll read it in a minute. What happened then?

A: Well, I call Emily up and say let's talk about price. I had it appraised for $100,000, but I figure I should get something for basically financing the sale, so I ask for $130,000. We agreed on $120,000. The other parts of the agreement are in that contract.

Q: Okay, let me read it. It says here that the seller is Adam. Who's he?

A: That's my younger son. When we bought the property we put it in his and my wife's name. We figured I'd go first and it would make things easier.

Q: Did you include Adam in the negotiations to sell the property?

A: No. Emily handled all that. I don't even think Adam knew he was on the deed at that point.

Q: You say Emily talked with the Belmonts, and they agreed to everything in the contract?

A: Yes.

Q: Then what happened?

A: Well, I had to tell my son, because he needed to sign the contract.

Q: I see that he did.

A: Yes, but that's where things started to unravel.

Q: Okay, what happened?

A: Emily gets $40,000 from Nicky and Marsha and takes it to my son, Adam. Emily gives Adam the $40,000 and Adam gives Emily the contract to be signed by the Belmonts.

Q: Adam got the money before the Belmonts signed the contract?

A: That's right. Forty thousand, like it called for.

Q: Okay, then what happened?

A: Well this was in March, and Nicky is on the road until October, so not much.

Q: Did you move out of the house?

A: Well actually, I had already done that. Nicky and his wife moved into the house in March.

Q: The month before the contract was agreed to?

A: Yes.

Q: Why?

A: Well, I was ready to move out, and it was only a matter of getting my son, Adam, to sign the contract and collect the down payment so I thought, what the heck.

Q: Did you ever get a copy of the contract signed by the Belmonts?

A: No.

Q: Why does the contract call for a $12,000 payment in November and the later payments of $1,000 each?

A: It's just the nature of the carnival business. Nicky would get a bonus at the end of the season in October and he could use the bonus to make the payment.

Q: What about the $40,000? Where is it?

A: Oh, we put that in a couple of mutual funds. I don't have a retirement plan, so we thought this would be a good investment and then I would live on Social Security and the $12,000 per year. When that ended, I would still have the $40,000 – if I'm still around.

Q: So how did the deal fall apart?

A: Nicky and Marsha called me and said that they had changed their mind, that I was too much trouble and they wanted me off the property or to give them their $40,000 back and call the whole deal off.

Q: What do you mean by too much trouble?

A: Marsha thinks I'm too nosey, that I say things that are none of my business. They even said I've been going into the house without their permission.

Q: Is there any truth to these claims?

A: No. Nicky and I get along fine. I did go into the house once, to get something out of a storage box and I will admit that I was shocked at the condition of the house and I guess I did say to Nicky that he was trashing the place.

Q: What did you do?

A: I tried to talk to Nicky, but he was never around.

Q: Have you been back in the house since then?

A: Heavens no. For one thing, they changed the locks on the house. For another, like I said, the place is trashed. They've got dogs that aren't house-trained, they never clean, the furniture is totally ruined. I don't want to go back.

Q: Is the furniture the same furniture that was in the house before you moved out?

A: Yes.

Q: Did they pay for it?

A: Not yet. They said they wanted to buy it, but they needed some time to get the money.

Q: How much did they agree to pay?

A: They haven't really agreed to buy it yet. I asked for $10,000, which is about what I paid for it.

Q: Why do you think the Belmonts want out of the deal?

A: My guess is that Nicky can't make the payment so Marsha's got lots of pressure. But I figure too bad. A contract's a contract.

Q: Is that what you want, to enforce the contract as written?

A: Absolutely.

Q: Other than talking to Nicky, have you done anything to try and enforce the contract?

A: No. I've just been living on the property. I've been meaning to go to a lawyer, but you know how it is. Then my son gets this letter from Nicky and Marsha's lawyer and you can imagine he's not thrilled with the prospect of being sued. He then tries to deal with the lawyer and we get the second letter.

Q: Where are you living now?

A: I'm in the motor home on the property here in Franklin. I expect to be moving to Columbia in about four weeks to spend some time there.

Q: Are the Belmonts still in the house?

A: Sure.

Q: What does your son think of this?

A: He's not happy, but he said to go to a lawyer and he'd sign whatever the lawyer and I wanted signed.

Q: Okay, I think I have an idea about where we stand. Is there anything else you want to tell me?

A: No. That's about it. Where do I stand? A contract's a contract, right?

Q: Well, Mr. Cox, I can't say right off the top of my head what your rights are. There are some complicated legal issues that affect the ability to enforce the contract, most notably, the fact that apparently the Belmonts did not sign the contract. Here's what I would like to do. I'd like to call your son and daughter and talk to them. Then I want to do a little legal research. After I've had a chance to look at the law, I want to get back together with you and I'll be in a better position to tell you what options we have. Is that okay?

A: Sure.

Dillard & Savim

Attorneys at Law

345 College Street

Shermer, Franklin

MEMORANDUM

To: Cox File

From: Logan Dillard

Re: Phone Conversations with Emily and Adam Cox

Date: July 18, 20X3

I spoke to both Emily Cox and Adam Cox today. Emily confirmed to me the substance of her father's story. Apparently Emily works with the Belmonts on occasion. This whole mess has hurt her business relationship, but says the Belmonts are the kind of people that if this didn't make them angry, something else would have at some point.

The Belmonts have a "noisy" relationship – lots of yelling. Emily thinks the second letter trying to cancel everything is Marsha saying "I told you so." She thinks Marsha believes Adam has taken advantage of the Belmonts. This according to Emily is a big joke, since Adam had nothing to do with it and wants nothing to do with the problem.

My conversation with Adam also confirmed the father's story. Adam said he was very surprised by the second letter from Vaughan, the Belmonts' lawyer. The big contention was his father's presence on the property. Marsha wants him off. He thought Vaughan would just come back and reiterate the demand to have complete title to the property. When I asked what was the reason his father was so adamant about not moving, Adam said he thought it was two things. First, "Dad's stubborn. I'm sure he gave you the 'contract is a contract' line." Second, the tools are not just any handyman's collection. There are lots of them and they are valuable. The pole barn is a former fire substation, big enough to hold two fire trucks. His parents bought the property, then had the house constructed behind the barn. Adam figures it will take a good size semi-truck to haul the equipment to Columbia – it would probably cost $15,000.

INSTALLMENT CONTRACT

Agreement made April 2, 20X3, between Adam F. Cox, of 876 Elm, Bradford, State of Columbia, Seller, and Nicholas and Marsha Belmont, Shermer, State of Franklin, Purchaser.

1. SALE. Seller, in consideration of the deposit made by Purchaser hereunder, and of the covenants and agreements on the part of Purchaser herein contained, agrees to sell to Purchaser, and Purchaser agrees to buy, that real property located at 11 Lake Road, Shermer, State of Franklin, together with the tenements, hereditaments, and appurtenances belonging or appertaining thereto.

2. PURCHASE PRICE. Purchaser agrees to pay to Seller the sum of $120,000, as follows:

The sum of $40,000 on execution of this agreement, receipt of which is acknowledged, and the balance of the purchase price, being the sum of $80,000, in 69 installments as follows:

The sum of $12,000, or more, on November 15, 20X3, and

The sum of $1,000, or more, on the 10th day of each month, beginning December 10, 20X3, and thereafter until the purchase price and interest are fully paid, provided that the purchase price shall be fully paid on or before July 10, 20X9.

The unpaid balance of the purchase price shall bear interest at the rate of zero percent (0%) per year until paid. All payments of principal shall, until further notice, be made to Seller at the address set forth above.

3. IN LIEU OF INTEREST. In lieu of interest on the outstanding balance as described in paragraph 2, Seller covenants that Ryan L. Cox, during his lifetime, shall:

    A. have the right to use the pole barn located on the property (a former substation of the fire department currently being used for the storage and use of woodworking tools) for the continued storage and use of his woodworking tools, with the right to ingress and egress and the right to exclude Purchaser from the structure; and

    B. have the right to maintain a motor home or trailer on the property as a residence, with the right to reasonable electricity, water and sewer connection at no cost.

4. TAXES AND ASSESSMENTS; INSURANCE. Purchaser shall pay all taxes and assessments on the above-described property levied, assessed, or accruing after the date of this contract, including the total of any payable in the 20X3 calendar year and beyond.

Initials: /s/ AFC

5. HAZARD INSURANCE/RISK OF LOSS. Upon the execution of this agreement, the Purchaser shall bear the risk of loss from all sources and shall keep the improvements on the property insured for an amount not less than the actual replacement costs of all buildings or the outstanding loan balance owing under this contract, whichever is greater.

6. ALTERATIONS TO THE PROPERTY. Purchaser shall not make any major alteration or additions or improvements to the property without first obtaining permission of Seller, which permission shall not be unreasonably withheld. All expenses in making alterations, additions or improvements to the property shall be promptly paid by Purchaser and Purchaser shall furnish copies of said paid bills to Seller together with executed lien releases or lien waivers.

7. FAILURE TO PAY TAXES OR INSURANCE. Should Purchaser fail to pay any taxes or assessments as herein provided, or fail to keep the property insured, Seller has the option to pay all or any of such taxes and assessments and to obtain such insurance. Purchaser shall repay to Seller, on demand, the amount of all moneys paid by Seller on account of such taxes, assessments, and/or insurance, together with interest thereon from the date of payment until repaid at the rate of 12 per cent per year.

8. FIXTURES. Purchase price shall include permanently attached fixtures, but does not include personal property.

9. NO RECORDING. Purchaser and Seller agree this contract shall not be recorded in public records, unless required by state statute. The recording of this agreement shall constitute a material breach of this agreement and Purchaser shall be liable to Seller for slander of title.

10. NO ASSIGNMENT. This agreement is personal to Purchaser and no conveyance may be made by Purchaser of the premises, or any part, or any beneficial interest thereof without first obtaining the prior written consent of the Seller. Any conveyance of the property made by Purchaser of the premises, or any part, or any beneficial interest thereof without first obtaining the prior written consent of the Seller shall entitle Seller to accelerate payment of the balance due on this agreement and, at the option of the Seller, all sums of money secured by this agreement become due whether or not they are due and payable under other terms of this agreement. Nothing contained herein shall be construed to constitute a novation or release of Purchaser or any subsequent owner of liability or obligation under this agreement.

Initials: /s/ AFC

11. OCCUPANCY. Purchaser shall occupy the premises as Purchaser's principal residence. Purchaser shall not rent or lease the property, or any part, without the express written permission of the Seller.

12. INSPECTION. Seller or his agent may make reasonable entries upon and inspections of the property. Seller shall give notice at the time of or prior to an inspection specifying reasonable cause for the inspection.

13. DELIVERY OF DEED. When the purchase price and all other amounts to be paid to Seller are fully paid as herein provided, and when all covenants and agreements on the part of Purchaser to be performed have been satisfactorily performed, Seller will execute and deliver to Purchaser a good and sufficient general warranty deed conveying the property free of all encumbrances made, done, or suffered by Seller.

14. POSSESSION. Purchaser shall be entitled to possession of the property from and after the date of this contract.

15. DEFAULT. If Purchaser shall fail for a period of 30 days to (1) pay Seller any of the sums herein agreed to be paid after such sums are due, or (2) pay taxes or assessments on the property after the same become due, or (3) comply with any of the covenants on Purchaser's part to be kept and performed, then Seller shall be released from all obligation to convey the property, and Purchaser shall forfeit all right thereto.

16. TIME OF ESSENCE. Time is of the essence of this agreement.

17. BINDING EFFECT. The terms, conditions, and covenants of this agreement shall be binding on and shall inure to the benefit of the heirs, executors, administrators, and assigns of the respective parties, but no assignment or transfer by Purchaser of this contract, or of an interest in the property described herein, shall be valid, unless made with the written consent of Seller.

Executed at the date first above written.

/s/ Adam F. Cox
Seller   Purchaser

Initials: /s/ AFC

James C. Vaughan
Attorney at Law

25687 Truman Street
Shermer, Franklin

May 2, 20X3

Mr. Adam F. Cox
876 Elm
Bradford, Columbia 39856

Re: 11 Lake Road, Shermer, Franklin

Dear Mr. Cox:

I have been retained by Marsha and Nicholas Belmont to finalize a sale of the above referenced real property or, in the alternative, obtain the return of the money they have paid. Specifically, my clients negotiated for the purchase of the property with your sister, Emily. The Belmonts delivered a down payment in the amount of $40,000.

My clients are ready, willing, and able to pay the additional money due and hereby offer such payment, at such time as you are prepared to deliver a recordable warranty deed free from any mortgage or other encumbrance other than current property taxes. In the alternative, please return my clients' payment of $40,000.

Please direct all communication directly to me. However, if I have not heard from you by June 1, 20X3, I will assume you have rejected each alternative. In that event I have been authorized to file an appropriate court action to resolve this matter. I trust you will honor your obligation in this matter so we all can avoid the expense and inconvenience of litigation. Please govern yourself accordingly.

Respectfully yours,

/s/ James C. Vaughan
James C. Vaughan

James C. Vaughan
Attorney at Law

25687 Truman Street
Shermer, Franklin

July 3, 20X3

Mr. Adam F. Cox
876 Elm
Bradford, Columbia 39856

Re: 11 Lake Road, Shermer, Franklin

Dear Mr. Cox:

I regret you have refused to see the mutually beneficial result from acceptance of either of the proposals contained in my letter of May 2, 20X3. Your demand that your father be able to retain possession of the storage barn for life is completely unacceptable to my clients.

I have been instructed by the Belmonts to withdraw their offer to purchase the property. I hereby demand return of the $40,000 previously submitted. Please remit a cashier's check to me at the above address. If I do not receive such check by August 10, 20X3, I have been authorized to file an appropriate court action to recover this money. Please govern yourself accordingly.

Respectfully yours,

/s/ James C. Vaughan
James C. Vaughan

Library

In re Ryan Cox

1. *Cavallaro v. Stratford Homes, Inc.*   3-192
2. *Binninger v. Hutchinson*   3-194
3. *Tanner v. Fulk*   3-196

CAVALLARO v. STRATFORD HOMES, INC.
Franklin Court of Appeal (2001)

The Cavallaros filed suit against Stratford Homes, Inc., seeking specific performance of an agreement for the purchase and sale of a lot and the construction of a home thereon, or, in the alternative, damages arising from Stratford's alleged breach of that agreement. The complaint alleged that the parties had executed a lot reservation agreement that reserved a particular lot and fixed the base price for the construction of one of Stratford's model homes until a sale and purchase agreement was executed.

The lot reservation provided, among other things, that: "Should [a sale and purchase] agreement not be executed within 14 days of this date, purchaser and/or seller may, at either's option, void this lot reservation." In consideration for the lot reservation, the Cavallaros gave Stratford a $500 deposit. The complaint alleged that, although the parties had subsequently executed an enforceable sale and purchase agreement, Stratford breached the agreement by improperly refusing to construct their home.

The undisputed record evidence established that the Cavallaros entered into negotiations with Stratford for the construction of a home, but that a meeting of the minds was never reached as to the price and the terms of construction of the home which were essential terms to an enforceable contract. The Cavallaros requested several changes to Stratford's basic model over a period of several months. Plans were redone and new pricing was formulated on a number of occasions. Because no final agreement was reached as to those essential terms, the entry of judgment in favor of Stratford was correct.

Even if the parties had reached a meeting of the minds as to the essential terms, any such contract would have been unenforceable under Franklin's statute of frauds. Pursuant to the statute of frauds, no action can be brought to enforce a contract for the sale of land unless the contract is in writing and signed by the party to be charged. In order to be an enforceable land sales contract, the statute of frauds requires the contract to satisfy two threshold conditions. First, the contract must be embodied in a written memorandum signed by the party against whom enforcement is sought. Second, the written memorandum must disclose all of the essential terms of the sale and these terms may not be explained by resort to parol evidence.

The Cavallaros contend there is evidence in the record demonstrating that the parties executed a written contract. More specifically, the Cavallaros maintain that the sale and purchase agreement and addendum which was signed by them, but not by Stratford, when read in conjunction with a price list which was signed by Stratford's agent four days later, satisfied the written memorandum requirement of the statute of frauds. We disagree. In order for documents to be read in conjunction with each other to constitute a sufficient memorandum for purposes of the statute of frauds, the law strictly requires some internal reference between the documents. To that end, there must be some reference to the unsigned writing in the signed writing. Here, the signed price list did not make reference to the unsigned sale and purchase agreement.

The Cavallaros next argue that the trial court improperly rejected their claim that the partial performance doctrine removed the parties' alleged oral agreement from the requirements of the statute of frauds. We disagree that partial performance would apply in this case even if an oral agreement had been reached by the parties. The established rule is that in order to constitute partial performance sufficient to take an oral agreement to devise real property out of the application of the statute of frauds requirements, delivery of possession of the real property is required. But the possession must be permissive and, most importantly, acquiescence by the parties to the terms of the agreement must be apparent. Here, a finding of partial performance could not be sustained because the Cavallaros never took possession of the property.

Having rejected all of the Cavallaros' claims of error, we affirm the trial court's judgment.

BINNINGER v. HUTCHINSON

Franklin Court of Appeal (1978)

Genise Tatum Binninger appeals a judgment granting specific performance to Ralph Hutchinson, the intended purchaser, based upon an oral agreement for the conveyance of real property. Binninger was the owner of improved property in Bay County, Franklin, which Hutchinson was interested in buying. Binninger was then living in Houston, Texas. There is a conflict of testimony, which the trial court resolved against Binninger, as to whether an agreement was reached between the parties. While Mrs. Binninger stated no bargain was struck, Hutchinson testified that during a long distance telephone conversation, she agreed to sell him the property for $15,000, provided he pay her $10,000 and give her an installment note for the remaining $5,000. Hutchinson stated Mrs. Binninger told him that upon his making the above payment, the property was his.

Following the conversation, Hutchinson forwarded a warranty deed, mortgage, note and a check in the amount of $2,000 payable to "Genise Tatum Bissonett." The named payee was an obvious error. Bissonett was the name of the street where Binninger resided. Upon receipt of the check she attempted to call Hutchinson to advise him she was not selling the property, but without success. When she later discovered Hutchinson had taken possession, and was making substantial improvements, she returned the check uncashed to her attorney, who also attempted to contact Hutchinson, but, being unable to, left a message for Hutchinson to call him. Hutchinson finally contacted Mrs. Binninger within one or two months after receipt of the papers by her.

When further negotiations between the parties failed, Hutchinson brought an action seeking specific performance of the oral contract. The court found the parties entered into an oral agreement for the sale of the property for a price of $15,000. The prayer for specific performance was granted and the property conveyed to Hutchinson upon payment of $15,000 together with accrued interest. We reverse.

Binninger argues (1) an oral agreement was never reached, and (2) the statute of frauds bars Hutchinson from relief. Hutchinson responds there was competent substantial evidence for the trial court to determine the contract had been formed between the parties and since proof of both possession and payment of some part of the consideration was made, partial performance of the agreement was made, thus bringing into operation the partial performance exception to the statute of frauds.

Before the partial performance exception may be applied, delivery of possession must be made pursuant to the terms of the contract and acquiesced to by the other party. Even construing the conflicting testimony in Hutchinson's favor, as we must, we find no evidence entitling him to possession of the property. His possession was known to Mrs. Binninger only after she received the deed, mortgage, note and check and after she was told by relatives Hutchinson was making improvements upon the property. Hutchinson's proof concerning Mrs. Binninger's acquiescence to his possession was hardly clear and positive. Before a plaintiff may be allowed to give evidence of a contract for the sale of land not in writing, it is essential that he establish, by clear and positive proof, acts which take the contract out of the statute. The statement attributed by him to Mrs. Binninger, that after he paid $10,000 down and gave her a note for $5,000 the property was his, cannot be reasonably relied upon by Hutchinson as acquiescence for him to move onto the property without title and begin extensive improvements. The oral agreement was within the statute of frauds and unenforceable.

Additionally we find Hutchinson's forwarding of a $2,000 check, rather than the $10,000 which even he said was agreed upon by the parties, was no more than a counteroffer. It is hornbook law requiring no citations of authority, except common sense, that a contract once entered into may not thereafter be unilaterally modified; subsequent modifications require consent and a meeting of the minds of all of the initial parties to the contract whose rights or responsibilities are sought to be affected by the modification.

REVERSED.

TANNER v. FULK

Franklin Court of Appeal (1985)

Plaintiff, George Tanner, filed an action against defendant, Michael Fulk, requesting that a land installment contract be terminated, that possession of the premises be restored to him, and that an additional judgment of $55,000 for deterioration and destruction of the premises be awarded.

A land installment contract is a type of conditional sale as, generally, possession is transferred immediately while legal title is held by the vendor until full payment of the contract price. A land installment contract means an executory agreement which by its terms is not required to be fully performed by one or more of the parties to the agreement within one year of the date of the agreement and under which the vendor agrees to convey title in real property to the vendee and the vendee agrees to pay the purchase price in installment payments, while the vendor retains title to the property as security for the vendee's obligation.

The court rendered a judgment which included findings of fact and conclusions of law. That judgment held as follows: 1) Fulk owed Tanner the actual amount called for in the land contract from its execution to the judgment canceling the contract and returning possession to Tanner, less payments made to Tanner; 2) Tanner was not entitled to any monies for destruction and deterioration of the property; 3) Tanner was not entitled to any monies based upon the fair rental value of the property; and 4) Fulk was not entitled to any monies from Tanner, and specifically could not recover the sum of $7,200 he had paid under the land contract prior to termination.

The election of the vendor to terminate the land installment contract is an exclusive remedy that bars further action on the contract unless the vendee has paid an amount less than the fair rental value plus deterioration or destruction of the property occasioned by the vendee's use. In such case the vendor may recover the difference between the amount paid by the vendee on the contract and the fair rental value of the property plus an amount for the deterioration or destruction of the property occasioned by the vendee's use. Where the vendor of the land installment contract brings an action for forfeiture for vendee's default under the contract, the vendor has elected an exclusive remedy which prohibits further action except to recover any amount paid by the vendee which is less than the fair rental value plus any deterioration or destruction of the property occasioned by the vendee's use. However, if the amount paid by the vendee exceeds fair rental value plus any deterioration or destruction, the vendor is permitted to retain the excess amount paid.

This measure of damages is also consistent with the general principle that specific performance is unavailable to the seller. In a typical case, where the buyer is in default of payment, monetary damages are adequate to compensate the seller since what the seller bargained for was money. As such, a monetary award is the equivalent of specific performance.

In the instant case, the trial court specifically placed a zero amount on the difference between the amount paid by Fulk on the land contract prior to termination and the fair rental value. The trial court also placed a zero amount on destruction and deterioration. Both of these determinations are supported by competent and credible evidence. Finally, the trial court found no reason to award Fulk any of the amount of $7,200 he had paid under the land contract prior to termination. Neither do we.

AFFIRMED.

VI. EDITORS' PREPARED GRADING GUIDE FOR PRACTICE QUESTION 1:

IN RE RYAN COX

Our editors have prepared a substantive grading guide outline to help you evaluate your answer. We have approached this from the perspective of the model answer structure typically used by a bar exam grader. After you complete a draft answer, compare and contrast it with the sample answer that follows this grading guide. If you missed any key issues in your analysis consider updating and perfecting your answer.

___ Enforceability of contract

   ___ *Cavallaro*: Meeting of the minds required

   ___ *Cavallaro*: Statute of Frauds

     ___ The Belmonts, the party being charged, did not sign the contract

     ___ Partial performance exception

       ___ Possession

       ___ Acquiescence

         ___ *Binninger*

       ___ Clear and positive proof required

       ___ May be inferred under these facts

         ___ Belmonts made the down payment and three monthly payments

         ___ Belmonts affirmatively took possession

         ___ Belmonts did not object to Cox staying on the property

   ___ *Tanner*: Funds not returned

VII. SAMPLE ANSWER TO PRACTICE QUESTION 1:

IN RE RYAN COX

MEMORANDUM OF AUTHORITY

TO: Logan Dillard
FROM: Applicant
RE: In re Ryan Cox
DATE: July 29, 20X3

INTRODUCTION

This memorandum addresses your questions concerning the legal position and options of Ryan Cox regarding the sale of real property in Franklin. Much turns upon the enforceability of the contract, particularly issues relating to the statute of frauds, part-performance and acquiescence.

DISCUSSION

Is there an enforceable land installment contract?

The first issue is whether the contract dated April 2, 20x3 signed by Adam Cox as seller is enforceable? If not, is there an oral agreement between the parties that satisfies the Statute of Frauds?

Agreement: Meeting of Minds

For a contract to be enforceable there must first be a valid agreement between the parties. This means there must be a "meeting of the minds" regarding all essential terms, including price of the land. If there is no such meeting of the minds, as was the case in Cavallaro, there is no agreement to serve as the basis of a contract.

The idea of selling the Franklin property to the Belmonts was first raised by Mr. Cox's daughter, Emily. She told Mr. Cox that the Belmonts "might be interested" in buying the house. However, at this point, an enforceable agreement was not reached. Neither party had clearly indicated their desire and intent to buy or sell.

The second exchange between the Belmonts and Emily came much closer to a legal agreement. As Mr. Cox described, he considered various options, including a land installment contract. This negotiation period resembles the dealings in Cavallaro when plans were redefined and new pricing formulated. Similarly, Mr. Cox and the Belmonts negotiated the price term. Mr. Cox initially asked for $130,000, but settled on $120,000.

According to Mr. Cox and confirmed by Emily, the Belmonts and Mr. Cox did reach a meeting of the minds. The price was set at $120,000. It seems that the Belmonts reviewed the written contract and affirmatively agreed to its terms. The essential terms included Mr. Cox's continued use of the barn and continued residence on the property in his motor home.

This agreement was made orally between the parties in March. Thus, the threshold issue of finding whether there was a meeting of the minds is met. The recognition of the agreement's terms in the letters from the Belmonts' lawyer is further evidence that an agreement had been reached.

Statute of Frauds

The agreement between the parties described above was oral. It was memorialized in a writing that was signed by Adam Cox. The Franklin Statute of Frauds specifies that a contract for the sale of land is unenforceable unless the essential terms are in writing, and the writing is signed by the party being charged. See Cavallaro.

Here, only Adam Cox signed the written contract. The Belmonts, against whom Mr. Cox wants to enforce the contract, did not sign anything. The contract cannot be enforced against them unless the Statute of Frauds is satisfied.

The Statute of Frauds could be satisfied through another written document signed by the Belmonts read in conjunction with the failed contract. Nothing in the facts indicates the existence of such a document. The letter from the Belmonts' attorney does seem to acknowledge the terms of the contract. However, there is no internal specific reference between the documents as required by Cavallaro. In addition, the Belmonts themselves did not sign the letter from the attorney.

Partial Performance

The Statute of Frauds may also be satisfied by the partial performance doctrine. An oral agreement to sell real property is enforceable if there is partial performance. This doctrine requires 1) delivery of possession of the property and 2) acquiescence by the parties to the terms of the contract. See Cavallaro.

This theory is helpful to Mr. Cox. He moved out of his house following the oral agreement, and the Belmonts moved in. The agreement was made in April and possession was delivered the month before. It is not clear whether the Belmonts actually lived at the house. From the interview, it seems that Marsha Belmont lived there, but her husband Nicky was traveling with the carnival until October. Nicky was present occasionally, as shown by the meeting with Mr. Cox in the house.

Possession alone, though, is not enough without acquiescence. In Binninger, the purchaser took possession of the property but the seller was not held to have acquiesced in either the possession or the contract terms.

In contrast, here Mr. Cox clearly acquiesced in the possession. The issue is whether the Belmonts acquiesced to the essential terms. The fact that the Belmonts paid the requested $40,000 down payment supports acquiescence. Had they paid less, as the purchaser in Binninger did, it would likely be considered a counteroffer because a unilateral subsequent modification of a contract requires consent.

In addition, the Belmonts did not object to Mr. Cox's remaining on the property in his motor home. More information is needed on whether they left the pole barn in his exclusive possession. The terms of the contract allowed Mr. Cox to remain on the property and retain sole access to the barn. If the Belmonts took possession and allowed these things to continue, their acquiescence may be inferred from their non-action. Mr. Cox must show acquiescence by clear and positive proof, as required by Binninger.

$40,000 Forteiture

Tanner suggest that the $40,000 payment does not have to be returned to the Belmonts as it is to be treated as a forfeiture.

CONCLUSION

In conclusion, Mr. Cox seems to have a reasonably strong case for proving that an enforceable contract exists. Although there were preliminary negotiations, the parties reached a meeting of the minds on the essential terms in May. This contract was oral and thus potentially unenforceable under the Statute of Frauds. However, because both possession and acquiescence seems applicable, the doctrine of part performance here seems to satisfy the statute. Given this, the $40,000 is properly treated as forfeited.

VIII. PRACTICE QUESTION 2:

U.S. v. ALEJANDRO CRUZ

TABLE OF CONTENTS

Documents Provided for Task	**Page**
Instructions	3-207
File	3-209
Task Memorandum	3-210
Transcript of Alejandro Cruz Interview	3-211
Letter from Office of Foreign Assets Control to Alejandro Cruz	3-215
Customs and Border Protection Report	3-217
Library	3-221
Selected Provisions of the Trading with the Enemy Act	3-222
United States v. Frade	3-224
United States. v. Macko	3-227
Editors' Prepared Grading Guide	3-231
Sample Answer	3-233

U.S. v. ALEJANDRO CRUZ

INSTRUCTIONS

1. You will have 90 minutes to complete this session of the examination. This performance test is designed to evaluate your ability to handle a select number of legal authorities in the context of a factual problem involving a client.

2. The problem is set in the fictional State of Franklin, one of the United States, located in the fictional Fifteenth Circuit. Franklin has District Courts (trial courts), Courts of Appeal (mid-level appellate courts), and a Supreme Court (Franklin's highest appellate court).

3. You will have two sets of materials with which to work: a File and a Library.

4. The File contains factual materials about your case. The first document is a memorandum containing the instructions for the tasks that you are to complete.

5. The Library contains the legal authorities needed to complete the tasks. The case reports may be real, modified, or written solely for the purpose of this performance test. If the cases appear familiar to you, do not assume that they are precisely the same as you have read before. Read each thoroughly, as if it were new to you. You should assume that cases were decided in the jurisdictions and on the dates shown. In citing cases from the Library, you may use abbreviations and omit page citations.

6. Your response must be written in the answer book provided. You should concentrate on the materials provided, but you should also bring to bear on the problem your general knowledge of the law. What you have learned in law school and elsewhere provides the general background for analyzing the problem; the File and Library provide the specific materials with which you must work.

7. Although there are no restrictions on how you apportion your time, you should probably allocate at least 45 minutes to reading and organizing before you begin writing your response. You may make notes anywhere in the test materials, but may not tear out pages from this booklet.

8. Your response will be graded on its compliance with instructions and on its content, thoroughness, and organization.

File

U.S.
v.
Alejandro Cruz

1. Memorandum to Applicant   3-210
2. Transcript of Alejandro Cruz Interview   3-211
3. Department of Treasury Letter   3-215
4. Department of Homeland Security Report   3-217

Law Offices of
Miles, Read and Paulete
605 Crawford Street

Carpenter, Franklin

TASK MEMORANDUM

To: Associate

From: Matt Mateo

Re: U.S. v. Alejandro Cruz

Date: July 29, 20X3

Our client, Alejandro Cruz, is threatened with criminal prosecution by the United States Department of the Treasury's Office of Foreign Assets Control (OFAC) following a trip to Cuba. OFAC has sent Mr. Cruz a letter requesting information concerning a possible criminal violation of Section 515.201 of the Trading With the Enemy Act.

Prepare a memorandum for me that: (a) identifies the elements of a criminal violation of Section 515.201 of the Trading With the Enemy Act; and (b) indicates the evidence the government now possesses to establish each element.

TRANSCRIPT OF
ALEJANDRO CRUZ INTERVIEW

Matt Mateo: OK, Alejandro, it was good to catch up on what you've been doing since we were in the Peace Corps in Nepal.

Alejandro Cruz: Indeed it was, Matt.

MATEO: Well, let's get to work. We've covered the basics, costs, retainer, and information that you and I will need to keep in touch. So, as I told you, I've turned on the tape recorder to get the full story. Do you have any questions before we start?

CRUZ: I don't think so. This whole thing is overwhelming. I don't feel that I'm on familiar or solid ground. I went on a tropical vacation and now I'm facing fines of six figures and even prison.

MATEO: I'm sure it is a shock. Thanks for the documents you've brought. We'll go over them in a minute. Let's go back to what's happened and start at the beginning.

CRUZ: Certainly. Many years ago, I began looking at taking a trip to Cuba. I was reading a lot of news stories about Cuba. There was the Pope's visit in 1998, the 40th anniversary of Castro's revolution the next year, and then all the news coverage on the little boy, Elían González, who was the center of the controversy involving Cuban-Americans in Miami. It seemed as though there was a news story every week about Cuba. I was curious about Cuba, and frankly I wanted to learn for myself what was left of communism in the 21st century. I'm not of Cuban extraction myself, but I was interested.

MATEO: Would it be fair to say that as a result of the news coverage you were aware of the U.S. embargo?

CRUZ: Yes. For example, in 2000 there were many stories about the possibility of the U.S. easing the embargo against the sale of food and medicine to Cuba, even though it didn't actually succeed. I definitely recall reading those with interest. Running my own business, I couldn't believe that the United States Congress would prohibit U.S. farmers from selling their agricultural commodities to Cubans.

MATEO: So you knew about the legal problems of going to Cuba before you went?

CRUZ: Let me think about that. There was extensive coverage on doing business with Cuba, for example, comparing the conflicting U.S. policies toward China and Vietnam and toward Cuba, but I can't recall ever reading about the travel restrictions. I don't think that many people in America realize that a trip to Cuba could land them in federal prison for 10 years.

MATEO: So you knew about the trade embargo, but perhaps not about the travel restrictions?

CRUZ: I think that I discovered those only after I decided to go, and began doing research on traveling there.

MATEO: What did you do?

CRUZ: I went to a bookstore and checked out the Internet. All the major guidebook publishers have guides to Cuba, and I scanned many of them.

MATEO: So, before going, how would you describe your understanding of the legality of traveling to Cuba?

CRUZ: That it was illegal, but that the travel restrictions were a relic of the long dead and buried Cold War, that thousands of Americans were going, and there was no punishment, not even a slap on the wrist. Everyone seemed to be going. I had received announcements of organized tours from my university alumni association.

MATEO: Did you keep any of them?

CRUZ: I don't think so. No, I didn't. I preferred to go on my own, traveling independently rather than on a packaged tour. Perhaps that was a mistake. Are the tours legal?

MATEO: I really don't know. So would it be fair to say that you understood that without some kind of permission, a license I think it says, it was illegal to go?

CRUZ: Yes.

MATEO: You knew the rules, you just did not think that there would be any consequences?

CRUZ: Yes, and, I guess, that it was so commonplace, that I would not be caught.

MATEO: So how did you go?

CRUZ: I followed the guide's instructions. I booked flights to Montego Bay and then to Havana. It's very easy to do on the Internet, except that you can't pay for the flight to Havana with a U.S. credit card. Only cash is accepted, but it's easy. It's the same in Cuba. You cannot use your American credit card, but the dollar is the common currency. There's no need to change any money for Cuban pesos.

MATEO: How long were you there?

CRUZ: Two weeks.

MATEO: Any idea what you spent?

CRUZ: Less than $2,000, including airfare.

MATEO: What was that for?

CRUZ: Hotel rooms, meals, and transportation, basically.

MATEO: Again, is it fair to say that those were the kinds of expenditures that you believed were prohibited?

CRUZ: Pretty much. I just did not think it mattered to anyone.

MATEO: Any records of your expenditures?

CRUZ: I can't recall any that I retained.

MATEO: So, when you came back to the U.S., what happened?

CRUZ: I was not even thinking that there would be a problem. I took a few precautions, and then forgot about it until I was suddenly searched and given the "third degree" by Customs.

MATEO: What precautions?

CRUZ: I stashed the Cuban cigars and rum I'd bought. And I removed the baggage tags from the flights to and from Havana.

MATEO: But they found the cigars and rum?

CRUZ: Just bad luck to be the one they picked out to search. As I said, I was not prepared for it. I tried to think of an explanation, but I did not do it very well. The Customs guy could tell I wasn't being straight.

MATEO: That comes through in his report.

CRUZ: I felt that he could see right through me. I finally decided to tell him the truth: I had been to Cuba. And then not say anything else. At least I had the presence of mind to remember that from the guidebook.

MATEO: I don't know how this is going to turn out, Alejandro, but I think that you made the right decisions on both counts. Is the officer's report accurate?

CRUZ: It embarrasses me to say that it is. He probably could have put in some more shuddering and stammering while I tried to think of something to say. I don't think that I raised my voice as he claims, but I did go through a phase of being angered that I was caught, because I recalled reading of Little Leaguers being able to get away with going to Cuba. I guess I thought of myself as an experienced world traveler, and I felt very foolish.

MATEO: Then what?

CRUZ: I thought that giving up 70 or 80 dollars worth of cigars and rum at the airport was the end of it. That's ironic: I bought them on the black market, so the money did not go to the Cuban government, but to some Cuban undercutting the government stores.

MATEO: Then what? You received the letter from OFAC?

CRUZ: Yes, the "Request to Furnish Information" from a "Sanctions Coordinator." That is when I decided that this was getting out of control and called you.

MATEO: This is obvious, but I assume that you don't have one of the licenses mentioned in the OFAC request?

CRUZ: No. I do not know who gets them or how. Although I guess the tour companies have that figured out.

MATEO: Probably. I notice that OFAC has to ask if you have a license. But I guess that's what they're stuck with. They can't send the FBI to Cuba to prove that you committed a crime. Are these then the only documents you have?

CRUZ: Yes. It's my entire Cuba file.

MATEO: I'll look it over. As I said, the Trading With the Enemy Act is not something I'm familiar with, so I'll probably ask one of our associates to look into it. We will probably want to respond in some way to the request, since criminal sanctions are being threatened. We'll draft something and be in touch.

CRUZ: Thank you.

DEPARTMENT OF THE TREASURY
Office of Foreign Assets Control
WASHINGTON, D.C.

OFAC No. X3-53-0798

July 16, 20X3

Alejandro Cruz
463 Cespedes
San Cabo, Franklin 60001

Request to Furnish Information Regarding Possible Criminal Violation of Section 515.201 of Trading With the Enemy Act

Dear Mr. Cruz:

This is in reference to your entry into the United States on July 2, 20X3, at Nelson City International Airport, State of Franklin. At that time, you acknowledged to a Customs and Border Protection Officer that you had been to Cuba. The Customs Report is enclosed. Section 515.201 of the Trading With the Enemy Act, administered by the Office of Foreign Assets Control (OFAC) of the United States Department of the Treasury, prohibits all persons subject to the jurisdiction of the United States from travel-related transactions in Cuba, unless authorized under a license.

The Trading With the Enemy Act provides that, unless otherwise authorized, any person subject to the jurisdiction of the United States who has traveled to Cuba shall be presumed to have engaged in prohibited travel-related transactions. This presumption may be rebutted by a statement signed by the traveler providing specific supporting documentation showing that (1) no transactions were engaged in by the traveler or on the traveler's behalf by other persons subject to the jurisdiction of the United States, or (2) the traveler was fully-hosted by a third party not subject to the jurisdiction of the United States, and payments made on the traveler's behalf were not in exchange for services provided to Cuba or any national thereof.

Accordingly, would you provide to this Office a signed statement under oath explaining whether you engaged in travel-related transactions in Cuba pursuant to a license? If you claim to have traveled pursuant to a license, provide documentation of the purpose and activities of your travel to Cuba; provide the number, date, and name of the bearer of the license; and, if still in your possession, provide a copy of the license itself. If you claim not to have engaged in travel-related transactions in Cuba, provide a statement under oath describing the circumstances of the travel and explain how it was possible for you to avoid entering into travel-related transactions such as payments for meals, lodging, transportation, bunkering of vessels, visas, entry or exit fees, and gratuities.

If you claim to have been a fully-hosted traveler to Cuba, provide a statement under oath describing the circumstances of the travel and explain how it was possible for you to avoid entering into travel-related transactions such as payments for meals, lodging, transportation, bunkering of vessels, visas, entry or exit fees, and gratuities. The statement should also state what party hosted the travel and why. The statement must provide a day-to-day account of financial transactions waived or entered into on behalf of the traveler by the host, including but not limited to visa fees, room and board, local or international transportation costs, and Cuban airport departure taxes. It must be accompanied by an original, signed statement from the host, confirming that the travel was fully-hosted and the reasons for the travel.

Since there is no question that you traveled to Cuba, the failure to establish that your travel was pursuant to a license, or that there were no travel-related transactions in Cuba, or that you were a fully-hosted traveler, could result in a criminal prosecution for violation of the Trading With the Enemy Act.

Your response should be mailed within 15 days to: Sanctions Coordinator, OFAC, U.S. Department of the Treasury, Washington, D.C.

OFFICE OF FOREIGN ASSETS CONTROL

/s/ Clara Charles
Clara Charles
Washington Sanctions Coordinator

DEPARTMENT OF HOMELAND SECURITY
Customs and Border Protection

Report (Customs Form 110 A)

Case No.: CS: X3-53-0798

Report Type: Seizure/Forfeiture of Cuban-origin commodities

Officer's Name/Badge No.: Customs Officer Paul Nardella, #36326

Office/Location: Nelson City International Airport, State of Franklin

Report Date/Time: July 2, 20X3, 3 p.m.

Suspect/Victim/Reporting Party: Alejandro Cruz, U.S. Passport #0534123132

Address: 463 Cespedes, Nelson City, Franklin 60001

Telephone: (555) 555-6034

Seized or Forfeited Property: 2 boxes, 25 cigars each of Cohiba Esplendidos. 1 box, 25 cigars of Cohiba Habanos. Total 75 cigars. 2 bottles Havana Club Anejo Reserva Rum. 5 "Che" key chains. One Cuban 3-peso coin.

Action Taken: Forfeiture of Cuban-origin commodities and referral to OFAC, Washington Office.

Narrative: On date of report, Customs and Border Protection Officer (CO) Nardella was assigned to an Inspector's secondary examination station, Nelson City Customs. Alejandro Cruz was selected for a random inspection by a roving Inspector and referred to CO's inspection station. Passport in order. Entry and exit stamps from Jamaica, Montego Bay, in accord with Customs Declaration (Form 6059B), listing arrival on Air Jamaica #319. No entry or exit stamps indicating travel to Cuba. Passport not retained. No commodities declared.

CO asked Cruz if he had anything to declare. Cruz responded no. "No tobacco or alcohol products?" CO asked. Cruz again responded no. CO performed hand search of luggage. Discovered Cuban-origin commodities listed above wrapped in dirty clothing and stuffed inside an empty camera bag. CO asked Cruz why he had not listed the commodities on Customs Declaration. Cruz said that he estimated that they were within $400 duty-free exemption and it was not necessary to write in. CO responded that that is correct if items are orally declared. Cruz responded, "That's been done now, right?"

CO responded that was correct but these are Cuban-origin commodities. Cruz volunteered that he had bought the Cuban-origin commodities in Jamaica, so he did not believe that they "were a problem with the Cuba embargo." CO responded, "So you did not buy these commodities in Cuba?" Cruz said, "No. I bought them in the duty-free store leaving Montego Bay, Jamaica." (This Customs Officer has observed the same items carried by passengers coming from Montego Bay.) CO informed Cruz that it did not matter where he bought them, as U.S. law does not permit the importation of Cuban-origin commodities even if purchased in another country.

CO informed Cruz that Cuban-origin commodities would have to be seized and that unless he was licensed to import or transport Cuban-origin commodities, he would be required to forfeit the Cuban-origin commodities. CO informed Cruz that he would have to wait while CO filled out a Seizure Report identifying the Cuban-origin commodities. Cruz was observed to be agitated and nervous. Cruz then volunteered that he "misspoke." He had not bought the items. They were gifts. He said several times, "I did not pay for them." Cruz said he had heard that the U.S. embargo of Cuba was "over" and that no one had ever been prosecuted for violating the embargo. "Why did you single me out?" Cruz said in a raised voice. CO said that he thought that Cruz said he had not been to Cuba. Cruz responded, "I did not spend any U.S. dollars" on the Cuban-origin commodities. CO responded OK, that he would put on the seizure form that the commodities had not been purchased in Cuba and that Cruz had not been in Cuba. Cruz responded the CO had "misunderstood me. I was in Cuba. I received the cigars as gifts in Cuba."

CO inquired what Cruz was doing in Cuba. Cruz responded that he thought he "better not say anything else." Thereafter Cruz refused to respond and repeated that he "better not say anything else." CO explained to Cruz that not all travel to Cuba was prohibited, that if he was in a category that qualified for a general license he could travel there and bring into the U.S. up to $100 worth of Cuban-origin commodities. CO explained that if he had family members in Cuba or was a journalist or a professor working in Cuba he could bring in the Cuban-origin commodities. CO asked Cruz whether he had traveled to Cuba as part of a specific license held in the name of another, such as an educational or professional tour. Cruz's response to each of these suggestions was that he "better not say anything else."

CO offered Cruz the opportunity to talk to the Customs supervisor on duty if he wanted to explain his presence in Cuba. Cruz declined. CO explained process to reclaim property or accept forfeiture. Cruz said, "Keep it. You and your buddies can enjoy the cigars." CO informed Cruz that the contraband would be smoked – in the Customs incinerators.

[End of Report]

Library

U.S.
v.
Alejandro Cruz

1. Selected Provisions of the Trading with the Enemy Act — 3-222
2. *United States v. Frade* — 3-224
3. *United States v. Macko* — 3-227

SELECTED PROVISIONS OF THE TRADING WITH THE ENEMY ACT

Section 515.201. Transactions involving designated foreign countries or their nationals.

(a) All of the following transactions are prohibited, except as authorized by the Secretary of the Treasury by means of licenses, if such transactions involve money or property in which any foreign country designated under this section, or any national thereof, has any interest of any nature whatsoever, direct or indirect:

(1) All dealings in, including, without limitation, transfers, withdrawals, or exportations of, any money, property, or evidences of indebtedness or evidences of ownership of property by any person subject to the jurisdiction of the United States; and

(2) All transfers outside the United States with regard to any money, property, or property interest subject to the jurisdiction of the United States.

(b) For the purposes of this section, and subject to the President's declaration, the term "foreign country designated under this section" includes . . . Cuba . . . .

(c) Any person subject to the jurisdiction of the United States who engages in any of the foregoing transactions is in violation of this section and is subject to civil action and remedies and, if such person engages in any such transaction willfully, to criminal prosecution and sanction.

Section 515.420. Fully-hosted travel to Cuba.

A person subject to the jurisdiction of the United States who is not authorized to engage in travel-related transactions in which Cuba has an interest will not be considered to violate the prohibitions of Section 515.201 when a person not subject to the jurisdiction of the United States covers the cost of all transactions related to the travel of the person subject to the jurisdiction of the United States.

Section 515.421. Presumption of travel-related transactions.

Unless otherwise authorized, any person subject to the jurisdiction of the United States who has traveled to Cuba shall be presumed to have engaged in travel-related transactions prohibited by Section 515.201. This presumption may be rebutted by a statement signed by the traveler providing specific supporting documentation showing that no transactions were engaged in by the traveler or on the traveler's behalf by other persons subject to the jurisdiction of the United States or showing that the traveler was fully-hosted by a third party not subject to the jurisdiction of the United States and that payments made on the traveler's behalf were not in exchange for services provided to Cuba or any national thereof.

The statement should address the circumstances of the travel and explain how it was possible for the traveler to avoid entering into travel-related transactions such as payments for meals, lodging, transportation, bunkering of vessels, visas, entry or exit fees, and gratuities. If applicable, the statement should state what party hosted the travel and why. The statement must provide a day-to-day account of financial transactions waived or entered into on behalf of the traveler by the host, including but not limited to visa fees, room and board, local or international transportation costs, and Cuban airport departure taxes.

Travelers fully-hosted by a person or persons not subject to the jurisdiction of the United States must also provide an original signed statement from their sponsor or host, specific to that traveler, confirming that the travel was fully-hosted and the reasons for the travel.

UNITED STATES v. FRADE

United States Court of Appeals, Eleventh Circuit, 1985

Father Joe Morris Doss, Rector of Grace Episcopal Church in New Orleans, and Father Leopold Frade, Curate of Grace Episcopal Church and Chairman of the National Commission for Hispanic Ministry, appeal their convictions for criminal violation of Section 515.415 of the Trading With the Enemy Act (TWEA). This provision makes unlawful any transaction "when in connection with the transportation of any Cuban national . . . unless otherwise licensed." The prohibited transactions included "transportation by vessel," the "provision of any services to Cuban nationals," and "any other transactions such as payment of port fees and charges in Cuba and payment for fuel, meals, lodging."

The events giving rise to the convictions are those of the now famous Mariel boatlift, or freedom flotilla, of spring 1980, by which some 114,000 Cuban refugees, in nearly 1,800 boats, crossed the 90 miles of ocean and great political divide between Cuba and the United States. In early April 1980, some 10,800 Cuban citizens claiming status as political refugees sought sanctuary in the Peruvian Embassy in Havana. On April 14, 1980, President Carter declared that up to 3,500 of these refugees would be admitted into the United States. An airlift was started, but within three days Castro stopped the flights, announcing that anyone who wanted to leave could do so through the harbor of Mariel. Almost immediately, small boats, funded by the members of the Cuban-American community, began leaving Key West.

Cuban-American parishioners of Grace Church implored Fathers Frade and Doss to help in arranging for a boat to bring their relatives from Cuba. A meeting held by the priests at Grace Church on May 3 to organize the rescue mission was attended by 650 people and met with immediate overwhelming response. Within forty-eight hours, $215,000 was raised.

Fathers Frade and Doss commenced negotiations with the Interest Section of the Cuban Government in Washington to obtain the release of family members and political prisoners. They obtained assurances that they would not be forced to bring back criminals, the mentally ill, or other undesirables that the Cuban government was then forcing into the Mariel boatlift. The Cuban Interest Section insisted that Fathers Frade and Doss turn over the list of the people they proposed to pick up. The priests submitted a list of 366 names, which were immediately telexed to Havana. Although Fathers Frade and Doss understood that, in the week following their meeting at the Cuban Interest Section, the Administration's attitude towards the boatlift had changed, they realized that, once the names had been telexed, they had passed the point of no return. Father Frade had been told by a Cuban official that a "national purge was taking place," those applying for permission to leave Cuba were losing jobs, houses, and ration cards, and sometimes being attacked, beaten, and killed. As the district judge observed at sentencing, "Once the list of names had been given over to the Cuban officials . . . it would have been very difficult, a very difficult decision of conscience to stop at that time."

On May 26, 1980, the *God's Mercy,* a large, safe vessel, equipped with $10,000 in added safety equipment, and manned by an experienced crew, including a doctor and a nurse, set sail for Mariel. After two weeks of intense negotiation, Fathers Frade and Doss succeeded in obtaining commitments to release the persons on their lists. On June 12, 1980, the *God's Mercy* arrived in Key West, with the priests and 402 refugees, including 288 persons from the lists.

The *God's Mercy* was escorted into Key West by two Coast Guard cutters. Fathers Frade and Doss were arrested immediately, and the indictment under the TWEA was brought. After trial, Fathers Frade and Doss received $431,000 in fines, and the *God's Mercy* was forfeited to the government.

Fathers Frade and Doss contend that the trial court erred in denying their motion for judgment of acquittal on the ground that there was no evidence to establish the requisite mental state for a criminal violation of Section 515.41 of the TWEA.

To be criminal, violation of the TWEA must be "willful." "Willfulness" is expressly required in some provisions of the act, such as Section 515.201, and impliedly required in the rest, including Section 515.415, with which we are concerned here. When used in a criminal statute, the word "willfully" generally connotes a voluntary breach of a known legal duty. Section 515.415, under which the priests were convicted, was enacted into its operative form unexpectedly and with little publicity on May 15, 1980 – after the list of names had been tendered to Cuba. It criminalized behavior (travel to, from, and within Cuba), which previously had been expressly authorized and which, in fact, remained lawful for a time, except when done in connection with the transportation of Cuban nationals, an activity which also is not generally criminal. It penalized the paying of port fees in a foreign harbor and duly incurred hotel, motel and restaurant bills if done to assist the transportation of Cubans to the United States.

These are activities that laymen do not consider wrong nor lawyers classify as *malum in se*. The government argues that the evidence demonstrated the necessary mental state for a criminal violation of Section 515.415 of the TWEA. The government relies principally on the testimony of government officials who stated that they had warned the priests that the venture *might* be against the law. The government also relies on the priests' knowledge that they *might* be liable for repeat trips or boat safety violations; that they *might* be subject to forfeiture of their vessel under civil statutes; and that the government *generally disapproved* of the boatlift as dangerous and inadvisable.

However, the finding that a defendant is aware of matters such as those stated above is insufficient to sustain a finding of guilt under a statute requiring a voluntary breach of a known legal duty. The government also argues that the priests' own behavior, including their fears and expressed concerns, indicated a voluntary breach of a known legal duty. The government relies on the priests' decision to captain the *God's Mercy* on the return voyage so that any possible onus might fall personally on them, and their own trial testimony that they would have gone ahead with the mission regardless of the law because of their moral commitment to those whose names were on the list submitted to the Cuban government. Their fears and expressed concerns, however, were understandable as normal caution and worry for the welfare of all concerned. They were simply insufficient to sustain a finding of a voluntary breach of a known legal duty. The judgment of the district court must be reversed.

UNITED STATES v. MACKO

United States Court of Appeals, Eleventh Circuit, 1999

Defendant Ralph Macko was accused of selling cigarette-packaging machinery and supplies to Cuba in violation of Section 515.201 of the Trading With the Enemy Act (TWEA). After a jury found Macko guilty, the district court held that the evidence was insufficient to support the guilty verdict. The United States appealed.

The evidence presented during the government's case-in-chief shows that the sales were through freight forwarders in Panama. The invoices did not disclose that Cuba was the ultimate destination. Macko visited Cuba by going through third countries.

In its order explaining the judgment of acquittal, the district court described the government's evidence as "primarily a paper case, made up of letters, faxes, shipping invoices, and other documents." This "paper trail," the court stated, "has too many twists and turns and dead ends to establish more than a tenuous inference that Macko acted with the requisite mental state for a criminal violation of Section 515.201 of the TWEA."

The district court observed that the circumstantial evidence against Macko "is susceptible of more than one interpretation." The jury could reasonably infer that Macko knew that his conduct was generally unlawful, the court says, but such a general awareness of illegality is not sufficient to establish guilt here. Only by "mere speculation" could a jury conclude that Macko acted with the mental state required.

According to the government, the evidence against Macko, though circumstantial, established that he was aware of the prohibitions of the Cuban trade embargo and that he acted with the intent to avoid them to his profit.

In Section 515.201, the TWEA prohibits the sale of merchandise to Cuba or Cuban nationals without a license from the Office of Foreign Assets Control. Though a child of the Cold War that ended seven years ago with the Soviet Union's extinction, the Cuban embargo remains very much alive. The TWEA limits transactions with Cuba for many purposes, including both trade and travel, although subject to many exceptions. Its primary purpose is to stop the flow of hard currency from the United States to Cuba. In *United States v. Frade* (11th Cir. 1985), we held that "willfulness" under the TWEA entails a voluntary breach of a known legal duty.

<u>To establish that Macko voluntarily breached a known legal duty, the government had to prove that he knew of the prohibition against dealings with Cuba and nevertheless violated it.</u>

In *United States v. Frade*, the defendants were two Episcopal priests who arranged for a ship to bring 402 Cuban refugees to the United States in 1980 during what became known as the Mariel boatlift. While the priests were laying their plans, President Carter's administration attempted to gain some control over the sudden mass immigration by amending the TWEA to generally criminalize travel to or from Cuba in connection with the transportation of Cuban nationals. We held that the evidence did not establish that the priests voluntarily breached a known legal duty, principally because the government failed to establish that the priests had knowledge of any such duty.

The case against Macko is more convincing than the case against the priests in *Frade*. Indeed, *Frade* recites considerable evidence that the priests did not know about the provision of the TWEA at issue there. That provision barred conduct that until then had been expressly authorized by a different provision. Although U.S. officials warned the priests that their boatlift *might* be illegal, that is all that they did, and that was insufficient. Furthermore, the priests did not attempt to hide their travel to and from Cuba.

In this case, on the other hand, the trade ban in Section 515.201 of the TWEA was promulgated neither quietly nor unexpectedly. It was in effect long before Macko involved himself in the Cuban cigarette plan, and it was widely publicized. The provision does not apply only to certain goods or activities but states a broad prohibition against transactions with Cuba or Cuban nationals. We also find it telling that Macko actively concealed his travel to Cuba as well as the final destination of the cigarette machinery and supplies. He did not attempt to shield his contacts with Panama or Panamanians, nor did he hide the fact that he was acquiring cigarette-packaging machinery and supplies.

The one aspect of the operation that he kept secret was the Cuban connection. Macko traveled to Cuba through Panama in a manner that left no reference to Cuba on his passport. Macko initially lied to U.S. Customs agents about traveling and sending equipment to Cuba. Macko's correspondence about the project with other participants scrupulously avoided mentioning Cuba by name. Macko had experience in exporting machinery from the United States and was involved in international sales of various goods.

The inference that Macko acted as though it was illegal to deal directly with Cuba would seem to satisfy the element of voluntary breach of a known legal duty. A jury could reasonably conclude that Macko's secrecy about this single fact resulted from his knowledge of the Cuban embargo. Consequently, the district court erred in granting Macko's motion for a judgment of acquittal on the charge of criminal violation of Section 515.201 of the TWEA.

Reversed.

IX. EDITORS' PREPARED GRADING GUIDE FOR PRACTICE QUESTION 2:

U.S. v. ALEJANDRO CRUZ

We have prepared a substantive grading guide outline to help you evaluate your answer. We have approached this from the perspective of the model answer structure typically used by a bar exam grader. After you complete a draft answer, compare and contrast it with the sample answer that follows this grading guide. If you missed any key issues in your analysis consider updating and perfecting your answer.

___ Trading with the Enemy Act (TWEA)

   ___ Elements

      ___ "any person"

      ___ "subject to the jurisdiction of the United States"

      ___ "willfully"

      ___ "engages in a transaction"

      ___ "involving money or property in which Cuba or any national thereof has any interest of any nature whatsoever, direct or indirect"

      ___ "including (A) transfers, withdrawals, or exportations of any money, property, or evidences of indebtedness or evidences of ownership of property by any person subject to the jurisdiction of the United States, and (B) transfers outside the United States with regard to any money, property, or property interest subject to the jurisdiction of the United States"

   ___ Statutory exceptions

      ___ License for Cuban travel

      ___ Fully-hosted travel

      ___ No-transactions travel

   ___ Evidence government possesses to establish each element

      ___ Person: Undisputed that Cruz is a person

      ___ Subject to U.S. jurisdiction: Cruz is a U.S. citizen, as evidenced by his U.S. passport number on the Customs Report

   __ Willfully

      __ *Macko* (citing *Frade*)

         __ "voluntary breach of a known legal duty"

         __ "knew of the prohibition against Cuba and nevertheless violated it"

         __ Customs Report

            __ Cruz concealed his travel (*Macko*)

               __ No Cuban stamps in passport

               __ Jamaican passport stamps show attempt to conceal travel by routing through third country

            __ Cruz initially lied to Customs about his travel (*Macko*)

__ Transaction: Cuban goods and coin seized by Customs

__ Cuban property or money: Cuban goods and coin seized by Customs

__ Transfer of money or property: Cuban goods and coin seized by Customs

X. SAMPLE ANSWER TO PRACTICE QUESTION 2:

U.S. v. ALEJANDRO CRUZ

MEMORANDUM

TO: Matt Mateo
FROM: Associate
RE: U.S. v. Alejandro Cruz
DATE: July 29, 20X3

INTRODUCTION

You have asked that I prepare a memorandum that: (a) identifies the elements of a criminal violation of Section 515.201 of the Trading with the Enemy Act; and (b) indicates the evidence the government now possesses which they could use to establish each element.

DISCUSSION

A. The elements necessary for a criminal violation of Section 515.201 of the Trading with the Enemy Act (TWEA) are as follows:

(1) "any person

(2) subject to the jurisdiction of the United States

(3) willfully

(4) engages in a transaction

(5) involving money or property in which Cuba or any national thereof has any interest of any nature whatsoever, direct or indirect,

(6) including (A) transfers, withdrawals, or exportations of any money, property, or evidences of indebtedness or evidences of ownership of property by any person subject to the jurisdiction of the United States, and (B) all transfers outside the United States with regard to any money, property, or property interest subject to the jurisdiction of the United States."

Three exceptions exist:

(I) transactions pursuant to license,

(II) "fully-hosted travel," that is, where a person not subject to the jurisdiction of the United States covers the cost of all transactions related to the travel of the person subject to the jurisdiction of the United States,

(III) "no transactions travel," that is, where a person travels to Cuba and no transactions were engaged in by the traveler or on the traveler's behalf by other persons subject to the jurisdiction of the United States.

In some sense items II and III *supra* are not really exceptions; when their requirements are met, it means that no prohibited transactions occurred so that element six was not met.

B. Evidence the government now possesses to establish each element:

1. "ANY PERSON"

This is not defined in the statute or materials in the file, but it seems likely that "any person" includes an individual human being and the government surely can prove Cruz is an individual, through his presence. That is, the fact finder will be able to observe that Mr. Cruz is an individual.

2. "SUBJECT TO THE JURISDICTION OF THE UNITED STATES"

This important operative phrase similarly is not defined. However, it is safe to assume that it includes a U.S. citizen. I assume that Mr. Cruz is a United States citizen. Although I cannot find a statement to that effect in the file, the Customs Report notes that Cruz has a U.S. Passport (#0534123132). The Customs Report says that Cruz's passport was returned to Cruz, but the government could obtain it from him by a subpoena. The 5th Amendment right against testimonial self-incrimination, which applies to the federal government, which would be the prosecuting government here, does not extend to non-testimonial articles like passports. Thus, the government can acquire the passport by subpoena and use it to prove Cruz is a U.S. citizen and subject to the jurisdiction of the United States.

3. "WILLFULLY"

This is the most important element in our case. The Macko and Frade cases interpreted the meaning of willfully in this context. Technically Frade, a 1985 case, interpreted "willfully" as used in Section 515.415 of the TWEA. However, Macko, a 1999 case, interpreted willfully as used in section 515.201 and cited Frade for authority. Hence it appears that willfully has the same meaning in both sections so that both cases are relevant in construing willfully as used in 515.201. Note as well that Macko and Frade are 11th Circuit cases. Florida is geographically close to Cuba and is located in the 11th Circuit, and many of these cases would be expected to arise there. However, Franklin is in the 15th Circuit.

The U.S. Constitution requires that a federal criminal trial be brought in the district in which the crime allegedly occurred. The crime/alleged crime here occurred in Cuba. I am not sure how this affects the venue. Venue would probably lie in the district in which the defendant resides. Cruz resides in Franklin, so he would be tried in federal district court in the relevant district of Franklin. Such court would be bound by the decisions of its circuit and not necessarily bound by the decisions of the 11th Circuit. Nonetheless the Macko and Frade cases are persuasive, if not binding, authority.

Macko, citing Frade, defines willfully as used in Section 515.201 as "the voluntary breach of a known legal duty." To prove that Macko voluntarily breached a known legal duty, the government had to prove that he "knew of the prohibition against Cuba and nevertheless violated it."

The Macko holding is very problematic for Cruz. The Macko court permitted an inference that the defendant knew of the prohibition against Cuba and nevertheless violated it under facts remarkably similar to ours.

Presently the government has the following evidence to prove that Cruz "knew of the prohibition against Cuba and nevertheless violated it."

First I note that, from the interview, Cruz has said that the Customs Report is embarrassingly accurate. This is accurate in at least four areas.

One, Cruz actively concealed his travel in two regards: Cruz traveled to Cuba in a manner that left no reference to Cuba in his passport and Cruz did not attempt to hide his travel to the third country, Jamaica, through which Cruz cleansed the taint of his Cuba travel. Macko did the exact same two things (his third country was Panama) and the court found this evidence of active concealment, that is, a scheme to make it appear that travel had been only to the third country. The government can prove these two elements from the Customs Report and Cruz's passport. According to the Customs Report, Cruz virtually admitted to traveling to Cuba (see discussion below), yet Cruz's passport did not bear any indicia of having visited Cuba.

Two, Cruz initially lied to U.S. Customs about his transactions involving Cuban acquired items. Macko identified this conduct as relevant evidence as to willfulness. The Customs Report shows that Cruz initially said, in answer to the question, "So you did not buy these commodities in Cuba?": "No, I bought them in the duty-free store leaving Montego Bay, Jamaica." Later, Cruz said that he had not bought the items, that they were gifts. Still later, "CO said that he thought that Cruz had said he had not been to Cuba."

Cruz did not answer that remark except to say that "I did not spend any U.S. dollars." The parsing of this language is intricate. From it, Cruz did not say, "I never have been to Cuba." However, Cruz did not affirmatively deny CO's statement, "I thought that you said you had not been to Cuba." Because Cruz did not deny traveling to Cuba, the statement could be regarded as an admission that Cruz had been to Cuba. However, that affirmation by silence cannot be inferred if the omitted statement would be incriminating, as it would have been here. Nonetheless, the statements in the Customs Report would be strong circumstantial evidence to allow a fact finder to conclude that Cruz had been to Cuba. Indeed, the government has so concluded. Its letter states, "You admitted going to Cuba; tell us how you did not violate the TWEA." Thus, while we could intricately parse the conversations between CO and Cruz and argue that Cruz never admitted going to Cuba, a fact finder could infer that he had been there.

Three, Cruz otherwise lied to and was deceitful with Customs. Cruz specifically denied that he had tobacco or alcohol products, but he possessed these articles. In addition, Cruz's statement that he thought these articles were within a $400 allowance is negated by the secretive nature in which he packed them – wrapped in dirty laundry, stuffed inside an empty camera bag. The lying and secretive evidence show knowledge of the prohibition and strongly point to Cruz's willful violation.

Fourth, Cruz is a well-versed traveler. <u>Macko</u> indicated that this was relevant to a conclusion that the defendant knew of the prohibition. The report also indicates that Cruz thought the US embargo of Cuba was over. That was not true, and even as the statement stands, it suggests that Cruz was aware of the embargo.

4. ENGAGES IN A TRANSACTION

The government has the following evidence: cigars, rum, and a Cuban three-peso coin. It also has the evidence discussed *supra*, which tends to prove that Cruz traveled to Cuba. The coin is the most damaging, as it gives a strong inference that Cruz engaged in a transaction with a Cuban national.

5. INVOLVING MONEY OR PROPERTY IN WHICH CUBA OR ANY NATIONAL THEREOF HAS ANY INTEREST WHATSOEVER, DIRECT OR INDIRECT

The government has the cigars, rum, and Cuban three-peso coin, so the evidence is in. It also has the other previously-discussed evidence that tends to prove Cruz traveled to Cuba.

6. INCLUDING (A) TRANSFERS, WITHDRAWALS, OR EXPORTATIONS OF ANY MONEY, PROPERTY, OR EVIDENCES OF INDEBTEDNESS OR EVIDENCES OF OWNERSHIP OF PROPERTY BY ANY PERSON SUBJECT TO THE JURISDICTION OF THE UNITED STATES, AND (B) ALL TRANSFERS OUTSIDE THE UNITED STATES WITH REGARD TO ANY MONEY, PROPERTY OR PROPERTY INTEREST SUBJECT TO THE JURISDICTION OF THE UNITED STATES

Again, the government has the cigars, rum, and Cuban three-peso coin, so the evidence is in. And again, it also has the other previously discussed evidence that tends to prove Cruz traveled to Cuba.

CONCLUSION

In conclusion, it appears that the government has sufficient evidence to indict our client.

RIGOS UNIFORM BAR REVIEW SERIES

MULTISTATE PERFORMANCE TEST (MPT) REVIEW

CHAPTER 4

OFFICE TASKS

Table of Contents

I.	**INTRODUCTION**	4-241
II.	**STRUCTURE OF THE QUESTION**	4-241
	A. Question Packet Instructions	
	B. Expected Answer Form	
	1. Technical Document	
	2. Client Letter	
	3. Default Form	
	C. Official Author	
III.	**ANSWERING THE QUESTION**	4-242
	A. Letters	
	1. Persuasive Letters	
	a. Examples	
	b. Unfavorable Facts or Law	
	2. Objective Letters	
	a. Opinion Positions	
	b. Conclusion Necessary	
	3. Know Your Audience	
	4. Active Voice Versus Passive Voice	
	a. Negative Facts	
	(1) Example – Active Voice	
	(2) Example – Passive Voice	
	b. Unimportant Actor	
	5. Wording Opportunities	
	6. Clarity	
	B. Wills	
	1. Format Provided	
	2. Objective Orientation	
	3. Explaining Your Finished Work Product	
	C. Other Tasks	
IV.	**WORKING THROUGH A SAMPLE QUESTION:**	
	IN RE PROGRESSIVE BUILDERS, INC.	4-244
	Instructions	4-247
	File	4-249
	Task Memorandum	4-250
	Editors' Summary of Task Memorandum	4-251
	Transcript of Interview of John May and Frank May	4-252
	Progressive Builders, Inc. Existing Contract	4-258

      Library...4-261
           Selected Provisions of the Franklin Codes...4-262
           Stirlen v. Supercuts, Inc...4-264
           Myers v. Scamardo Termite Control..4-268
      Editors' Summary of Key Facts and Legal Authority 4-272
      Sample Answer 4-273
      Working Practice Questions..4-277

V. PRACTICE QUESTION 1:
IN RE SNOW KING MOUNTAIN RESORT   4-279
      Instructions..4-281
      File...4-283
           Task Memorandum 4-284
           Memorandum from Sally Johnson, Mountain Operations Director.....................4-285
           Memorandum from Kyle Mills, Marketing Director 4-286
           Letter from National Life and Casualty Insurance Company 4-287
      Library...4-289
           Franklin Civil Code § 846..4-290
           Schneider v. Mount Desert Island Land Trust..4-291
           Gerkin v. Saint Clara Valley Water District..4-294
      Editors' Prepared Grading Guide 4-297
      Sample Answer 4-299

VI. EDITORS' PREPARED GRADING GUIDE FOR
PRACTICE QUESTION 1:
IN RE SNOW KING MOUNTAIN RESORT   4-297

VII. SAMPLE ANSWER TO PRACTICE QUESTION 1:
IN RE SNOW KING MOUNTAIN RESORT   4-299

VIII. PRACTICE QUESTION 2:
IN RE WINSTONS   4-301
      Instructions..4-303
      File...4-305
           Task Memorandum 4-306
           Transcript of Interview of Ralph and Margaret Winston.....................................4-307
      Library...4-311
           Selected Provisions of the Franklin Fair Housing Act..4-312
           Project HOME v. City of Catalina..4-314
           Townley v. Rocking J Residential Community..4-318
      Editors' Prepared Grading Guide 4-323
      Sample Answer 4-325

IX. EDITORS' PREPARED GRADING GUIDE FOR
PRACTICE QUESTION 2:
IN RE WINSTONS   4-323

X. SAMPLE ANSWER TO PRACTICE QUESTION 2:
IN RE WINSTONS   4-325

RIGOS UNIFORM BAR REVIEW SERIES

MULTISTATE PERFORMANCE TEST (MPT) REVIEW

CHAPTER 4

OFFICE TASKS

I. INTRODUCTION

An "Office Tasks" assignment is the third most common type of MPT question. Almost any of these assignments may require drafting an opinion letter to be presented to the client, usually under your supervising attorney's name. The NCBE has released questions requiring the applicant to draft a document such as a last will and testament which we categorize as an office task. The examiners could require the drafting of other documents, such as a prenuptial agreement or a simple contract.

II. STRUCTURE OF THE QUESTION

A. Question Packet Instructions

As in persuasive briefs and objective memoranda assignments, your question packet will contain instructions, a File, and a Library. Take your book pages apart and lay out these three resources into separate sections for working convenience.

B. Expected Answer Form

1. Technical Document: If your task involves drafting a technical document, you can expect to find a secondary "pointer" memorandum specifying the format the document should follow. The detail will depend on the complexity of the assigned task. See page 4-250 *infra* for an example.

2. Client Letter: On the other hand, if your assigned task is to write the usual letter to a client, you will likely not receive any guidance as to layout form. In that case, use a standard, simple business letter format such as the headings To, From, Date, Subject, etc. The headings in the example questions and answers in this text will suffice. See page 4-273 *infra* for an example.

3. Default Headings: As in the previous chapters, if the instructions contain guidance as to headings, use them. If not, remember our organizational section's default trio of Introduction, Discussion, and Conclusion.

C. Official Author

If you are asked to draft a letter, you will usually be instructed to prepare it for your supervising attorney's signature. In that case, end the signature block with his or her name. If you are simply told to draft a letter, without instructions as to who will be the "official" author, the best position is probably to use the name of your imaginary law firm (*e.g.*, "Holmes Law Firm").

> **MPT Tip:** As stated in the previous chapter, do not write your real name anywhere in your answer. Don't even put your initials below the signature.

III. ANSWERING THE QUESTION

A. Letters

When drafting a letter, consider two main questions: First, is it intended to be persuasive or objective? Second, who is the recipient?

1. Persuasive Letters: A persuasive letter is generally addressed to opposing counsel. As such, the document is not intended to be objective.

a. Examples: These types of letters include demand letters, affirmative settlement offer letters, and letters rejecting demands or settlement offers made by opposing counsel. Your main goal is to convince opposing counsel of the weakness of his case and reasons why it is in his client's best interest to accept your client's present generous offer of settlement.

b. Unfavorable Facts or Law: If there are facts or law unfavorable to your client, you should attempt to deemphasize the harmful facts and/or distinguish the unfavorable law. It is a mistake to disregard these negative issues, as the graders will look to see how well you handle this paradox and mitigate the damage. If you do not deal with the negative issues, your letter will not be very persuasive.

> **MPT Tip:** The NCBE's Point Sheets indicate that citations to legal authority are expected in letters addressed to other lawyers.

2. Objective Letters: An objective letter is generally addressed to a layperson client and intended to provide legal advice or assist her in resolving a legal problem.

a. Opinion Positions: These letters are sometimes referred to as "opinion letters." This task calls for a similar approach to that you might use in drafting an objective memorandum. An example is the task of preparing a client letter explaining the statute of limitations tested in February, 2012. Analyze both the pros and cons of the issues presented.

b. Conclusion Necessary: As is the case with objective memoranda, your exposition must usually reach a conclusion. Without a summation, you have not provided your client all the information s/he needs to decide the best course of action.

> **MPT Tip:** Even in a letter to a layperson, you should cite the legal authority on which you rely. The task memorandum may explicitly tell you to do this.

3. Know Your Audience: A letter to a lawyer calls for a more sophisticated tone than a letter to a layperson. When writing to a layperson, you must be able to explain legal concepts in a way that she/he can understand them. Regardless of who will receive your letter, always write in a concise, professional manner. "Padding" your letter by using needlessly complicated words or repeating yourself will not impress the hypothetical reader, who in reality is your grader.

4. Content and Organization: If the office task letter assignment memorandum specifies a form, follow it. If not, consider using three heading sections of:

  a. Opening: Identify the parties and purpose of the letter.

  b. Discussion: Break this down into subsections to cover all the concerns.

  c. Summary and Go-Forward Plans: Here you need to sum up and suggest what go-forward steps are necessary.

> **MPT Tip:** Headings in your task answer portray to the grader an organized communication.

5. Active Voice Versus Passive Voice: In general, you should write directly by using sentences framed in the active voice. This usually promotes clarity, conciseness, and maximum readability. Exceptions to this "no passive voice" rule include:

  a. Negative Facts: In a persuasive letter, stating harmful facts in the passive voice can make them seem less important.

    (1) Example – Active Voice: "Ms. Johnson filed her reply brief late."

    (2) Example – Passive Voice: "The reply brief was filed late by Ms. Johnson." Notice that the untimely nature of the filing has a little less emphasis when the word "late" is stated in the passive voice and buried in the middle of the sentence.

  b. Unimportant Actor: The passive voice also may be helpful and appropriate when the act is significantly more important than the subject actor. An example would be, "Gotrocks Jewelry Store was burglarized on June 7, 20X2, by unknown persons."

6. Wording Opportunities: Your choice of wording to describe the facts may mitigate harshness, and it may be possible to emphasize or de-emphasize background facts.

  a. Example 1: If the facts state that the defendant was arrested and taken into custody, the prosecution may state that "the accused was arrested by the police," while the defense might state that "the suspect was taken into custody by the authorities."

  b. Example 2: Another example is a traffic fender-bender incident fact pattern described by the plaintiff as a "collision" rather than an "accident" description used by the defendant. The first wording suggests reckless behavior while the second suggests mere fortuity.

7. Clarity: In general, if a reader will need to read a sentence more than once to understand it, you should revise it to increase clarity. If you need to make such a revision, it is occasionally possible the sentence would actually be clearer if written in the passive voice. Think before you write.

> **MPT Tip:** Since all the controlling law is usually provided in the task assignments, your organization and wording choice are quite important to your grade.

B. Wills

Preparing a last will and testament is a possible office task on the MPT. This is somewhat of a cross-over question opportunity, since the controlling legal rules vary between jurisdictions and are usually also tested in essay questions. This includes subjects such as wills, trusts, and family law agreements.

1. Format Provided: If you are asked to draft or create a last will and testament, most likely you will receive a pointer memorandum setting forth the format you should use. Such a pointer memorandum will probably contain instructions not to draft various "boilerplate" provisions.

2. Objective Orientation: In this type of question, you will probably be informed of your client's desired asset disposition plan and named beneficiaries or groups. Other estate goals and objectives may also be stated in the task assignment. You should receive all the necessary state law to ensure that you draft a last will and testament that, from a legal perspective, is consistent with your client's wishes.

3. Explaining Your Finished Work Product: Most recent last will and testament MPT questions have also asked the applicant to write a drafting letter explanation. For example, one task involved a primary task of drafting a will in accordance with the client's wishes, which included disinheriting a son and vesting control of the family business in his daughter. The secondary task assigned the applicant was to explain how she approached drafting the provisions of the will to meet the client's two objectives.

> **MPT Tip:** Will validity requirements is one of the few instances on the MPT where state law could matter. If so, the grader will want you to demonstrate your knowledge of the particular local law. Most required law will be provided in the Library, but an applicable on point state deviation will score points.

4. Explain Reasons for Redraft: The secondary task is to provide the reasons the author changed the original contract. This may be designed as a guide to assist a senior partner in marshalling their arguments and/or presentation for a client.

C. Other Tasks

There have also been other office tasks required such as in 2013 requiring an analysis and re-draft of a trademark agreement and redrafting a significant contractual provision. Read the task memorandum assignment carefully to determine the objective and parameters of your assignment.

IV. WORKING THROUGH A SAMPLE QUESTION:

IN RE PROGRESSIVE BUILDERS, INC.

We will now turn to a sample MPT question, *In re Progressive Builders, Inc.* The table of contents begins on the next page.

IN RE PROGRESSIVE BUILDERS, INC.

TABLE OF CONTENTS

Documents Provided for Task	**Page**
Instructions	4-247
File	4-249
Task Memorandum	4-250
(Editors' Summary of Task Memorandum)	4-251
Transcript of Interview of John May and Frank May	4-252
Progressive Builders, Inc., Contract	4-258
Library	4-261
Selected Provisions of the Franklin Codes	4-262
Stirlen v. Supercuts, Inc.	4-264
Myers v. Scamardo Termite Control	4-268
(Editors' Summary of Key Facts and Legal Authority)	4-272
Sample Answer	4-273

IN RE PROGRESSIVE BUILDERS, INC.

INSTRUCTIONS

1. You will have 90 minutes to complete this session of the examination. This performance test is designed to evaluate your ability to handle a select number of legal authorities in the context of a factual problem involving a client.

2. The problem is set in the fictional State of Franklin, one of the United States, located in the fictional Fifteenth Circuit. Franklin has District Courts (trial courts), Courts of Appeal (mid-level appellate courts), and a Supreme Court (Franklin's highest appellate court). Additionally, the question refers to the fictional State of Columbia, which is another one of the United States and is also located in the Fifteenth Circuit.

3. You will have two sets of materials with which to work: a File and a Library.

4. The File contains factual materials about your case. The first document is a memorandum containing the instructions for the tasks that you are to complete.

5. The Library contains the legal authorities needed to complete the tasks. The case reports may be real, modified, or written solely for the purpose of this performance test. If the cases appear familiar to you, do not assume that they are precisely the same as you have read before. Read each thoroughly, as if it were new to you. You should assume that cases were decided in the jurisdictions and on the dates shown. In citing cases from the Library, you may use abbreviations and omit page citations.

6. Your response must be written in the answer book provided. You should concentrate on the materials provided, but you should also bring to bear on the problem your general knowledge of the law. What you have learned in law school and elsewhere provides the general background for analyzing the problem; the File and Library provide the specific materials with which you must work.

7. Although there are no restrictions on how you apportion your time, you should probably allocate at least 45 minutes to reading and organizing before you begin writing your response. You may make notes anywhere in the test materials, but may not tear out pages from this booklet.

8. Your response will be graded on its compliance with instructions and on its content, thoroughness, and organization.

File

In re Progressive Builders, Inc.

1. Memorandum to Applicant — 4-250
2. Editor's Summary — 4-251
3. Transcript of Interview of John May and Frank May — 4-252
4. Customer Progressive Builders, Inc. Contract — 4-258

COYLE & COOPER, LLP
6620 DWIGHT PROMENADE
SPRING VALLEY, FRANKLIN 55510

TASK MEMORANDUM ASSIGNMENT

To: Applicant
From: Vivian Coyle
Subject: *In re Progressive Builders, Inc.*
Date: July 29, 20X3

We have been retained by John May, the owner of Progressive Builders, Inc. (PBI), a residential property construction company, to give ongoing legal advice.

In the course of my initial interview with Mr. May, a question arose about a form contract that PBI has used for the past several years outside of Franklin, and specifically about its provision for arbitration of disputes. Mr. May has tentatively agreed to build a house in Franklin for the restaurateur Pier Nittardi and thinks he may need to use the arbitration provision in this agreement. I have made an appointment to discuss the matter with him tomorrow, and have told him that I will have a letter delivered to him beforehand to help guide our discussion.

Please prepare, for my signature, a pre-counseling letter for delivery to Mr. May, in which you explore the following two questions:

1. State our understanding of the objectives and goals that Mr. May seeks to achieve by using the arbitration provision.

2. In light of Mr. May's objectives and goals, discuss the likely consequences of keeping the arbitration provision as-is.

In preparing the pre-counseling letter, remember that Mr. May is a layperson. Although you must discuss the law, you should do so as clearly and concisely as possible, and in a manner that a non-lawyer can understand.

EDITORS' SUMMARY

A. The Task Memorandum

1. Assignment: Here, the task memorandum is quite clear. Your assignment is to draft an objective opinion letter to a business owner client of the law firm. Our client is a contractor with a concern about the legal issues associated with an arbitration clause contained in a form contract.

2. Writing Style: The supervising attorney has even reminded you about writing in a manner so that a layperson can evaluate the advice. Keep it simple – this is not a law review article.

3. Two Objectives: Note that your assignment has two main objectives.

   a. Advantage Focus: First, you must explain your understanding of the client's reasons for and advantages in using the arbitration clause.

   b. Likely Legal Consequences: Second, while keeping those reasons in mind, you need to explain the probable consequences of leaving the arbitration clause unchanged. Be sure to address both prongs of this objective; otherwise, your answer will be incomplete.

4. If the court determined the contract to be unconscionable it would be struck. This would potentially open the client up to punitive damages under Franklin Civil Code Section 3294.

Now, we will look at the rest of the File and the Library.

TRANSCRIPT OF INTERVIEW OF JOHN MAY AND FRANK MAY

VIVIAN COYLE: With your permission, I'll be tape-recording our conversation today?

JOHN MAY: Yes.

FRANK MAY: Of course.

COYLE: Let's back up and summarize how we got to where we are now. John, you were referred to our firm by Peter Padilla, of Padilla Construction Company, one of our clients.

JOHN MAY: That's right. I wanted to establish an ongoing relationship with a law firm in Franklin that had experience with the residential property construction industry. I, of course, hope to avoid any legal problems in the first place, you understand. But if a problem develops, then I want to minimize unnecessary time and money in educating some lawyer on an emergency basis.

COYLE: Prior to turning on the tape recorder, John, you and I executed the standard written retainer agreement approved by the Franklin State Bar Association.

JOHN MAY: Yes, we did.

COYLE: Why don't you state the gist of what you told me about PBI?

JOHN MAY: Sure. Frank and I started PBI here in Spring Valley in Franklin in the mid-1970's. We incorporated it here; we'd always been its sole shareholders, 50-50; I'd always been the President and he'd always been the Vice-President.

COYLE: And what does PBI do?

JOHN MAY: We're a construction company that does residential property. Earlier on, we did small repairs, a bit more complex than handyman work, but then we started to do remodels and eventually construction of new houses.

FRANK MAY: By the early 1980's, we had concentrated on major remodels and new construction. That's all we've done ever since.

COYLE: Just to clarify, you work only on residential property?

FRANK MAY: That's right. When we first started out, we took any job we could get, doing anything we could do, or thought we could do, whether it was residential or commercial or even industrial. But not since the early '80's.

COYLE: More clarification: You work on single-family residences or duplexes or apartments . . . ?

FRANK MAY: No, just single-family residences. Again, in the early days we did anything and everything. But since the early '80's, only residential, and only single-family.

Sample Question 4-252   Course 5329. Copyright 2018 by Rigos UBE Review Series – MPT.

COYLE: By the '90's, what had happened?

JOHN MAY: Politics were heating up here in Franklin and so were property values. Each of us was married by then and had children. With the cost of housing, the only way we could move up was to move out. And there was the State of Columbia right next door. It was somewhat backward. But you could buy land for a song.

COYLE: And the politics?

JOHN MAY: Right. With the tightening of building requirements and environmental regulations and assorted red tape, it took more time and money to get anything built. And that meant that the business was becoming less profitable.

FRANK MAY: So, we both moved to Columbia with our families and moved the business there too. Our first major jobs were building our own houses.

COYLE: Let me return to the politics. Didn't one of you mention something about what you called the "litigation climate"?

JOHN MAY: I did. The "litigation atmosphere." When we started out in the mid-'70's, there was relatively little suing and being sued involving contractors. I'm not saying there were no disputes. In construction, there're always disputes, especially when you're remodeling someone's house or building him a new one. But we just worked things out, working with each other, the builder and the owner. As the '90's rolled around, that had begun to change. At job sites you'd hear, "See you in court," more often, I'll bet, than you hear it here at your law firm.

COYLE: Well . . . .

FRANK MAY: John's exaggerating somewhat, but not much.

COYLE: But did you two have any bad experiences?

JOHN MAY: We didn't, but our friends in the business did, including Pete Padilla, who recommended you to me. Look, our business is construction and not law. From what I've heard, legal problems don't simply cost you a lot of money for lawyers. What's worse, they can pull you away from work for a huge amount of time, and then distract you when you finally get back to work and make you much less efficient.

COYLE: And so . . . .

JOHN MAY: And so, we went to Columbia, where the atmosphere wasn't so sue-crazy, at least not then.

COYLE: You went there in the early '90's?

FRANK MAY: That's right. Since then, we continued our concentration on major remodels and new construction, but moved to the higher end – contract prices of between $450,000 and

$850,000 and up – as more and more wealthy people from around the country have looked to Columbia for their second or third homes.

COYLE: Okay. Your work has been in Columbia exclusively?

JOHN MAY: Yes, except for a job or two now and again in Franklin, as a favor for a friend, like the house we built two years ago for Pete Padilla's daughter Sophia, who is Frank's goddaughter.

COYLE: What about your subcontractors, have you drawn them exclusively from Columbia?

JOHN MAY: Just about. We've always subcontracted as little work as possible. It's sometimes been a pain to do a lot ourselves, but it's more of a pain to lose control of quality. Of course, we still had to subcontract, particularly the specialty trades, like plasterers and ornamental metal workers. Also foundation work, which demands heavy equipment and lots of concrete and rebar. But all that's mostly local.

COYLE: But here you are in Franklin.

JOHN MAY: Right. Demand for our kind of high-end residential construction has been heating up in this area in Franklin for quite some time. The rich folks who were flocking to Columbia from around the country for their second or third homes have started flocking here as well. Demand hasn't cooled down much in Columbia – but this business is cyclical. So I decided to move back into the Franklin market.

FRANK MAY: Not me, though. John moved back with his family. He's already set up an office here in Spring Valley. I sold him my interest in PBI. With the money, I've started my own business in Columbia, Frank May Construction, Inc.; I'm working out of our old office there. Now PBI is all John's.

COYLE: That's about all of the background, isn't it? John, your move back led you to talk to Pete Padilla, and Pete Padilla led you to our firm.

JOHN MAY: Right.

COYLE: And in the course of our conversation, you told me about some of your general concerns.

JOHN MAY: Right again. I'm a builder, not a lawyer, and I need to avoid litigation and its costs if I want to stay profitable. Even Franklin's become more sue-crazy. I just want to make sure I don't make any missteps as I come back here.

COYLE: It was in this connection that you happened to mention your customer contract form and to give me this copy of it. Right?

JOHN MAY: Yes. We've been lucky over the years. The contract's been part of our luck. You might not believe it, but we've never been sued. The main reason is that we've done very good work, and done it on time and within budget. We've also made sure that we fix our own mistakes on our own initiative. We provide old-fashioned honest value, and that's our reputation. Our contract is simple and uncluttered, and communicates the message of honest value: It specifies what you pay and what we do. That's just about it.

COYLE: Plus arbitration.

JOHN MAY: Plus arbitration. That's important to me. I've just got to avoid the costs of litigation, both the money costs and the time costs. I've seen how they've eaten up friends of ours, builders whose businesses were more profitable than ours, until one or two big lawsuits hit. What I also worry about are punitive damages. All the time I read about some business that screws up a few thousand dollars' worth, and then has to pay a few million in punitive damages. I couldn't survive that. You can't run a business with an open-ended risk like that. You know I can't get insurance to cover that, don't you?

COYLE: Yes, I do. But let me ask you this question: Why do you specify arbitration by the National Arbitration Organization ("NAO")?

JOHN MAY: Two reasons. One is that the NAO was founded in Franklin around the time we started out in the mid-'70's, and we wanted to support a local business. The other is that it focused on construction disputes.

COYLE: How much does the NAO charge for arbitration?

JOHN MAY: You know, I really don't know. Years ago, the first time I tinkered with the arbitration provision and inserted the NAO clause, I think I had a list of charges. But we never became involved in any arbitration with our clients. Whatever disputes arose, we settled them ourselves, by give and take.

COYLE: Let me back up for a moment. You said you "tinkered" with the arbitration provision. Did you actually draft the arbitration provision or any other part of the contract?

JOHN MAY: I wouldn't use the word "draft." Over the years, I've seen lots of contracts. I just took shreds and patches and tried to sew them together to make a whole contract. And I'd mend those pieces from time to time. Basically, over the years, I took out as many words as I could, and simplified the ones that were left.

COYLE: Did you, or do you, negotiate with clients about the terms of the contract?

JOHN MAY: Well, there are all those blanks – you have to come to some agreement with the client on the work to be done, the cost, the schedule, you know.

COYLE: I know. But in addition to filling in the blanks, do you negotiate with clients about the terms of the contract?

JOHN MAY: I can't remember anybody wanting to change anything. If they get the work they want, at the price they want, on the schedule they want, well, that's about it.

COYLE: What about the arbitration provision? It requires the client to arbitrate but not you.

JOHN MAY: No, I can't remember anybody wanting to change that either. I'd never thought about whether I'd be required to arbitrate if I had a claim. The arbitration provision doesn't say so, but I'd never thought about it.

COYLE: Before I forget, let me add that it's my understanding that your concerns about the contract have not arisen in the abstract.

JOHN MAY: Sorry. That's right. I'm finalizing an agreement which I hope to wrap up in a week or two, to build a house for Pier Nittardi in Bradfield, which is only a few miles away from Spring Valley, here in Franklin.

COYLE: Nittardi is the chef and owner of Il Pavone, a restaurant there, isn't he?

FRANK MAY: Yes. John and I have known him for quite some time. He's remarrying his ex-wife Jean.

JOHN MAY: This project will be bigger than any of the jobs Frank and I did together. It couldn't be more important.

COYLE: And before you reduce it to contract, you want to know what contract to reduce it to?

JOHN MAY: That's right.

COYLE: Fine. Before we conclude, let's sum up what you want to do, and what you want me to do, with respect to the contract.

JOHN MAY: Basically, I want to use the contract in Franklin, just as we used it in Columbia, and of course I want to use it for Pier's house.

COYLE: Without modification?

JOHN MAY: Yes, without modification, if possible. I want the contract to change only as necessary. The important thing is for the contract to be understandable and to get the job done.

COYLE: I understand. But Franklin's law is different from Columbia's. So even if it didn't need any fixing there, it might need some fixing here. That will depend on all sorts of things. For instance, will your subcontractors come from Franklin? What about your suppliers?

JOHN MAY: Who knows? As I said, in Columbia we used mostly Columbia subs. Also mostly Columbia suppliers. It's conceivable I could use some of those Columbia folks in Franklin, but it's 200 miles away, so I don't know how likely it is.

COYLE: Give me some time to research the issues. Can you come by again perhaps on August 4th so that we can discuss the matter?

JOHN MAY: Sure. How about 2 o'clock?

FRANK MAY: There's no need for me to return. I'm the fifth wheel, since PBI is all John's now. I just came today because John asked me, to help him with any background you might need to know. Also, I've got to get back to a job in Columbia.

COYLE: Frank, that's fine with me. Thanks for coming. John, two o'clock is good for me too. By noon on August 4th, I'll have a letter delivered to you to assist in focusing the discussion in the meeting.

JOHN MAY: That'll be fine. Thanks so much.

COYLE: You're welcome. Good-bye.

FRANK MAY: Good-bye.

JOHN MAY: Bye.

PROGRESSIVE BUILDERS, INC. CUSTOMER CONTRACT

1. Parties to this Contract:

    A. Contractor:

       Progressive Builders, Inc.

       4333 Broadway, Woodhaven, Columbia 65377

       (555) 555–7900, (555) 555–7905 (fax)

    B. Customer Property Owner:

       (Name) _____

       (Address) _____

       (City, State, Zip) _____

       (Telephone, Fax, and Email) _____

2. Location of Work:

   _____

3. Completion Dates:

    A. Estimated date of commencement: _____

    B. Estimated date of completion: _____

4. Contract Price: $_____

5. Method and Schedule of Payment:
   _____
   Note: The initial down payment must equal at least one-third of the contract price.

6. Description of the Work:
   _____
   _____
   _____

7. Warranty: Contractor provides the following warranty to Property Owner, to the exclusion of all other warranties, express or implied. Contractor warrants that the work will be free from faulty materials; constructed according to the standards of the building code applicable to this location; and constructed in a skillful manner and fit for habitation.

8. Arbitration of Disputes: If a dispute arises concerning the provisions of this contract or its performance, Property Owner agrees: (1) to submit any such dispute to binding and final arbitration under the rules of the National Arbitration Organization (NAO); and (2) to limit any relief that may be awarded by the NAO to compensatory damages. Contractor and Property Owner agree to bear the costs of arbitration equally.

9. Additional Provisions:

    A. _____

    B. _____

    C. _____

10. Contract Acceptance:

Signature of Contractor:
_____

Date: _____

Signature of Property Owner:
_____

Date: _____

Library

In re
Progressive Builders, Inc.

1. Selected Provisions of the Franklin Codes   4-262
2. *Stirlen v. Supercuts, Inc.*   4-264
3. *Myers v. Scamardo Termite Control*   4-268

SELECTED PROVISIONS OF THE FRANKLIN CODES

Section 3282 of the Franklin Civil Code. Compensatory Damages.

Every person who suffers detriment from the unlawful act or omission of another, may recover from the person in fault a compensation therefor in money, which is called compensatory damages.

* * * * * * *

Section 3294 of the Franklin Civil Code. Punitive Damages.

In an action sounding in tort, where it is proven by clear and convincing evidence that the defendant has been guilty of oppression, fraud, or malice, the plaintiff, in addition to compensatory damages, may recover punitive damages for the sake of example and by way of punishing the defendant.

* * * * * * *

Section 1281 of the Franklin Code of Civil Procedure. Policy in Favor of Arbitration.

A written agreement to submit to arbitration an existing controversy or a controversy thereafter arising is valid, enforceable, and irrevocable, save upon such grounds as exist for the revocation of any contract.

* * * * * * *

Section 7191 of the Franklin Business and Professions Code. Arbitration and Residential Property Work and Construction.

(a) If a contract for construction of, or work on, residential property with four or fewer units contains a provision for arbitration of a dispute between the parties, the provision shall be clearly titled "ARBITRATION OF DISPUTES," and shall be set out in capital letters.

(b) Immediately before the line or space provided for the parties to indicate their assent or nonassent to the arbitration provision described in subdivision (a), and immediately following that arbitration provision, the following shall appear, and shall be set out in capital letters:

"NOTICE: BY INITIALING IN THE SPACE BELOW YOU ARE AGREEING TO HAVE ANY DISPUTE ARISING OUT OF THE MATTERS INCLUDED IN THE 'ARBITRATION OF DISPUTES' PROVISION DECIDED BY NEUTRAL ARBITRATION AS PROVIDED BY FRANKLIN LAW AND YOU ARE GIVING UP ANY RIGHTS YOU MIGHT POSSESS TO HAVE THE DISPUTE LITIGATED IN A COURT OR JURY TRIAL. BY INITIALING IN THE SPACE BELOW YOU ARE GIVING UP YOUR JUDICIAL RIGHTS TO DISCOVERY AND APPEAL, UNLESS THOSE RIGHTS ARE SPECIFICALLY INCLUDED IN THE 'ARBITRATION OF DISPUTES' PROVISION. IF YOU REFUSE TO SUBMIT TO ARBITRATION AFTER AGREEING TO THIS PROVISION, YOU MAY BE COMPELLED TO ARBITRATE. YOUR AGREEMENT TO THIS ARBITRATION PROVISION IS VOLUNTARY."

(c) Notwithstanding any law to the contrary, a provision for arbitration of a dispute between parties to a contract for construction of, or work on, any residential property with four or fewer units that does not comply with this section is not enforceable against any party other than the party performing the construction or work.

* * * * * *

Section 7195 of the Franklin Business and Professions Code. Residential Property Work and Construction and Treble Damages as Punitive Damages.

In an action sounding in tort arising from construction of, or work on, residential property with four or fewer units, where it is proven by clear and convincing evidence that the person or entity performing the construction or work has been guilty of oppression, fraud, or malice, the person or entity for which the construction or work is performed, in addition to compensatory damages, may recover an additional amount up to three times the amount of compensatory damages as punitive damages for the sake of example and by way of punishing the person or entity performing the construction or work.

STIRLEN v. SUPERCUTS, INC.

Franklin Court of Appeal (1997)

The District Court of Santa Fe County denied a motion to compel arbitration pursuant to the arbitration provision of an employment contract on the ground that that provision was unenforceable because it was unconscionable. We find its order correct and affirm.

Defendant Supercuts, Inc. ("Supercuts"), a Delaware corporation that conducts a national hair care franchise business, appeals from an order, which is statutorily appealable in advance of final judgment, by which the District Court denied its motion to compel arbitration of a dispute relating to its termination from employment of plaintiff William N. Stirlen, its Vice-President and Chief Financial Officer.

Stirlen commenced this action with a complaint that alleged causes of action based on various contract and tort theories, and that sought compensatory damages in contract and punitive as well as compensatory damages in tort.

Supercuts moved to compel arbitration under the arbitration provision of its employment contract with Stirlen. The District Court denied the motion, as we have said, on the ground that the arbitration provision was unenforceable as unconscionable. Supercuts timely appealed.

We shall assume, as have Stirlen and Supercuts, that the arbitration provision of Stirlen's employment contract with Supercuts is subject to the Federal Arbitration Act inasmuch as the employment contract itself evidences a transaction involving interstate commerce within the meaning of Section 2 of the Act.

But we note that, under the Federal Arbitration Act, the question whether, in the words of Section 2, a particular arbitration provision is "valid, irrevocable, and enforceable," or instead presents "grounds . . . for [its] revocation," is answered not by the act itself, but in the first instance by the law of the forum – which in the present case is Franklin.

The arbitration provision of Stirlen's employment contract with Supercuts – which Supercuts itself drafted in its entirety – states, in pertinent part, as follows: "In the event there is any dispute arising out of Executive's [*i.e.*, Stirlen's] employment with Company [*i.e.*,

Supercuts], the termination of that employment, or the employment contract itself, whether such dispute gives rise or may give rise to a cause of action in contract or tort or based on any other theory or statute, Company and Executive agree that exclusive recourse for Executive shall be to submit any such dispute to final and binding arbitration and to obtain, if Executive prevails, compensatory damages only."

Under the law of Franklin, a contract, or a provision of a contract, is unenforceable if it is unconscionable. Unconscionability has both procedural and substantive aspects. The procedural aspect has to do with lack of meaningful freedom of assent, whereas the substantive aspect has to do with the imposition of harsh or oppressive terms. The view that prevails in Franklin is that both procedural and substantive aspects must be present, each at least in some degree, for unconscionability to be present.

The District Court determined that the arbitration provision of Stirlen's employment contract with Supercuts was procedurally unconscionable because the contract itself evidenced lack of freedom of assent, and it was a contract of adhesion. We agree.

A contract of adhesion is a contract, usually with standard terms, that is drafted and imposed by a party of superior bargaining strength, and that allows a party of lesser bargaining strength only to take it or leave it.

Supercuts maintains that its employment contract with Stirlen is not a contract of adhesion because it did not have superior bargaining strength. Supercuts emphasizes that Stirlen was not a person desperately seeking employment, but a successful and sophisticated corporate executive. Supercuts sought him out and "hired" him "away" from a highly paid position with a major corporation "by offering him an annual salary of $150,000, and then agreeing to remunerative 'extras' not included in the standard executive employment contract," such as generous stock options, a bonus plan, a supplemental retirement plan, and a $10,000 "signing bonus."

We are not persuaded that this was a bargained-for agreement. Stirlen appears to have had no realistic ability to modify the terms of his employment contract with Supercuts. Undisputed evidence shows that the terms of the contract, which were cast in generic and gender-neutral language, were presented to him after he accepted employment and were described as standard provisions that were not negotiable. The only negotiating between

Supercuts and Stirlen regarding the conditions of Stirlen's employment related to the stock options, bonus and retirement plans, and other "extras," but these matters were the subject of a separate letter agreement Stirlen executed more than a month before he signed the employment contract. Moreover, the letter agreement referred to the "standard employment contract" Stirlen would be required to sign, noting that the terms of the letter agreement did not supplant but were "in addition to the standard provisions of the contract." Supercuts does not dispute Stirlen's assertions that the employment contract was presented to him on a "take-it-or-leave-it basis," and that every other corporate officer was required to sign, and did in fact sign, an identical agreement.

The District Court also determined that the arbitration provision of Stirlen's employment contract with Supercuts was substantively unconscionable because the provision itself was harsh and oppressive, and unduly favored only the employer. Here too, we agree.

The arbitration provision of Stirlen's employment contract with Supercuts cannot be characterized other than as unduly one-sided. We shall overlook the fact that the provision expressly requires Stirlen to arbitrate any dispute that he may have with Supercuts, but impliedly allows Supercuts either to arbitrate or to litigate any dispute that it may have with Stirlen, as it chooses. Instead, we shall focus on this fact alone: The provision allows Supercuts – in effect, if not in terms – to engage in any and all "oppression" and "fraud" and "malice" against Stirlen, without running the risk of any liability award of even the most minimal punitive damages under Section 3294 of the Franklin Civil Code. Such a provision is unduly one-sided as a matter of law. It is settled in Franklin that any and all contracts or contractual provisions that exempt a contracting party from responsibility for its own oppressive, fraudulent, or malicious conduct are against the policy of the law.

In arguing to the contrary, Supercuts relies on several decisions of courts of sister states. Its reliance is misplaced. Each of those decisions involves the law of a state other than Franklin. More importantly, each deals with an arbitration provision that contains a mechanism for the award of treble damages, which are a species of punitive damages, inasmuch as by definition they amount to three times the compensatory damages in question, and are apparently given "for the sake of example and by way of punishing the defendant" (Frank. Civ. Code, § 3294). No such mechanism, however, is present here.

Lastly, we note that the District Court was not obligated to attempt to salvage any part of the arbitration provision of Stirlen's employment contract with Supercuts that might itself not be unconscionable. It has long been established that a court need not aid a party who has drafted an unconscionable contract, or contractual provision, by effectively redrafting what is objectionable into something unobjectionable. Indeed, we believe that a court should not provide any such aid even if it were otherwise minded to do so. A party who seeks the unmerited benefit of unconscionability must not be allowed to avoid its deserved burden.

For the reasons stated above, we conclude that the District Court correctly denied Supercuts' motion to compel arbitration because the arbitration provision of Supercuts' employment contract with Stirlen was unconscionable and therefore unenforceable.

Affirmed.

MYERS v. SCAMARDO TERMITE CONTROL
Franklin Court of Appeal (1998)

In this action under the Franklin Consumer Sales Act, the District Court of Lucas County issued an order (1) granting a motion by the plaintiff for partial summary judgment declaring that an arbitration provision of a contract was unenforceable on the ground of unconscionability, and (2) denying a motion by the defendant to stay the action pending arbitration pursuant to that provision.

Under the Franklin Consumer Sales Act, an order determining the enforceability of an arbitration provision of a contract against a claim of unconscionability is appealable.

The defendant timely appealed the District Court's order.

For the reasons set out below, we shall affirm.

The plaintiff, Judith Myers, an elderly woman with limited resources, and defendant, Scamardo Termite Control (STC), entered into a contract: STC agreed to eradicate termites that had infested Myers' house; and, in exchange, Myers agreed to pay STC $1,300. The contract contained an arbitration provision, which reads as follows: "The Consumer and STC agree that any controversy or claim between them arising out of or relating to this contract shall be settled exclusively by arbitration. Such arbitration shall be conducted in accordance with the rules and procedures of the National Arbitration Organization then in force."

Having become dissatisfied with STC's service when termites reinfested her house, Myers brought this action under the Franklin Consumer Sales Act seeking, among other relief, (1) an award of $41,000 in compensatory damages, an award of $123,000 in treble damages as authorized by the act itself, and an award of $2,000,000 in punitive damages; and (2) a declaration that the arbitration provision of her contract with STC was unenforceable on the ground of unconscionability.

Thereupon, STC moved to stay the action pending arbitration pursuant to the arbitration provision of its contract with Myers, and Myers moved for partial summary judgment declaring that the provision was unenforceable on the ground of unconscionability.

As noted, the District Court issued an order granting Myers' motion and denying STC's. It did so because it concluded that the arbitration provision was indeed unenforceable as unconscionable.

On appeal, both Myers and STC agree that the soundness of the District Court's order depends on the correctness of its conclusion on the unconscionability of the arbitration provision of their contract. To that question, we now turn.

The following facts are undisputed for present purposes: The arbitration provision of Myers' contract with STC requires that arbitration must be "conducted in accordance with the rules and procedures of the National Arbitration Organization [now] in force." A party seeking arbitration with the National Arbitration Organization must pay a filing fee – for example, $2,000 for a claim between $100,000 and $250,000, and $7,000 for a claim between $1,000,000 and $2,500,000. Because Myers is asserting a punitive damages claim in the amount of $2,000,000, she would have to pay a $7,000 filing fee. Even if Myers should choose to forgo her perhaps overly optimistic punitive damages claim, she still has a not unreasonable claim for treble damages under the Franklin Consumer Sales Act itself, in the amount of $123,000 – for which she would have to pay a $2,000 filing fee. A filing fee paid by Myers in the amount of $2,000 would exceed the sum of $1,300 that she paid on her contract with STC by a large percentage. Myers did not know at the time of contracting that she would be required to pay any filing fee whatsoever, less still one that would be so high. Although the National Arbitration Organization had, and still has, a published schedule of filing fees, none was attached to the contract or otherwise disclosed to Myers.

Under the law of Franklin, which Myers and STC agree applies here, a contract, or a provision of a contract, is unenforceable if it is unconscionable. As the court in *Stirlen v. Supercuts, Inc.* (Frank. Ct. App. 1997) recently held: "Unconscionability has both procedural and substantive aspects. The procedural aspect has to do with <u>lack of freedom of assent</u>, whereas the substantive aspect has to do with the imposition of harsh or oppressive terms. The view that prevails in Franklin is that both procedural and substantive aspects must be present, each at least in some degree, for unconscionability to be present."

In our judgment, unconscionability taints the arbitration provision of the contract between STC and Myers in both its procedural and substantive aspects.

As for procedural unconscionability, the contract between STC and Myers as a whole is plainly a contract of adhesion – that is to say, an instrument with standard terms, drafted and imposed by a party of superior bargaining strength, allowing a party of lesser bargaining strength only to take it or leave it. Perhaps more significantly, the arbitration provision contains an unfair surprise – the undisclosed requirement that Myers would have to pay what must be characterized as arbitration fees that are exorbitant as to her. Such an unfair surprise could have been avoided by disclosure on the part of STC. But STC made no such disclosure.

As for substantive unconscionability, the arbitration provision of the contract between STC and Myers is harsh and oppressive because it effectively requires Myers to pay arbitration fees that are themselves harsh and oppressive because, as stated, they are exorbitant as to her. We do not dwell in a fool's paradise, thinking that the National Arbitration Organization should provide arbitration without cost. Nor do we mean to suggest that its arbitration fees are out of line with the value of the services it provides. Rather, we conclude only that requiring a consumer in Myers' situation to pay such fees is harsh and oppressive. Harshness and oppressiveness could have been avoided by STC's agreement fee to pay such fees on Myers' behalf. But STC made no such agreement.

In sum, because the District Court was correct in its conclusion that the arbitration provision of the contract between STC and Myers is unconscionable, its order denying STC's motion to stay the action pending arbitration pursuant to that provision, and granting Myers' motion for partial summary judgment declaring that that provision was unenforceable on the ground of unconscionability, was altogether sound.

In this court, however, Myers seeks to obtain more than she received below, asking us to enjoin STC from attempting to enforce the arbitration provision here at issue against any consumer in the future. Her request comes too late. But even had it been timely, we would have rejected it. We would be reluctant to find the arbitration provision unconscionable, always and everywhere, and in the abstract, with respect to any and all consumers, no matter what their resources, with whom STC has contracted or may contract. First, and manifestly, unconscionability is in large part a judgment that arises from the unique facts of each individual case. Second, many, or at least some, consumers might in fact prefer arbitration over litigation might also prefer to avoid the premium that STC would presumably build into the contract price if it had to cover the risk of litigation and its costs.

For present purposes, however, all that we need do, and shall do, is to uphold the District Court's order denying STC's motion to stay the action pending arbitration and granting Myers' motion for partial summary judgment.

Affirmed.

EDITORS' SUMMARY

Below we have summarized your resources and tried to focus the analysis.

A. The Facts

1. Interview Transcript: Determining the client's objectives and goals requires a careful reading of the interview transcript. After reading it, you will realize that much of the fact pattern the examiners have provided is unnecessary to answer the homebuilder's question about their customer contract.

2. Arbitration Clause: On the other hand, the arbitration clause – which, as the task memorandum notes, is the primary reason why the client is seeking a legal opinion – is easy to locate quickly by scanning the client's form contract.

3. Objective: The danger the client needs to avoid is a too aggressive contract that is declared unconscionable. If this occurs, it could open Progressive Builder up to a normal one-sided civil court proceedings which could include a punitive damage award.

B. The Law

1. Statutes: While it is not necessary to cite every statute in the Library, all of them provide some information that is helpful to the outcome, at least to some degree. Here, Franklin Code 7191 authorizes arbitration agreements; they do not generally violate the doctrine of unconscionability.

2. Cases: Here, the library provides two cases, both authored by the Franklin Court of Appeals that reviewed decisions below applying the doctrine of unconscionability. Both cases should be cited somewhere in the letter to the client.

3. Enforceability Focus: Both the cases here are relevant and deal with the enforceability of arbitration clauses in Franklin.

C. Sample Letter

The letter that begins on the next page is an example of a reasonably good answer to this question.

COYLE & COOPER, LLP
6620 DWIGHT PROMENADE
SPRING VALLEY, FRANKLIN 55510

John May, Progressive Builders, Inc.
1234 Main Street
Spring Valley, Franklin 55510

July 29, 20X3

Re: Contract Arbitration Clause

Dear Mr. May:

Enclosed please find my preliminary opinion regarding Progressive Builders, Inc.'s (PBI) objectives and goals in using an arbitration clause in its customer contracts. Franklin authorizes arbitration of disputes. Analyzed below are the potential consequences of leaving your Customer Contract language as is without changes

DISCUSSION

I. Goals Sought Through The Arbitration Clause

Based upon our meeting the other day it seems to me there are three primary goals PBI wishes the arbitration clause to achieve. First it seems PBI wishes to reduce any likelihood of formal litigation and prefers that all disputes be resolved through arbitration. Second, to limit any costs that might arise from any damages award, particularly the possibility of punitive damages. Third, there is a desire to limit any business time lost to any disputes and other disruptions resulting from any adverse decision. If you have any additional goals that I have not addressed, please contact me regarding those goals.

II. Consequences of Leaving Arbitration Agreement As Is

The primary risk associated with leaving the arbitration clause as it is today is that a court may refuse to enforce the clause and PBI would be forced to litigate the matter. Also, an arbitrator may refuse to limit damages to compensatory damages and there is some risk punitive damages could be imposed if there was a finding of oppression.

A. Risk Arbitration Clause Will Be Unenforceable

There are two general grounds on which a court may find the present arbitration clause unenforceable. The first risk is that the clause is written in the wrong format. The second risk is that the clause is determined to be unconscionable.

1. Form of the Clause

As an initial matter, Franklin Business and Professions Code Section 7191 requires that all arbitration clauses regarding contracts for construction of residential property of four or fewer units be clearly titled "ARBITRATION OF DISPUTES" and be set out in capital letters. Furthermore, there is specific language that must be used and this language must be entirely in capital letters. And immediately following this language there must be a line or space provided for the parties to indicate their assent or non-assent to the provision. Where a builder does not follow this required format, the arbitration agreement is only enforceable against the builder and the customer retains the right to sue in civil court.

2. Unconscionability

Even if a court accepts the form of the present arbitration clause, it is possible that it will deem the clause unconscionable and therefore refuse enforcement. In Franklin, contracts must be both procedurally unconscionable and substantively unconscionable before a court will find them unenforceable. Our research indicates that the current arbitration clause risks being found to be both procedurally and substantively unconscionable.

a. Contracts of Adhesion

Franklin courts have found arbitration clauses in contracts of adhesion procedurally unconscionable. A contract of adhesion is a contract, usually containing standard terms, that is drafted and imposed by a party of superior bargaining strength. The opposing party of lesser bargaining strength must be required to take or leave the bargain without an opportunity for reasonable negotiation. See Stirlen v. Supercuts. It is not clear if your contract is a contract of adhesion. While your current form contract contains some standard terms, on the whole your customers are able to negotiate significant portions of the contract including the location of work, completion dates, contract price, method and schedule of payment, the description of work, and may include additional provisions.

However, if a court were to find your contract a contract of adhesion, there is a reasonable likelihood the court would find the arbitration clause substantively unconscionable and therefore unenforceable. In the case of Stirlen v. Supercuts, a Franklin court refused to enforce an arbitration clause that prohibited a customer from receiving any punitive damages and only required one party to submit to arbitration. Under Franklin Code Section 3294, punitive damages may be awarded where a defendant engages in an act of fraud, malice or oppression. Contracts that limit liability for fraud, malice, or oppression are considered to be against public policy. Thus, an arbitration clause that limits recovery to compensatory damages, even though fraud, oppression, or malice occurred, is against public policy, and will likely not be enforced.

b. Unfair Surprise

Furthermore, even if your contract is held not to be a contract of adhesion it may be found to be procedurally unconscionable because it implicitly contains undisclosed, required fees to be paid for the arbitration. In the case of Myers v. Scamardo Termite Control, the plaintiff, an elderly lady in Franklin, signed a contract that contained an arbitration clause that required arbitration in compliance with the rules and procedures of the National Arbitration Organization. The National Arbitration Organization requires customers filing for arbitration to pay a filing fee based upon the amount of damages sought. In the Myers case, the necessary filing fee was $7,000 even though the original contract was only for $1,300. Because the fees charged were undisclosed and plaintiff's share of $3,500 is exorbitant for the average layperson, the court decided that this provision constituted an unfair surprise depriving the consumer of a judicial remedy. That conclusion rendered the clause unconscionable.

Again it is not clear if your failure to disclose the fees would constitute unfair surprise to your customers. The construction contracts you presently perform are unlikely to result in customer filing fees above $3,500. Your contract offers to split the costs of arbitration and presumably filing fees equally, which arguably is an equitable distribution. However, it is still possible that a court could determine that the current arbitration clause is an unfair surprise, the disclosure was inadequate, and therefore the contract is unenforceable.

B. Risk an Arbitrator Will Award Punitive Damages

As described above, contracts that exclude punitive damages may be determined to be against public policy in Franklin if too harsh and oppressive. Accordingly, it is possible an arbitrator may refuse to deny the elimination of potential punitive damages.

CONCLUSION

Thank you for coming to see me. I hope this letter gives you a sense of the legal variables and structure helpful to analyze the decision you have to make in this matter. Please call me with any questions. I look forward to discussing these issues with you further, including how I can help you improve your Customer Contract.

Sincerely,

Vivian Coyle, Partner
Coyle & Cooper, LLP

E. Working Practice Questions

1. Begin Testing Yourself: Now that you've examined a typical office task MPT question and answer, you should complete the following two practice questions on your own. Afterwards, compare your office task memorandum with the sample grading guide and narrative answer provided.

> **MPT Tip:** One of the major mistakes students make in preparing for the MPT exam is to eliminate self-testing. It is too easy to read the Library and File and then refer to the answer and say to yourself "yep, that's how I would have done it." You need to gain experience in actually creating the task answer.

2. Learning-Testing Conditions: You should create your own conditions as close to those of the MPT bar exam as possible. This would mean you should allocate a minimum of a full 90-minute time block for the question. You will have to work up to this time limit and to start perhaps allow yourself a full 120 minutes.

3. Concentration Objective: Ideally, you should complete the answer without taking a break. Again, you may have to work up to this. Concentration during your writing time is critical. Turn off all phones and do not answer email during this testing period.

4. Grading Your Answer: After you have completed the task, use our grading guides to objectively evaluate your answer coverage. Also, you should compare your answers with the sample answers provided for substance, organization, form, structures, and overall presentation. Don't be discouraged if your answer is missing something important or if it contains a significant mistake. Use this as a learning opportunity to figure out how and why you went wrong so you can improve your future MPT performance.

5. Re-Write Helpful: Many candidates find correcting and supplementing their first answer helpful. If you typed your answer this is quite easy, but even if your answer was in long hand it may be worth redoing at least portions. Add to your first edition any omissions you feel are important. Redoing your answer allows you to create an office task "model answer" to refer back to later. It also reduces the chance you will repeat similar errors on other office tasks.

> **MPT Tip:** Some students find it too difficult to actually spend the full 90 minute time creating their own complete answer to the questions before looking at our Editor's Summary and Sample Answer. If that temptation applies to you, you may not get the task creation practice you need to pass the MPT. Consider enrolling in our supplemental personal MPT Service described in the foreword information just before the introductory chapter 1.

V. PRACTICE QUESTION 1:

IN RE SNOW KING MOUNTAIN RESORT

TABLE OF CONTENTS

Documents Provided for Task	**Page**
Instructions	4-281
File	4-283
Task Memorandum	4-284
Memorandum from Sally Johnson, Mountain Operations Director	4-285
Memorandum from Kyle Mills, Marketing Director	4-286
Letter from National Life and Casualty Insurance Company	4-287
Library	4-289
Franklin Civil Code § 846	4-290
Schneider v. Mount Desert Island Land Trust	4-291
Gerkin v. Saint Clara Valley Water District	4-294
Editors' Prepared Grading Guide	4-297
Sample Answer	4-299

IN RE SNOW KING MOUNTAIN RESORT

INSTRUCTIONS

1. You will have 90 minutes to complete this session of the examination. This performance test is designed to evaluate your ability to handle a select number of legal authorities in the context of a factual problem involving a client.

2. The problem is set in the fictional State of Franklin, one of the United States, located in the fictional Fifteenth Circuit. Franklin has District Courts (trial courts), Courts of Appeal (mid-level appellate courts), and a Supreme Court (Franklin's highest appellate court).

3. You will have two sets of materials with which to work: a File and a Library.

4. The File contains factual materials about your case. The first document is a memorandum containing the instructions for the tasks that you are to complete.

5. The Library contains the legal authorities needed to complete the tasks. The case reports may be real, modified, or written solely for the purpose of this performance test. If the cases appear familiar to you, do not assume that they are precisely the same as you have read before. Read each thoroughly, as if it were new to you. You should assume that cases were decided in the jurisdictions and on the dates shown. In citing cases from the Library, you may use abbreviations and omit page citations.

6. Your response must be written in the answer book provided. You should concentrate on the materials provided, but you should also bring to bear on the problem your general knowledge of the law. What you have learned in law school and elsewhere provides the general background for analyzing the problem; the File and Library provide the specific materials with which you must work.

7. Although there are no restrictions on how you apportion your time, you should probably allocate at least 45 minutes to reading and organizing before you begin writing your response. You may make notes anywhere in the test materials, but may not tear out pages from this booklet.

8. Your response will be graded on its compliance with instructions and on its content, thoroughness, and organization.

File

In re Snow King Mountain Resort

1. Memorandum to Applicant — 4-284
2. Memorandum to Manuel Lopez – 7-18-x3 — 4-285
3. Memorandum to Manny Lopez – 7-19-x3 — 4-286
4. Insurance Letter to Manuel Lopez – 7-22-x3 — 4-287

Law Offices of Spence and Hawks
San Obispo, Franklin

TASK MEMORANDUM

TO: Applicant
FROM: Margaret Thompson, Partner
DATE: July 29, 20X3

RE: Snow King Mountain Resort

Our client, Snow King Mountain Resort (SKMR), needs assistance in dealing with its insurance carrier. Yesterday, I spoke to SKMR's CEO, Manuel Lopez. We've done corporate and real estate work for them in the past, but because they've grown tremendously and this will be a new operation, I asked Manuel to describe the current operations and proposed program in some detail.

SKMR is a ski area and vacation second-home resort complex, which wants to add recreational mountain biking to the list of activities available to its summer guests. Their plans include bike trails, aerial tram rides, and trail fees. Everything was set until SKMR's insurer informed them that mountain biking would require the highest risk rating, possibly leading to prohibitively high premiums that probably would make the mountain biking plans infeasible.

Franklin has a recreational use statute, Franklin Civil Code, Section 846, which protects from liability a landowner who permits recreational use of her or his land. I'm familiar with the statute, and the insurance company is correct that the statute doesn't specifically refer to mountain biking. However, the statute also says that "any recreational purpose" is covered.

The insurer's letter is attached. It invites a response, if we believe that the recreational use statute applies. Please draft a persuasive argument, in letter form, arguing that the recreational use statute will apply.

Also, in drafting the letter, do not address issues of conduct that could result in negligence, or willful or malicious failure to guard or warn against a dangerous condition, use, structure, or activity.

SNOW KING SKI MOUNTAIN

TO: Manuel Lopez
FROM: Sally Johnson, Mountain Operations Director
DATE: July 18, 20X3

RE: Snow King Mountain Biking Sales and Trail Fees

This will sum up what I've reported at the staff meetings. We can easily have a mountain biking program for next summer. Most of the mountain's ski trails are too steep for ascent and descent, except perhaps for extreme games fanatics. However, the mountain is crisscrossed by snow-groomer access roads and beginner ski trails that would make excellent natural terrain for mountain biking.

You may recall that the idea for mountain bike trails came from discussions I had last summer with many of the mountain bikers who are already using the mountain for riding. They've given me good information on the best rides, trail links that could be added, trouble spots (usually encounters with hikers at high speed or blind spots). They also have ideas on where we could build some single-track trails, about 30" wide, which are very popular for mountain biking and would link up existing trails. Most of the trail building could be done by our own work crews, and would help provide them more off-season work. I'd budget an additional $35,000 of capital expenditures the first year for trail building, trail maps, and signage, and about $5,000 a year thereafter for maintenance. That would give us the minimum program: no trail fees, equipment sales or rentals, or tram ticket sales, but also very low cost, and assuming that we don't patrol the trails, almost no additional personnel costs.

A mountain bike trail fee would require a minimum of 4 access kiosks, costing around $144,000 in construction, and $172,000 annually to operate, assuming a 7-day, 12-hour operation from June through September. This includes one bike-patroller to prevent access to nonpaying cyclists and for safety.

Snow King Mountain Resort

"The Place To Come Home To"

MEMORANDUM

TO: Manny Lopez

FROM: Kyle Mills, Marketing Director

DATE: July 19, 20X3

RE: Mountain Biking at Snow King Mountain Resort

Manny, it's great that SKMR will be offering mountain biking to our guests. Marketing-wise, I don't see any down-side.

Up-front, mountain biking fits the target demographics of our year-round development plan. Industry research has confirmed the Marketing Department's assumptions. Mountain bike enthusiasts aren't as young as the snowboard crowd. The majority are in the target 25-34 age group, and 35-44 is the second largest grouping. Average incomes and shopping expenditures are second only to golf and tennis guests (average annual income: $58,500). Education: 16.5 years. For casual riders, bike and accessories expenditures average $500. Self-described "serious" riders spend $1,000 to $2,000.

More importantly, mountain biking long-term growth projections are excellent, exceeding all other seasonal participation sports and are almost as strong as snowboarding. Image-wise mountain biking is again on-target. It will make great visuals for promotions and appeal to the 20-somethings attracted to the image of extreme sports. Next year the producers of the Summer Extreme Games will visit SKMR, and, with mountain biking and perhaps paragliding, we could make a viable pitch to be on their venue schedule. The Extreme Games could be our biggest seasonal attraction!

National Life and Casualty Insurance Company
One City Center Plaza
Suite 1400
Saint Francis, Franklin 99900
(555) 555-8200

July 22, 20X3

Mr. Manuel Lopez
President and Chief Executive Officer
Snow King Mountain Resort
Snow King Village, Franklin 99014

Reference: Snow King – Policy No. 2877408569867

Dear Manuel:

Thanks for giving us the opportunity to bid on insurance coverage for the new mountain biking operations.

Mountain biking at Snow King, with its unique natural beauty and congenial atmosphere, could be a huge success. My partner and I love mountain biking, and are out riding almost every weekend. I'm going to talk to Jen about coming up for Memorial Day.

After our conversation, I sent a memorandum to our Rating Department in Colorado and just received a call from them. It's not good news. Rating thinks that mountain biking requires the highest risk rating. Of course, I can't give you an exact premium quote until we get some usage numbers, but for budgeting purposes I fear that you can assume that it will be in the same ballpark as the skiing operations.

I'd suggest that you consider having your lawyer review Rating's conclusions, and, if they think that Rating is incorrect, that they address a letter to me, which I'll pass along to Rating, stating Snow King's position. For your lawyer's information, here's what our Rating Department states.

They acknowledged that Franklin has a recreational use statute, Franklin Civil Code Section 846, which could significantly reduce the risk of liability, and thus the risk rating. However, mountain biking is not one of the enumerated recreational activities, and they believe that the statute will likely apply only to the specifically named recreational activity. *Gerkin v. Saint Clara Valley Water District*, Franklin Court of Appeal, 1982.

We value our relationship as the insurer for Snow King, and will do all we can to provide coverage as you continue to grow the business. Please let me know how you decide to proceed.

Best wishes.
Sincerely,
/s/ Tamara Scott
Tamara Scott

Library

In re Snow King Mountain Resort

1. Franklin Civil Code   4-290

2. *Schneider v. Mount Desert Island Land Trust*   4-291

3. *Gerkin v. Saint Clara Valley Water District*   4-294

FRANKLIN CIVIL CODE

§ 846. Permission to Enter for Recreational Purposes

An owner of any estate or any other interest in real property, whether possessory or nonpossessory, owes no duty of care to keep the premises safe for entry or use by others for any recreational purpose or to give any warning of hazardous conditions, uses of, structures, or activities on such premises to persons entering for such purpose, except as provided in this section.

A "recreational purpose," as used in this section, includes such activities as fishing, hunting, camping, water sports, hiking, spelunking, sport parachuting, animal riding, snowmobiling, and all other types of vehicular riding, rock collecting, sightseeing, picnicking, nature study, nature contacting, recreational gardening, gleaning, hang gliding, winter sports, and viewing or enjoying historical, archaeological, scenic, natural, or scientific sites.

An owner of any estate or any other interest in real property, whether possessory or nonpossessory, who gives permission to another for entry or use for the above purpose upon the premises does not thereby (a) extend any assurance that the premises are safe for such purposes, or (b) constitute the person to whom permission has been granted the legal status of an invitee or licensee to whom a duty of care is owed, or (c) assume responsibility for or incur liability for any injury to person or property caused by any act of such person to whom permission has been granted except as provided in this section.

This section does not limit the liability which otherwise exists for willful or malicious failure to guard or warn against a dangerous condition, use, structure or activity.

Nothing in this section creates a duty of care or ground of liability for injury to person or property.

SCHNEIDER v. MOUNT DESERT ISLAND LAND TRUST
Supreme Court of Franklin, 1997

The State of Franklin is blessed with an abundance of scenic treasures. Its natural landscape contains over 250 miles of shoreline, massive mountains, magnificent lakes and sweeping deserts. Such diversity and contrast lend to its appeal as a place where recreational pursuits may flourish, at times on realty owned by others.

In this case we address questions about the scope of Civil Code Section 846, which immunizes landowners from liability for injuries sustained by recreational users of their property. We conclude, under settled principles of statutory construction, that the Legislature defined "recreational purpose" so broadly as to apply to plaintiff's conduct here.

While driving along the coast, plaintiff stopped at Thunder Hole, a spectacular spot within Mount Desert Island Preserve. The Preserve is owned by the Mount Desert Island Land Trust, a private foundation, and is open to the public. Plaintiff parked her car at one of the lots maintained by the Preserve, and she followed the steps down to Sand Beach. She tripped, allegedly because of a defect in the steps, and brought this suit against the Preserve for her resulting injury.

Before entering the Preserve plaintiff had stopped for a cup of coffee and, rather than drink it there (wherever that was) or in the car, she saw a sign ("Sand Beach") and decided to go there to drink it. The Preserve, pleading the statute, sought and obtained summary judgment. Plaintiff appeals. We affirm.

On appeal, plaintiff makes two contentions. First, plaintiff contends that coffee drinking is not within the statutory list, and, second, that she intended none of the named activities. The short answer to the first is that the list does not purport to be complete, but is only illustrative. Any number of clearly recreational activities suggest themselves, from birdwatching to sunbathing, to playing ball on the beach. Neither as a matter of grammatical construction, nor common sense, is the statute to be read as applying only to the recreational activities expressly named.

Section 846 establishes limited liability on the part of a landowner for injuries sustained by another from recreational use of the land. The statute provides an exception from the general rule that a private landowner owes a duty of reasonable care to any person coming upon the land. Under Section 846, an owner of any estate or other interest in real property owes no duty of care to keep the premises safe for entry or use by others for recreational purposes or to give recreational users warning of hazards on the property, unless: (1) the landowner willfully or maliciously fails to guard or warn against a dangerous condition, use, structure or activity; (2) permission to enter for a recreational purpose is granted for a consideration. The landowner's duty to the nonpaying recreational user is, in essence, that owed a trespasser under the common law as it existed prior to *Rowland v. Christian*, Frank. Sup. Ct., 1968; *i.e.*, absent willful or malicious misconduct, the landowner is immune from liability for ordinary negligence.

Thus, the Legislature has established only two elements as a precondition to immunity: (1) the defendant must be the owner of an "estate or any other interest in real property, whether possessory or nonpossessory"; and (2) the plaintiff's injury must result from the "entry or use [of the 'premises'] for any recreational purpose."

Turning first to the "recreational" element of Section 846, we have little difficulty in upholding the trial court's implicit finding that plaintiff entered or used defendant's property for a recreational purpose within the meaning of the statute.

Plaintiff contends that the list of activities set forth in Section 846 is exhaustive. The plain language of the statute does not support such a claim. The statutory definition of "recreational purpose" begins with the word "includes," ordinarily a term of enlargement rather than limitation. To be sure, the principle of *ejusdem generis* provides that "when a statute contains a list or catalogue of items, a court should determine the meaning of each by reference to the others, giving preference to an interpretation that uniformly treats items similar in nature and scope. [Citations.]" The examples included in Section 846, however, do not appear to share any unifying trait which would serve to restrict the meaning of the phrase "recreational purpose." They range from risky activities enjoyed by the hardy few (*e.g.*, spelunking, sport parachuting, hang gliding) to more sedentary pursuits amenable to almost anyone (*e.g.*, rock collecting, sightseeing, picnicking). Some require a large tract of open space (*e.g.*, hunting) while others can be performed in a more limited setting (*e.g.*, recreational gardening, viewing historical, archaeological, scenic, natural and scientific sites). Moreover, the statute draws no distinction between natural and artificial conditions; it specifically mentions "structures," and it obviously encompasses improved streets. Thus, it is not limited to activities which take place outdoors, and does not exclude recreational activities involving artificial structures.

Accordingly, because the list of examples provided by the Legislature does not effectively limit the meaning of "recreational purpose," we conclude that entering and using defendant's property whether to sightsee, drink coffee, or just relax invoked the immunity provisions of Section 846. Therefore, for our purposes here, walking down the beach steps is no different in kind from scaling a cliff or climbing a tree. Each is clearly recreational in nature.

Second, plaintiff contends that she raised a triable issue as to whether she entered the property for recreation. She claims that it could be found that she was not engaged in any recreational activity at all; that the weather was "cool, drizzly, overcast," and she was going "not to swim, sightsee or have a picnic lunch," and that only to drink coffee under such circumstances could be found not recreational. Generally, whether one has entered property for a recreational purpose within the meaning of the statute is a question of fact, to be determined through a consideration of the "totality of the facts and circumstances, including . . . the prior use of the land. While the plaintiff's subjective intent will not be controlling, it is relevant to show purpose." (*Gerkin v. Saint Clara Valley Water Dist.*, Frank. Ct App., 1982)

The consequences of plaintiff's approach would be absurd. The manifest purpose of the Preserve is recreational. Whether plaintiff entered the property to drink coffee or hike is immaterial. In either case, her presence was occasioned by the recreational use of the property, and her injury was the product thereof.

The judgment of trial court, accordingly, is affirmed.

GERKIN v. SAINT CLARA VALLEY WATER DISTRICT

Franklin Court of Appeal, First District, 1982

Jo Ann Gerkin through her guardian *ad litem* appeals from a summary judgment in dismissing her action against Saint Clara Valley Water District ["Water District"] and other defendants for personal injuries. Gerkin suffered personal injuries when she fell from a bridge located at Little Llagas Creek in the City of Morgan Creek. According to the complaint, Gerkin was injured because the Water District negligently permitted the bridge to remain in a dangerous condition.

In support of the motion for summary judgment, the Water District presented excerpts from the depositions of Gerkin and her younger sister showing that Gerkin was walking with her bicycle across the two planks that constituted the bridge when she slipped and fell into a dry creek below. In opposition to the motion, Gerkin submitted the declarations of herself, her mother and her sister averring that (1) on the date in question there was no telephone at the apartment where Gerkin was living, (2) Gerkin's mother gave Gerkin and her sister permission to cross the area in order to use the telephone at a market and to buy a candy bar there, (3) Gerkin's purpose in making the trip was to make a phone call and buy a candy bar, and (4) Gerkin walked across the bridge with her bicycle both to and from the store. The trial court granted the motion for summary judgment on the ground that Gerkin "was engaged in conduct specified by Civil Code Section 846."

Section 846 provides that, in the absence of willful or malicious failure to guard or warn of a dangerous condition, an owner of "any estate in real property" owes no duty of care to keep the premises safe for entry by trespassers or licensees who engage in certain specified recreational activities. Included among these specified activities are "hiking," but not bicycle-riding. On summary judgment, Gerkin's claim that she was walking over the bridge when the accident occurred must be accepted.

However, relying on dictionary definitions of "to hike" as "to walk or tramp" and "to go for a long walk," the Water District argues that Gerkin's activity was encompassed within the statute and that summary judgment was therefore proper. It is contended that any test which hinges upon the user's subjective "recreational" intent would read into Section 846 a requirement not stated by the Legislature and lead to "diverse, arbitrary and unjust results."

Section 846 must be construed in light of the legislative purpose behind it. It is a cardinal rule that statutes should be given a reasonable interpretation and in accordance with the apparent purpose and intention of the lawmakers. The purpose of Section 846 was to encourage landowners to keep their property open to the public for recreational activities by limiting their liability for injuries sustained in the course of those activities. The Water District is therefore incorrect when it contends that to walk across their property necessarily constitutes "hiking" within the meaning of the statute. Both the language and the historical background of Section 846 compel the conclusion that the Legislature did not intend to immunize landowners from liability for all permissive or nonpermissive use of their properties, but only those uses which could justifiably be characterized as "recreational" in nature.

The Water District's contention that "walking" falls within the scope of "hiking" under Section 846 is contrary to principles of statutory construction: First, a construction which implies that words used by the Legislature were superfluous is to be avoided wherever possible. If "hiking" were to be read as including the act of "walking," it would have been unnecessary for the Legislature thereafter to enumerate other types of activities which necessarily involve walking such as camping, rock collecting and hunting. Obviously, "hiking" was intended to denote more than just traveling on foot.

Second, a purely literal interpretation of any part of a statute will not prevail over the purpose of the legislation. This principle is vividly illustrated by that portion of Section 846 which, at the time of the events in question, extended a landowner's immunity to "all types of vehicular riding." Read literally, the statute would preclude anyone traveling in a car from suing the owner for injuries caused by a dangerous condition on his property. It is apparent from the purpose of the enactment, however, that the Legislature was intending to reach only recreational vehicular activity such as motorcycling for pleasure or dune buggying. Likewise, to equate the word "hiking" with mere "walking" or traveling on foot apart from any recreational context would be to ignore the legislative purpose of Section 846 and, in effect, broaden the statute in a manner not contemplated by the lawmakers.

And finally, this court has in past cases applied the rule that statutes in derogation of the common law must be strictly construed. This maxim of construction provides that where there exists a common law doctrine relevant to the issue presented by the parties and the statute which would change the common law, the legislative intent to change the common law must be clearly expressed. In changing the common law rules applicable to the tort liability of the landowner to the entrant, the legislature has, in Section 846, made a new accommodation of the conflicting rights and interests of landowner and entrant. In Section 846, the legislature has shifted some of the risk from the landowner to the entrant, apparently having decided that the social good of encouraging landowners to open their land to the public for recreational purposes outweighs the social cost of imposing the expense of injuries on the entrant to the land rather than on the landowner who may be in a position to prevent the injury. Section 846 is a statute in derogation of the common law, and should be narrowly interpreted.

We conclude that for an activity to fall within the term "hiking" as it is used in Section 846, it must be proved not merely that the user was "walking" across the property, but that the activity constituted recreational "hiking" within the commonly understood meaning of that word, *i.e.*, to take a long walk for pleasure or exercise.

We agree with the Water District that the test should not be based on the plaintiff's state of mind. We believe, however, that such a determination must be made through a consideration of the totality of facts and circumstances, including the path taken, the length and purpose of the journey, the topography of the property in question, and the prior use of the land. While the plaintiff's subjective intent will not be controlling, it is relevant to show purpose.

There is no showing that Gerkin was "hiking" within the commonly understood recreational sense of the word. On the contrary, Gerkin and her sister crossed the Water District's property because it was the shortest route between their apartment and the supermarket and was a method regularly used by residents in the area. A triable issue of fact was raised as to whether Gerkin was engaged in "hiking" on the subject property such as to permit the Water District to invoke the immunity of landowners set forth in Section 846. It was error to grant summary judgment.

Reversed.

VI. EDITORS' PREPARED GRADING GUIDE FOR PRACTICE QUESTION 1:

IN RE SNOW KING MOUNTAIN RESORT

Our editors have prepared a substantive grading guide outline to help you evaluate your answer. We have approached this from the perspective of the model answer structure typically used by a bar exam grader. After you complete a draft answer, compare and contrast it with the sample answer that follows this grading guide. If you missed any key issues in your analysis consider updating and perfecting your answer.

__ Persuasive letter to insurance company

   __ Recreational use statute (Section 846): No duty of care (or duty to warn) recreational land users unless conduct is willful or malicious, or consideration is paid for use of land applies to mountain biking

      __ Applies to mountain biking

         __ *Schneider*: List of specific activities in statute is not exclusive

      __ *Gerkin* is distinguishable

         __ Plaintiff was walking across land to visit store, and not for a recreational purpose

         __ *Schneider* has more precedential value

            __ *Gerkin* was decided 15 years before *Schneider*

            __ *Schneider* is from a higher court

VII. SAMPLE ANSWER TO PRACTICE QUESTION 1:

IN RE SNOW KING MOUNTAIN RESORT

Dear Ms. Scott:

Given the potential for accidents, we understand the concern you may have with regard to the high risk associated with creating a mountain biking path for Snow King Mountain Resort ("SKMR") ski area's summer guests. Based upon our legal research and survey of relevant case law, we believe that the recreational use statute will apply to SKMR. Application of this statute should substantially reduce or even eliminate your concerns.

DISCUSSION

You have suggested that Franklin Civil Code Section 846, the recreational use statute, may not apply to mountain biking. Section 846 provides a landowner an exception from the general rule that a private landowner owes a duty of reasonable care to any person coming upon the land. Under Section 846, an owner owes no duty of care to keep the premises safe for entry or use by others for recreational purpose or to give recreational users warning of hazards unless there is willful or malicious conduct or there was consideration for the use of the land.

The Supreme Court of Franklin has stated with regard to Section 846 that "the list does not purport to be complete, but is only illustrative . . . . Neither as a matter of grammatical construction, nor common sense, is the statute to be read as applying only to the recreational activities expressly named." Schneider v. Mount Desert. The Schneider court found that the statutory definition of "recreational purpose" begins with the word "includes" which the court noted is "ordinarily a term of enlargement rather than limitation." Thus, the statute encompasses all recreational activities. In Schneider, the plaintiff was on the land to drink a cup of coffee, but the Supreme Court found that the manifest purpose of the preserve is recreational and whether the plaintiff entered to drink coffee or hike is immaterial.

The Schneider statutory construction may be inconsistent with the findings of the Franklin Court of Appeal, which in 1982 found that Section 846 should be narrowly interpreted. Gerkin v. Saint Clara. However, the Gerkin court distinguished between walking across the property for some separate purpose from taking a long walk for pleasure or exercise. The latter would be considered recreational. The Gerkin plaintiff prevailed because she was walking across the defendant's land to get to a store and not for leisure or enjoyment. Thus even then the statute is narrowly constructed, mountain biking would nonetheless likely be considered a recreational activity since there is little utilitarian purpose in taking a bike up the mountain to ride it back down. Furthermore, Schneider is a Franklin Supreme Court case that was decided 15 years after the Franklin Court of Appeal issued its decision in Gerkin, and thus Schneider would likely carry more weight as precedent.

CONCLUSION

Therefore, absent any willful or malicious failure to guard or warn against a dangerous condition, use, structure or activity, SKMR would have no liability for injuries.

Sincerely,

Associate

cc: Manuel Lopez, Snow King Mountain Resort

VIII. PRACTICE QUESTION 2:

IN RE WINSTONS

TABLE OF CONTENTS

Documents Provided for Task	**Page**
Instructions	4-303
File	4-305
Task Memorandum	4-306
Transcript of Interview of Ralph and Margaret Winston	4-307
Library	4-311
Selected Provisions of the Franklin Fair Housing Act	4-312
Project HOME v. City of Catalina	4-314
Townley v. Rocking J Residential Community	4-318
Editors' Prepared Grading Guide	4-323
Sample Answer	4-325

IN RE WINSTONS

INSTRUCTIONS

1. You will have 90 minutes to complete this session of the examination. This performance test is designed to evaluate your ability to handle a select number of legal authorities in the context of a factual problem involving a client.

2. The problem is set in the fictional State of Franklin, one of the United States, located in the fictional Fifteenth Circuit. Franklin has District Courts (trial courts), Courts of Appeal (mid-level appellate courts), and a Supreme Court (Franklin's highest appellate court).

3. You will have two sets of materials with which to work: a File and a Library.

4. The File contains factual materials about your case. The first document is a memorandum containing the instructions for the tasks that you are to complete.

5. The Library contains the legal authorities needed to complete the tasks. The case reports may be real, modified, or written solely for the purpose of this performance test. If the cases appear familiar to you, do not assume that they are precisely the same as you have read before. Read each thoroughly, as if it were new to you. You should assume that cases were decided in the jurisdictions and on the dates shown. In citing cases from the Library, you may use abbreviations and omit page citations.

6. Your response must be written in the answer book provided. You should concentrate on the materials provided, but you should also bring to bear on the problem your general knowledge of the law. What you have learned in law school and elsewhere provides the general background for analyzing the problem; the File and Library provide the specific materials with which you must work.

7. Although there are no restrictions on how you apportion your time, you should probably allocate at least 45 minutes to reading and organizing before you begin writing your response. You may make notes anywhere in the test materials, but may not tear out pages from this booklet.

8. Your response will be graded on its compliance with instructions and on its content, thoroughness, and organization.

File

In re Winstons

1. Memorandum to Applicant   4-306
2. Transcript of Interview of Ralph and Margaret Winston   4-307

Franklin Center for Disability Law
Protection and Advocacy System for Franklin

645 Walther Way, Suite 319

Santa Clarita, Franklin 55515

TASK MEMORANDUM

To: Associate

From: Ginny Klosterman

Date: July 29, 20X3

Subject: In re: Ralph, Margaret and Clint Winston

The Winstons have asked us to represent them in their attempt to purchase a home in Pinnacle Canyon Estates, a "55-and-older" residential community. Ralph and Margaret Winston have a 23-year-old developmentally disabled son, Clint, who lives with them. When Ralph and Margaret tried to purchase a house in Pinnacle Canyon Estates, they were told that Clint couldn't live there because the residential community has a minimum age of 55 for residents.

Please draft the body of a letter to Emma Zucconi, Pinnacle Canyon's attorney, that argues persuasively that Pinnacle Canyon Estates Homeowners Association is legally required to waive the age restriction for Clint. Ms. Zucconi is familiar with the dispute, so you need not inform her of the basic factual situation.

Also, Ms. Zucconi has indicated to me that her client's position is supported by *Townley v. Rocking J Residential Community*, a case handed down by the Franklin Court of Appeal a few years ago. In a nutshell, Ms. Zucconi believes that while *Townley* may create an obligation to make a disability accommodation for homeowner/residents who qualify for initial admission under their criteria, they are not required to do so for those who, like Clint, are not qualified for admission as residents.

Transcript of Interview of Ralph and Margaret Winston

Ginny Klosterman (Ginny): Mr. and Mrs. Winston, do you mind if I tape record our interview? It will help me remember what you tell me. I won't do it if you are not comfortable with it.

Margaret Winston (Margaret): No, it is fine with us if you record it.

Ginny: Thanks. Why don't you tell me your full name, your ages, and what is going on that brought you to me?

Mr. Winston (Ralph): My name is Ralph Winston, and I am 59. My wife is Margaret Winston, and she is . . . 57?

Margaret: No dear, I'm still only 56. (Laughs.) We are here because we tried to buy a house but were rejected. We have a developmentally disabled son who lives with us, and we think they don't want us to live there because of that.

Ginny: What do you mean, you were rejected?

Margaret: The homeowners' association for the community told us that our son couldn't live in the house with us because it is an over-55 only community, and our son is much younger than 55. He has to live with us. He has severe developmental disabilities, and if he didn't live with us he would have to be in some sort of institution, and that is out of the question.

Ginny: What is your son's name?

Ralph: Clint.

Ginny: Can you tell me a bit about your son?

Margaret: He is a wonderful loving person, and we are very proud of him. He was born with serious developmental problems. He functions pretty well, but he can't be safely left alone and can't live without us. He is 23 years old but functions at a level well below that. He has a lot of trouble learning, remembering, and he has some communication difficulty, of course.

Ginny: Ok. What is the name of the community?

Ralph: Pinnacle Canyon Estates.

Ginny: Did you have a particular house in mind?

Margaret: Yes. We saw a listing in the paper for a house for sale by the owner, and when we looked, the house was just perfect. Both Ralph and I are getting a little older, and now that our other children have moved out we don't need all the space just for the three of us. The seller was very nice and very reasonable concerning the price of the house.

Ginny: What was the seller's name?

Margaret: Her name is, I've got it written down here, Pamela Garcia. Pamela wanted to sell because her husband had died and she wants to move to Tucson. So it was a good match. The house has a nice arrangement with a bedroom on one side that would work well for Clint. And it is a very nice community, with a lot of people about Ralph's and my age.

Ginny: When did you find out that the community didn't want you to buy?

Ralph: We had set everything up, and it was a few days before escrow was going to close. At that time, a representative from the Pinnacle Canyon Estates Homeowners' Association, Phyllis Lim, told us that our son couldn't live in the home with us because it is a 55-and-over community and he isn't 55 or older. She was very nice, actually. She said they were very sorry, that it had nothing to do with the fact that Clint is developmentally disabled, and that there are in fact a lot of disabled people in the neighborhood. She said something about them having to maintain their situation under the law as housing for a 55-and-over community and that letting anyone under 55 live there is not permitted by something called "the C C and Rs." I didn't know what that meant, and I didn't really believe that had anything to do with it. We thought they just didn't want anyone with disabilities to live there.

Ginny: Yes, it is confusing. The letters C C and R are an abbreviation for covenants, conditions and restrictions. They are very common community requirements for property in a neighborhood and include a bunch of stuff. Some neighborhoods want to be for older residents only and put age requirements in the CC&Rs.

Ralph: Oh, I see. Is it legal for them to do that?

Ginny: That's hard to say. Sometimes 55-and-over communities are allowed in effect to discriminate on the basis of age. But it is not permissible for housing communities to make it hard for people with disabilities to select the housing they want. What did you do when she told you that?

Ralph: Well the seller, Pamela Garcia, got pretty mad and said that was ridiculous, the rules were silly, and where was Clint supposed to live? But we cancelled the closing. She said if we could get the community to agree to let Clint live with us, she will be happy to sell us the house. She also suggested we see a lawyer because she thinks the community should be sued, or something. She was very supportive of us. Of course, she probably wants the sale, but it's not like the price is a great deal for her. So is there anything that can be done?

Ginny: What are your goals at this point? Is it really to find another house somewhere else?

Ralph: We'd like to move into that house if we could. We aren't in an incredible hurry, but we need to move eventually. And I'm kind of worried, because we'd like to live in a community where people are our age, but, if they are all going to do this, we won't be able to do so unless we have Clint institutionalized, and we don't want that and can't afford it.

Ginny: Tell me more about why Clint can't live on his own.

Margaret: He can't prepare meals. He might burn himself on the stove. He needs help with basic housekeeping and hygiene. He can't handle his own finances, things like paying bills and having a checking account. People could easily take advantage of him when it comes to handling money.

Ginny: Does he have a job?

Ralph: He works in a sheltered workshop, you know, where they hire disabled people. But he can't safely use public transportation, so one of us has to drive him there and back.

Ginny: Do you think he would pose difficulties for the other people living in the neighborhood?

Margaret: Oh my goodness, no. Clint is quiet and shy, kind and very gentle. He doesn't really approach strangers and doesn't leave the house without one of us.

Ginny: Has there ever been a problem at any of the places you've lived before?

Margaret: With Clint? No, never.

Ginny: Ok. I think that the appropriate first step is for me to research this a bit more, because I've never run into a situation exactly like yours. But if things are as I think, I can send a letter to the Pinnacle Canyon Estates Homeowners' Association and request that it waive the 55-and-over age restriction. I've made requests similar to that before for various clients with disabilities, and some homeowner associations are quite flexible about it, while others are not. So they might agree to that. If not, we could go to court to seek a ruling that their refusal to grant your requested waiver violates the Franklin Fair Housing Act. Going to court wouldn't be as extreme as it might sound. Hopefully, we will be able to resolve it with a letter. Does that sound like a good way to proceed?

Margaret: Yes, that is what we would like you to do, isn't it, Ralph?

Ralph: Yes, I think so. I'd like to work it out if we could, and if we can't, well then let's make Pamela Garcia happy, and sue them. It is worth it to see if we can live there.

Ginny: Ok, then I'll get started with some research and then send them a letter.

Ralph: Thank you very much for spending time with us.

End of Interview

Library

In re Winstons

1. Selected Provisions of the *Franklin Fair Housing Act* 4-312

2. *Project Home v. City of Catalina* 4-314

3. *Townley v. Rocking J Residential Community* 4-318

SELECTED PROVISIONS OF THE FRANKLIN FAIR HOUSING ACT

§ 41 Definitions

In this article, unless the context otherwise requires:

1. "Disability" means a mental or physical impairment that substantially limits at least one major life activity, a record of such an impairment or being regarded as having such an impairment.

2. "Dwelling" means any building, structure or part of a building or structure that is occupied as, or designed or intended for occupancy as, a residence by one or more families.

3. "Familial status" refers to the status of one or more individuals being younger than the age of eighteen years and domiciled with a parent or another person having legal custody of the minor or minors.

4. "Person" means one or more individuals, corporations, partnerships, associations, legal representatives, mutual companies, trusts, trustees, receivers, and fiduciaries.

§ 42 Housing for older persons exempted; rules; definition

A. The provisions of this article relating to familial status do not apply to housing for older persons.

B. Housing qualifies as housing for older persons if:

1. At least eighty percent of the units are occupied by at least one person fifty-five years of age or older per unit, and

2. The housing community demonstrates, by publication of and adherence to policies and procedures, an intent by the owner or manager to provide housing for persons fifty-five years of age or older.

§ 43 Discrimination in sale or rental

A person may not refuse to sell or rent after a *bona fide* offer has been made, or refuse to negotiate for the sale or rental of or otherwise make unavailable, or deny a dwelling to any

person because of race, color, religion, sex, familial status or national origin. A person may not discriminate against any person in the terms, conditions or privileges of sale or rental of a dwelling, or in providing services or facilities in connection with the sale or rental, because of race, color, religion, sex, familial status or national origin.

§ 44 Discrimination due to disability; definitions
* * *

B. A person may not discriminate against any person in the terms, conditions or privileges of sale or rental of a dwelling or in the provision of services or facilities in connection with the dwelling because of a disability of:

    1. That person;

    2. A person residing in or intending to reside in that dwelling after it is so sold, rented or made available;

    3. A person associated with that person.

C. For the purposes of this section, "discrimination" includes:

    1. A refusal to permit, at the expense of the disabled person, reasonable modifications of existing premises occupied or to be occupied by the person if the modifications may be necessary to afford the person full enjoyment of the premises.

    2. A refusal to make reasonable accommodations in rules, policies, practices or services if the accommodations may be necessary to afford the person equal opportunity to use and enjoy a dwelling.

PROJECT HOME v. CITY OF CATALINA

Franklin Court of Appeal (1998)

This is an appeal from the trial court ruling granting summary judgment for Project HOME and denying summary judgment for the City of Catalina ("City"). This case arises under the Franklin Fair Housing Act ("FFHA"). The plaintiff alleges that the defendant City's failure to grant a requested zoning permit for a proposed home for homeless persons constitutes "a refusal to make reasonable accommodations in the rules, policies, practices, or services, when such accommodations may be necessary to afford such person equal opportunity to use and enjoy a dwelling. . . ."

Plaintiff Project HOME is a Franklin nonprofit corporation that provides a continuum of services to homeless persons who are mentally ill and/or recovering substance abusers. The organization operates emergency shelters open to any chronically homeless person in the City and offers treatment at two drug- and alcohol-free transitional homes. Recognizing that many residents of the transitional homes would benefit from more privacy and independence than the two homes afford, Project HOME sought to create a "Single Room Occupancy" ("SRO") facility with small individual rooms and community kitchen facilities that would give the resident a sense of control over his or her environment.

Project HOME acquired a building on Fairmount Avenue to use for its proposed SRO. The property includes a substantial side yard which extends the entire depth of the block, but no rear yard. When Project HOME applied for a zoning and use permit for the Fairmount Avenue property, two civic associations opposed the introduction into the neighborhood of a new residential facility for persons beset with handicaps, and the City denied the zoning and use permit application on the ground that the Fairmount property has no rear yard. Under the Catalina Zoning Code, a commercial building or a residential building housing families must have a rear yard. Project HOME sought a waiver from the back yard requirement on the ground that the ample side yard is an adequate substitute. The City refused.

Project HOME and potential residents seek a declaration that as a matter of law the City's conduct constitutes a violation of 44C(2) of the FFHA, which provides that unlawful discrimination includes failure to make "reasonable accommodations in rules, policies, practices or services . . . necessary to afford [a disabled] person equal opportunity to use and enjoy a dwelling." They argue that the reasonable accommodation they seek, that the back yard requirements are waived because the side yard is adequate, is necessary in order to provide their disabled residents with the housing of their choice. The City seeks a ruling that as a matter of law it need not waive the requirement.

The FFHA is copied from its federal counterpart. In creating the FFHA, the Franklin legislature expressed its intent "that the state undertake vigorous steps to provide equal opportunity in housing . . . extend housing discrimination protection to the disabled, exempt housing for the elderly from the provisions prohibiting discrimination against families with children . . . and obtain substantial equivalency with the federal government's housing discrimination enforcement efforts."

We are mindful of the FFHA's stated policy "to prevent housing discrimination and provide for fair housing throughout Franklin." One of the purposes of the FFHA is to "integrate people with disabilities into the mainstream of the community." The FFHA is a broad mandate to eliminate discrimination against and equalize housing opportunities for disabled individuals. Because it is a broad remedial statute, its provisions are to be generously construed, and any exemptions must be construed narrowly in order to preserve the primary operation of the purposes and policies of the FFHA.

Concerning the reasonable accommodation requirement, we stress the FFHA's imposition of an affirmative duty to reasonably accommodate disabled persons. A facially neutral requirement that affects disabled and non-disabled individuals alike implicates the reasonable accommodation section of the FFHA when it prevents a disabled individual from gaining access to proposed housing. The legislative history of the reasonable accommodation portion of the FFHA indicates that one of the purposes behind the reasonable accommodation provision is to address individual needs and respond to individual circumstances and that the concept of reasonable accommodation has a long history in regulations and case law dealing with discrimination on the basis of a person's disability. A discriminatory rule, policy, practice or service is not defensible simply because that is the manner in which such rule or practice has traditionally been constituted. This section would require that changes be made to such traditional rules or practices if necessary to permit a person with disabilities an equal opportunity to use and enjoy a dwelling.

The City argues that there is no FFHA violation because there is no "causal nexus" between the section of the Zoning Code provision at issue – the rear yard requirement – and the handicaps of the prospective residents. The City contrasts the case at hand with a situation in which a zoning code barred the installation of elevators in three-story buildings. In such a case, a disabled person who sought to install an elevator so that he could live in a three-story building would be able to show a direct causal link between the Zoning Code and a City action that bars him from residing in this dwelling because of his handicap. Although the City acknowledges that "discrimination" is defined in § 44C as a refusal to make a reasonable accommodation, it argues that what is unlawful under the FFHA is discrimination "because of disability." § 44B (emphasis added).

The City reads the statute too narrowly. The FFHA provision concerning discrimination based on a refusal to make a reasonable accommodation contains an independent definition of "discrimination" – a definition not modified by the phrase "because of a disability" found in § 44B. Thus the language of § 44C does not suggest that, to establish a FFHA violation on the basis of discrimination against a person with a disability, a plaintiff must show a "causal nexus" between the challenged provision and the disabilities of the prospective residents. Cases that have interpreted § 44C also provide strong support for the conclusion that no such causal nexus is required.

In addition, according to the legislative history of the FFHA, one method of making housing unavailable to people with disabilities has been the application or enforcement of otherwise neutral rules and regulations on land use in a manner that discriminates against people with disabilities. Such discrimination often results from false assumptions about the needs of disabled people, as well as unfounded fears of difficulties about the problems their tenancies may pose. These and similar practices are prohibited by the FFHA. The City's argument that the statute only reaches special restrictions that specifically prohibit the sale or rental of a dwelling to disabled individuals is thus without merit. So is the City's argument that prohibiting the SRO facility from operating would have no discriminatory effect on plaintiffs or disabled persons in general because there are other facilities in Franklin.

Enforcement of a restrictive covenant or ordinance can, despite the apparent neutrality of the covenant or ordinance toward people with disabilities, constitute discrimination because of a disability. A reasonable accommodation would have been to waive enforcement of the covenant. Such an accommodation would not impose an undue financial or administrative burden on the private defendants nor would it undermine the basic purpose behind the practice of enforcement, namely, to maintain the residential nature of the neighborhood.

A plaintiff can thus establish a violation of the FFHA by showing that the defendant failed to make reasonable accommodations in rules, policies or practices, including rules, policies or practices that do not themselves discriminate on the basis of disability. If a restriction is an impediment to the disabled
person's ability to obtain equal housing opportunity, the disabled person is permitted to invoke the "reasonable accommodation" requirement of the FFHA so long as the accommodation "may be necessary" to afford that person equal opportunity to use and enjoy a dwelling.

In this case, a waiver of the back yard requirement is necessary to afford the plaintiffs the equal opportunity to use and enjoy the Project HOME dwellings envisioned for the property. While an accommodation is not reasonable if it imposes a fundamental alteration or substantial administrative or financial burdens on the accommodating party, the City does not appear seriously to dispute that the requested substitution of side yard for rear yard is reasonable. Substituting side yard for rear yard would impose no financial or administrative burden on the City. Nor does it appear that granting the accommodation requested would require a fundamental alteration of the Zoning Code.

Affirmed.

TOWNLEY v. ROCKING J RESIDENTIAL COMMUNITY

Franklin Court of Appeal (2003)

In this case we are asked to decide whether a community permitted by an exemption in the Franklin Fair Housing Act ("FFHA") to exclude persons under the age of 55 violates the FFHA's disability discrimination provisions by refusing to waive its minimum age requirement for an over-55 prospective resident with a disability who requires a live-in caretaker under the age of 55.

According to undisputed facts, plaintiff Art Townley ("Townley"), a 68-year-old man who has a disability that renders him unable to live independently, agreed to purchase from seller Dina Whitmore a home in Rocking J Residential Community ("Rocking J") housing development. Rocking J requires at least one person fifty-five years of age or older to reside in each unit. The Rocking J covenants, conditions and restrictions ("CC&Rs") state that no person under the age of 55 may reside in the community. Townley's live-in caregiver, Frank Johnson ("Johnson"), who has lived with and taken care of Townley for the past five years, is currently 32 years old. When Ms. Whitmore notified the Rocking J Homeowners Association (the "Association") of the purchase and that the buyer would have a 32-year-old live-in caregiver, the Association told Ms. Whitmore and Townley that Townley was welcome as a resident but Johnson would not be permitted to live in any home at Rocking J.

Townley and Ms. Whitmore filed suit to enjoin Rocking J from refusing to permit Townley's live-in caregiver to live in the home. They alleged that Rocking J is required under the FFHA to permit underage caregivers to live with over-55 residents, in order to allow adults with serious disabilities opportunities to live in the housing community of their choice. The trial court granted summary judgment for Rocking J.

Rocking J argues that because Rocking J qualifies as a "55 and over" community under the FFHA, the community is entitled to enforce its CC&R concerning the age requirement. Its position is that if it lets anyone under the age of 55 live in the community, the community will lose its status as exempt "housing for older persons," resulting in a fundamental alteration in the nature of the community. It also argues that permitting the plaintiff buyer to have a 32-year-old living in his home would result in granting to the plaintiff buyer greater than equal opportunity to use and enjoy a dwelling, while the FFHA does not require anything more than equal treatment. It also argues that it does not discriminate against Townley on the basis of disability because it already has many disabled elderly residents living there.

The FFHA's "housing for older persons exemption" does not exempt the defendants from its FFHA-imposed obligation to reasonably accommodate persons with disabilities. Section 41 of the FFHA prohibits discrimination against families with children. At the same time, however, Section 42 of the FFHA explicitly exempts "housing for older persons" from the prohibition against familial status discrimination. In other words, if an over-55 housing community abides by the FFHA's requirements regarding occupancy by persons over the age of 55, such qualifying communities are free to exclude underage persons from the housing community and not be found liable for familial status discrimination. This exemption, however, only protects the housing community from liability for status discrimination. See § 42. It does not protect the over-55 community from discrimination claims based upon race, color, national origin, religion, gender or disability.

The Supreme Court of Franklin, adopting United States Supreme Court interpretations of the identical Federal Fair Housing Act, has held that an accommodation is not reasonable (1) if it would require a fundamental alteration in the nature of a program, or (2) if it would impose undue financial or administrative burdens on the defendant. Defendant argues that the waiver would fundamentally alter the nature of the community by jeopardizing its "55 and over status."

Under the "55 and over" housing exemption, an over-55 housing community is exempt from familial status discrimination if: (1) at least eighty percent of the units are occupied by at least one person who is fifty-five years of age or older per unit, and (2) the housing community publishes and adheres to policies and procedures that demonstrate the intent to maintain the community as 55 or over, only. Nothing in the statute requires that all occupants of a unit be over the age of 55 in order to obtain or maintain eligibility for a "55 and over" exemption. The statute specifically requires only "one person who is fifty-five years of age or older. . ." § 42 (B)(1). The federal regulations promulgated by The Department of Housing and Urban Development (HUD), which we find useful and persuasive, fully contemplate situations where persons under the age of 55 will reside in over-55 housing communities. Under those regulations, a community will meet the 80% occupancy rule where there are units occupied by persons under 55 who are necessary to provide reasonable accommodation to disabled residents. Thus the HUD regulations implicitly contemplate that an over-55 community does not lose its status as "housing for older persons" if a caretaker under the age of 55 resides with an over-55 resident.

Accordingly, Rocking J is not correct that the community will jeopardize its status as a "55 and over" community if it waives the age requirement for Townley's live-in caregiver. A waiver will not have any impact on the "55 and over" status of the community. Townley's household will still count toward the 80% occupancy requirement, because there will be one person over 55 living in his unit. And the waiver would not indicate that Rocking J had failed to publish and adhere to policies and procedures that demonstrate the intent that Rocking J be housing for older persons and is not inconsistent with the community's intent to remain an over-55 community. A waiver granted in order to comply with a state law that requires reasonable accommodation for a disabled person's need for a live-in caregiver can not be interpreted as an intent to relinquish its status as "housing for older persons." As long as Rocking J's general policies, practices, procedures and services are specifically aimed at providing compatible housing for older persons, the waiver will not jeopardize the community concerning the intent requirement for the exemption.

Nor will the waiver inevitably cause a fundamental change by resulting in a "flood" of people wishing to share a residence with underage individuals. Reasonable accommodations vary depending on the facts of each case, and what is reasonable in a particular circumstance is a fact-intensive, case-specific determination. The FFHA allows Rocking J to consider each request individually and to grant only those requests that are reasonable. Presumably, only a narrow group of persons would be entitled to the limited exception to the CC&Rs necessitated by disabled individuals' need for an underage live-in caretaker.

Defendant also argues that a waiver is unreasonable because the FFHA requirements that people with disabilities be given equal treatment does not require giving the plaintiff-buyer greater than equal opportunity to use and enjoy a dwelling. Defendant's argument might be persuasive if the definition of "discrimination" under the disability prohibitions of the FFHA were the same as the definitions prohibiting "discrimination" due to an individual's race, color, religion, sex, national origin or familial status. The FFHA prohibition on "discrimination in the sale or rental of housing" has been interpreted to require entities to provide "equal treatment" in their dealing with (for examples) men and women, Hispanics and non-Hispanics, African-Americans and Caucasians.

In interpreting this requirement, courts have clearly distinguished "equal treatment" from the affirmative duty to provide a "reasonable accommodation" and an "equal opportunity." Thus the discrimination provisions that require "equal treatment" under this portion of the FFHA have not been interpreted to impose on housing providers a duty of greater than equal treatment to avoid or to rectify discrimination in housing on the basis of an individual's race, color, religion, sex, national origin or familial status. In contrast, the FFHA's provisions defining discrimination due to disability require more of housing providers than to maintain equal treatment to disabled and non-disabled persons alike. These FFHA provisions place on housing providers an affirmative duty to, among other things, "reasonably accommodate" a person with a disability if the accommodation may be necessary to afford the person "equal opportunity" to use and enjoy a dwelling. § 44C(2). "Equal opportunity" under this portion of the FFHA gives the disabled the right to live in the residence and community of their choice because that right serves to end their exclusion from mainstream society.

Accordingly, although Defendant is correct that the FFHA's general prohibitions concerning housing discrimination do not require an entity to provide anything more than "equal treatment," Defendant is not correct that they have no obligation to give more than "equal treatment," because the FFHA's "reasonable accommodation" requirement concerning housing for people with disabilities by its very nature may impose a duty of more than equal treatment. To reasonably accommodate a disabled person, an individual or group may have to make an affirmative change in an otherwise valid policy. Thus the Rocking J community's FFHA imposed-obligation is more than to provide "equal treatment" for all disabled residents. It is to make necessary alterations in its rules so as to allow Townley "equal opportunity" to live in the residence of his choice.

Similarly, the fact that the Defendant does not generally discriminate against residents with disabilities does not insulate Defendant from its obligation to make a reasonable accommodation to Townley. Defendant's argument that it could not be found to have discriminated against Townley on the basis of disability because it already has many disabled elderly residents living there misses the point. The issue here is not whether the Defendant excludes or discriminates against residents with disabilities in general, but whether it failed to provide a reasonable accommodation to a particular individual who needed it in order to live in the Rocking J community. The fact that other disabled persons already live in the community does not relieve the community from its obligation to make reasonable accommodations to permit another disabled individual to live there.

This state has adopted the public policy of assisting the physically and developmentally disabled by promoting their deinstitutionalization and encouraging community integration. The overriding policy of the FFHA, which is to ensure equal opportunity to disabled persons to have adequate opportunities to select the housing of their choice, requires that Rocking J waive the age requirement. Consequently, state policy reflected in the FFHA and other statutes concerning disabled persons requires Rocking J to reasonably accommodate Townley by waiving its age requirement for a live-in caretaker for Townley.

Reversed.

IX. EDITORS' PREPARED GRADING GUIDE FOR PRACTICE QUESTION 2:

IN RE WINSTONS

Our editors have prepared a substantive grading guide outline to help you evaluate your answer. We have approached this from the perspective of the model answer structure typically used by a bar exam grader. After you complete a draft answer, compare and contrast it with the sample answer that follows this grading guide. If you missed any key issues in your analysis consider updating and perfecting your answer.

__ Franklin Fair Housing Act (FFHA) § 44 forbids housing discrimination on the basis of disability

  __ "Discrimination" includes failure to make reasonable accommodations

  __ "Disability" includes any physical or mental impairment that substantially limits at least one major life activity

    __ No dispute that Clint is disabled by virtue of his mental impairment

    __ No dispute that Clint cannot live independently

  __ "Equal treatment" is not the same as "reasonable accommodation" and "equal opportunity" (*Townley*)

  __ *Project Home*

    __ Facially-neutral requirement may nonetheless violate the FFHA

    __ Waiver of facially-neutral requirement may be required as an accommodation

      __ Test is whether accommodation would create "unreasonable burden"

        __ Clint is at work during the day

        __ His parents will supervise him when he is at home

        __ Clint is quiet and shy, and thus unlikely to disturb other residents

  __ Granting waiver will not endanger community's 55+ status because only one resident over 55 is needed for the unit to count toward the 80% threshold, and both of Clint's parents qualify (*Townley*)

X. SAMPLE ANSWER TO PRACTICE QUESTION 2:

IN RE WINSTONS

Dear Ms. Zucconi:

It is with great regret that I write this letter concerning the Winstons.

INTRODUCTION

The Winstons, naturally, still wish to enjoy life as residents in the fine community of Pinnacle Canyon Estates. But the denial by the Homeowners' Association of their request for a simple waiver, preventing them from completing the sale of the property from Pamela Garcia, represents a considerable blow to their aspirations, as they could hardly be expected to place Clint Winston in an institution.

We believe that a close examination of the applicable law will lead you to the same conclusion we have reached: that the denial of the waiver is in violation of the provision of the Franklin Fair Housing Act. We have no desire, of course, to be forced to pursue litigation, even though the case is appropriate for summary judgment given the undisputed facts. When you consider the applicable precedents and statutes one is led to the same conclusion we have reached: a waiver for Clint is a "reasonable accommodation" which is required under the Act.

DISCUSSION

The Controlling Statute

Perhaps, in your excitement over this case, and your obvious concern over maintaining the character of the community, you neglected a few of the finer points of the statute. The Franklin Fair Housing Act (FFHA) is concerned with any sort of discrimination that results in the denial of equal opportunity to enjoy a community, and the age-restrictive nature of Pinnacle Canyon Estates is not a defense to a disability discrimination claim.

Statutory Language

We would like to draw your attention to Section 44 of the FFHA, which bans discrimination on the basis of disability in any of the "terms, conditions or privileges of sale or rental of a dwelling . . . because of a disability" either of the person directly purchasing or renting, or because of the disability of a person "residing in or intending to reside in that dwelling." Additionally, "discrimination" is defined as including a "refusal to make accommodations in rules, practices or services" if the accommodations are "necessary to afford the person equal opportunity to use and enjoy a dwelling." The statute defines a disability as any "mental or physical impairment that substantially limits at least one major life activity" and "dwelling" as "any building . . . designed for occupancy." And the "condition" – the minimum 55 year age requirement – is equally obvious.

The Statutory Requirements Are Satisfied

While we appreciate your acknowledgment of Clint's disabled status, we would like to make it clear that Clint's disability would not be at issue in this dispute: Clint cannot handle basic housekeeping or cooking. He cannot manage his own finances, and he cannot safely use public transportation – that is, he is restricted in ordinary domestic activities, economic life, and transportation, and these are clearly "major life activities." Similarly, living in a single-family house at Pinnacle Canyon is clearly a "major life activity." A single-family house at Pinnacle Canyon is clearly a "dwelling" as it is a building designed for occupancy. Additionally, Clint would, naturally, be a resident in the building, so he falls under 44B2 of the FFHA. So the basic provisions are clearly satisfied.

Because Clint is so clearly disabled, a "refusal to make reasonable accommodations in rules," such as the "covenants, conditions, and restrictions" that the homeowners' association refers to, could potentially implicate FFHA – 44C2. As we will explain below, Franklin law clearly supports modification or waiver of age requirements; similarly, case law defines "equal opportunity" much more broadly than strictly "equal treatment."

Facially Neutral Requirements Can Implicate Disability

Thankfully, we have more cases for guidance than <u>Townley</u>, which you erroneously believe to support your client's position. The <u>Project Home</u> case dealt with reluctance by a government, under pressure from various homeowners' associations, to provide accommodations in their zoning codes for persons with disabilities. The court there was dealing with a facially neutral statute that resulted in a denial of a permit for a facility because it lacked a backyard – a neutral statute that resulted in people with disabilities being denied housing. The court indicated that any sort of "facially neutral requirement" – such as a minimum age of 55 – that "prevents a disabled individual from gaining access to proposed housing" would violate the FFHA. The court additionally commented that "traditional" requirements may have to be changed to accommodate those with disabilities.

Enforcement of Facially Neutral Restrictive Covenants Can Be Discriminatory

We would certainly hope that the application of this binding precedent to the case would be obvious to you. It should be clear that under Franklin law, courts have interpreted neutral restrictions that result in individuals with disabilities being denied housing as discriminatory. Disabilities are entitled to reasonable accommodations. Clint Winston is disabled, and the refusal of the community to waive the requirement can constitute discrimination. The fact that it is a neutral rule and perhaps applied fairly and broadly is, unfortunately, likely not a defense. Of course, while the court in Project Home was dealing directly with zoning, it also explicitly ruled that enforcing a "restrictive covenant or ordinance, can despite the apparent neutrality of the covenant . . . constitute discrimination because of a disability" as part of its holding (emphasis added).

Equal Opportunity Is More than Equal Treatment

As the Court in Townley indicated, the requirement of "equal treatment" under FFHA-43 is different from "reasonable accommodation" and "equal opportunity" under FFHA-44. The Court in Townley found the "equal opportunity" provisions create an affirmative duty to reasonably accommodate, even when dealing with neutral rules and regulations. Equal opportunity incorporates an affirmative duty to waive a general rule in a specific case. In this case, to avoid discriminating against an individual with a disability, Pinnacle Canyon Estates is obliged to make all reasonable accommodations for Clint Winston.

Waiving Enforcement of a Covenant Can Be Reasonable

An individual with a disability, such as Clint Winston, is allowed to invoke the "reasonable accommodation" requirement if the accommodation "may be necessary" to allow that individual full and fair access to housing. The court has expressly found that a "reasonable accommodation would have been to waive enforcement of the covenant;" this is especially true when it would not "impose an undue financial or administrative burden . . . nor would it undermine the basic purpose behind the practice of enforcement." Similarly, to "reasonably accommodate a disabled person, an individual or group may have to make an affirmative change in an otherwise valid policy."

The test as outlined in Project Home indicates what is "reasonable" only in the negative. It defines an unreasonable burden as an undue financial or administrative burden or an accommodation that would undermine the basic purpose behind the practice of enforcement. In this case, we are merely asking that one developmentally disabled individual, so disabled that he is effectively unable to function without adult supervision at all times, be allowed to live with his parents. As Clint has something of an outside occupation in the workshop, he would not be present during the day, and Margaret and Ralph Winston would be available during the evenings to supervise him and make sure he does not disturb the other residents. Moreover, Clint is quiet and shy, so he would be unlikely to disturb the peace of the other residents.

In this instance, the waiver of the age requirement would not lead to a fundamental change, nor would it even lead to minor children residing in the community, but simply one quiet, loving, disabled adult. Specifically, it would not be a financial or administrative burden, because the Winstons would be responsible for caring for Clint. It would also not undermine the basic purpose of enforcing the age restriction, because the Winstons themselves would still meet the age restriction. Clint is not a minor so the PCE cannot discriminate against him. Therefore, the waiver should be granted.

Granting a Waiver Will Not Endanger Pinnacle Canyon's "Over-55" Status

<u>Townley</u> indicated that the 80% requirement applies only to units, not individuals. As the "unit" the Winstons will be purchasing would have not one, but two, individuals over 55 living in the unit, a waiver of the age requirement for Clint would have no effect and would maintain Pinnacle Canyon at its current level of 80% of units being inhabited by those over 55.

CONCLUSION

Pinnacle Canyon is under a duty not to discriminate against the disabled, even in its applications of neutral rules. Clint is disabled; he is being denied reasonable accommodations, which would not impose a financial burden or change the nature of the community or undermine the purpose of the restriction. Pinnacle Canyon has an affirmative duty under the law to avoid discriminating. Their present position on the waiver issue results in discrimination and a denial of Clint's rights to "equal opportunity" for housing. Moreover, as Clint's parents are both over 55, allowing Clint to live with them will not endanger the community's status as "housing for older persons."

Thank you for considering our position in this matter.

Truly Yours,

The Franklin Center for Disability Law

RIGOS UNIFORM BAR EXAM (UBE) REVIEW SERIES

MULTISTATE PERFORMANCE TEST (MPT) REVIEW

CHAPTER 5

LITIGATION TASKS

Table of Contents

I.	**INTRODUCTION**	5-333
	A. Exam Frequency	
	B. Different Tasks	
II.	**STRUCTURE OF THE QUESTION**	5-333
	A. File	
	1. Task Memorandum	
	2. Pointer Memorandum	
	3. Pointer Memorandum Substitutes	
	a. The Task Memorandum	
	b. Secondary Authority and Other Documents	
	B. Library	
	1. Content	
	2. Relevancy	
III.	**ANSWERING THE QUESTION**	5-334
	A. Planning Your Answer	
	B. It Depends on the Task	
	C. Remember You Are an Advocate	
	1. Dealing with Facts	
	a. Relevance	
	b. Helpful Facts	
	c. Harmful Facts	
	(1) Handling Unfavorable Facts Implicitly	
	(2) Handling Unfavorable Facts Explicitly	
	(a) Placement	
	(b) Wording	
	(c) Use of the Passive Voice	
	(3) Compare	
	(a) Example – Active Voice	
	(b) Example – Passive Voice	
	2. Dealing with the Law	
	a. Unfavorable Law	
	(1) Distinguishing Cases	
	(2) Precedential Value of Case Law	
	(3) Recent Authority Usually Trumps Older Authority	
	(4) Older Authority May Still Be Controlling	
	b. Analyzing Statutes and Similar Sources of Law	
	c. Applying Other Sources of Law	
	d. Secondary Authority	

IV.	**WORKING THROUGH A SAMPLE QUESTION:** *STATE v. SIZEMORE*	5-336
	Instructions..	5-339
	File...	5-341
	Task Memorandum	5-342
	Pointer Memorandum...	5-343
	Editors' Summary of Task Memorandum and Pointer Memorandum....	5-345
	Trial Transcript..	5-346
	Library...	5-357
	Selected Provisions of the Franklin Penal Code	5-358
	Selected Provisions of the Franklin Rules of Evidence	5-360
	State v. Smith...	5-361
	State v. Cameron	5-363
	Editors' Summary of Key Facts and Legal Authority	5-366
	Sample Answer	5-367
	Working Practice Questions..	5-370
V.	**PRACTICE QUESTION:** *PEABODY v. MIDDLETOWN*	5-371
	Instructions..	5-373
	File...	5-375
	Task Memorandum	5-376
	Pointer Memorandum...	5-377
	Excerpts from Complaint for Violation of Civil Rights.....................	5-378
	Transcript of Interview with Joe Peabody and Jeff Whittaker............	5-380
	Library...	5-387
	Amendment IV, United States Constitution.......................................	5-388
	United States Code, Title 42, Section 1983	5-389
	Bishop v. Carter	5-390
	Editors' Prepared Grading Guide	5-393
	Sample Answer	5-395
VI.	**EDITORS' PREPARED GRADING GUIDE FOR** **PRACTICE QUESTION:** *PEABODY v. MIDDLETOWN*	5-393
VII.	**SAMPLE ANSWER TO PRACTICE QUESTION:** *PEABODY v. MIDDLETOWN*	5-395

RIGOS UNIFORM BAR EXAM (UBE) REVIEW SERIES

MULTISTATE PERFORMANCE TEST (MPT) REVIEW

CHAPTER 5

LITIGATION TASKS

I. INTRODUCTION

"Litigation Tasks" are the least common of the MPT questions.

A. Exam Frequency

The NCBE has asked candidates to perform a litigation task about once every other year since 2000. These tasks were to draft interrogatories, write a closing argument, draft part of a Complaint in a cause of action for fraud, and write a proposed finding of fact and conclusions of law. Preparing interrogatories or a discover plan is possible. A demand or settlement letter to opposing party combines litigation and office tasks.

B. Different Task

It is quite possible that the NCBE would ask candidates to perform a different type of litigation task. However, given the relative rarity of these questions, you should not spend much time worrying about the myriad of possible litigation task questions. What you learn in this section of the Rigos review will prepare you to answer any MPT question.

II. STRUCTURE OF THE QUESTION

Similar to all other MPT questions, your question packet will contain instructions, a File, and a Library. Separate and lay out these three separate sections on your desk for convenience when you work through the practice questions leading to your answer.

A. File

As usual, the File will contain a task memorandum and other documents needed to complete your assignment.

1. Task Memorandum: The task memorandum provides the requirements or "call of the question." The required format is usually specified and included in a memorandum from a supervising attorney containing your assigned task. Be alert for instructions not to address a certain issue, not to prepare things like captions, or otherwise refrain from doing something relevant to your assignment.

> **MPT Tip:** Specific instructions to exclude a subject or work product must be followed. If you discuss an excluded area or issue, it will create a negative impression on the grader. Your goal is to keep the grader smiling as she reads your answer.

2. Pointer Memorandum: It is quite rare for a litigation task question to include in the File a pointer memorandum with formatting instructions for the answer. Absent instruction, use the general presentation headings and organization discussed in the introductory chapter. If some form requirement such as litigation work-product is specified, think of your organizing and sequencing.

3. Pointer Memorandum Substitutes: To provide applicants with necessary instructions as to form, the MPT has typically included this information elsewhere in the File.

a. The Task Memorandum: The prior MPT task asking applicants to create a closing argument did not include a pointer memorandum. However, that task memorandum provided the same type of instructions typically included in a pointer memorandum.

b. Secondary Authority and Other Documents: The prior MPT interrogatories task also did not include a pointer memorandum. However, the File contained three sample interrogatories drafted by the supervising attorney and a treatise excerpt that provided guidance on preparing interrogatories. These items provided the necessary formatting information assigning the form of the expected answer.

B. Library

Like other MPT questions, all legal authority needed to complete the task will be contained in the Library. The Library is usually much larger than the File, so it may take extra time to review.

1. Content: Do not go beyond the materials presented in the Library or cite other "real world" legal authority.

2. Relevancy: Remember that not all of the authorities provided will be relevant. Some may be more compelling or persuasive than others. As always, be on the lookout for red herrings and seductive distracters that could take you off point.

III. ANSWERING THE QUESTION

A. Planning Your Answer

We covered this on page 1-11 and the planning time allocation system involving multiple steps that make a good answer a great answer.

B. It Depends on the Task

How you answer the question will depend on what task you are asked to perform. The rarity of these questions makes it difficult to predict what task might be assigned and the resulting preferred answer approach. Therefore, we do not believe it would be an efficient use of your study time to memorize suggestions specific to certain litigation tasks. The general instructions in this chapter will help you handle any question that comes your way.

C. Remember You Are an Advocate

Keep in mind that a litigator is an advocate, and you should adopt an advocate's mindset when performing litigation tasks. The persuasive tone may vary somewhat depending on the assigned litigation task. For example, interrogatories would be written with a less persuasive tone than, for example, an opening or closing argument that is advocacy in nature and very fact based.

1. Dealing with Facts: Like other types of MPT questions, you will need to read and analyze the facts carefully.

a. Relevance: Some of the facts given may be of little or no consequence to the assigned task. Be alert for red herrings that have the potential to distract you from addressing the primary issue(s) presented.

b. Helpful Facts: Take note of and make use of all facts that are helpful and relevant to your client's position.

c. Harmful Facts: Similarly, you will need to identify relevant facts that are unfavorable to your case.

(1) Handling Unfavorable Facts Implicitly: If your litigation task is to prepare discovery requests or some other "one-sided" document, such as an affidavit, you probably will not have to state harmful facts explicitly. However, they may still be of use in completing your task. For example, if they are appropriate for your assigned task, you might be able to draft interrogatories having the potential to uncover other facts and circumstances that mitigate the impact of the harmful facts.

(2) Handling Unfavorable Facts Explicitly: On the other hand, if your litigation task is to draft a closing argument or something similar, you will likely need to address explicitly any relevant facts that are harmful to your case. You cannot simply ignore them; however, you can and should de-emphasize these facts or otherwise present them in a light that is as favorable to your client as possible.

(a) Placement: Harmful facts usually have less impact when they are "buried" in the middle of a sentence or paragraph.

(b) Wording Opportunities: Your choice of wording to describe the facts may mitigate harshness, because it may be possible to emphasize or de-emphasize background facts.

(1) Example 1: If the facts state that the defendant was arrested and taken into custody, the prosecution may state that "the criminal accused was arrested by the police," while the defense might state that "the suspect was taken into custody by the authorities."

(2) Example 2: Another example is a traffic fender-bender incident fact pattern described by the plaintiff as a "collision" as opposed to an "accident" description used by the defendant. The former suggests reckless behavior while the latter descriptive characterization suggests mere fortuity.

(3) Use of the Passive Voice: Reversing the sentence active voice structure is usually discouraged but it may be useful to use the passive voice to de-emphasize unfavorable or negative facts. Compare the following.

(a) Example – Active Voice: "The Franklin State Highway Patrol arrested and took into custody Ms. Deam for violating Franklin's reckless driving statute, Franklin Motor Vehicle Code § 99.02."

(b) Example – Passive Voice: "Ms. Deam was taken into custody by two Franklin State Highway Patrol officers who alleged a violation of the state's reckless driving statute, Franklin Motor Vehicle Code § 99.02." Notice in this passive voice example that the violation of the statute has less emphasis. Also note that "taken into custody" is less harsh a characterization than "arrested."

2. Dealing with the Law: Remember that the MPT is primarily a test of legal reasoning. Therefore, you must analyze the law presented in the Library carefully.

a. Unfavorable Law: If the Library contains legal authority that is harmful to your client, chances are good that the task will expressly or implicitly require you to address it. The graders will want to see how well you handle and mitigate the damage. Do not simply ignore unfavorable law.

(1) Distinguishing Cases: Are there relevant facts that distinguish your client's case from a harmful case in the Library? If so, be sure to discuss the factual differences and why the unfavorable case should be deemed inapplicable to your case.

(2) Precedential Value of Case Law: As is true in all MPT questions, only cases from Franklin state courts, the fictitious federal 15th Circuit, or the U.S. Supreme Court are binding. All other things being equal, a favorable binding case will trump an unfavorable non-binding case.

(3) Recent Authority Usually Trumps Older Authority: Please look for and consider the dates of the cases. If one decision was handed down after the other and the second decision is more favorable to your client, you might suggest that the judge who wrote the later decision was likely aware of the previous decision and therefore intended to change the controlling law.

(4) Older Authority May Still Be Controlling: Conversely, if the previous decision is more favorable, note whether the more recent decision specifically overruled or even mentioned the prior decision. If the later decision neither mentions nor overrules the prior decision, it is likely that the older case remains, at least in part, good law.

b. Analyzing Statutes and Similar Sources of Law: If the Library contains multiple statutes, administrative regulations, court rules, or similar types of legal authority, chances are very good that not all of what is presented is necessary to complete your task. The same warning that applies to analyzing facts also applies to analyzing law.

c. Applying Other Sources of Law: The Library may contain other sources of law, such as court rules; *e.g.*, those governing evidence or legal ethics. If so, the task memorandum will probably indicate that you need to resolve an evidentiary or ethical issue. Be sure any rule you use is appropriate for the situation.

d. Secondary Authority: Your Library may contain some secondary authority, such as an excerpt from a treatise or law review journal article. Usually this material is included to help you understand the legal issues or provide a format for your answer. In the latter case, the task memorandum may explicitly tell you to follow the treatise's suggested form. Incorporate any relevant suggestions or approaches that you feel are helpful.

> **MPT Tip:** Be on the lookout for red herrings with the potential to steer you away from writing an answer that is responsive to your assigned task.

IV. WORKING THROUGH A SAMPLE QUESTION

Here, we will turn to a sample MPT question, *State v. Sizemore*. The table of contents begins on the next page.

STATE v. SIZEMORE

TABLE OF CONTENTS

Document Provided for Task	**Page**
Instructions	5-339
File	5-341
Task Memorandum	5-342
Pointer Memorandum	5-343
(Editors' Summary of Task Memorandum and Pointer Memorandum)	5-345
Trial Transcript	5-346
Library	5-357
Selected Provisions of the Franklin Penal Code	5-358
Selected Provisions of the Franklin Rules of Evidence	5-360
State v. Smith	5-361
State v. Cameron	5-363
(Editors' Summary of Key Facts and Legal Authority)	5-366
Sample Answer	5-367

STATE v. SIZEMORE

INSTRUCTIONS

1. You will have 90 minutes to complete this session of the examination. This performance test is designed to evaluate your ability to handle a select number of legal authorities in the context of a factual problem involving a client.

2. The problem is set in the fictional State of Franklin, one of the United States, located in the fictional Fifteenth Circuit. Franklin has District Courts (trial courts), Courts of Appeal (mid-level appellate courts), and a Supreme Court (Franklin's highest appellate court).

3. You will have two sets of materials with which to work: a File and a Library.

4. The File contains factual materials about your case. The first document is a memorandum containing the instructions for the tasks that you are to complete.

5. The Library contains the legal authorities needed to complete the tasks. The case reports may be real, modified, or written solely for the purpose of this performance test. If the cases appear familiar to you, do not assume that they are precisely the same as you have read before. Read each thoroughly, as if it were new to you. You should assume that cases were decided in the jurisdictions and on the dates shown. In citing cases from the Library, you may use abbreviations and omit page citations.

6. Your response must be written in the answer book provided. You should concentrate on the materials provided, but you should also bring to bear on the problem your general knowledge of the law. What you have learned in law school and elsewhere provides the general background for analyzing the problem; the File and Library provide the specific materials with which you must work.

7. Although there are no restrictions on how you apportion your time, you should probably allocate at least 45 minutes to reading and organizing before you begin writing your response. You may make notes anywhere in the test materials, but may not tear out pages from this booklet.

8. Your response will be graded on its compliance with instructions and on its content, thoroughness, and organization.

File

State

v.

Sizemore

1. Memorandum to Applicant   5-342
2. Memorandum to All Office Attorneys   5-343
3. Editors' Summary of Assigned Tasks   5-345
4. Trial Transcript – *State v. Sizemore*   5-346

STATE'S ATTORNEY'S OFFICE

County of Marion

10 The Green

Benton, Franklin

Theodore LeBlang
State's Attorney

To: Associate
From: Theodore LeBlang
Date: July 29, 20X3
Subject: State v. Sizemore
Closing Arguments

As you know, this office is prosecuting Jerry Martin Sizemore on a charge of attempted murder. The trial was completed yesterday, and closing arguments were scheduled for this morning. Unfortunately, Bonnie Miller, the Assistant State's Attorney trying the case, has gone into the hospital for an emergency appendectomy. The court has given us an extension of time until tomorrow to present closing arguments.

I will present the closing argument, but I want you to outline and draft part of the argument for my review.

Specifically, please draft the portions of the closing argument that will address the problematic testimony of Katie Wendell and expert witness Dr. Harold Beatty as they relate to the defenses of abandonment and intoxication.

Please write out the argument exactly as you would present it in court. I want to see bolded headings within the document to facilitate my presentation. Beyond that follow the guidelines contained in the office memo on Closing Arguments/Bench Trials.

STATE'S ATTORNEY'S OFFICE

County of Marion

10 The Green

Benton, Franklin

Theodore LeBlang

State's Attorney

To: All Office Attorneys

From: Theodore LeBlang

Date: February 22, 20X0

Subject: Closing Arguments/Bench Trials

Your closing argument should begin with an understanding of the legal principles that will be applied to the facts of the case. In jury trials, you will have jury instructions. In bench trials, however, you must rely on your analysis of legal authority (statutes and case law) during closing argument. The legal authority in bench trials (just as the instructions in jury trials) will give you the framework for your closing argument.

The argument must show how the evidence admitted during the trial meets the legal standards established by the statutes and case law. While in a jury trial you do not ordinarily discuss or make reference to legal authorities, in a bench trial you have more latitude in referring to the legal authority. Indeed, in the absence of jury instructions, you may find it necessary to explain to the court finer points of the law. But, you must not lose sight of the fact that a closing argument is not a legal brief or an essay. The argument is based on the evidence presented, not histrionics or personal opinion.

Your job is to help the judge understand how the law relates to the facts presented and to persuade the judge that he or she has no choice but to find in favor of our position. In doing that, you may want to do some or all of the following:

- State explicitly the ultimate facts that the court must find for us to prevail.
- Explain how the evidence fits the ultimate facts.
- Use relevant legal principles to support your argument.

- Discuss the sufficiency of the evidence and the credibility of the witnesses.
- Draw reasonable inferences from the evidence to support your position.
- Anticipate opposing counsel's arguments and point out weaknesses in his or her case.
- Refer to equities or policy considerations that merit finding for your position.
- Never hold back any argument because you anticipate having a second opportunity to make it in rebuttal.

Not all of the items in this list fit every case, but they are things you should at least think about in creating closing arguments. Organization and persuasiveness are very important. If you immerse the court in a sea of unconnected details, the judge may not be able to follow your argument. Your goal is to present a coherent picture of the facts and controlling law that persuades the court to rule in your client's favor.

EDITORS' SUMMARY

A. The Task Memorandum

The task memorandum requirement here is relatively simple.

1. Closing Arguments: Your job is to draft a portion of a closing argument to rebut testimony that is potentially harmful to the prosecution.

2. Opponent's Expected Argument: Further, you need to cover the defendant's expected argument in its closing concerning two specific affirmative defenses to the attempted murder charge. An argument is by definition persuasive, not objective.

B. The Pointer Memorandum

For this question, the pointer memorandum is crucial.

1. Inexperience: If you are a recent law school graduate, it is likely that you have not had any meaningful experience with a closing argument presented in trial court. The pointer memorandum explains the basic structure of a closing argument, gives you numerous tips, and stresses the importance of organization.

2. Persuasive Tone: While it should be obvious that a closing argument is intended to persuade the trier of fact, the pointer memorandum also explicitly states that your work product should be persuasive in nature.

It is now time to examine the rest of the File, as well as the Library.

TRIAL TRANSCRIPT
STATE v. SIZEMORE

EXAMINATION OF B.J. ATWOOD

B.J. Atwood, a witness called by the State, first being duly sworn, testified as follows:

DIRECT EXAMINATION BY MS. MILLER

Q: Would you tell us your name?

A: B.J. Atwood.

Q: Where do you work?

A: I am a Trooper with the State Police.

Q: Were you on duty September 19, 20X2?

A: Yes.

Q: Did you investigate a possible hit and run on that date?

A: Yes, it was on September 19th, while on patrol, I came upon a black 1987 BMW model 325 on Tower Drive.

Q: Did you notice anything unusual about the car?

A: The car had clearly been in an accident and was abandoned. It also matched the description of the car that had been involved in an accident and possible hit and run about two hours earlier.

Q: What did you do?

A: I determined that the car belonged to Jerry Martin Sizemore.

Q: Then what happened?

A: I knew Sizemore lived with his parents. I went to their home to interrogate the defendant.

Q: At what time was that?

A: Approximately 4:15 p.m.

Q: Where is the house located?

A: 9873 Pine Street, Benton, Franklin.

Q: What happened when you went to the house?

A: I knocked at the door of the Sizemore home. The defendant responded and admitted me into the house.

Q: What happened then?

A: I interviewed the defendant.

Q: Was anyone else present during this interview?

A: The interview started in the presence of Katie Wendell, a friend of Sizemore's.

Q: Did you ask Sizemore about the accident?

A: Yes.

Q: What did he say?

A: Sizemore denied any involvement in the accident and claimed that his car had been stolen earlier in the day and that his sister, Pamela, was supposed to have reported the theft.

Q: Hearing this, what did you do?

A: I asked to speak to Pamela, and Sizemore brought her into the room.

Q: And then?

A: When the young girl came into the room I asked if I could talk to her outside. She said yes, so we went outside.

Q: Where did you go?

A: I took her to my police car.

Q: How long did you talk with Pamela?

A: We talked for about five or ten minutes.

Q: Did you talk about the defendant's car?

A: Yes, and during my conversation in the police car Pamela told me her brother's car had not been stolen.

Q: Did you finish your conversation with Pamela?

A: No.

Q: Why not?

A: While we were talking I heard someone say in a loud tone of voice, "Pam, get out of that car."

Q: What did you do?

A: I looked in the direction the voice came from and saw Sizemore standing in front of the house, approximately 20-25 feet from the police car, with a .22 caliber rifle to his left shoulder, pointed straight at me.

Q: Did he say anything?

A: He said, "I'm going to kill you, cop," and Pam started hollering, "No, Jerry, No, Jerry, No," and he hollered at her and said, "Get out of that car."

Q: Did she leave the car?

A: She jumped out the door and started running. She ran toward Mrs. Combs' house, which is back behind her house and to the right.

Q: Then what happened?

A: The defendant said, "Damn you, I'm going to kill you."

Q: What did you do?

A: I said, "Put your gun down," and he said, "No, I'm going to kill you."

Q: Was he still on the porch?

A: Well, after he said that, he started off the porch and he said, "You move, and I'm going to kill you."

Q: What were you doing as he came off the porch?

A: I had my right hand on the steering wheel and I had my left hand up on the door post. He said, "If you move, I'll kill you. You put your hands up."

Q: What did you do?

A: I just raised them up like this, and then he walked on up to about five feet of the car, and I said, "Put your gun down and let's talk."

Q: What did he say?

A: He said, "No, I'm going to kill you." I said, "If you kill me, you go to the execution chamber."

Q: Was anyone else present while this was going on?

A: About this time, Katie Wendell, the other person who was in the house, came out and Sizemore told her, "Go around and get his gun."

Q: What did Ms. Wendell do?

A: Wendell said, "No, I'm not going to get involved in it. I'm not going to spend the rest of my life in the penitentiary." I then told Sizemore again, I said, "Put your gun down. When you shoot me, you don't go to the penitentiary. You go to the execution chamber."

Q: What was the defendant's response?

A: He said, "I'm going to kill you," and he told Wendell again "I told you to get his gun," and Wendell said, "No, I'm not going to get his gun." I told Sizemore, "You had better give her the gun because when you pull the trigger and kill me, that's cold-blooded murder," and I said, "You'll die in the execution chamber for it."

Q: What happened next?

A: I heard a small "click" noise, and then Sizemore said, "Trigger must be jammed." He hit the side of the rifle a few times and then tried to pull the trigger again. I heard another click, and Sizemore muttered, "Piece of junk won't fire."

Q: Did he then put the gun down?

A: Not right away. I said, "Right now you're just involved in an automobile accident charge." That was the only thing I was investigating, but I said, "You're getting yourself into some serious trouble." I told him again, "When you fire that gun and kill me, you'll go to the execution chamber," and I told him this two or three different times. Finally he just dropped the gun down and I said, "Give it to your friend," and he handed the gun to Katie Wendell.

Q: Do you know what provoked this confrontation?

A: Well, it was pretty obvious. There was no unpleasantness when we were in the house. It was obviously my request for a private conversation with Sizemore's sister that provoked the defendant and triggered his actions.

BY MS. MILLER: That's all I have, Your Honor.

CROSS-EXAMINATION BY MS. JANE

Q: Trooper Atwood, Mr. Sizemore smelled like he had been drinking, didn't he?

A: Yes.

Q: Before Mr. Sizemore gave up the gun, he pointed it toward the ground, then pushed the safety back on it and handed it to Ms. Wendell, correct?

A: Yes.

Q: Ms. Wendell then took the gun and ejected the shells onto the ground, is that right?

A: Yes.

Q: Now, after Mr. Sizemore gave the gun to Ms. Wendell, without even getting out of the car, you said to Sizemore, "Come around and have a seat," and he came around and sat beside you in the patrol car, is that correct?

A: Yes.

Q: You questioned Mr. Sizemore in the car about the accident?

A: Yes.

Q: After talking about the car accident, that's when you arrested him and took him to the Marion County Jail?

A: Yes.

Q: You didn't handcuff Mr. Sizemore, did you?

A: No.

REDIRECT EXAMINATION BY MS. MILLER

Q: Trooper Atwood, did Mr. Sizemore appear to be drunk?

A: The defendant did not appear to be drunk when he came out of the house. While Sizemore had the odor of alcohol about his person, he answered all questions clearly and intelligently. He never staggered; he walked steadily; the gun he was holding on me never wavered any appreciable amount, and he appeared to be very much in control of himself.

Q: Thank you, Trooper Atwood.

BY MS. MILLER: Your Honor, the prosecution rests, subject to rebuttal.

EXAMINATION OF JERRY SIZEMORE

Jerry Martin Sizemore, a witness called by the Defendant, first being duly sworn, testified as follows:

DIRECT EXAMINATION BY MS. JANE

Q: Would you tell us your name?

A: Jerry Martin Sizemore.

Q: Where do you live?

A: 9873 Pine Street, Benton, Franklin.

Q: Mr. Sizemore, do you recall your activities on September 19, 20X2?

A: Not really.

Q: What do you mean?

A: Well, I don't really remember much other than that I got up in the morning and had been drinking beer and whiskey, and driving my BMW around.

Q: Do you remember meeting Trooper Atwood that day?

A: No.

Q: Do you remember anything about that day other than drinking beer and whiskey and driving around?

A: I remember waking up in the county jail.

Q: Would it be fair to say you were intoxicated on September 19th?

A: Yes.

Q: Have you ever intended to kill Trooper Atwood?

A: No.

BY MS. JANE: No further questions, Your Honor.

CROSS-EXAMINATION BY MS. MILLER

Q: Mr. Sizemore, this isn't the first time you've been arrested is it?

A: No.

Q: In fact, isn't it true that you were arrested for shoplifting?

BY MS. JANE: Objection, your Honor. Use of an arrest is improper impeachment. Likewise, shoplifting is an act that, even if leading to a conviction, is improper impeachment under Franklin Rules of Evidence 609.

BY MS. MILLER: Your Honor, this is not for the purpose of impeachment. Rather, it is related to Rule 404(b) intent. If you will allow me to make a few more questions to make the point . . . .

BY THE COURT: Go ahead.

BY MS. MILLER: Isn't it true that you were arrested for shoplifting?

A: Yes.

Q: You went to jail?

A: Yes.

Q: While in jail were you accused of attacking a jail guard?

A: Yes, but that was just Johnny Simms. We'd been friends for years. Besides which, I told people that I didn't throw that fan at Johnny, that fan fell off the shelf.

Q: You were tried and convicted of a felony arising out of that altercation weren't you?

BY MS. JANE: Objection, your Honor. I renew my previous objection and now object to the introduction of the felony conviction. Both are improper impeachment and irrelevant under Rule 404(b).

BY MS. MILLER: Again, your Honor, this is not for the purpose of impeachment. Further, the felony conviction is admissible under Rule 609 and I gave Ms. Jane notice long before the trial that I intended to introduce this evidence.

BY THE COURT: I'll overrule the objection.

BY MS. MILLER: Mr. Sizemore, let me ask you again, you were tried and convicted of a felony arising out of that altercation at the county jail, weren't you?

A: Yes.

Q: You were sentenced to a year in jail, weren't you?

A: Yes, but 6 months were suspended.

BY MS. MILLER: Nothing further, your Honor.

EXAMINATION OF KATIE WENDELL

Katie Wendell, a witness called by the Defendant, first being duly sworn, testified as follows:

DIRECT EXAMINATION BY MS. JANE

Q: Where did you spend September 19, 20X2?

A: Mr. Sizemore and I spent the day together.

Q: What did you do?

A: I went over to his house about 9:30 in the morning. Most of the time we were just hanging out.

Q: Did you ever leave Mr. Sizemore's house?

A: Yeah. About 2:00 we went out to buy some more beer.

Q: Did you use Mr. Sizemore's car?

A: No, we used mine.

Q: Why was that?

A: Jerry said his was stolen, so I drove.

Q: Did you pick up more beer?

A: Yeah.

Q: How much?

A: I think it was two 12 packs.

Q: Had you been drinking before 2:00 p.m.?

A: Yes.

Q: How much?

A: Well, I'd brought over two 12 packs and we finished those. That's why we had to go out to get some more.

Q: Were you present when Trooper Atwood came to the Sizemore house on September 19, 2007?

A: Yes.

Q: By that time, how much beer had you drunk?

A: We had pretty much gone through a total of three 12 packs.

Q: How much of that had Mr. Sizemore drunk?

A: At least half of it.

Q: When Trooper Atwood arrived at the house, did he ask Sizemore about the accident?

A: Yes.

Q: What did he say?

A: Just that the car was stolen, and that Pammy was supposed to have reported the theft.

Q: Did Trooper Atwood ask to speak to Pamela?

A: Yes.

Q: Did he?

A: Yes, out in the patrol car.

Q: Where did you go?

A: I stayed in the house with Jerry.

Q: What happened in the house?

A: Jerry was kind of annoyed that the Trooper had stopped the party and that apparently Pam had not reported the car theft.

Q: Did anything happen?

A: Jerry said, "Let's go have some fun and scare Pammy."

Q: Then what happened?

A: Jerry took his .22 rifle off the rack and went out front.

Q: Did he say anything?

A: He said, "I'm going to kill you."

Q: When he said "you" who did he mean?

BY MS. MILLER: Objection. Calls for speculation.

BY THE COURT: Overruled.

BY MS. JANE: You can answer.

A: Well, it was clear from what he had said about scaring Pam, he meant Pam. But it was just to scare her.

Q: Did Pam do anything?

A: She starts yelling, "No, Jerry, no, Jerry, no, please." Then she jumps out of the car and runs over to the neighbors.

Q: Then what happened?

A: The policeman says, like, "Put the gun down and let's talk."

Q: What did Mr. Sizemore do?

A: He handed me the gun and then went into the patrol car with the policeman.

BY MS. JANE: That's all I have your Honor.

CROSS-EXAMINATION BY MS. MILLER

Q: Isn't it true that Mr. Sizemore asked you to get Trooper Atwood's gun?

A: No.

Q: In response to Mr. Sizemore's request, you said, quote, "No, I'm not going to get his gun. I'm not going to get involved with it. I'm not going to spend the rest of my life in the penitentiary."

A: No.

Q: After Pamela left the car, Mr. Sizemore said to Trooper Atwood, "I'm going to kill you."

A: No.

Q: Trooper Atwood told Mr. Sizemore, "You had better give Katie the gun because when you pull the trigger and kill me, that's cold-blooded murder."

A: No.

Q: Let's try this, then. You've been a friend of Jerry Sizemore's for a long time haven't you?

A: Since high school.

Q: That would be what, 7 or 8 years?

A: About that.

Q: You hang out together?

A: Yes.

Q: Drink together?

A: Some.

Q: Actually, you were arrested once together, weren't you?

BY MS. JANE: Objection.

BY THE COURT: Overruled.

Q: You've been convicted of a felony yourself, haven't you?

A: Yes.

Q: That was two years ago?

A: I think that's right.

Q: The conviction was for assault and battery, is that right?

A: I believe that's what they called it.

BY MS. MILLER: No further questions.

Sample Question 5-354   Course 5329. Copyright 2018 by Rigos UBE Review Series – MPT.

EXAMINATION OF HAROLD BEATTY

Harold Beatty, a witness called by the Defendant, first being duly sworn, testified as follows:

DIRECT EXAMINATION BY MS. JANE

Q: Would you tell us your name and occupation, please.

A: Dr. Harold Beatty. I am a physician at Marion Community Hospital.

Q: Are you licensed to practice medicine in this state?

A: Yes.

BY MS. JANE: Your Honor, rather than prolong this, I ask the Court to recognize Dr. Beatty as an expert on the effect of alcohol on the human body.

BY MS. MILLER: Your Honor, I have no objection to Dr. Beatty's qualifications to testify about the effect of alcohol, but do object to the relevancy of this testimony.

BY THE COURT: I'll accept the agreement that Dr. Beatty is an expert. Ms. Jane, will the doctor's testimony be lengthy?

BY MS. JANE: Just a couple of questions, your Honor.

BY THE COURT: I'm going to allow it. Ms. Miller, this is a bench trial. You can make your relevancy point on closing, if you like.

BY MS. MILLER: Thank you, your Honor.

BY MS. JANE: Now, Dr. Beatty. Let me ask you, imagine a 26 year old man, who is 5 feet 10 inches tall and weighs 160 pounds. Assume that man consumes 18 cans of beer over a period of 6 hours. Each can of beer contains 12 ounces. Do you have an opinion to within a reasonable degree of medical certainty whether that person would have a blood alcohol content in excess of .08 percent?

A: The individual would be lucky to be able to stand up at all. The alcohol content would be far in excess of .08 percent.

Q: Would it be conceivable that the person would have a diminished capacity to function?

A: Yes.

Q: Would the person be unable to recall what happened during that six-hour period?

A: Most certainly.

Q: Thank you doctor.

CROSS-EXAMINATION BY MS. MILLER

Q: Dr. Beatty, you've never examined the defendant Jerry Sizemore have you?

A: No.

Q: You've never even met Mr. Sizemore, have you?

A: No.

Q: Thank you, doctor. I have no further questions, your Honor.

BY MS. JANE: Your Honor, the defense rests.

BY MS. MILLER: Your Honor, the prosecution has no rebuttal witnesses. We rest.

BY THE COURT: Thank you. Given the late hour, I think we will recess until tomorrow at 9:30 a.m. At that point, I will hear closing arguments. Good afternoon.

Library

State

v.

Sizemore

1. Selected Provisions of the
   Franklin Penal Code — 5-358

2. Selected Provisions of the
   Franklin Rules of Evidence — 5-360

3. *State v. Smith* — 5-361

4. *State v. Cameron* — 5-363

SELECTED PROVISIONS OF THE FRANKLIN PENAL CODE

§ 128. Criminal attempt

a. *Definition of attempt.* A person is guilty of attempt to commit a crime if, acting with the kind of culpability otherwise required for commission of the crime, s/he:

(1) Purposely engages in conduct which would constitute the crime if the attendant circumstances were as a reasonable person would believe them to be;

(2) Does or omits to do anything with the purpose of causing a particular result without further conduct on his/her part, when causing a particular result is an element of the crime; or,

(3) Purposely does or omits to do anything which, under the circumstances as a reasonable person would believe them to be, is an act or omission constituting a substantial step in a course of conduct planned to culminate in his commission of the crime.

b. *Conduct which may be held substantial step under subsection a.(3).* Conduct shall not be held to constitute a substantial step under subsection a.(3) of this section unless it is strongly corroborative of the actor's criminal purpose.

* * *

d. *Renunciation of criminal purpose.* When the actor's conduct would otherwise constitute an attempt under subsection a(2) or (3) of this section, it is an affirmative defense which s/he must prove by a preponderance of the evidence that s/he abandoned his/her effort to commit the crime or otherwise prevented its commission, under circumstances manifesting a complete and voluntary renunciation of his criminal purpose.

Within the meaning of this chapter, renunciation of criminal purpose is not voluntary if it is motivated, in whole or in part, by circumstances, not present or apparent at the inception of the actor's course of conduct, which increase the probability of detection or apprehension or which make more difficult the accomplishment of the criminal purpose.

m§ 140. **Murder**

    a. Criminal homicide constitutes murder when:

        (1) The actor purposely causes death or serious bodily injury resulting in death; or

        (2) The actor knowingly causes death or serious bodily injury resulting in death.

* * *

§ 148. **Intoxication**

    a. Except as provided in subsection d of this section, intoxication of the actor is not a defense unless it negates an element of the offense.

    b. When recklessness establishes an element of the offense, if the actor, due to self-induced intoxication, is unaware of a risk of which s/he would have been aware had he been sober, such unawareness is immaterial.

    c. Intoxication does not, in itself, constitute mental disease.

    d. Intoxication which is not self-induced or is pathological is an affirmative defense if by reason of such intoxication the actor at the time of his/her conduct lacks substantial and adequate capacity either to appreciate its wrongfulness or to conform his/her conduct to the requirement of law.

    e. *Definitions*. In this section, unless a different meaning plainly is required,

    (1) "Intoxication" means a disturbance of mental or physical capacities resulting from the introduction of substances into the body;

    (2) "Self-induced intoxication" means intoxication caused by substances which the actor knowingly introduces into his/her body, the tendency of which s/he knows or ought to know causes intoxication, unless s/he introduces them pursuant to medical advice or under such circumstances as would afford a defense to a charge of crime;

    (3) "Pathological intoxication" means intoxication grossly excessive in degree, given the amount of the intoxicant, to which the actor does not know s/he is susceptible.

SELECTED PROVISIONS OF THE FRANKLIN RULES OF EVIDENCE

Rule 404. Character Evidence Not Admissible to Prove Conduct; Exceptions; Other Crimes.

* * *

(b) Other crimes, wrongs, or acts. Evidence of other crimes, wrongs, or acts is not admissible to prove the character of a person in order to show action in conformity therewith. It may, however, be admissible for other purposes, such as proof of motive, opportunity, intent, preparation, plan, knowledge, identity, or absence of mistake or accident, provided that upon request by the accused, the prosecution in a criminal case shall provide reasonable notice in advance of trial, or during trial if the court excuses pretrial notice on good cause shown, of the general nature of any such evidence it intends to introduce at trial.

Rule 609. Impeachment by Evidence of Conviction of Crime.

(a) General rule. For the purpose of attacking the credibility of a witness, (1) evidence that a witness other than an accused has been convicted of a crime shall be admitted, unless unduly prejudicial, if the crime was punishable by death or imprisonment in excess of one year under the law under which the witness was convicted, and evidence that an accused has been convicted of such a crime shall be admitted if the court determines that the probative value of admitting this evidence outweighs its prejudicial effect to the accused; and (2) evidence that any witness has been convicted of a crime shall be admitted if it involved dishonesty or false statement, regardless of the punishment.

STATE v. SMITH

Supreme Court of Franklin (1980)

This is an appeal from a judgment directing a verdict in favor of the defendant, Richard Kevin Smith (Smith), at the close of the State's evidence upon the charge of attempted murder. We reverse.

On the evening of August 10, 1979, Smith and his uncle, Melvin Howell, were heavily engaged in a drinking bout. They fell to quarreling. Smith grabbed a jackknife and stabbed his uncle in the chest twice, but the blade was too dull to penetrate the uncle's skin. Smith then pursued him up the street shouting unintelligible epithets at his uncle as they ran.

The uncle collapsed from weakness a block away, and when Smith approached, his mood had changed. He was remorseful and wept. Smith then dragged his uncle into the uncle's car, threw away the knife, sped up Pearl Street to the police station, and turned himself in. Ultimately, Smith was charged with attempted murder.

After the State had rested its case-in-chief, the trial court granted Smith's motion for a directed verdict on the basis of abandonment. The sole question on appeal is as follows:

> *Whether the trial court erred in ruling that Smith had abandoned the crime of attempted murder after he had tried to inflict serious knife wounds upon his intended victim, but found that the blade was not capable of inflicting serious injury.*

The thrust of Smith's argument, and the theory relied upon by the trial court, is that after the stabbing, and after the uncle had collapsed and was at Smith's mercy, Smith abandoned the effort to commit the underlying offense of murder and voluntarily prevented its commission.

The State argues that the defense of abandonment is not available in a case of attempted murder where the defendant's attempt was thwarted only by circumstances, not previously known to the defendant, that made commission of the underlying crime impossible. In such a case, the effort to commit the underlying crime has been completed and cannot be abandoned.

It is generally true that attempted murder cannot be purged after the defendant has thrust a knife toward his intended victim with intent to kill, no matter what may cause the plan to be abandoned later. On the other hand, although a criminal plan has proceeded far enough to support a conviction of criminal attempt, it would be sound to recognize the possibility of a *locus penitentiae* so long as no substantial harm has been done and no actual danger committed.

In any event, abandonment must occur before the crime is completed or the harm is done. Furthermore, under Franklin Penal Code § 128(d), the defense of abandonment is not available when the renunciation of criminal purpose is completely or partially motivated "by circumstances, not present or apparent at the inception of the actor's course of conduct, which . . . make more difficult the accomplishment of the criminal purpose." In this case, the offense charged was attempted murder, which was completed when, acting with the culpability required for the commission of the crime, the perpetrator engages in conduct that constitutes a substantial step toward the commission of the crime.

The offense here was completed with the first thrust of Smith's knife. This was followed by a second thrust of the knife and further pursuit of the uncle. Two attempts were completed and Smith abandoned the third attempt. But here, the abandonment is no defense, because it was prompted by unforeseen circumstances that made accomplishing the criminal purpose more difficult; *i.e.*, the knife was too dull to kill the intended victim.

The trial court erred in entering a judgment for the defendant at the close of the State's case-in-chief. Accordingly, we reverse.

STATE v. CAMERON
Supreme Court of Franklin (1986)

The appeal presents a narrow, but important, issue concerning the role that a defendant's voluntary intoxication plays in a criminal prosecution. The Court of Appeal reversed defendant's convictions. We now reverse the Court of Appeal.

Defendant, Michele Cameron, age 22 at the time of trial, was indicted for aggravated assault and possession of a weapon, a broken bottle, with a purpose to use it unlawfully, and resisting arrest. A jury convicted defendant of all charges.

The appellate court reversed the conviction on the ground that voluntary intoxication is a defense when it negates an essential element of the offense – here, purposeful conduct. We agree with that proposition. Likewise we are in accord with the determinations of the court below that all three charges of which this defendant was convicted – aggravated assault, the possession offense, and resisting arrest – have purposeful conduct as an element of the offense and that a person acts purposely "with respect to the nature of his conduct or a result thereof if it is his conscious object to engage in conduct of that nature or to cause such a result" (quoting Franklin Penal Code § 135(b)(1)). We part company with the Court of Appeal, however, in its conclusion that the circumstances disclosed by the evidence in this case required that the issue of defendant's intoxication be submitted to the jury.

Under the Franklin Penal Code, self-induced intoxication is not a defense unless it negates an element of the offense. *See* § 148(a). The Code permits evidence of intoxication as a defense to crimes requiring either "purposeful" or "knowing" mental states, but it excludes evidence of intoxication as a defense to crimes requiring mental states of only recklessness or negligence. Intoxication is admissible to disprove the culpability factors of purpose or knowledge, but for crimes requiring only recklessness or negligence, exculpation based on intoxication should be excluded as a matter of law.

Under the Code, proof of voluntary intoxication would negate the culpability elements of the offenses of which this defendant was convicted. The charges – aggravated assault, possession of a weapon with a purpose to use it unlawfully, and resisting arrest – all require purposeful conduct (aggravated assault uses "purposely" or "knowingly" in the alternative).

The question is what level of intoxication must be demonstrated before a trial court is required to submit the issue to a jury. What quantum of proof is required?

The mere intake of even large quantities of alcohol will not suffice. Moreover, the defense cannot be established solely by showing that the defendant might not have committed the offense had she been sober. The Code's definition of intoxication is "a disturbance of mental or physical capacities resulting from the introduction of substances into the body." Franklin Penal Code § 148(e)(1). This is often interpreted as showing a great prostration of the faculties such that the requisite mental state was totally lacking. Such a state of affairs will likely exist in very few cases.

In general, the factors that should be used include: the quantity of intoxicant consumed, the period of time involved, the actor's conduct as perceived by others (what he said, how he said it, how he appeared, how he acted, how his coordination or lack thereof manifested itself), any odor of alcohol or other intoxicating substance, the results of any tests to determine blood-alcohol content, and the actor's ability to recall significant events. Cases in which evidence of intoxication was deemed sufficient to present a jury question include *State v. Frankland* (1968) (defendant consumed fifteen drinks of scotch and water and could not remember the events of the evening); and *State v. Polk* (1977) (defendant drank beer and wine from 9 a.m. until sometime in the afternoon; drinking companion had blood-alcohol concentration of 0.158; defendant acted irrationally, hitting baby with his fist and throwing baby down onto a porch). Cases holding that the evidence was insufficient to warrant a jury charge on intoxication are *State v. Selby* (1981) (defendant shared with three others a marijuana pipe for about ten minutes, as a result of which he felt "high" and "pretty good"); *State v. Kinlaw* (1977) (defendant drank beer between 11 a.m. and 2 p.m. and described himself as "drunk") and *State v. Ghaul* (1975) (defendant testified he had been "drinking all day").

Measured by the foregoing standard and evidence relevant thereto, it is apparent that the record in this case is insufficient to have required the trial court to grant defendant's request to submit the issue of intoxication to the jury. True, the victim testified that defendant was drunk, and defendant herself said she felt "pretty intoxicated," "pretty bad," and "very intoxicated." But these are no more than conclusory labels, of little assistance in determining whether any drinking produced a prostration of faculties. Defendant's conduct was violent, abusive, and threatening. But with it all there is not the slightest suggestion that she did not know what she was doing or that her faculties were so beclouded that she was incapable of engaging in purposeful conduct. That the purpose of the conduct may have been bizarre, even violent, is not the test. The question is whether defendant was capable of forming that bizarre or violent purpose, and we do not find sufficient evidence to permit a jury to say she was not so capable.

Reversed.

EDITORS' SUMMARY

C. The Facts

The task memorandum on page 5-342 indicates the key facts that you must gather from the lengthy trial transcript: those concerning Jerry Sizemore's asserted defenses of intoxication and abandonment.

1. Testimony Focus: The requirements indicate that you need to focus on the problematic testimony of Katie Wendell and Dr. Harold Beatty. Your portion of the closing argument is intended to minimize and/or mitigate the harmful impact of that expected adverse testimony. Dr. Beatty's testimony is quite short and easy to read. On the other hand, Ms. Wendell's testimony requires you to identify the key facts contained within her testimony, including her felony conviction (see below) and her friendship with Mr. Sizemore.

2. Officer of the Law Focus: You should also focus on the testimony of Trooper Atwood, as it is the most favorable to your position as prosecutor. Furthermore, there appear to be no credibility or other problems with the Trooper's statements from the witness stand.

D. The Law

Franklin Rule of Evidence 609 is your best legal (as opposed to factual) way to attack and discredit Katie Wendell's testimony, as her felony conviction can be used to impeach her. (Rule 404 is a red herring, at least for purposes of your assigned task here.) You can then summarize Trooper Atwood's testimony as a more accurate version of the facts.

1. Witness Testimony: As for Dr. Beatty, first note that his testimony concerning the effects of alcohol is predicated on Ms. Wendell's testimony. Her credibility is vulnerable under Rule 609, which allows impeachment of a witness by introducing evidence of certain criminal convictions. This is not made explicit in the trial transcript. Instead, you have to make the connection yourself

2. Case Authority: The *Smith* case construes Franklin's statute on abandonment of criminal intent. Under this case, Mr. Sizemore's alleged abandonment of his activities was insufficient to invoke that affirmative defense. *Cameron* is important to completing this task because it construes Franklin's statute on intoxication.

3. Extraneous Authorities: The remaining law in the Library provides some background concerning the legal issues involved, but is largely unnecessary for purposes of your task.

E. Sample Closing Argument

The closing argument that begins on the next page is an example of a good answer to the task assigned in this question.

State v. Sizemore
Closing Argument

Your Honor, thank you for the time extension to allow me to review the trial record so I can present the State's closing argument. I will focus on the two most important issues of abandonment and persuasiveness of the defendant's paid expert witness upon which their case is based.

<u>I. First, according to the Most Credible Source, Defendant Sizemore Did Not Voluntarily Abandon His Attempt to Murder Trooper Atwood.</u>

<u>Ms. Wendell's Testimony Should Be Discounted Because She Is Not a Credible Witness.</u>

Ms. Wendell was arrested and convicted of a felony two years ago. Rule 609 specifies that a witness' testimony may be impeached by providing evidence of a prior conviction. The prior conviction must have been punishable by death or imprisonment in excess of one year. Ms. Wendell was charged and convicted of assault and battery, felonies in Franklin, and sentenced to more than one year in jail. Thus, Ms. Wendell's statement that the Defendant abandoned his attempt voluntarily, and without prompting from outside sources is not credible. Ms. Wendell's testimony concerning the intended target of the gun and whether the Defendant intended to scare or shoot the targeted person is likewise not credible.

Furthermore, Ms. Wendell is biased towards the Defendant because of the long-term and ongoing friendship with the Defendant. As such, Ms. Wendell's testimony should be rejected in favor of Trooper Atwood's more credible and objective testimony.

<u>The Lack of Credibility Is Reinforced Because Defendant Sizemore Withdrew Only After He Pulled the Trigger, but the Rifle Did Not Fire.</u>

Defendant ceased his course of action only after he twice pulled the trigger and found that the rifle would not fire. Defendant did not withdraw voluntarily because of his own conscience. The Defendant continued to point the rifle at Trooper Atwood and yelled that he would kill the Trooper. The Defendant abandoned his plan only because it was impossible to carry out.

Under Franklin Penal Code § 128(d), as construed in Smith, "The defense of abandonment is not available when the renunciation of criminal purpose is completely or partially motivated 'by circumstances, not . . . apparent at the inception of the actor's course of conduct, which . . . make more difficult the accomplishment of the criminal purpose.'" Accordingly, even if the Defendant did not complete the crime of murder because the gun jammed and would not fire, the defense of abandonment will not excuse his actions.

II. The Second Important Issue Is that the Court Should Reject the Expert Testimony of Dr. Harold Beatty, and Accordingly, the Defense of Intoxication Will Not Shield the Defendant.

While the Defendant's expert, Dr. Beatty, offered an opinion concerning the effect of the alcohol allegedly consumed by the Defendant, the Court should reject it. First, Dr. Beatty's opinion was predicated on the consumption of "18 cans of beer over a period of 6 hours." The only testimony regarding the quantity of beer consumed and the time span during which that beer was consumed was provided by Katie Wendell. As discussed *supra*, Ms. Wendell's testimony is not credible and should not be believed.

Cameron set forth six factors to be considered when a defendant pleads the affirmative defense of intoxication: 1) how much intoxicant the defendant consumed; 2) the amount of time it took for the defendant to consume the intoxicant; 3) how others perceived the actor's conduct; 4) any odor of an intoxicating substance; 5) blood-alcohol test results; and 6) the ability of the defendant to remember significant events. Regarding factors 1 and 2, again, the sole testimony concerning quantity and time is not credible. As such, Dr. Beatty's opinion amounts to nothing more than speculation concerning a hypothetical scenario. Dr. Beatty's opinion concerning factor 6 is predicated upon the unreliable testimony concerning factors 1 and 2, and is thus equally speculative and hypothetical. Having neither examined nor even met the Defendant, Dr. Beatty did not and could not offer any testimony related to factor 3. Finally, with no blood-alcohol test results introduced into evidence, Dr. Beatty could offer no testimony concerning factor 5. To be sure, Trooper Atwood did note an odor of alcohol when he encountered the Defendant, but this single factor is severely outweighed by the other five factors.

If the Court properly rejects Ms. Wendell's testimony concerning the Defendant's intoxication and Dr. Beatty's testimony, the defense cannot establish the affirmative defense of intoxication. Cameron, citing Franklin Penal Code § 148(e)(1), is instructive on this point. The court noted that intoxication "is often interpreted as showing a great prostration of the faculties such that the requisite mental state was totally lacking. Such a state of affairs will likely exist in very few cases." Trooper Atwood testified that Mr. Sizemore "answered all questions clearly and intelligently," "never staggered," "walked steadily," "never wavered the gun," and "appeared to be very much in control of himself." In light of this testimony and the lack of sufficient, credible evidence concerning the Defendant's alleged intoxication, the Court should find that the Defendant was not "intoxicated" for purposes of that affirmative defense.

In summary, the most credible witness, Trooper Atwood, testified that Mr. Sizemore pointed the gun at him, repeatedly threatened to kill him, never appeared drunk, and gave up the gun only because the weapon was malfunctioning and would not fire.

The State therefore respectfully asks the Court to convict Mr. Sizemore of attempted murder and reject his proffered affirmative defenses.

I thank the court for its attention.

F. Working Practice Question

1. Begin Testing Yourself: Now that we've finished looking at a litigation task MPT question and answer, you should complete the following practice question on your own. Afterwards, compare your answer with the sample grading guide and answer provided.

> **MPT Tip:** One of the major mistakes students make in preparing for the MPT exam is to eliminate self-testing. It is too easy to read the Library and File and then refer to the answer and say to yourself "yep, that's how I would have done it." You need to gain experience in actually creating the task answer.

2. Learning-Testing Conditions: You should create your own conditions as close to those of the MPT bar exam as possible. This would mean you should allocate a minimum of a full 90-minute time block for the question. You will have to work up to this time limit and to start perhaps allow yourself a full 120 minutes.

3. Concentration Objective: Ideally, you should complete the answer without taking a break. Again, you may have to work up to this. Concentration during your writing time is critical. Turn off all phones and do not answer email during this testing period.

4. Grading Your Answer: After you have completed the task, use our grading guides to objectively evaluate your answer coverage. Also, you should compare your answers with the sample answers provided for substance, organization, form, structure, and overall presentation. Don't be discouraged if your answer is missing something important or if it contains a significant mistake. Use this as a learning opportunity to figure out how and why you went wrong so you can improve your future MPT performance.

5. Re-Write Helpful: Many candidates find correcting and supplementing their first answer helpful. If you typed your answer this is quite easy, but even if your answer was in long hand it may be worth doing. Add to your first answer any omissions you feel are important. Redoing your answer allows you to create a litigation task "model answer" to refer back to later. This self-correction also reduces the chance you will repeat similar errors on other litigation tasks.

> **MPT Tip:** Some students find it too difficult to actually spend the full 90 minute time creating their own complete answer to the questions before looking at our Editor's Summary and Sample Answer. If that temptation applies to you, you may not get the task creation practice you need to pass the MPT. Consider enrolling in our supplemental personal MPT Writing Program Service described in the foreword information just before the introductory chapter 1.

V. PRACTICE QUESTION:

PEABODY v. MIDDLETOWN

TABLE OF CONTENTS

Documents Provided for Task	**Page**
Instructions	5-373
File	5-375
Task Memorandum	5-376
Pointer Memorandum	5-377
Excerpts from Complaint for Violation of Civil Rights	5-378
Transcript of Interview with Joe Peabody and Jeff Whittaker	5-380
Library	5-387
Amendment IV, United States Constitution	5-388
United States Code, Title 42, Section 1983	5-389
Bishop v. Carter	5-390
Editors' Prepared Grading Guide	5-393
Sample Answer	5-395

PEABODY v. MIDDLETOWN

INSTRUCTIONS

1. You will have 90 minutes to complete this session of the examination. This performance test is designed to evaluate your ability to handle a select number of legal authorities in the context of a factual problem involving a client.

2. The problem is set in the fictional State of Franklin, one of the United States, located in the fictional Fifteenth Circuit. Franklin has District Courts (trial courts), Courts of Appeal (mid-level appellate courts), and a Supreme Court (Franklin's highest appellate court).

3. You will have two sets of materials with which to work: a File and a Library.

4. The File contains factual materials about your case. The first document is a memorandum containing the instructions for the tasks that you are to complete.

5. The Library contains the legal authorities needed to complete the tasks. The case reports may be real, modified, or written solely for the purpose of this performance test. If the cases appear familiar to you, do not assume that they are precisely the same as you have read before. Read each thoroughly, as if it were new to you. You should assume that cases were decided in the jurisdictions and on the dates shown. In citing cases from the Library, you may use abbreviations and omit page citations.

6. Your response must be written in the answer book provided. You should concentrate on the materials provided, but you should also bring to bear on the problem your general knowledge of the law. What you have learned in law school and elsewhere provides the general background for analyzing the problem; the File and Library provide the specific materials with which you must work.

7. Although there are no restrictions on how you apportion your time, you should probably allocate at least 45 minutes to reading and organizing before you begin writing your response. You may make notes anywhere in the test materials, but may not tear out pages from this booklet.

8. Your response will be graded on its compliance with instructions and on its content, thoroughness, and organization.

File

Peabody

v.

Middletown

1. Memorandum to Applicant   5-376

2. Central Franklin Legal Services Memorandum to all Attorneys & Paralegals   5-377

3. Complaint for Violation of Civil Rights   5-378

4. Transcript of Interview with Peabody and Jeff Whittaker   5-380

# CENTRAL FRANKLIN LEGAL SERVICES

Middletown Office
1407 Main Street
Middletown, Franklin

TO: Associate

FROM: Sandy Kramer

DATE: July 29, 20X3

RE: *Peabody v. Middletown*

As you know, a few weeks ago we filed a Complaint against the City on behalf of a class of homeless individuals challenging the Mayor's "Clean Sweep" policy, which we allege is deliberately intended to drive the homeless out of Middletown. Counsel for the defendant moved to dismiss our claims on the ground that we had failed to state a cause of action on any claim, and yesterday that motion was heard. Judge Harris ruled that on the facts alleged we had stated valid claims. She went on to say that our third cause of action, regarding the seizure and destruction of property, turns largely on Fourth Amendment issues, and she believes the issues can be resolved at an early stage. She said she would treat defendant's original motion as a motion for partial summary judgment on the property claim, and I told the judge we would file a cross-motion for partial summary judgment.

The attached file consists of the relevant portion of our Complaint and a transcript of the intake interview I conducted with named plaintiff Joe Peabody and homeless activist Jeff Whittaker.

My research turned up a case, *Bishop v. Carter*, that seems at first to be directly against us, but I think we can distinguish it.

Here is what I want you to do. Please prepare an affidavit for Peabody that can be used in support of the Third Cause of Action. A copy of our office memorandum on affidavits is attached. Also, if your examination of the materials turns up any key facts that cannot be included in Peabody's affidavit, but nonetheless should be brought to the court's attention, please state what they are, indicate why they are important, and explain why they should not be set forth in Peabody's affidavit.

CENTRAL FRANKLIN
LEGAL SERVICES

MEMORANDUM REQUIREMENTS

TO: All Attorneys & Paralegals

FROM: Executive Committee

RE: Affidavits in Support of Motions or Other Requests for Judicial or Administrative Action

Affidavits should meet the following requirements:

1. Affidavits are to be limited to statements of fact. The facts should be those necessary to support the legal position asserted in the motion or other request.

2. The facts should be presented in numbered paragraphs, and each numbered paragraph, to the extent possible, should contain only one factual statement.

3. Only those facts that are personally known to the affiant and which are truthful, logically relevant, and material shall be included.

Assume the person signing the affidavit will be subject to cross-examination concerning the contents of the affidavit. Particular care must be taken to ensure that his or her credibility will not be impeached.

The materials you rely upon may not always contain precisely the facts you need. There often are, however, other facts that can be inferred from existing statements of the person who will sign the affidavit. If you have a good-faith basis to believe that he or she has personal knowledge of those inferred facts, include them. We will then check with the person to confirm he or she actually does have personal knowledge of the inferred fact.

Captions, signature lines, and sworn acknowledgement will be added by support staff.

Sandra Kramer
Central Franklin Legal Services
1407 Main Street
Middletown, Franklin

Attorney for Plaintiff
JOE PEABODY

UNITED STATES DISTRICT COURT

for the

CENTRAL DISTRICT OF FRANKLIN

JOE PEABODY, on behalf of himself and all others similarly situated, Plaintiff, v. CITY OF MIDDLETOWN, Defendant.	No. 07-491-KRI **COMPLAINT FOR VIOLATION OF CIVIL RIGHTS SEEKING INJUNCTIVE AND DECLARATORY RELIEF**

Plaintiff Joe Peabody alleges as follows:

1. This action arises under the First, Fourth, Eighth and Fourteenth Amendments of the United States Constitution and 42 USC Sections 1983 and 1988.

2. This Court has jurisdiction over the claims arising under federal law pursuant to 28 USC Sections 1331 and 1343.

3. Plaintiff Joe Peabody is a homeless resident of the City of Middletown, Franklin. He brings this action on behalf of himself and other homeless persons in the City of Middletown.

4. Defendant City of Middletown is a municipality incorporated under the laws of the State of Franklin. The city has adopted and implemented the "Clean Sweep Program" described below.

5. The Clean Sweep Program is a police enforcement program directed at minor offenses committed by homeless persons such as sleeping or camping in public parks or obstructing sidewalks. The Program in all its aspects is the official policy of the city and endorsed by its mayor.

* * * *

THIRD CAUSE OF ACTION: CONFISCATION OF PROPERTY IN VIOLATION OF FOURTH AMENDMENT OF THE UNITED STATES CONSTITUTION

32. Plaintiffs incorporate the allegations of the preceding paragraphs.

33. As part of the Clean Sweep Program, defendant has confiscated the property of numerous homeless persons.

34. The property so confiscated is not used as evidence of any crime, but is simply discarded at the time of confiscation.

35. The property so confiscated has often consisted of all the worldly possessions of homeless persons, including necessities of life such as clothing and bedding.

36. Defendant has advanced no justification for the seizure and destruction of plaintiffs' property, and its presumed interest in maintaining the aesthetic appearance of its streets and parks cannot outweigh the interest of plaintiff class members in retaining their right to privacy and the exclusive possession and control of their property.

37. Defendant's confiscation of property of homeless persons violates the Fourth Amendment of the United States Constitution as incorporated in and applied to the states through the Fourteenth Amendment.

* * * *

TRANSCRIPT OF INTERVIEW WITH JOE PEABODY AND JEFF WHITTAKER

ATTORNEY KRAMER (Q): This is an initial interview with Jeff Whittaker, director of the Middletown Homeless Coalition, and Joe Peabody, a homeless Vietnam veteran who has identified himself as a willing plaintiff should we decide to file a lawsuit. Both Jeff and Joe have given their permission for this session to be recorded and possibly transcribed. Is that right, gentlemen?

JEFF WHITTAKER (W): Right.

JOE PEABODY (P): Right.

Q: So, let's get started. Jeff, you said on the phone that you wanted to discuss filing a lawsuit challenging the city's Clean Sweep Program. I must say I've been giving that some thought myself. From what I've heard, it's making things pretty miserable for the homeless.

P: You heard that right, ma'am. They're trying to drive homeless folks out of Middletown, and they're just about succeeding. Believe me, if I had some other place to go, I'd be out of here myself.

W: The newspapers don't know half of what's going on. You wouldn't believe some of the stories I've heard.

Q: Why don't you give me some examples. You know, the worst things you've heard – things you think might be illegal.

W: It's hard to know where to start, so much is going on. Like, people have these arrest warrants over their heads, now, so they never know when they might get picked up and hauled down to the jail. So they're afraid to ask for a handout or do anything, except kind of sneak around.

Q: They're issuing arrest warrants for sleeping in the park or obstructing a doorway?

P: Not the first time. That's not how it works. Sometimes they take you downtown and book you, but sometimes they just cite you. You know, give you this ticket that says you've gotta go down to the court or send in an $80 fine by mail. As if a homeless guy is gonna have $80 to stick in the mail. And even if they book you, you get released unless there's a warrant out, and then they might hold you for a day or two.

Q: So the warrant is issued . . . when?

P: About the tenth time you don't show up at court or pay the fines. See, the judge just keeps track of how many fines you got, and when it gets to $800 or $900, then they put out this arrest warrant on you, and then they got it to use against you whenever they want.

Q: So are people serving jail time? That's what I thought this thing was all about: getting people off the street and into jail, so they won't bother other people.

W: No way. They don't have room in the jail, and they know the fines aren't gonna get paid. Half the time the charges are dismissed if they do take somebody in. This is about harassment, man. They want people to leave.

Q: So let me get this straight. If somebody is picked up and taken down to the jail and there is a warrant out, they might hold him a day or two, you said.

W: Right. Until he goes to court. But then most of the time it's either dismissed or he gets "time served." You know, he gets sentenced to two days in jail, but he's already done that, so he gets to walk.

Q: I see. So the warrant offenses are taken care of, and . . . .

W: It starts all over again.

Q: I get it. Joe, has this happened to you?

P: In the last few months, sure. Before that, you had to do something really dumb to get arrested. I've been on the streets for six years, and I've never seen it like this. Used to be the cops would kind of look out for you; you know, take you over to detox if you were really out of it, but basically leave you alone.

Q: So we've got these arrests that sound like they're mainly meant to hassle you. What else?

P: Well, people are most upset about losing their stuff. I mean, it's no fun to have some cop roust you at five in the morning and take you down to the jail, but then people have to try to replace their stuff. You know, scrounging a sleeping bag or something so they can get through the night. I know a guy whose wheelchair got thrown away, and we've had people lose their family pictures and their medicine – all kinds of stuff.

Q: And the police are doing this? Or is it that the stuff gets left behind and disappears or something?

P: Oh, no. They're doing it. I mean, sometimes stuff gets stolen, but we try to look out for that. You can always get somebody to watch your stuff. But see, when they sweep the park and make everybody leave, then the stuff you can't carry, or other people's stuff, that goes right to the dump, as far as I know.

Q: So it's not just the police? I mean, somebody else comes and hauls it away?

P: Guys in those orange jumpsuit things. You know, the guys that collect garbage.

Q: Right. Sounds like city sanitation workers, all right. And you've seen this?

P: Lots of times. The worst was when I was the one who was supposed to watch everybody's stuff while they all went to eat breakfast at the mission, and the police vans come up with a garbage truck right behind them and order us out of the park. I took my shopping cart and as much as I could carry of my friend's stuff, but the other six carts I was guarding, and the piles of stuff on the ground, were thrown right into the dump truck. They didn't even bother going through it. The landfill where they take the stuff is way the hell out – must be in the next county – but even if you make it out there, there's no use. The stuff is gone, man. Even if you can dig something out that you recognize, anything valuable is long gone.

Q: Jeff, have you seen belongings just thrown away like that, too?

W: Oh, yeah, we've got plenty of people who can testify to that. I mean, if you've got a backpack or an iPod or something like that on you when they arrest you, you get that back. But if they take you to the jail, they don't let you take a shopping cart, or a duffel bag, or even a sleeping bag, man. They make you leave it behind, and then they either throw it in a dump truck or leave it there to be stolen.

Q: And do the police ever look for drugs or anything?

W: Well, that varies. If they think somebody's dealing, they'll go through his stuff with a fine-tooth comb, and if they find anything, that guy's likely to do real time. But on this Clean Sweep thing, mostly they don't bother.

Q: Even though sometimes, I imagine, somebody might have some drugs along with their other stuff?

W: Well, not that many of the people we work with use drugs, and the ones who do are wise to what might happen; you know, that they might be arrested for camping or urinating in public or whatever at any time. So you aren't gonna find many people who actually carry drugs on them these days.

Q: So if the police did go through shopping carts or duffel bags or whatever, they might turn up some drugs, sometimes, but most likely that just gets thrown away too?

W: Right. That's not what this is about. This is about getting rid of the homeless, man. However you have to do it.

Q: And you've personally seen the police – or sanitation workers – take people's stuff and throw it away?

W: Yeah, because the Coalition has been documenting what the city is doing. We have people stationed at certain parks and other places two or three times a week – taking pictures, talking to people, just watching what goes on. And I go out myself as often as I can. I used to be homeless myself, you know. I know what it's like.

Q: We'll no doubt have to get back together at some point, but I'd like to get as much detail as I can today, to help me decide which of the possible legal theories is going to fit. And if we're going to try to get an injunction, I have to show that Joe and other people you guys know about really do stand to lose some property, because of where they've been sleeping during the day, and where the police are coming through with these sweeps and so forth.

P: So, do you want me to talk about that?

Q: Yeah, I do. Why don't you start with where you were the times you've been arrested or moved out of an area.

P: Okay. Up until about four months ago I used to sleep in Founder's Park most nights. There was a group of us who hung together and had a certain area where we kept our stuff and went to sleep when it got dark.

Q: Uh-hmm. And Clean Sweep started four months ago?

P: It was like war had been declared, man. Five o'clock in the morning, bullhorns and everything. I didn't see 'em, but somebody said they even had dogs in the police car.

Q: And did they arrest you that time or just move you out?

P: We were all cited for sleeping in a park, which is a crime, you know, only they never cite people who go over there to sunbathe, or the ones who fell asleep at those outdoor concerts.

Q: I'm sure you're right. So they just cited you the first time?

P: Yeah. And made us get out of there. They said they'd arrest us if we didn't move fast, and they meant it. The vans were all ready to go.

Q: And do you happen to know what date that was?

W: I do. It was March 18th.

Q: Was any property taken that time?

P: Yeah. We'd been there for a while, and there was too much to carry. We left some tents we'd rigged up, some extra blankets, a couple of boxes of canned food, and a lot of the cans and bottles we'd been collecting to take to the recycling center.

Q: Which is one of the ways you get cash, right?

P: About the only way, for the guys I hang out with.

Q: I think you said you had actually been taken into custody at one point. When and where was that?

P: It's happened a few times. The first time was about three months ago. I was taken down to the jail and released without them even citing me, but they made me leave my stuff, and by the time I got back, most of it was gone. Not the personal stuff I care about most, because that was in the backpack I took with me, but I lost an almost-new sleeping bag somebody gave me, and my warm jacket and some food and stuff.

Q: And where did that happen?

P: About a block from the state employment office. I go down there every week to see if there's any jobs opened up that I can do. You know how it works. You have to sign up on a list when you get there, and then you have to wait two or three hours to see one of the counselors. They don't let you bring shopping carts inside, so after I signed the list I went back outside and sat down in the doorway of this empty building to wait.

Q: What kind of building?

P: I think the state owns it, but like I said, it's empty. I don't know what it used to be. Some kind of offices, maybe.

Q: And they arrested you for what? Blocking the doorway?

P: Well, they said that, but they didn't book me. I think they took me in just to teach me a lesson about not moving fast enough. They do that a lot, you know – take you a couple miles away so you lose your place in line or lose your stuff or whatever.

Q: But some other times you've actually been charged?

P: Right. I've been cited a lot – maybe ten times, now. And I've been taken to the jail two other times. The first time I was released after a few hours, but the second time there was an outstanding warrant, and I stayed in for the weekend. Then that Monday I was let out for time served.

Q: So you've had contact with the police 10 or 12 times in the last four months?

P: Yep. They got cops that do nothing but hassle people, all day long, on this Clean Sweep thing.

Q: Tell me all the different locations where this happened, if you can.

P: Okay. Twice in Founder's Park. Three or four times in that little park across from City Hall. What's it called?

W: Jefferson Square.

P: Right, Jefferson Square. A couple of times under the freeway that runs along Oak Street – you know, where it crosses Thirteenth. I usually try to sleep there if it rains, only lately you can't go there too early, and you have to be out right after daylight. Another time next to the Main Street bridge. And the rest have been doorways, I think. I don't know the addresses. But there are some doorways down around First and Second Street that are pretty sheltered, and lots of times they don't check down there, since it's deserted at night.

Q: These are the doorways of businesses, or what?

P: I guess so. I'm not sure on all of them. Nobody lives there, I know that, but they are more like office buildings.

Q: Okay, we can track down more on that later if we need to. So as I understand it, you don't try to set up camp or sleep in any one spot like you used to, but just sort of move around and try to keep ahead of the cops.

P: Yeah, as best we can. There's a group of us that tries to stick together.

Q: And you mostly bed down in parks or on other public property, but sometimes you're on some portion of private property that's open to the public?

P: Right.

Q: If we could get back to the property losses for a minute. Did you lose any property the time they arrested you for a warrant, and kept you for the weekend?

P: No, a buddy of mine was watching it at the time. I don't have anything that won't fit into my backpack and one shopping cart anymore. See, somebody can at least take one other shopping cart if they have to move, so now me and my friends try to leave enough guys with the stuff so they can actually move it if the cops come along.

Q: But there's still the danger those people could be arrested, and everybody's stuff dumped or left unprotected, right?

P: Right. And that's what's happening. A lot. When our money runs out and the guys are trying to get by on the free meals that are provided by the mission and other places, they're having to take turns eating. There's no way you can eat in shifts, most places, 'cause they let everybody in at once. So, like, if people get hungry enough they might take a chance on leaving their stuff, with maybe one guy to keep scroungers away, and then they find out it was hauled to the dump while they were gone.

Q: Okay. Let's talk about your shopping cart a bit. Since we're going to be arguing that the stuff in it is valuable, at least to you, maybe I could get a little inventory. Could you tell me in some detail what's in there?

P: Sure. I've got a good sleeping bag – dirty, but not ripped or anything – and that's kind of rolled up with this piece of foam I use as a mattress and tied with a piece of rope. I've also got a jug of water in there, just a plastic jug, and usually I kind of shove my coat in there too, unless I'm wearing it. And I have an old duffel bag, where I store books, papers, my mess kit, and stuff I find in the garbage that I think I might be able to sell to somebody.

Q: Anything else?

P: Well, I've got a flashlight. I used to keep some tools in there too, for when I could find work, only those got stolen that time they took me down to the jail. There's also a little one-burner cookstove and some fuel. And on top of all that stuff is a double garbage bag with my extra clothes, some towels, and a kind of ratty blanket. And then in that little rack at the back, the child seat, I guess it is, that's where I keep my backpack. My backpack has the most valuable stuff, because usually I can take that with me.

Q: Why don't you tell me the kinds of things you carry in your backpack, because there's no guarantee that they won't make you leave that behind in the future.

P: Well, extra cash, if I have any. And I was married for a while, so I've got some old letters, and a few pictures. My parents died when I was a kid, but I've even got a few pictures of them, and an old address book that has the names of some of my parents' friends, and relatives I've never met and stuff. Someday I'm going to go back and see if I can find any of them. And then I've got some medical records and cards I have to have when I go to the county hospital, and some prescription medicine I have to take . . . .

Q: It might be helpful to know more about the medicine. Like, if it was for a serious condition that might be life-threatening if you didn't have it . . . .

P: I got some pills and an inhaler I have to use for asthma, and this new tranquilizer I take – I forget the name of it – because I have post-traumatic stress disorder from the time I was in Vietnam.

Q: Okay. Anything else in the backpack?

P: Some prescription glasses, paper towels, some shampoo and toothpaste and stuff . . . that's it, I think.

Q: Thanks. I'm sorry to have to get into so much detail, but that's what we need if we're going to convince the court that these things are essential to you, and that it's outrageous for the city to take them and just throw them away.

P: I sure hope you can stop it. Believe me, if I could afford a room, I'd be off the streets in a minute, but I haven't had more than a few days of work since I came here, six years ago. There's no place else I can go.

Library

Peabody

v.

Middletown

1. The Constitution of the
   United States of America   5-388

2. United States Code   5-389

3. *Bishop v. Carter*   5-390

THE CONSTITUTION OF THE UNITED STATES OF AMERICA

Amendment IV

The right of the people to be secure in their persons, houses, papers, and effects, against unreasonable searches and seizures, shall not be violated, and no warrants shall issue, but upon probable cause, supported by oath or affirmation, and particularly describing the place to be searched, and the persons or things to be seized.

UNITED STATES CODE

Title 42, Section 1983

Every person who, under color of any statute, ordinance, regulation, custom, or usage, of any State or Territory or the District of Columbia, subjects, or causes to be subjected, any citizen of the United States or other person within the jurisdiction thereof to the deprivation of any rights, privileges, or immunities secured by the Constitution and laws, shall be liable to the party injured in an action at law, suit in equity, or other proper proceeding for redress, except that in any action brought against a judicial officer for an act or omission taken in such officer's judicial capacity, injunctive relief shall not be granted unless a declaratory decree was violated or declaratory relief was unavailable. For the purposes of this section, any Act of Congress applicable exclusively to the District of Columbia shall be considered to be a statute of the District of Columbia.

BISHOP v. CARTER

United States Court of Appeals for the Fifteenth Circuit (2003)

William Bishop brought an action against Alvin Carter, Mayor of Garden City, Franklin; James Reilly, Chief of Police of Garden City; and Garden City itself alleging that the defendants violated his constitutional rights by his arrest and confiscation of his property. The complaint sought damages and an injunction against further violations. The District Court granted summary judgment for the defendants. On this appeal by Mr. Bishop, we affirm the judgment.

According to his affidavit, Bishop was a homeless person living on the streets of Garden City, making a living as a street musician. In April 2001, he became "the Homeless Task Force Coordinator," *i.e.*, an apparently self-appointed spokesman for homeless persons, speaking for six evenings in April on KGC TV in opposition to Mayor Carter's homeless policy.

Bishop lived in a tent at Civic Center Plaza, a public square owned by the city. One evening in April, two Garden City police officers seized his tent and took it away in a police vehicle. The officers told Bishop that Mayor Carter had "directed the immediate removal of tents of homeless people from the plaza."

On the morning of July 6, 2001, police arrived in force at the plaza and, pursuant to earlier notices, told the persons who slept in the plaza that they must leave it. Bishop told the police that the shelters were full and there was no place to go. The police insisted that he leave. When the media arrived, Bishop made a public statement in opposition to the mayor's homeless policy. He continued to refuse to leave. His personal property was then seized, including a guitar and case, bedding, clothes, toiletries, food preparation items, a radio, cash, some jewelry, books, and papers. He was also arrested and jailed for four days. Much of the property was destroyed. The criminal case against him was later dismissed.

Bishop sued the defendants alleging that Mayor Carter and Chief Reilly "deliberately and intentionally conspired" to violate his right to privacy and to assemble, associate and express his views in support of the homeless in violation of the First Amendment to the United States Constitution; that these defendants also deliberately and intentionally conspired to violate his right to be secure in person and property against unreasonable seizure and arrest in violation of the Fourth Amendment; and that the defendants also deliberately and intentionally conspired to deprive him of liberty and property in violation of the Due Process and Equal Protection Clauses of the Fourteenth Amendment. Bishop alleged that this conspiracy, conducted under color of state law, violated 42 USC Sections 1983 and 1985.

The defendants submitted the affidavit of Police Captain Arturo Medina stating that he arrested Bishop on July 6, 2001, after Bishop had been advised four times to leave the civic center area and had also over a period of one and one-half hours refused to do so. Medina attested that Bishop's property had been confiscated but not destroyed. He further stated that he had made the decision to have Bishop arrested and that "neither Mayor Carter nor Chief Reilly had any role in the decision to arrest Mr. Bishop." The district court granted summary judgment for the defendants, and Bishop appeals.

Bishop first argues on appeal that his arrest violated the First Amendment because it was a suppression of his right of free speech. He contends that his sleeping in the park as well as his communications to the media were expressions protected by the First Amendment; that his sleeping in a public place "dramatized" the plight of the homeless.

Although sleeping would seem to be the antithesis of speaking, we need not determine whether Bishop's conduct was a form of expression. Bishop claims he was arrested in retaliation for his speech, in violation of the First Amendment. To support the claim, Bishop has produced not the slightest evidence that his arrest by Captain Medina was for any communication made by him or that his arrest was ordered by Mayor Carter and Chief Reilly. Bishop's continued presence in the plaza was a violation of Franklin Penal Code Section 647(i), which makes it a misdemeanor to lodge in any place, whether public or private, without the permission of the owner. As far as the record shows, Captain Medina alone decided to arrest him for this crime.

Second, Bishop argues that his arrest was a violation of the Fourth Amendment. This argument presupposes that he was arrested for exercising his right of free speech. The argument fails with his failure to produce evidence to substantiate his free speech claim and his failure to implicate either the mayor or the police chief.

Bishop additionally contends that the destruction of his property violated the Fourteenth Amendment. Accepting for the purposes of summary judgment that much of his property was destroyed, we find no evidence it was destroyed in violation of the Fourteenth Amendment. Bishop asserts no facts showing that the police behaved unreasonably. To sustain the claim he must show that the taking of the property was unreasonable. Mere negligence of the police would not violate the Due Process Clause, and he would have no federal claim for such negligence if it occurred. Nor does Bishop make any showing whatsoever that the mayor or police chief effected the destruction, which Bishop concedes was contrary to city policy.

AFFIRMED.

VI. EDITORS' PREPARED GRADING GUIDE FOR PRACTICE QUESTION:

PEABODY v. MIDDLETOWN

Our editors have prepared a substantive grading guide outline to help you evaluate your answer. We have approached this from the perspective of the model answer structure typically used by a bar exam grader. After you complete a draft answer, compare and contrast it with the sample answer that follows this grading guide. If you missed any key issues in your analysis consider updating and perfecting your answer.

___ Affidavit

    ___ Background: Peabody is a homeless resident of Middletown

    ___ Personal property

        ___ All belongings contained and transported in shopping cart

        ___ Property is valuable to Peabody

        ___ Inventory of property in shopping cart

    ___ Peabody's observations

        ___ Homeless person's wheelchair seized
        ___ Homeless people's family pictures seized
        ___ Homeless people's medication seized
        ___ Incident where police and sanitation workers confiscated property belonging to multiple homeless individuals who were inside the mission eating breakfast
        ___ Seized property is simply discarded

    ___ Arrests and citations

        ___ Peabody never arrested or charged with a crime until recently
        ___ During the past few months, multiple arrests and citations
        ___ Seized property not kept as evidence of crime
        ___ Forced to relocate constantly to avoid arrest/citation or property seizure

___ Additional relevant key facts that should not be included in Peabody affidavit

    ___ Peabody lacks personal knowledge of certain facts regarding illegal drugs
        ___ Police discard any illegal drugs found
        ___ Police do not retain any such drugs for evidence of crime
        ___ Whittaker knows that most homeless people who receive services from the Coalition do not use illegal drugs, and the few who do use them generally do not carry the drugs with them

    ___ Even if Peabody were a user of illegal drugs, including such information in his affidavit could harm his credibility

VII. SAMPLE ANSWER TO PRACTICE QUESTION:

PEABODY v. MIDDLETOWN

AFFIDAVIT OF JOE PEABODY

1. My name is Joe Peabody.

2. I am an adult over the age of 18 years.

3. I have been a homeless person in Middletown, Franklin, for six years.

4. I own a shopping cart containing property that is valuable to me, including bedding (sleeping bag, foam pad, and blanket), clothing (including my coat), towels, and a plastic water jug, a duffel bag containing my mess kit, books, personal papers.

5. I also have some discarded property that I found and believe to have resale value, including a flashlight, one-burner cookstove, and fuel for the stove.

6. I use a backpack to hold what I believe to be my most valuable possessions, including any cash I have at the time, photographs (including pictures of my deceased parents), personal correspondence, an old address book with contact information for relatives and family friends, personal hygiene materials (toothpaste, shampoo, and paper towels), medical records, cards that allow me access to health care at the county hospital, and prescription medications.

7. I use my shopping cart to store and transport all of my other possessions, which are listed above in Paragraphs 4 and 5.

8. The prescription medication mentioned in Paragraph 6 includes tablets and an inhaler to treat my asthma.

9. The prescription medication mentioned in Paragraph 6 also includes a tranquilizer that I take because of the post-traumatic stress disorder I suffer from as a result of my military service in Vietnam.

10. I personally know a homeless person whose wheelchair was seized and discarded by the Middletown police and city sanitation workers.

11. I personally know a homeless person whose family pictures were seized and discarded by the Middletown police and city sanitation workers.

12. I personally know a homeless person whose medication was seized and discarded by the Middletown police and city sanitation workers.

13. On one occasion, when I was watching the property of other homeless persons while they went to eat a free breakfast at the mission, I personally witnessed the Middletown police

and city sanitation workers seize all property that I was unable to carry. The police and sanitation workers did not inventory the seized property. Instead, the property was merely thrown into a garbage truck.

14. During the past four months, Middletown police have issued me approximately ten citations and arrested me three times.

15. Prior to receiving the citations and arrests mentioned above, I had never been cited or arrested by Middletown police.

16. On every occasion when I was arrested, any property seized was not used as evidence of any crime, but simply discarded.

17. Because of the actions of the Middletown police and city sanitation workers, I am forced to relocate constantly to avoid citation or arrest.

18. I personally know other homeless people who are forced to relocate constantly to avoid citation or arrest.

19. I have never refused to comply with a police order to vacate a specific location.

ADDITIONAL RELEVANT KEY FACTS

The information provided by Jeff Whittaker in the intake interview concerning the police's treatment of illegal drugs (in particular, their general practice of merely discarding any drugs found) when confiscating homeless persons' property is important because it strongly supports Paragraph 34 of the Complaint; *i.e.*, the allegation that confiscated property is discarded immediately and not used as evidence of crime. We should not include this information in Peabody's affidavit, however, because it seems that he probably lacks the required personal knowledge of this police practice as required by law. Peabody never stated that he observed anything pertaining to illegal drugs, nor did he say anything about use of illegal drugs by himself or others, or suggest that he had knowledge of such use. Furthermore, even if Peabody does or did use illegal drugs, including this information in his affidavit may harm his credibility.

By contrast, Whittaker appears to have personal knowledge of these facts due to his work as director of the Middletown Homeless Coalition. More generally, Whittaker has personal knowledge that most of the homeless people served by the Coalition do not use illegal drugs, and those who do use illegal drugs generally do not carry the drugs with them.

RIGOS UNIFORM BAR REVIEW SERIES

MULTISTATE PERFORMANCE TEST (MPT) REVIEW

CHAPTER 6

TABLE OF REFERENCES TO THE ABA

MODEL RULES OF PROFESSIONAL CONDUCT

Title 1	***Client-Lawyer Relationship***	*Page*
1.1	Competence	401
1.2	Scope of Representation and Allocation of Authority	402
1.3	Diligence	403
1.4	Communication	403
1.5	Fees	404
1.6	Confidentiality of Information	407
1.7	Conflict of Interest: Current Clients	410
1.8	Conflict of Interest: Current Clients: Specific Rules	412
1.9	Duties to Former Clients	415
1.10	Imputation of Conflicts of Interest: General Rule	416
1.11	Former and Current Government Officers and Employees	417
1.12	Former Judge, Arbitrator, Mediator or Other Third-Party Neutral	417
1.13	Organization as Client	418
1.14	Client with Diminished Capacity	418
1.15	Safekeeping Property	419
1.16	Declining or Terminating Representation	420
1.17	Sale of Law Practice	422
1.18	Duties to Prospective Client	422

Title 2	***Counselor***	
2.1	Advisor	423
2.2	(Intermediary)	423
2.3	Evaluation for Use by Third Persons	424
2.4	Lawyer Serving as Third-Party Neutral	424

Title 3	***Advocate***	
3.1	Meritorious Claims and Contentions	424
3.2	Expediting Litigation	425
3.3	Candor Toward the Tribunal	425
3.4	Fairness to Opposing Party and Counsel	426
3.5	Impartiality and Decorum of the Tribunal	427

3.6	Trial Publicity	427
3.7	Lawyer as Necessary Witness	428
3.8	Special Responsibilities of a Prosecutor	429
3.9	Advocate in Nonadjudicative Proceedings	430

Title 4 — *Transactions With Persons Other Than Clients*

4.1	Truthfulness in Statements to Others	430
4.2	Communication with Person Represented by Counsel	430
4.3	Dealing with Unrepresented Person	431
4.4	Respect for Rights of Third Persons	431

Title 5 — *Law Firms and Associations*

5.1	Responsibilities of Partners, Managers, and Supervisory Lawyers	431
5.2	Responsibilities of a Subordinate Lawyer	432
5.3	Responsibilities Regarding Nonlawyer Assistants	432
5.4	Professional Independence of a Lawyer	432
5.5	Unauthorized Practice of Law; Multijurisdictional Practice of Law	433
5.6	Restrictions on Right to Practice	434
5.7	Responsibilities Regarding Law-related Services	434

Title 6 — *Public Service*

6.1	Voluntary *Pro Bono* Publico Service	434
6.2	Accepting Appointments	434
6.3	Membership in Legal Services Organization	435
6.4	Law Reform Activities Affecting Client Interests	435
6.5	Nonprofit and Court-Annexed Limited Legal Services Programs	435

Title 7 — *Information About Legal Services*

7.1	Communications Concerning a Lawyer's Services	435
7.2	Advertising	435
7.3	Direct Contact with Prospective Clients	436
7.4	Communication of Fields of Practice and Specialization	437
7.5	Firm Names and Letterheads	437
7.6	Political Contributions to Obtain Government Legal Engagements or Appointments by Judges	438

Title 8 — *Maintaining the Integrity of the Profession*

8.1	Bar Admission and Disciplinary Matters	438
8.2	Judicial and Legal Officials	438
8.3	Reporting Professional Misconduct	438
8.4	Misconduct	439
8.5	Disciplinary Authority; Choice of Law	440

OPENING ARGUMENT AND PRIMARY ISSUES

ABA MODEL RULES OF PROFESSIONAL CONDUCT (RPC)

The following material is a brief overview of most of the key issues of the lawyer's Professional Responsibility (PR) rules. NCBE directly tests these PR rules in performance task questions and many states still incorporate a lawyer's professional restraints in traditional essay question subjects. These professional rules are important to consider if the tasks indicate a lawyer is personally involved in a representation capacity.

The following ethical performance task questions and answers assume the state in question follows the ABA's current model rules as of the previous ABA annual meeting date. Candidates should check with their local state bar authority to determine if the individual jurisdiction's ethics rules are tested and if they vary from the ABA model rules.

Candidates in jurisdictions that test professional responsibility using the MPRE should consult the *Rigos UBE Review Series – MPRE* for complete textual coverage, Magic Memory Outlines® software, and over 350 multiple-choice questions with Make Your Own Exam software drills. This book and other Primer Series publications are sold at law school bookstores throughout the nation and online at http://www.rigos.net/register_v2.asp.

If the call of the essay task assignment is general – "create a memorandum opinion why the law firm should be disqualified from the representation" – the on-point ABA Rule's technical language should be stated in your answer. These will score you easy points, let the grader know you are proficient in the right professional responsibility section, and understand the essence of the ethical rule possibly at play.

Many frequently tested ethical Rules have an "opening argument." Such a brief, focused rule statement shows you understand the detailed significance of an ethical subject. The opening argument also suggests to the grader that she is about to read a well-organized and thoughtful recitation of the applicable rules. The below primary issue statements can be discussed up front or integrated into your task answers.

- **Professional Responsibility Opening Argument:** The Rules of Professional Conduct (RPCs) set the minimum standard that no lawyer may fall below without being subject to professional discipline.

- **Sample Primary Issue Statements:**

  - A lawyer must provide a client reasonably competent representation, which requires the legal knowledge, skill, thoroughness, and preparation necessary for the representation. Here, . . .

  - A lawyer must communicate sufficiently to allow the client to make informed decisions about objectives and settlement offers and report errors to the client. Here, . . .

  - A lawyer's fees shall be reasonable considering the skills required, amount involved, novelty and difficulty, time involved, opportunities foregone, average customary fee in the locale, relationship, expertise, reputation, experience, and result achieved in the representation. Here, . . .

  - Retainers are fully earned when received and client prepayments and advances must go into the trust account in most states. Here, . . .

- A lawyer may reveal client confidential information to the extent necessary to prevent reasonably certain death or substantial bodily injury. Here, . . .

- A lawyer may reveal confidential information to prevent the client from committing a crime or fraud resulting in substantial injury in furtherance of which the client has used or is using the lawyer's services. Here, . . .

- A lawyer shall not act as an advocate against a person the lawyer is representing in another matter. Here, . . .

- A lawyer shall not represent a client if that representation is materially limited by other clients' interests or the lawyer's personal considerations unless all clients consent which is confirmed in writing. Here, . . .

- A lawyer who has formerly represented a client in a matter shall not represent another person with adverse interests in the same or substantially related matter. Here, . . .

- While lawyers are associated in a firm, none of them shall knowingly represent a client when any one of them practicing alone would be so prohibited. Here, . . .

- A lawyer shall withdraw if the representation would result in a violation of the RPCs, if the lawyer has developed an impaired ability, or is affirmatively discharged by a client. Here, . . .

- A lawyer may withdraw if the client is pursuing criminal action and the lawyer is being used in the commission thereof, the client's objective is extremely repugnant, the burden on the lawyer is unreasonable, or other good cause for withdrawal exists. Here, . . .

- A lawyer may withdraw if there is a reasonable time for the client to retain succeeding counsel, client papers are returned, and all unearned fees refunded. Here, . . .

- In domestic relations representation, a lawyer may not usually charge fees on a contingency basis, have sexual relations with the client, have opposing counsel who is related, or have only an oral agreement with the client. Here, . . .

- A lawyer shall not knowingly make a false statement of fact or law to a tribunal and must promptly notify the court to correct any significant past falsity. Here, . . .

- A lawyer shall not falsify evidence or counsel, assist, or induce a witness to testify falsely or flee the jurisdiction. Here, . . .

- A lawyer is responsible for the improper conduct of subordinates if they directly order the conduct or with knowledge of the specific conduct fail to avoid, correct, or mitigate the consequences. Here, . . .

- A lawyer with actual personal knowledge of a committed violation of the MRPCs that raise a substantial question as to another lawyer's honesty, trustworthiness, or fitness shall inform the appropriate professional authority. Here, . . .

- A lawyer is in violation of MRPCs if they engage in conduct involving dishonesty, fraud, deceit, or misrepresentation even if such conduct is not related to the practice of law. Here, . . .

RIGOS PRIMER SERIES UBE REVIEW

MULTISTATE PERFORMANCE TEST (MPT) REVIEW

CHAPTER 6

ABA MODEL RULES OF PROFESSIONAL CONDUCT (RPC)

> **MPT Tip:** While professional responsibility is not usually separately tested, candidates should always be on the lookout for these issues any time a lawyer is involved in the fact pattern.

This material is a summary of the ABA's Model Rules and includes current (2017) Ethics Committee statements and recommendations including the 20/20 amendments. The MPT tests the professional responsibility (PR) subjects as a part of performance task questions about once a year. Look for the word "lawyer," "attorney," or "law firm" in the facts. Examples include a corporate governance question in which a lawyer is advising both the entity and another adverse constituent, conflicting shareholders or evaluate whether a motion to disqualify a law firm will be successful. Discuss the PR issues either before or after the substantive portion; do not usually mix the two.

I. COMPETENCE, SCOPE OF REPRESENTATION, AND FEES

The following group of ethical rules are often combined on the UBE.

> **MPT Tip:** A lawyer-client relationship may be express or implied and may be created by a failure to affirmatively reject a prospective client's reasonable belief of professional representation.

A. Competence – MRPC 1.1

Lawyers must competently represent their clients. This requires the legal knowledge, skill, thoroughness, and preparation reasonably necessary for the legal matter handled.

1. Proficiency Required: Competent representation is usually based on personal experience and lawyers should not accept employment beyond their competency. Lack of experience in a given area is not conclusive evidence of incompetence because all persons who pass the bar exam are presumed competent to research and practice any general area of law. However, a lawyer cannot charge the client for excessive research time spent learning details of the substantive law that an experienced lawyer would know. With client prior informed consent a lawyer may associate with another attorney who has the necessary competency, but the client must agree to accept the association arrangement.

2. Required Standard: The standard is usually that of a general practitioner, but may be elevated if the lawyer held himself out as an expert such as an LL.M. in taxation.

3. Emergency Situation: In an emergency, a lawyer may make a best effort until it is possible to refer the client to a more competent practitioner.

4. Maintaining Competence: A lawyer must keep abreast of changes in the area of practice. Usually this means participating in relevant continuing legal education (CLE).

> **MPT Tip:** Incompetence is often combined on the exam questions with delay (MRPC 1.3) and a failure to communicate with the client (MRPC 1.4).

5. Legal Malpractice Relationship: Legal malpractice theories include breach of contract (reasonable care implied), tort (misrepresentation or negligence), or breach of fiduciary duty (confidentiality, loyalty, and honest dealings).

a. Standards Differ: The MRPCs do not create a private cause of action or necessarily set the standards of practice for purposes of civil liability. Evidence of a disciplinary violation or alleged violation may not be introduced in a malpractice lawsuit. However, an expert may incorporate the concepts underlying the MRPCs into an opinion on the reasonable legal standard of care to which the lawyer should have adhered.

b. Proof Required: The client generally must prove that "but for" the lawyer's malpractice, the client would have prevailed in the underlying matter ("case within a case").

B. Scope of Representation and Authority Allocation – MRPC 1.2

This Rule includes a variety of representation matters including who – the client or lawyer – makes which decisions and addresses related ethical restrictions on the client's directions over the lawyer. The scope of the lawyer's undertaking is also examined.

1. Representation Objectives: The client has the ultimate authority in determining the substantive objectives in the representation. This includes all of the major outcome-determinant decisions.

2. Lawyer's Decisions: Unless specified to the contrary, the lawyer has implied authorization to decide the means and tactics to achieve the objectives. This includes making most strategic and procedural decisions such as which causes of action to plead, the extent of discovery, professional courtesy to be extended to opposing counsel, and trial witness presentation choices. The lawyer should consult with the client on such details.

3. Client's Decisions – AJET: The client has the ultimate authority to make major litigation decisions. These include the questions of whether to (1) **a**ccept or reject a settlement offer; or in a criminal case, (2) **j**ury trial waiver, (3) **e**ntering a plea, or (4) **t**estifying at trial.

4. No Endorsement: A lawyer's representation of a client does not constitute approval or an endorsement of the client's political, social, or moral views and activities.

5. Counsel a Crime or Fraud: A lawyer shall not counsel or assist a client in perpetrating conduct that the lawyer knows is criminal or fraudulent. Prohibitions include planning and concealing ongoing unlawful activities, which is aiding and abetting; the lawyer must withdraw. However, the lawyer may attempt to determine the validity, scope, meaning, or application of the law to a past offense and discuss the legal consequences. A lawyer may in good faith counsel a client on how to gain legal standing necessary to challenge the law.

6. Client Urging MRPC Violation: If the client insists upon assistance from the lawyer not permitted by the MRPCs, the lawyer must consult with the client concerning the ethical limitations on the lawyer's conduct. The lawyer must tell the client that he cannot violate the disciplinary rules. If the client insists, the lawyer must attempt to withdraw.

7. Client Authority: In some states, a lawyer shall not willfully purport to act as a lawyer for any person without the prior authority of that person.

8. Limit of Scope Representation: Clients usually contractually retain a lawyer to handle all aspects of a matter, such as pursuing or defending all legal representation in a pre-defined cause of action. In many states, the scope of representation by a lawyer may be "limited" to a particular discrete aspect of a matter, such as only the trial court representation, but not an appeal or an expert arguing a highly technical motion. Scope restrictions must be reasonable under the circumstances, and the client must give informed consent after consultation.

> **MPT Tip:** A lawyer unilaterally making the client's **AJET** decisions is frequently tested.

C. Diligence – MRPC 1.3

A lawyer shall act with reasonable diligence and promptness in representing a client.

1. Dilatory Practices: The lawyer must act promptly and forcefully in pursuing the client's interests. Dilatory practices include an unreasonable delay in filing a lawsuit, procrastination in following up on a matter, or neglecting to return the client's calls or requests for information concerning the status of their case. If a lawyer is leaving the practice of law, substituted counsel must be appointed to handle the ongoing client representation. The client must be informed of the situation and the succeeding attorney. The client may decide to go elsewhere.

2. Legal Rules: Court deadlines control. A plaintiff's lawyer's worst nightmare is a statute of limitations (SOL) violation – failure to formally file a claim timely is ordinarily automatic malpractice. Effective calendaring and docket control systems are critical.

3. Representation Completion: Diligence includes carrying through the representation until the case is complete and/or the lawyer properly withdraws. The client must be informed of completion and any appeal possibility – preferably in writing – so she reasonably understands the lawyer's responsibility has ended and she needs to look elsewhere for advice and monitoring.

> **MPT Tip:** To violate MRPC 1.3, the lawyer's delay must be patently unreasonable.

D. Communication – MRPC 1.4

A lawyer shall regularly keep active clients reasonably informed about progress and developments in the status of their matter, any issues requiring informed consent, and any limitations on the lawyer. This includes notification that their electronic data may have been hacked. Any MRPC limitations should be explained if the client's expectations could involve a violation. All *bona fide* offers of settlement must be communicated to the client.

1. Informative Explanations: An explanation may be necessary so that clients can participate in making informed decisions and have a full understanding upon which informed consent is based. Any request for information by the client should be answered timely. Client telephone calls, emails, and letters should be returned promptly. If for some reason the time schedule or agreed timeline slips, the lawyer should inform the client before the due dates.

2. Written v. Oral: Oral communications are worth the paper they are written on. While the expectations of both parties start with the representation agreement, it is also a good idea to send a letter at various intervals summarizing the status of the matter and what is ahead.

3. Special Situations: There are two exceptions to the communication duty.

a. Court Order or Rules: A court order may prohibit or limit the lawyer from sharing sensitive information with the client. For instance, a judge may issue a protective order forbidding the lawyer from communicating to their client trade secrets of a competitor that the lawyer learned in the discovery process.

b. Client Imprudent Reaction: If the disclosure of adverse information would cause the client to harm herself, the lawyer may delay the communication.

4. Communicate Mistakes: Ethical rulings direct that any mistake a lawyer makes must be communicated to the client. This could create a conflict of interest requiring client consent to allow the lawyer to go forward in the representation. See MRPC 1.8(h) infra at 414.

5. Communicate Termination: The client must ordinarily be informed when the attorney-client relationship has ended. This closing requirement intends to make it clear to the client that the lawyer's responsibility has terminated, and she is no longer monitoring the client's situation or possible changes in the law that may have adverse consequences.

> **MPT Tip:** Grievances involving a failure to communicate (MRPC 1.4) and failure to act in a diligent manner (MRPC 1.3) both suggest an incompetent lawyer (MRPC 1.1).

E. Fees – MRPC 1.5(a)

A lawyer may not charge an unreasonable fee (or recover unreasonable expenses), regardless of how characterized or calculated. Fee arrangements include fixed, flat hourly time, contingent, or blended. Fee dispute mediation or arbitration contract requirements in a fee agreement are usually enforceable in most states (ABA Op 02-425).

1. Reasonable Factors: In determining the reasonableness of a fee, there is no single bright-line test. Rather there is a multifactor analysis in most states. Consider the following multi-factor **SANTA** (case-related) and **REBER** (attorney-related) factors.

a. Skill Required: A complex antitrust class action will require more skill than an uncontested divorce and thus may be billed at a higher rate.

b. Amount Involved: Value added is currently a favored justification for higher fees. An attorney pursuing a personal injury case seeking millions of dollars in damages could bill more per hour than for a small dollar collection action.

c. Novelty and Difficulty: The novelty and difficulty of prevailing in the case is a factor in determining appropriate fee levels.

d. Time Involved / Opportunities Foregone: The time and labor required are probably the most widely accepted factors in setting fees. A case that the client knows will absorb all a lawyer's time and preclude other employment may be billed at a higher rate.

e. Average Customary Fee: This is the amount normally charged in the locality for similar legal services.

f. Relationship: The nature and length of the attorney's professional relationship with the client is a factor in determining the fee level. Satisfied long-term clients may pay more. Frequently a lawyer demands a fee and cost advance from a new client.

g. Expertise: An attorney who is the world's expert on corporate tax-free reorganizations would command a higher billing rate than a novice.

h. Basis of Fee: Whether the fee is fixed, hourly, or contingent is an important factor in determining the reasonableness question. Retainers and flat fees are now approved if agreed to in advance in a writing signed by the client.

i. Experience / Reputation of Lawyer: The more experience in the area and better the reputation of the attorney, the higher the usual expected fee.

j. Result: The result achieved in the controversy matters; winning attorneys are usually paid more than losing attorneys.

> **MPT Tip:** No one factor is conclusive in the **SANTA REBER** analysis. If the fee is questioned, the burden is on the lawyer to show that the fee is not unreasonable.

2. Double Billing: The ABA in Formal Opinion 93-379 stated that double billing the same time or work product to two clients is improper. This may involve billing two clients for the same research or the same transportation time.

3. Fee Agreement Required – MRPC 1.5(b): Fee and related cost agreements (alone or as a part of a more inclusive representation agreement) are often quite important to a determination of the reasonableness of the amount to be charged the client for the representation.

a. Includes: There must always be a fee agreement that allows the client to receive a reasonable and fair disclosure of all material elements of the engagement fee and cost billing practices. Some states require a writing if the fee exceeds a threshold amount, such as $1,000 or involves a flat fee or nonrefundable arrangement. The MRPC commentary suggest a simple memorandum avoids misunderstandings and clarifies expectations. Still, the Rule does not preclude an oral agreement as long as the lawyer is able to prove that the oral agreement gave the required reasonable and fair disclosure.

b. New Client: When the lawyer does not have an established business relationship with the client, an agreement is required. This communication will preferably be communicated before or within a reasonable time after commencing the representation.

c. Substantially Different: If the services to be performed or the fee details are substantially different from a previously-existing arrangement between the lawyer and client, the new factors involved in determining the charges must be communicated to the client.

d. Change in Circumstances: If developments occur that make an earlier fee estimate impossible, a revised estimate should be timely submitted to the client.

e. External Fee Split: There must be client informed consent if a fee split involves a lawyer external to the firm, and it is not proportional to services performed. All associated lawyers must take joint responsibility for the matter. The client's agreement must be confirmed in writing, and the total fee may not be substantially increased. See *infra* under G2 at 6-407. Fee splits with non-lawyers are not allowed. See MRPC 5.4(a) *infra* at 6-432.

f. Writing Request: Upon the request of the client, the lawyer shall communicate in writing the details requested. This may include the time spent, cost itemization, the hourly rate, and the basis of the fee.

g. Withdrawal Writing: Depending on the particular situation at hand, the lawyer may conclude that the safest course of action is to withdraw rather than complete the representation. The client's non-payment of fees, failure to provide required information, or expressed intent to defraud the court may create such a situation. Termination of the professional relationship is best expressed in writing. If the matter is in litigation, a formal motion to withdraw may be necessary. See also MRPC 1.16 *infra* at 439 for additional detail concerning withdrawals.

4. Client Fee Objection: The question of fee reasonableness usually develops when a client objects to a billing. The lawyer is entitled to fair compensation for work performed. If there was a client fee prepayment, the disputed amount should usually remain in trust pending a resolution. Be cautioned that a lawsuit by a lawyer to collect a fee from a client usually draws both a counterclaim for malpractice and a complaint to the disciplinary authority alleging the fee is unreasonable.

> **MPT Tip:** Any disputed portion of client advances and prepayment funds should be left in trust pending a resolution.

F. Contingency Fee Agreement – MRPC 1.5(c)

A fee may be contingent in whole or in part on the outcome of the matter except in the two situations where a contingency fee is prohibited; see subsection 3 below.

1. Writing Requirement: A contingent fee is determined by the outcome of the representation. Such an agreement must always be in writing and signed by the client. A contingent fee cannot be unreasonable in amount considering the effort and outcome. The writing should clearly state the method by which the lawyer's fee is to be determined. Details of the percentages that would accrue to the lawyer in the event of client discharge, case settlement prior to trial, full trial verdict, or appeal should be explained. Examples, including case outcome dollar hypotheticals, may also be helpful.

2. Treatment of Costs: The agreement must set forth litigation and other expenses to be deducted from the recovery. In addition, whether such expenses are to be deducted before or after the contingent fee is calculated must be disclosed.

3. Prohibited Matters – MRPC 1.5(d): A lawyer cannot enter into a contingency fee arrangement for the following matters:

a. Domestic Relations: This includes an attempt to secure a dissolution of marriage, custody of children, property division, alimony and child support awards. In contrast, a contingent fee may be proper for collection of delinquent alimony or support in arrears.

> **MPT Tip:** Domestic relation questions are one of the examiners' favorite topics.

b. Criminal Matter: Representation in a criminal case may not be undertaken on a contingency basis.

4. Client Termination: The client may terminate an "at-will" lawyer at any time. Substantial completion is usually achieved if the lawyer obtains a firm settlement offer in an amount that the client had approved. If substantial completion has been delivered, a recovery may be allowed under *quantum meruit* for the reasonable value of the services rendered.

5. End of Case: Upon conclusion of a contingency matter, the lawyer must provide the client with a written statement of account. This should itemize the dollar recovery outcome, all chargeable costs, and the calculation of amounts going to both the lawyer and the client.

> **MPT Tip:** Common fact patterns include contingency oral agreements that are not allowed in domestic or criminal cases. Also tested is the lack of a written final accounting to the client showing the details of costs and fees after the contingency representation was concluded.

G. Division of Fees – MRPC 1.5(e)

Division of fees rules between lawyers depends on whether they practice in the same law firm.

1. In Same Firm: There are no restrictions on intra-firm split of fees paid by a client for representation. Many firms have formula revenue and expense allocation systems. For example, a rainmaking partner may receive some portion of the billing for supervising the law firm's representation of certain of her clients. Similarly, the firm may pay a former partner a percentage of fees earned after her retirement or sale of her interest.

2. Not in Same Firm: This involves a single fee billing to a client when the lawyers are not in the same firm. This facilitates association of external expertise on a client's matter. There are two allowed methods of permissive fee splits.

    a. Proportional: Fees proportional to services each lawyer performs, or

    b. Non-Proportional: An external fee division not proportional to services performed by each lawyer may also be proper if each lawyer assumes joint responsibility for the whole representation, and the total fee is not substantially increased.

    c. Client Consent: Under either of the above arrangements, the client must consent to the arrangement, including the specific non-proportional share each lawyer is to receive. The agreement must then be confirmed in writing. The client disclosure should include the inherent risks of divided responsibility and advantages of specialized expertise. For instance, the client could agree that her friend, the overseeing lawyer, would receive a substantially higher fee per hour than the lawyer doing most of the work.

> **MPT Tip:** Splitting a fee with an external lawyer who neither works on the case nor assumes responsibility creates a potential disciplinary action against both lawyers involved.

3. Referral Services: External referral fees may be paid only to a bar association or local bar-approved referral service. Any other forwarding, referrals, or commissions on fees may not be paid to any person, even if that person is another lawyer.

4. Overall Reasonable Restraint: Finally, the total fee all the lawyers receive in the matter and the fee allocation scheme must be reasonable. Some states, such as New York, have statutes limiting attorney contingency fees to a particular percentage of recovery.

II. CONFIDENTIALITY AND CONFLICTS OF INTEREST

A. Confidentiality of Information – MRPC 1.6

1. In General: This topic includes the evidence rules of both the attorney-client privilege and work-product doctrine, as well as the ethical rule of confidentiality.

> **MPT Tip:** Attorney confidentiality exceptions have been tested on the MPT.

a. Core Values: The core legal professional value here is to promote candid and complete communications from the client to the attorney so all the details and complexities may be considered. Full information allows the lawyer to provide the best possible comprehensive advice to their clients. If a client believes the lawyer will reveal her representation information to third parties, it necessarily puts a chilling effect upon the desirable candid communications. Confidential information usually may be shared within the firm for consultation or to prepare for trial, but communication to outside entities requires express client consent.

b. Attorney-Client Privilege: The attorney-client privilege is an evidence rule of exclusion for non-public communications that an actual or potential client communicates to his lawyer. Pre-existing documents do not become subject to the privilege merely by transmitting them to an attorney, but all work product created by a lawyer or her subordinates generally is privileged. The confidential privilege survives the death of the client. The general rule is there is no attorney-client privilege as between jointly-represented clients.

2. Representation Information: In some jurisdictions, the rule distinguishes between confidences and secrets. "Confidences" include the substance of client communications to the lawyer and a lawyer's work product protected by the evidentiary attorney-client privilege. "Secrets" refers to other information gained in the professional relationship concerning the client, the disclosure of which would be embarrassing or would likely be detrimental to the client. Profits made by the lawyer or third party tippee from the use of confidential not generally known client information may be disgorged.

> **MPRE Tip:** ABA Formal Opinion 11-459 requires lawyers to warn clients about the confidentiality risks inherent in using unencrypted electronic communications including e-mail.

3. Exceptions: There are important policy exceptions to the general rule of non-disclosure outside the law firm absent informed client consent. The lawyer should usually first seek to persuade the client to take the action necessary to obviate the need for disclosure and, if unsuccessful, warn the client that a lawyer must reveal such confidential information. If disclosure is still necessary, the extent and scope of any disclosure should be minimized.

a. Future Death or Substantial Bodily Injury: A lawyer may reveal confidential information to the extent necessary to prevent the client from committing a future crime causing certain death or substantial bodily harm of a human. This includes a client's plan to take his own life. The overriding value of life controls. Even if the lawyer concludes that disclosure should be made, it is permissible only to the extent necessary to prevent the offense. This might not even require disclosure of the identity of the client.

> **MPT Tip:** A growing number of states elevate the future death and substantial bodily harm confidentiality permissive disclosure exception "may" to "must" or "shall" reveal.

b. Lawyer Being Sued or Related: A lawyer may also reveal relevant client confidential information only to the extent necessary concerning a:

(1) Claim or Defense Against Client: Limited disclosure is allowed to establish a "claim or defense" on behalf of the lawyer in a legitimate dispute between the lawyer and the client. If the client brings a malpractice claim against a lawyer, she waives the confidentiality right, at least as it relates to the relevant details of the representation. A lawyer entitled to a fee may reveal client confidences to the extent reasonably necessary to effectuate collection, but should avoid disclosing confidential information.

(2) Lawyer's Involvement: A lawyer may disclose client crimes, fraud, or substantial financial injury in which the client used the lawyer's services. Such involvement could create legal complicity and lead to a criminal charge or civil claim against the lawyer resulting from client wrongful activities. A lawyer may also make disclosures in the process of securing professional advice about his own degree of compliance with the MRPCs.

(3) Bar Complaint: Disclosure of confidential information may be made to respond to allegations in any proceeding concerning the lawyer's professional representation of the client (such as a bar association grievance filed by a client).

(4) Joint Clients or Court Order: Disclosure may be made when representing joint clients who later litigate among themselves or pursuant to a court order.

c. Sarbanes-Oxley Act (SOX): The ABA Model Rule now allows federal securities lawyers to disclose publicly-traded corporate client frauds externally.

(1) Breadth: Disclosure may be made to prevent the client from committing a crime, financial fraud, or breach of fiduciary duty that involved the lawyer's services, if reasonably certain to result in substantial injury to the financial interests or property of another.

(2) Corporate Reporting Up: SOX § 307 states that a lawyer learning of evidence of (1) material, clear violations of federal securities laws or (2) significant breach of fiduciary duty must disclose such evidence internally within the company. If the corporate chief legal officer (CLO) or CEO does not "appropriately respond" – basically stop the wrongdoing – the lawyer is required to then report the matter to the company's board of directors disclosure and/or audit committee. If that internal reporting fails to result in a corporate "appropriate response," external disclosure to the SEC is authorized to the extent necessary to prevent material and certain injury to the corporation or its investor-owners. See also MRPC 1.13 *infra* for organizational reporting and whistleblowing issues.

d. Third Party Notice: The lawyer may give reasonable notice to a third party of the fact that she has withdrawn. Also, any relevant opinion document or other "questionable information" prepared by the lawyer based on client provided fraudulent information may be withdrawn or disaffirmed.

e. IRS Form 8300: Another "no reveal" exception involves IRS Form 8300, which must usually be filed if the client pays the lawyer $10,000 or more in cash. The ABA suggests that unless the client approves, the lawyer can file the form but must leave the secret of the client's name and Social Security number off the form. The IRS can issue a summons, and if the U.S. District Court judge so orders, the lawyer could then make full disclosure.

f. Client Waiver: If the client communication is not private or the client releases a substantial portion of the information to third parties, confidentiality may be legally waived. If a client claims as a defense reliance upon advice of counsel, the privilege is also usually deemed waived at least as to details of the matter in controversy.

g. Breach of Fiduciary Responsibility: Many states also allow a lawyer to reveal to the tribunal information that discloses significant breach of fiduciary duty responsibility by a client who is a guardian, personal representative, receiver, or other court-authorized fiduciary. Danger to a child may also be grounds for disclosure.

MPT Tip: Confidentiality issues are heavily tested. The extent and manner of disclosure under the above exceptions must be the minimum necessary under the circumstances.

B. Conflict of Interest: Current Clients – MRPC 1.7

MRPC 1.7, 1.8, and 1.9 have a variety of restraints intended to ensure there are no impairments to a lawyer giving undivided representational loyalty and diligent services to a client. A lawyer must decline new representation for a person whose interest concurrently conflicts with that of an existing client or a lawyer's personal interest. If the conflict becomes apparent later after the representation is underway, the lawyer must withdraw from representing both clients. Under MRPC 1.10, this conflict disqualification is imputed to all lawyers in a firm.

1. Client-to-Client: There are two degrees of present and potential concurrent client conflicts. The lawyer's benefit to one client is also a detriment to the other client.

a. Representation Directly Adverse – MRPC 1.7(a)(1): "Direct Adversity" is the highest level of present client-based conflict of interest and usually applies to a matter in which the lawyer is acting as a litigation advocate against the interest of another of the clients that the lawyer currently represents in another matter.

> **MPT Tip:** Representation while simultaneously opposing the same client puts a client in the difficult position of considering the same lawyer as both trusted confidant and frightening foe.

b. Lawyer's Responsibilities Materially Limited – MRPC 1.7(a)(2): This potential conflict applies if there is significant risk that a lawyer's representation on behalf of one client will materially limit her future effectiveness in representing other existing client(s). Another client may be adversely affected by the resolution of the matter or the precedent set.

(1) Lower Level: "Materially limited" is a lower level of conflict than present "direct adversity," and formal litigation may not be involved. The conflict may arise because of the lawyer's responsibilities to another client, a third party, or her own interests.

(2) Examples: Examples include the conflicts that could result from joint representation of the driver and passenger against a common defendant in an automobile accident. Creating a precedent for one client that may adversely affect another client is another example of a material limitation. Representing one client against a second client in an unrelated matter, representing both a buyer and seller in the same transaction, or mediating a dispute between clients are favorite exam facts.

c. Exception – MRPC 1.7(b): Dual representation may be allowed if:

(1) No Harm to Attorney-Client Relationship: The lawyer must reasonably believe that the representation of one client would not adversely affect the competent and diligent representation relationship with the other client. This is an objective foreseeability standard of a prudent, disinterested lawyer.

> **MPT Tip:** The lawyer's belief that there will not be an adverse effect on the representation of either client must be objectively reasonable. Would a disinterested lawyer so conclude?

(2) Informed Consent Confirmed in Writing: Each affected client must give a prior informed consent "waiver" after receiving full disclosure of all material risks and dangers that the lawyer's conflict could create. General consent may be insufficient. Presenting alternatives such as "these questions are avoided if you both have your own counsel" is best. The oral informed consent must then be signed by the client or confirmed in writing by the lawyer.

(a) Adverse Clients Identification: The lawyer's disclosure to the clients must usually include the identification of the other conflicting client(s) and lack of the attorney-client privilege between clients in jointly represented matters.

(b) Confidential Information Authorization: Full disclosure to one client in securing the conflict informed consent may require the other client's authorization if the disclosure contains his confidential information.

(c) Revoking Consent: Conflict consent may subsequently be withdrawn by either client. The employment of the lawyer may also be terminated by either client. The lawyer will usually be forced to withdraw from representing any of the clients if the joint representation fails. This danger should be explained in advance to both clients.

> **MPT Tip:** Look for a situation in which an incident occurred that strongly suggests future representation of a client may be materially limited by the duty of loyalty to another client. The lawyer must withdraw from representing both clients without disclosing any confidences.

(3) Same Litigation Prohibition: The ABA Model Rule does not allow the above consent waiver to abate a present directly adverse conflict if the matter is in litigation.

> **MPT Tip:** To abate a 1.7 conflict, remember the acronym **NIC**: **N**o harm will result to either client, **I**nformed consent waiver by clients is secured, and the consent is **C**onfirmed in writing.

(4) Fundamentally Antagonistic: The comments to the Model Rules state that if the clients' interests are fundamentally antagonistic and aligned directly against each other, the conflict facing the lawyer may be realistically nonconsentable. Joint representation of both spouses in a marital dissolution proceeding may be a good example due to the high level of animosity that frequently develops between the parties in a divorce.

d. Related Attorneys: A possible conflict of interest relates to personal relationships between opposing counsel. A lawyer is prohibited from representing a party if an attorney who is related to the first lawyer represents a directly adverse party. Related attorneys include spouses, domestic partners, parent-child, or two siblings. The informed consent of both clients may abate this restriction, and a writing is not required. The prohibition is not imputed firm-wide so another lawyer in the firm could handle one of the representation positions.

e. Organizational Clients: This conflict rule addresses organizational groups. Examples include a lawyer for one corporation in a corporate-affiliated group or one governmental agency that is a part of an upstream government control organization.

(1) General Rule: A lawyer representing one corporate or governmental unit does not necessarily represent any other constituent or affiliated organization. Thus, such a lawyer may accept representation of a case adverse to the affiliate.

(2) Exceptions: The no-conflict outcome does not apply if (1) the related affiliate is considered to be a client of the lawyer, (2) there is a prior understanding that the lawyer will avoid representation adverse to the affiliate, or (3) the representation would in fact place a material limitation on the loyalty afforded to either client.

f. Lawyer Board Member: A lawyer for an entity who is also an official member of the board of directors may be conflicted in advising board actions when the lawyer's prior work is at issue. This could create a go-forward conflict for the lawyer. The lawyer may be required to withdraw from the board to eliminate the conflict. Further, other board members should be advised that the attorney-client privilege does not apply if the lawyer is in a director's capacity. (See MRPC 1.13 *infra* on page 6-418 for additional details.)

> **MPT Tip:** MRPC 1.8, discussed in detail below, contains a variety of restrictions and/or prohibitions where the conflict of interest is between the lawyer and the client. The client trust inherent in the fiduciary relationship creates a disparity in bargaining power. Any prohibition on a lawyer is generally imputed to all the lawyers associated in the law firm.

      2. Current Client / Prohibited Transactions: Business transactions between a lawyer and a client could create divided loyalties and thus are subject to special scrutiny.

      a. No Business Relationship Unless TICC – MRPC 1.8(a): The lawyer shall not enter into a business relationship with a client (including an estate) she represents in the same transaction because there is a clear possibility of overreaching. Examples are loaning to or borrowing money from a client or entering into a partnership with a client. An exception allows the client transaction if all three **TICC** transaction elements are met:

      (1) Terms of Transaction Are Fair: The financial transaction and all material terms must be fair at a reasonable market price and fully disclosed to the client in writing. The disclosure must be stated in language that the client can clearly understand.

      (2) Independent Counsel: The client must be advised in writing to seek the advice of independent counsel in the transaction. Notice it is only required that the client has a reasonable opportunity to seek advice from another attorney, not that he actually receives it. Certainly, the safest posture is if the client secures independent advice and financial valuation.

      (3) Client Consent in Writing: The client must consent in a signed writing. The informed consent must go to both the transaction's essential terms and the lawyer's conflict of interest disclosure, not only the terms of the underlying transaction.

> **MPT Tip:** The disparity in bargaining power is significant since the client inherently trusts the lawyer to protect her financial and legal interests. This creates a presumption of overreaching and undue influence justifying setting aside a client-to-lawyer transaction, such as a bargain purchase or loan from a client.

      b. Information Disadvantaging the Client – MRPC 1.8(b): The lawyer must not use information to a client's disadvantage unless the client gives informed consent. For instance, a lawyer may not purchase assets in competition with a client she is representing. In a later transaction or business dispute, the lawyer cannot use information derived from a prior representation to the client's disadvantage unless informed consent was given. If no client disadvantage results, client information use is generally permitted.

      c. No Gifts from Clients – MRPC 1.8(c): A lawyer may accept a gift from a client only if the transaction meets general standards of fairness and does not involve overreaching. However, a lawyer cannot solicit a gift or prepare an instrument bestowing upon herself or her family members a substantial gift from a client. This includes a testamentary device, such as a will, unless the lawyer is related to the donor. Lawyers can prepare their parents' wills and name themselves and their children as takers. Gifts given to a lawyer without a prepared instrument – say a cash bonus at the end of a case – are not *per se* improper as they are for a judge.

d. No Agreement for Literary or Media Rights – MRPC 1.8(d): A lawyer may not negotiate an agreement to receive the client's publication rights to information based in substantial part on the lawsuit prior to the conclusion of the representation. A client waiver and consent is ineffective. A lawyer has to wait until the case is over before the client can agree to give the lawyer the book and movie rights of the trial. This rule guards against a lawyer trying to publicize an upcoming book during a trial, which could jeopardize the client's position.

e. No Financial Assistance – MRPC 1.8(e): A lawyer shall not advance or guarantee financial assistance to a client for living expenses, advances for family support, or medical treatment because this would be acquiring an interest in litigation. There are three exceptions:

(1) Litigation Expenses: A lawyer may lend a client funds to pay or guarantee a third party's payment of litigation costs – such as expert witness fees, court costs, medical examinations, and discovery costs – but the client must remain responsible for those costs. Still, repayment of these costs may be contingent on the outcome of the matter.

(2) Contingency Cost Allocation: There are three possible ways to charge costs in a contingency recovery. First, the costs come off the top before the percentage split between the attorney and client. That's probably permissible because the client bears most of the costs. Second, the client bears 100% of the costs from his portion – that's permissible even though the client may not like it. Third, the lawyer bears all the costs from her share – in theory, that is a violation even though the client would usually prefer it.

(3) Indigent Client: Court costs and expenses may be paid on behalf of an indigent client regardless of whether these funds will be repaid. Some jurisdictions also have a class-action exception, which is justified because of the public service aspect, since it otherwise might be too difficult to get plaintiffs to join the class.

> **MPT Tip:** A lawyer may refer a client seeking funds to a financing institution or bank as long as the lawyer does not guarantee the loan.

f. No Fee Payment by Third Parties – MRPC 1.8(f): Payment of attorney fees by a third party is not allowed. Examples include parents who pay for their child's DUI defense or the corporate payment of attorney fees incurred by a co-defendant officer. Another example is the defendant's insurance company that may be responsible for the ultimate damage claim and is also paying for the defendant's legal defense. Exceptions to this rule apply if:

(1) Informed Consent and No Interference: The primary client may consent to the lawyer also representing an interested third party after consultation. A writing is not required. There must be no interference by the third-party payor with the lawyer's independence, professional judgment, or loyalty to the client. A future conflict waiver demanded by an insurance company third party payor is problematic. It may be ineffective because the client may lack sufficient information about possible future third-party interference acts to give an informed consent until a fact-specific conflict actually develops.

(2) Confidentiality: The client's confidential information must not be compromised. This may be tricky because information the lawyer conveys to the fee paying third party in a billing statement is protected by the confidentiality rules. The lawyer cannot disclose sensitive client information that could damage the client. An example is a "reservation of rights" notice being issued by the insurance company based on the billing information. Insurers may not impose "litigation management guidelines" on a lawyer if it will interfere with independent judgment. If any of these conditions occur, a lawyer may have to withdraw.

> **MPT Tip:** Legal fees paid by a third party (such as parent or insurance company) require **INC** – **i**nformed consent by client, **n**o interference with the lawyer's independent judgment, and **c**lient confidentiality must be maintained.

g. No Aggregate Settlement if Multiple Clients – MRPC 1.8(g):

(1) Criminal Case: When a lawyer represents more than one client in a criminal matter, the lawyer must not participate in making an aggregate agreement as to guilty or *nolo contendere* pleas. The potential for conflict in representing multiple criminal defendants is grave – they may need to take inconsistent positions because what is good for one may be bad for another. Ordinarily a lawyer should decline to represent more than one co-defendant. An exception applies if each client gives informed, written consent. The lawyer must make disclosure of the existence and nature of all the claims or pleas involved and the participation of each person in the settlement agreement.

(2) Civil Case: This lawyer representation restraint applies to multiple clients who would share as plaintiffs in an aggregate dollar settlement or co-defendants in a civil case with joint and several liability. There may be cross-claims or disputes relating to award recovery or cost allocations between the clients. Again, there is an exception if each client gives informed consent in a signed writing after disclosure that includes all information about the claims being settled and the amount each client will receive or be required to pay.

h. Limiting Liability – MCPR 1.8(h):
A lawyer shall not prospectively limit the client's right to file a bar complaint or pursue a claim for future or past malpractice.

(1) Prospective Limitation: The lawyer's representation agreement cannot state that the "client agrees not to sue for malpractice if the lawyer fails to exercise reasonable care" unless the client is separately represented by counsel in the negotiation. Even adding mandatory arbitration clauses to the representation agreement may be deemed improper because the client is giving up the right to a jury trial. A mere warning that "you should talk to a lawyer" is insufficient; actual client independent representation is required.

(2) Malpractice Settlement: A client may assert a malpractice claim against her lawyer, for example, because the lawyer complied with the requirement that he communicate his lack of competent performance and the client is unhappy about damages the lawyer has created. The attorney and client may reach agreement as to an equitable settlement of the resulting damages and the portion the lawyer should bear. The client must be advised in writing to seek independent counsel, but need not do so. However, there must be reasonable opportunity to seek such advice; settlement cannot be made "on the spot."

> **MPT Tip:** Notice the client must actually have independent representation to agree to prospective malpractice limitations. In contrast, after-the-fact liability settlements only require the client to receive such advice and a reasonable opportunity to seek representation.

i. No Proprietary Interest in Cause of Action – MRPC 1.8(i):
A lawyer shall not acquire an actual ownership interest in the client's cause of action or legal claim. There is no exception, even if the client agrees. Still allowed are:

(1) Fee Security: A lawyer may take a promissory note or acquire a lien allowed by law to secure the lawyer's fee or expenses. This is a business or financial transaction with a client requiring the three **TIC** transaction elements.

(2) Contingent Fee: A lawyer may contract with a client for a reasonable percentage contingent fee in a civil case, and such is not usually deemed a proprietary interest.

j. Sexual Relations with Clients – MRPC 1.8(j): Lawyers in most jurisdictions are prohibited from having sexual relations with current clients or representatives of their clients, such as the parent of a child in a personal injury action. This restriction is not imputed to other firm members who are not working on the representation. An exception also exists if there was a prior consensual relationship between the lawyer and client before the lawyer undertook the case. This sexual relationship prohibition terminates at the end of the representation.

(1) Definition: The definition of "sexual relationship" is not in the Model Rule – and many people differ in their views of how much it takes to have a "sexual relationship." Some states attempt a definition such as California's "sexual intercourse or the touching of an intimate part of another...." Disciplinary cases focus on lawyers going to bed with their clients; in most states this meets the threshold definition.

(2) Consent Ineffective: A client's informed consent or waiver, even in writing, does not abate the violation. In such a situation, there could easily be overreaching by the lawyer where a client is emotionally vulnerable and therefore might feel forced to accept an imposed *quid pro quo* personal relationship. A sexual relationship could impact the attorney's fiduciary duty, in which the lawyer occupies the highest position of trust and confidence. From a lawyer's standpoint, your independence and objectivity may be put at risk – can you tell a lover client that her case objectively lacks merit or that she would make a bad witness?

(3) Client Affections: If the client wants an affair, the attorney needs to say no. Explain to the client that you could get disciplined. Say no to gifts and invitations for dinner or drinks after work. If the client's aggressive affections do not stop, it would be prudent to transfer the client to another attorney in the firm.

> **MPT Tip:** The 1.8 restrictions (except 1.8(j)) usually are imputed to all lawyers in the firm.

C. Conflict of Interest: Duties to Former Clients – MRPC 1.9

Lawyer loyalty and confidence rules survive the representation, and these ongoing duties to a former client may conflict with a current client's interests. Is confidentiality at risk? Under MRPC 1.10, the conflict disqualification is imputed to every lawyer in a law firm, unless the imputation can be overcome by effective screening.

1. Subject Matter Relationship: The current matter must be substantially related to the factual context of the prior client's matter. This provision relates to MRPC 1.7 in that if a lawyer withdraws from representing one client, the client then becomes a prior client.

2. Informed Consent Possible: A lawyer usually cannot, in the same or a substantially related legal dispute, represent another person who has an adverse interest to her prior client. Representation in different unrelated matters against a former client is usually allowed. This conflict may be waived if the former client gives informed consent after full disclosure, confirmed in writing, and the new client agrees.

3. Substantially Related Example: Suppose a lawyer represented both spouses in a property transaction, and three years later, the wife wants the same lawyer (or the lawyer's partner) to represent her in a divorce. If the same property is subject to the dissolution proceeding, the matter may be sufficiently factually related to disqualify the lawyer. The lawyer needs to secure informed consent from both parties, or the attorney is conflicted out.

4. Confidential Information Restriction: Even if the former client consents to the representation, and it is confirmed in writing, there is a separate restriction on using the former client's material confidential information to his disadvantage. The duty of protecting information confidentiality continues after the client-lawyer relationship has terminated unless the information in question has become generally known public knowledge.

5. Example: Suppose a corporate client asked a lawyer's opinion about hiring an employee whom the lawyer had defended in an embezzlement case five years ago. The lawyer probably cannot disclose to the corporation what she knows about her former client's fraud potential even though one could argue the matter is not exactly the same. The test is "substantial subject matter relationship." Still, the common nexus concerns the former embezzlement, so the similar subject matter test is arguably satisfied in this fact pattern.

> **MPT Tip:** For purposes of former client disqualification under Rule 1.9, the matter at issue must be substantially related to the prior client's matter. Note this subject-matter nexus is not necessary to create a disqualifying conflict under Rule 1.7 for present "direct adversity" and future "materially limited" conflicts where mere adverse client identity may be sufficient.

III. DISQUALIFICATION, CLIENT FUNDS, AND WITHDRAWAL

A. Imputed Disqualification – MRPC 1.10

1. Conflicts of Interest: While lawyers are associated in a law firm, none of them shall knowingly represent a client when any one of them practicing alone would be prohibited from doing so by the conflict of interest rules. If any one lawyer is disqualified, this disqualification is traditionally imputed to all other lawyers in the firm.

2. Joining a Firm: When a lawyer who, as opposing counsel, represented an adverse party at their old firm becomes associated with a new firm, both the new firm and all members in it are disqualified. Neither the firm nor the "**p**ersonally **d**isqualified **l**awyer" – **PDL** – may knowingly represent a person with adverse interests to the prior represented client in any same or substantially related matter unless:

a. Screening: The PDL must be timely and effectively screened from participating in or discussing the matter with the litigation team at the new firm. No material confidential information can be revealed by the personally disqualified lawyer and she may not be apportioned any part of the fee obtained from that representation.

b. Written Notice to Former Client: The former client of the PDL must receive written notice. This must include the details of the screening mechanism used to prohibit the PDL's disseminating the prior firm trial strategy and confidential information.

c. Certification: The PDL and a new firm partner must serve on her former law firm and the client a periodic certification of compliance. Judicial review and supervision of the screening procedures is possible to ensure compliance and may follow a court's denial of the motion to disqualify.

> **MPT Tip:** Many of NCBE's performance tasks focus on lawyer or law firm disqualification.

3. Leaving a Firm: A law firm may represent a person with interests directly adverse to a former client represented by a lawyer who has left the firm. Representation is only precluded if (1) the matter is the same or substantially related and (2) any lawyer remaining in the firm has relevant confidential information protected by RPC 1.6.

B. Successive Government and Private Employment – MRPC 1.11

This applies to a government attorney who goes into private practice, such as a prosecutor, public defender, or representative attorney for a government agency.

1. Personal and Substantial Participation: Such a previous government lawyer may not represent a private client in a matter in which she previously **p**ersonally **a**nd **s**ubstantially – **PAS** – participated in while employed by the government, unless the agency gives informed consent which is confirmed in writing. The "matter" must involve the same or closely related parties. This disqualification is imputed to any other lawyer in the firm, but (1) a screening arrangement is possible with (2) written notice to the agency of the screening procedures employed, if (3) the screened lawyer does not share in the fee. The prohibition extends to use of or disclosure to third parties of any agency confidential information.

2. Employment Negotiation: A government lawyer may not negotiate for private employment with parties and attorneys appearing before the agency if the lawyer participated personally and substantially. If the lawyer did not participate in the matter for or against the party – she only worked for the same agency – it is not improper to pursue such employment.

3. Confidential Government Information: In subsequently representing a client in private practice, a lawyer may not use "confidential government information" that was prohibited by law from disclosure to the public. The prohibition extends to confidential government information about a person who is an adversary of the client. Information available under the Freedom of Information Act is not deemed confidential.

C. Former Judge, Arbitrator, Mediator, or Third Party Neutral – MRPC 1.12

This provision parallels MRPC 1.11.

1. Restrictions: A former or retired judge, adjudicative officer, or third-party neutral (including their law clerks) may not act as a lawyer in a matter in which she formerly served as a judge. Prior participation in the matter must have been **PAS** – **p**ersonal **a**nd **s**ubstantial – to disqualify the former judge – for example, she personally adjudicated a case where the client was a party. Mere remote involvement or incidental administrative responsibility is normally insufficient to create a conflict of interest. A partisan member of an arbitration panel is not prohibited from subsequently representing that party.

2. Employment Negotiation: A judge or law clerk shall not negotiate for private employment with parties appearing in her court. This restriction does not block all work for a former litigant in front of the judge – only those matters in which the former judge or law clerk was involved. A law clerk nearing the end of a clerkship may negotiate for employment with a law firm appearing in the court; however, the clerk must first tell the judge of the employment search and specifically identify the law firms with which she is interviewing.

3. Consent or Screening Exception: Subsequent representation is permitted if all parties to that proceeding give informed consent confirmed in writing. Even if no consent is given, a law firm may not be disqualified if its tainted lawyer is timely screened and written notice is promptly given to the parties and appropriate tribunal.

D. Organization as Client – MRPC 1.13

A corporate attorney owes the primary duty of loyalty to the organizational entity, not the Board as a whole or individual directors, officers, employees, shareholders, or other human constituents. A lawyer for a business entity may usually also represent a majority owner.

1. Dual Representation: Dual representation of both the corporation and a human constituent may be a RPC 1.7 conflict, but informed consent by both clients may avoid the disqualification. A lawyer may not concurrently represent a constituent whose interest the lawyer determines is adverse to the organization, such as an employee accused of committing a criminal act involving the corporation. The lawyer must state that s/he cannot represent them, is not giving them advice, that no attorney-client privilege exists as to anything they disclose, and that they should obtain their own independent representation.

2. Private Organization Internal Reporting: A lawyer should report violations of law to the involved wrongdoer(s). If not corrected, and the matter is clearly a violation of law that will result in substantial injury to the organization, the lawyer "may" (not "must") reveal "up the ladder" to the chief executive officer or full Board of Directors. The lawyer must minimize any risk of the information being revealed externally. A lawyer discharged by a corporate manager for revealing such wrongdoing shall inform the Board of the discharge or withdrawal details.

3. Public Organization External Reporting: If the corporation is publicly-traded, the lawyer may report to the SEC under the Sarbanes-Oxley Act. While noisy withdrawals are not encouraged, a lawyer may externally withdraw his own prior writings relied upon by third parties, even if this is not normally permitted by Rule 1.6.

4. Governmental Organizational Client: When a lawyer who is not a public officer or employee represents a discrete governmental agency that is part of a broader governmental entity, the lawyer's client is the particular governmental agency or unit represented, not the broader upstream governmental entity. An exception may apply if provided otherwise in writing by both governmental agencies.

E. Client with Diminished Capacity – MRPC 1.14

Usually we assume a client has the ability and intellectual decision-making capacity to maintain a normal client-lawyer relationship, including making adequately considered decisions and assisting in preparation of her case.

1. Disability: If the client cannot adequately act in her own interest because she is under a significant disability – *e.g.*, incapacity, minority, unconsciousness, mental impairment, elderly with diminished capacity – the lawyer may take reasonably necessary protective actions such as seeking court appointment of a guardian *ad litem*.

2. Preserve Confidences: The application for guardian appointment should not disclose any unnecessary client confidences protected under MRPC 1.6.

F. Safeguarding Property – MRPC 1.15

1. Separation Required: All property of clients and third persons must be safeguarded and held separately from the lawyer's own property. Client property may not be used, commingled, converted, borrowed from, or pledged by the lawyer. A separate trust account is required. A small exception is that a lawyer's funds may be used to pay bank service charges. Commingling is a serious fiduciary offense even if the client approves of the "loan" and all funds are repaid.

2. Retainers and Trust Advances: The ABA Model Rules do not distinguish between retainers and advances. In many jurisdictions, availability retainers are client payments that are fully earned when received as compensation for taking on the case and being available concerning the matter. Such retainers are non-refundable and should not be deposited in a trust account. All other funds that clients advance for future fees and costs must be deposited in trust accounts in the state where the lawyer's office is situated, and must be kept separate from the law firm's regular operating account. In most states, split deposits (part retainer and part already earned fees in one check) must be deposited into a trust account.

3. Transfers from Trust: As lawyers bill, they should withdraw that portion from the trust account unless the client objects. The usual prudent approach is to wait 10 to 20 days after sending out a fee statement before transferring the funds between accounts; this gives the client a reasonable time to contest the billing. A lawyer's failure to withdraw uncontested billed fees from the trust account results in impermissible commingling.

> **MPT Tip:** Any client disputed amount must be left in trust until the dispute is resolved.

4. All Client Property Kept Identifiable and Accountable: Client property must be identifiable, segregated, and held in a secure place such as a locked safe deposit box. Complete accounting records of all client property shall be preserved for five years minimum. An attempt should be made to contact the clients before any of their files are destroyed.

a. Notice of Receipt of Property and Funds: A lawyer shall promptly notify a client of the receipt of funds, securities, or other property, including a settlement check.

b. Identify and Label Securities and Properties: A lawyer shall identify and label securities and properties of a client promptly upon receipt. Such assets shall be placed in a locked safe deposit box or other place of safekeeping as soon as practicable.

c. Third Parties' Claims: If a third party has an apparent lawful claim – usually a lien or unsatisfied judgment – against client funds or other property in the lawyer's possession, the lawyer may file an action to have a court resolve the dispute. The funds at issue in the controversy should be interpleaded into the registry of the court for a judicial determination of the third party's claims.

d. Promptly Return Property: At the client's request or at the end of the representation, a lawyer must promptly deliver to the client all the client's property. This includes all client-related assets in the lawyer's possession and any interest earned during custody of the client's funds. If the client disputes the fee and / or other split amount items as calculated by the lawyer, the client should be paid any undisputed portion. If the dispute cannot be liquidated, the balance may be interpleaded into the registry of a court.

5. Escrow Funds: Escrow and other funds held by a lawyer involving multiple party transactions are treated as client funds subject to these rules. Examples include funds for the closing of a real estate property transfer, or the sale and purchase of a business. This applies regardless of whether the lawyer, the law firm, or the parties view the funds as belonging to clients or non-clients. Many jurisdictions require Bar authorities to perform random audits to promote proper client funds management.

G. Declining or Terminating Representation – MRPC 1.16

The rule on declining or terminating representation has two sections – one where the lawyer must withdraw and another where withdrawal is optional.

1. Must Terminate / Withdraw – VID: Withdrawal is mandatory if any of the following three **VID** reasons apply.

a. Violate MRPCs or Law: A lawyer shall withdraw from the representation of a client if continued representation would result in a violation of the MRPCs, a court order, or other laws. Examples include a client's malicious harassment of an opponent or the lawyer's conclusion that the client's case cannot be supported by a good faith argument for the extension, modification, or reversal of existing law. [MRPC 3.1]

b. Impaired Ability to Represent: A lawyer must decline or withdraw from the representation of a client if the lawyer's physical or mental condition materially impairs the ability to represent the client. This includes a lawyer's physical or mental decline.

c. Discharged by Client: A lawyer must withdraw if discharged by the client.

> **MPT Tip:** The **VID** "must" withdraw rules, especially MRPC violations, are frequently tested.

2. May Terminate / Withdraw – CURBSO: The second prong of the Rule gives a lawyer discretion to withdraw from representing a client. The withdrawal usually must be accomplished without a material adverse effect on the client's interests, but certain specifically approved **CURBSO** grounds allow withdrawal notwithstanding adverse effects. These include:

a. Client Pursuing Criminal Action: A lawyer may withdraw if the client intends to persist in a course of action involving the lawyer's services that the lawyer reasonably believes is criminal or fraudulent (future actions).

b. Used Lawyer to Commit Crime: A lawyer may withdraw if the client has used the lawyer's services to perpetrate a crime or fraud (past actions).

c. Repugnant Objective: A lawyer may withdraw if the client insists on pursuing an objective the lawyer considers repugnant or very imprudent.

d. Burden on Lawyer Unreasonable: A lawyer may withdraw if the representation will result in an unreasonable financial burden on the lawyer or the client has been unreasonably difficult.

e. Serious Client Failure: This includes a client's unsatisfied commitment to pay fees, refusal to obey a court order, or failure to comply with required discovery. The lawyer should warn the client that withdrawal will occur unless the obligation is satisfied timely. Still, a failure to pay fees when due may be insufficient alone to justify withdrawal.

f. Other Good Cause for Withdrawal Exists: This is a catchall category where the burden is on the attorney asserting the good cause argument. Client difficulties short of actual discharge, such as non-cooperation in preparing for trial, may fall into this category.

> **MPT Tip:** Distinguish between the **VID** reasons for which a lawyer must withdraw (especially RPC violations) and those **CURBSO** reasons in which she may withdraw but it is not required even in situations that arise suspicion.

3. Court Order: Formal withdrawal may be required if the matter is in litigation. Where ordered by a tribunal, a lawyer must continue representation notwithstanding a good cause for terminating the representation.

4. Notice, Surrender, and Refund: A lawyer must take reasonable steps to protect a client's interests. This includes giving the client reasonable notice of intent to withdraw, allowing time to hire other counsel, surrendering appropriate papers and property to the client, and refunding any unearned advance payment of fees.

a. No Client Prejudice: The withdrawal should not prejudice the client's rights or create a material adverse effect on her interests. A withdrawing lawyer must usually allow sufficient time before trial so the client can get a new attorney.

b. Surrender Papers and Property: The lawyer must surrender papers and property to which the client is entitled. The files belong to the client unless the retainer agreement specifically states to the contrary. It makes no difference if the document is the lawyer's work product or not. Any unearned balance in the trust account shall be refunded.

c. File Lien: In many jurisdictions an attorney's possessory lien provision may apply to the client's judgment award. This lien provision may not be used to hold the client's legal files hostage unless the retention would not prejudice the client and/or it is allowed by state law. This is rare if the litigation is still going forward with new counsel. If withholding the file materially interferes with the ability of a new lawyer to represent the client, the court or professional authority may order the file transferred to the succeeding attorney.

d. Other Lien Restraints: A lawyer seeking or enforcing a lien to tie up the client's judgment or property must be sure the underlying proceeding is not frivolous [MRPC 3.1] or interposed strictly to embarrass or burden a person [MRPC 4.4].

5. Formal Notice: Many jurisdictions require filing of a formal motion and Notice of Withdrawal with the tribunal a minimum of 10 days before withdrawal may be effective. The notice must specify the trial date and identify any succeeding lawyer. If the client does not have a new lawyer substituting in, the address of the client must be stated. If anyone objects to the withdrawal, the court will hold a hearing. If it is too close to trial or other foreseeable prejudice will result, the court may deny the motion, and the lawyer must stay on the case.

6. Malpractice Concern: Prudence suggests that a lawyer with any concern about a possible present or future malpractice claim should copy the file at her own expense.

7. "Noisy" or "Flag-Waving" Withdrawals: To alert third parties, the federal Sarbanes-Oxley Act (SOX) allows a noisy withdrawal for a corporate attorney learning of an ongoing client fraud. This aspect of SOX is controversial because most jurisdictions require that a lawyer's withdrawal not create a material adverse effect on a client. A lawyer can withdraw any of her own prior opinions given to third parties that now appear to be fraudulent. A lawyer may write to a third party stating that "facts have come to my attention such that you should not rely on my prior opinions," without saying anything negative about the client.

> **MPT Tip**: A good summary of a lawyer's **4Re's** withdrawal requirements are that a lawyer must allow a **re**asonable time for the client to **re**tain succeeding counsel, **re**turn client papers and property, and **re**fund all unearned fees.

H. Sale of Law Practice – MRPC 1.17

This rule focuses on the sale of a law practice by a retiring lawyer or by the estate of a deceased attorney. There are confidentiality restrictions imposed on potential buyers making a purchase investigation. Notice must be given to clients of the transfer and client consent for file transfer is required. This may be inferred if the client does not affirmatively object within 90 days after receiving notice of the practice sale. A single buyer or group must purchase the entire practice or an entire substantive practice area; cherry-picking and piecemeal sale of client accounts is not allowed in most states. The sales price may be set at a percentage of future fees collected from the book of business the buyer purchased. The purchaser of the practice cannot increase client charges to finance the acquisition.

I. Duties To Prospective Client – MRPC 1.18

A growing number of jurisdictions recognize some professional duty to a prospective client. A typical example is a potential client telephones a lawyer to discuss and/or determine whether the lawyer will take on the representation of their case.

1. Conflict Question: The prospective client must always reveal enough information to allow the lawyer to perform a conflict check and determine if the lawyer is competent and willing to undertake representation of the matter. As long as the discussion stops before "significantly harmful" information is shared, the lawyer will not be personally disqualified from later representing the other side in the same or a substantially related controversy.

2. Screening Possible: Even if "significantly harmful" information has passed and both the existing and prospective clients do not consent, the Rule allows a "screening" procedure of the **p**ersonally **d**isqualified **l**awyer (PDL). This isolation treatment requirement permits others in the firm to undertake representation of someone on the other side of the controversy. The prospective client must receive written notice of the screening.

3. Fair Warning: A lawyer receiving a prospective representation inquiry usually may avoid disqualification by affirmatively stating that "our law firm has many clients who may be adverse to your interest in this dispute. Therefore, nothing you disclose in this prospective conversation is confidential unless we subsequently enter into a formal written representation agreement." Website inquiry submission forms should contain a specific disclaimer disavowing an attorney-client relationship until an actual writing is signed.

4. Duty Not to Mislead: If the client expects that a lawyer will represent her in a matter, the lawyer must affirmatively reject the association expectation.

5. Confidential Information Protected: Even if the lawyer disavows the representation, and therefore the attorney-client privilege does not attach, MRPC 1.6 protects preliminary discussions with the prospective client of any harmful non-public information.

IV. COUNSELOR, ADVOCATE, AND THIRD PARTY DEALINGS

A. Counselor – TITLE 2

Title 2 focuses on a lawyer functioning not as a partisan, but rather as an advisor, intermediary, preparer of an evaluation for use by a third party, or neutral.

1. Advisor – MRPC 2.1:

a. Independence: A lawyer in an advisory role shall exercise independent professional judgment and present the client with both favorable and unfavorable facts and considerations. The lawyer must give the client honest and candid advice, which may refer to relevant moral, economic, social and political factors, as well as ethical considerations. If the necessary objective advice is unpleasant, try to put it in as acceptable a form as honesty permits. Sometimes lawyers have to tell their clients what they don't want to hear.

b. Offering Advice: There is normally no duty to give advice until asked by the client. If the client's action is likely to result in substantial adverse legal consequences, there may be a communication duty under MRPC 1.4. A lawyer should attempt to tell the client that such activity is likely to result in serious legal or ethical problems.

2. Intermediary: The ABA has deleted MRPC 2.2 (intermediary between clients) and now treats the intermediary role as a MRPC 1.7(b) conflict where there is a "material limitation" on the lawyer concurrently serving as an advocate for two clients. See *supra*. Many jurisdictions have retained this intermediary role and related restraints in a separate rule.

a. General Rule: A lawyer may act as intermediary between existing clients. The general conflict of interest rules still apply here since parties may have or develop adverse interests; the theoretical difference is that the lawyer is functioning as a counselor, not as an advocate. Examples include putting a transaction together for both a seller and a buyer, or representing two individuals in forming a corporation or partnership without any apparent adverse interest in sight. The lawyer seeks common ground between clients where both benefit rather than seeking to obtain an advantage for one party over the other.

(1) Consultation and Consent: The lawyer consults with each client concerning the implications of the common representation, including the advantages and risks involved and the effect on the attorney-client privilege. Each client must give written consent to the common representation.

(2) Client's Best Interests: The client's best interests control. The lawyer must reasonably believe the matter can be resolved on terms compatible with each client's best interests. This is an objective standard. The lawyer must also believe that each client will be able to make adequately informed decisions in the matter and there is little risk of material prejudice to any of the clients if the contemplated resolution is unsuccessful.

(3) Impartiality: The lawyer must also reasonably believe that the common representation can be undertaken impartially and without improper effect on other responsibilities the lawyer has to any of the clients.

(4) Attorney-Client Privilege: The prevailing view is that the evidentiary privilege and duty of confidentiality do not attach to communication with commonly represented clients as to one another. Both affected clients should be so advised in advance.

b. Withdrawal: A lawyer shall withdraw as intermediary if one of the clients so requests or any of the above conditions is no longer satisfied. Upon withdrawal, both clients receive Rule 1.9 prior client protections, and the lawyer cannot continue to represent any of the clients in any matter that was a subject of the intermediation.

3. Evaluation for Use by Third Party – MRPC 2.3:

a. Role: This is preparing an evaluation or opinion letter for the primary use of a third party. An example is a lawyer giving an opinion on a client's property title for a buyer or lender. Another is a corporate client planning to sponsor a public stock offering who wants its lawyer to author an opinion letter that states the corporation is current on all its state filings. Factual matters limited or excluded, or scope restrictions should be disclosed in the evaluation.

b. Two Requirements: The lawyer must reasonably believe that making the opinion letter evaluation is compatible with other aspects of the attorney-client relationship. If the evaluation may create adverse effects, the client must give informed consent. The consent to disclose confidential information and secrets in an evaluation may be oral.

c. Uncertainties: The attorney function is much like a CPA in an audit role. There is potential negligent misrepresentation liability to third parties who rely on the lawyer's evaluation and thereby suffer losses. Some jurisdictions authorize withdrawing a false evaluation relied upon by a third party. See also MRPC 1.6, 4.1, and 8.4(c).

4. Lawyer Serving as Third-Party Neutral – MRPC 2.4:
Lawyers serving non-clients as neutrals in mediation, arbitration, conciliation, or in a similar capacity must inform unrepresented parties that the lawyer is not representing them and it might be prudent to seek independent legal advice. A former neutral may not later become an advocate in the same or related dispute unless all the parties give full informed consent that is confirmed in writing. However, a partisan member of an arbitration panel is not prohibited from subsequently representing their party. [MRPC 1.12]

> **MPT Tip:** The treatment of subsequent representation of a party involved in a prior intermediary and neutral role is related to MRPC 1.9 prior client protections.

B. Advocate – TITLE 3

1. Meritorious Claims and Contentions – MRPC 3.1:

a. Civil Case: The required ethical basis in bringing or defending a civil lawsuit is that lawyers must present a non-frivolous good faith argument in support of their clients' positions. This is similar to Civil Rule 11, under which the court may impose sanctions when an attorney signs a pleading lacking minimal merit and upon notice does not promptly make correction. To avoid sanctions, Civil Rule 11 requires a "reasonable basis," while MRPC 3.1 requires a basis that is "not frivolous." The required ethical standard thus appears lower than the legal threshold.

(1) Not Frivolous: It is not frivolous to advance an action merely because the facts have not been fully substantiated, discovery is necessary to develop vital evidence, or it involves a new legal theory. The fact that the lawyer believes that the client's position ultimately will not prevail also does not necessarily mean a claim or defense is frivolous.

(2) Is Frivolous: The action is frivolous if the lawyer is unable to make a good faith argument for the extension, modification, or reversal of existing law. Also, if the claim was asserted merely to delay a trial or harass or maliciously injure the opposing party, it is frivolous. If the client insists on a frivolous position, the lawyer must withdraw. [MRPC 1.16]

b. Criminal Case: This standard is somewhat relaxed in a criminal case. A frivolous defense may be asserted at least to the extent it forces the state to prove every element required to prosecute the crime.

> **MPT Tip:** If the client insists on a frivolous position or extreme delay, the attorney must withdraw.

2. Expediting Litigation – MRPC 3.2: A plaintiff is entitled to obtain her day in court. Dilatory practices done with no intent besides delaying proceedings or harassing the opposing side are not allowed. Multiple postponements are to be avoided. Defendant counsel's dilatory actions must thus have some substantial purpose and rationale other than naked intent to delay.

> **MPT Tip:** This lawyer litigation violation is often combined with inadequate competency (1.1) and diligence (1.4). Try **DEC** – **d**iligence, **e**xpediting litigation, and **c**ompetency.

3. Candor Toward the Tribunal – MRPC 3.3: These restraints focus on the duty of utmost candor the lawyer owes the tribunal as an officer of the court.

a. False Statements of Law / Fact: A lawyer shall not knowingly make a false statement of law or material fact to a tribunal or fail to correct a previous false statement. Although the lawyer may not have personal knowledge of all factual matters, he should verify legal authority. For example, a lawyer cannot cite or quote a case for controlling authority when the case held to the contrary or was overruled. The lawyer may also refuse the client's request/demand to offer evidence that the lawyer reasonably believes to be false.

b. Facts Believed False: A lawyer may not offer evidence that the lawyer reasonably believes or actually knows to be false. It is also improper for a lawyer to facilitate a client or witness giving false testimony. This includes narrative answers the lawyer knows will be false such as asking, "What happened next?" The lawyer's duty is less clear if the client or a witness commits perjury when called by the opposing party since the lawyer is not "offering" anything.

c. Later Falsity Discovery: If the client or lawyer offers material evidence that later is discovered to have been false, the lawyer must take reasonable remedial measures.

(1) Persuade Client: The lawyer should first make reasonable efforts to persuade the client to consent to a curative disclosure procedure.

(2) Withdrawal: If the client refuses, the lawyer should seek to withdraw.

(3) Required Tribunal Disclosure: Disclosure of the falsity to the tribunal is required if the motion to withdraw is denied or the lawyer's withdrawal will not undo the effect of the false evidence.

d. Continuing to End of Proceeding: The duty to make disclosure to the court continues to the end of the proceeding, including the trial court appeal period. Thus, withdrawal does not necessarily terminate the duty to disclose to the court. If the lawyer first learns of the fraud after final judgment, the Rule 1.6 confidential duty precludes disclosure.

e. *Ex Parte* Proceeding: In some states, a lawyer may appear *ex parte* before a judge without the opposing party or his attorney present. The appearing lawyer shall inform the *ex parte* tribunal of all material facts reasonably necessary to make an informed decision, even if such facts are adverse to the lawyer's client. This enhanced duty of candor is necessary because the usual checks and balances of the adversarial process are missing.

> **MPT Tip:** Every exam has numerous questions focusing on the above restraints. In the end, the lawyer's duty as an officer of the court prevails over blind obedience to the client's cause.

4. Fairness to Opposing Party and Counsel – MRPC 3.4: These restraints focus on litigation discovery abuses and a lawyer's improper statements at trial.

a. Cannot Interfere with Evidence: A lawyer shall not unlawfully suppress or obstruct another party's pre-trial access to relevant evidence or participate in the altering, destroying (spoliation), or concealing of a document or physical instrument having potential evidentiary value. The duty to preserve evidence arises when the commencement of a relevant proceeding becomes reasonably foreseeable. A lawyer also may not counsel or assist another in doing such an act. There is no duty to disclose voluntarily the existence of evidence, only to preserve it.

b. Falsify Evidence or Witness Inducement: A lawyer shall not falsify evidence or counsel, assist, or induce a witness not to give relevant information, to testify falsely, or to flee the jurisdiction to avoid testifying. Subornation of perjury is the corrupt procurement of false testimony; this is also a crime in most jurisdictions.

> **MPT Tip:** The ethical dilemma between a lawyer's duty not to reveal client secrets (1.6) and the duty not to offer false testimony (3.4) is usually resolved in favor of candor to the court.

c. Witness Matters: Agents, employees, and relatives of clients may properly be instructed not to voluntarily give information to an opposing party or attorney unless formerly subpoenaed. Only payments of usual expenses, including loss of time, are proper for fact witnesses. In contrast, expert witnesses may be paid at a usual professional hourly rate. Neither type of witness may be paid on a contingent testimony or outcome basis.

d. Discovery Standards: In pretrial procedure, a lawyer shall not make a frivolous or unduly burdensome discovery request for facts or documents. A lawyer must also not frustrate the discovery rules and must reasonably comply with a legally proper discovery request propounded by an opposing party. Litigation sanctions may be imposed for discovery non-compliance and discipline referral is possible for repeated non-compliance.

e. At Trial:

(1) Improper Arguments: A lawyer shall not allude to any matter that is not relevant or that has not been or will not be supported by admissible evidence. Examples include mentioning the defendant's previous settlement offers to imply culpability or referring to the opposing party's enormous wealth in an attempt to inflame the jury.

(2) Closing Arguments: In summing up, a lawyer must not refer to evidence not introduced during the trial, including a criminal defendant's refusal to testify.

f. Personal Opinion During Trial: At trial, a lawyer may usually argue on the analysis of the evidence for or against any position or conclusion, but should not assert personal knowledge or related opinions on the facts, unless the lawyer is also a trial witness.

(1) Prohibited Statements: During trial, a lawyer shall not state a personal opinion as to the justness of a cause, credibility of a witness, culpability of a civil litigant, or the guilt or innocence of the accused. The lawyer should not use or imply the word "I," "me," or "we" during trial argument. An example is "Everyone in this courtroom believes the defendant is a liar and not credible." "Everyone" includes the lawyer, so this is improper.

(2) Witness Questions: A lawyer may not ask a witness questions that will draw answers that imply another witness was or was not credible. An example is, "Do you think witness B was testifying truthfully?" But in closing arguments, it would not be improper for a lawyer to sum up to the jury with "You saw in cross-examination that C was not truthful."

> **MPT Tip:** Watch for a lawyer using "I," "we," or "everyone here" in the closing argument, such as, "We all know that the defendant is guilty . . ." This goes beyond the scope of permissible evidentiary argumentation.

5. Impartiality and Decorum of the Tribunal – MRPC 3.5:

a. Improper Conduct: A lawyer ordinarily must obey the orders of the tribunal and shall not seek to illegally influence a judge, juror, or potential juror. Gifts or loans to judges are only allowed if permitted by state judicial conduct rules. Disruptive, harassing, or abusive or belligerent conduct in court is also prohibited.

b. *Ex Parte* Communications: *Ex parte* communications with the court or an actual or potential juror is ordinarily prohibited because the opposing party lawyer's position cannot be considered by the person receiving the communication. An exception applies if the lawyer's *ex parte* communication was purely procedural, such as inquiring about a scheduling matter. Even a lawyer not connected with a case must not discuss the matter with an impaneled juror. Post-trial communication with jurors in an attempt to prove juror impropriety is allowed unless it involves misrepresentation, coercion, duress, or harassment.

> **MPT Tip:** A lawyer's *ex parte* communications with the court or attempts to create judicial partiality in a question usually involves several violations of candor to the tribunal and fairness to opposing party and counsel.

6. Trial Publicity – MRPC 3.6:
Extrajudicial trial publicity by lawyers and prosecutors is restricted if it would be disseminated and materially prejudice the proceeding.

a. Prohibited Criminal Case Statements – TOPIC: Prohibited extrajudicial statements and comments by a lawyer that are too prejudicial and may impair selection of an impartial jury include the **TOPIC** subjects of:

(1) <u>T</u>est Results: The performance or results of any investigative test, such as a polygraph examination (lie detector test) or a lab test or failure to submit to such a test.

(2) Opinion of Guilt or Future Witness Testimony: Any opinion as to the guilt or innocence of any suspect or defendant, or the credibility or anticipated testimony of a prospective witness.

(3) Plea or Confession: The possibility of a guilty plea or the existence or contents of a confession, admission, or statement given by a suspect or defendant or that person's refusal or failure to make such a statement.

(4) Inadmissible Evidence: Information the lawyer knows or reasonably should know is likely to be inadmissible as evidence in a trial, such as prior convictions.

(5) Character: Statements about the character, credibility, reputation, or past criminal record of a witness, suspect, or defendant are generally prohibited (except for impeachment purposes in some circumstances).

> **MPT Tip:** The **TOPIC** prohibited extrajudicial statements made by a lawyer or their subordinate are heavily tested on the exam.

b. Permitted Disclosures: A lawyer's out-of-court statements should be limited to the general nature of the claim or defense, the procedural or scheduling status of the case, and public record information, including identities of designated witnesses. A lawyer also has a right to publicly rebut the prejudicial effect of negative publicity generated by another.

c. Safety Information: The public has a right to know about threats to its safety and measures aimed at assuring public security. A public prosecutor involved in a criminal case may state publicly that **IIPAW** – an **i**nvestigation is in progress, **i**dentify parties involved (if allowed by law), **p**ublic record information, request **a**ssistance in obtaining evidence and information, and **w**arn the public of danger concerning the behavior of a person of interest. There must be reason to believe there is a likelihood of substantial harm to an individual or to the public interest.

d. Civil Case Statements: A lawyer's statements that have a substantial likelihood of materially prejudicing an adjudicative proceeding are prohibited in civil matters. This usually involves a lawyer's discussion of inadmissible evidence or evidence of negative statements about an opposing party's character or credibility.

> **MPT Tip:** Any extrajudicial publicity by an attorney or their subordinates beyond IIPAW that could materially prejudice the proceeding deserves a full paragraph in your answer.

7. Lawyer as Witness – MRPC 3.7: The role of a trial partisan-advocate may conflict with that of an independent witness. Serving as a fact witness subject to cross-examination may also reduce the effectiveness of the lawyer's advocacy role.

a. Improper to Act as Advocate and Witness: A lawyer shall not act as advocate at a trial where the lawyer is likely to be a necessary witness concerning a material contested question of fact. Some states limit this prohibition to jury trials.

b. Exceptions: An attorney may be a witness and an advocate in the same matter if any **HULA** reason applies:

(1) Hardship on Client: A lawyer may testify when the evidence is otherwise unobtainable or the lawyer has been called by the opposing party. Another valid factor for the court to consider is whether disqualification of the lawyer as an advocate would work a substantial hardship on the client. Some states also require that the likelihood of the lawyer being a necessary witness was not reasonably foreseeable before trial.

(2) Uncontested or Formality: A lawyer may testify if the testimony relates to a minor factual issue that is not critical because either uncontested or a mere formality. An example is testifying as a witness to the execution of a will or a corporate document.

(3) Legal Services Rendered Value: A lawyer may testify if the testimony relates to the nature and value of legal services rendered in the case.

(4) Another Firm Lawyer Witness: Unlike the firm-wide disqualification provisions of MRPC 1.10, a lawyer is not disqualified as an advocate merely because another lawyer in the same firm is a witness unless the firm itself has a Rule 1.7 or 1.9 conflict.

8. Special Responsibilities of a Prosecutor – DASH PET - MRPC 3.8: A prosecutor in a criminal case has several elevated duties as the role turns from being an advocate of a private client to being an advocate of the public in the pursuit of justice.

a. Discovery on Lawyer: Prosecutors shall not subpoena a lawyer to secure client evidence in a grand jury or criminal proceeding. An exception allows such discovery on a lawyer if the evidence is not privileged, it is essential or extremely important, and there is no feasible alternative source. Lawyers assisting in client criminal activities may be at risk here.

b. Accused's Right to Counsel: Except for grand jury appearances, a prosecutor has a duty to advise the accused of the right to counsel and provide the opportunity to obtain a lawyer. The absence of *Miranda* warnings is usually grounds for reversal of a subsequent conviction based upon admissions made during unrepresented interrogation.

c. Supported by Probable Cause: A prosecutor cannot bring a charge or prosecute a criminal case that the prosecutor knows is not supported by probable cause. This includes being able to present believable evidence on every element of the offense.

d. Honor Pretrial Rights of Accused: The prosecutor has a duty to refrain from seeking a waiver of important pretrial rights from an unrepresented accused (rights against self-incrimination, waiver of preliminary hearing, or demand for jury trial).

e. Post-Conviction Duty: Prosecutors are required to take affirmative steps to remedy a clearly wrongful prior conviction. This corrective requirement applies if new credible legal or factual evidence later comes to light that clearly and convincingly creates substantial doubt about the fundamental fairness of the defendant's conviction. There must be reasonable grounds to now believe the person was innocent of committing the crime. A prosecutor must promptly disclose such information to an appropriate court or other authority. *Brady*. Some argue this puts prosecutor immunity at risk.

f. Extrajudicial Statements: The prosecutor shall not make prohibited extrajudicial statements and must supervise subordinates. Investigators, law enforcement personnel, employees, or other persons assisting or associated with the prosecutor in a criminal case likewise are prohibited from making extrajudicial statements that the prosecutor would be prohibited from making. (See also MRPC 3.6 *supra* at 6-427.)

g. Timely Disclosure of Exculpatory Evidence: The prosecutor must make timely disclosure to the defense of all material exculpatory evidence or information known to the prosecutor that tends to negate the guilt of the accused or tends to mitigate the severity of the offense. During sentencing, the prosecutor has a duty to disclose to the defense and the tribunal all unprivileged mitigating information known to the prosecutor. (*Brady*)

> **MPT Tip:** Look for fact patterns where the prosecutor over-reaches the scope of probable cause to bring charges, fails to preserve the defendant's right to counsel, fails to disclose to the defendant's attorney exculpatory or mitigating information, or fails to prevent subordinates from making inappropriate remarks.

9. Advocate in Nonadjudicative Proceeding – MRPC 3.9: A legislative or administrative tribunal or agency will likely give special weight to a lawyer's opinions on a question of law or rulemaking. If the lawyer is giving opinion testimony and simultaneously representing a client with an interest in the subject, disclosure of the attorney-client relationship is required. This permits the agency to make an assessment of any relevant biases of the lawyer. If the jurisdiction allows practicing lawyers to hold public office concurrently, they may not use their public positions to obtain special advantage that is clearly contrary to the public interest.

C. Transactions with Persons Other than Clients – TITLE 4

1. Truthfulness in Statements to Others – MRPC 4.1

a. False Statement: A lawyer shall not knowingly make a false statement of material fact or law to a third person in the course of representing a client that significantly influence the third party's decision. Third parties include opposing counsel. Misrepresentations can also occur by partially true but misleading statements. While a lawyer need not disclose all facts, material omissions that are the equivalent of affirmative false statements are improper. A lawyer's puffery to opposing counsel in representing estimates of price, value, or dollar settlement maximums are not usually considered statements of fact.

b. Duty to Disclose: There is also a duty to make disclosure of a material fact to a third party when disclosure is necessary to avoid assisting a client's criminal or fraudulent act. Most jurisdictions do not allow disclosures violating MRPC 1.6, but withdrawal may be required. Beyond withdrawal, a lawyer may have to disaffirm affirmatively documents she created that now appear to be fraudulent to avoid being deemed to have personally assisted.

c. Liabilities to Third Parties: Some jurisdictions, including California, have adopted a multi-factor test and held there is potential legal liability to unrepresented third parties if it is clear they will rely to their detriment on the lawyer's statements.

2. Communication with Persons Represented by Counsel – MRPC 4.2:
A lawyer shall not communicate with a person represented by another lawyer in the same matter unless that person's lawyer consents or direct communication is authorized by law or court order. If the lawyer is called or emailed directly by the opposing party, she should say, "I cannot talk to you directly; you need to talk to your own lawyer." Simultaneous communication, such as mailing a letter directed to both the opposing party and his lawyer, is still usually considered to be a violation.

a. Includes: Direct communications by a lawyer about the subject of the representation are prohibited. This might include a lawyer using an investigator to record conversations surreptitiously to obtain damaging admissions from a represented opposing party. If an organization such as a corporation is a party, the Rule protects all directors and employees with managerial responsibility and those personally involved in the wrongdoing.

b. Limited Representation: An opposing party with only limited representation is considered unrepresented unless the opposing lawyer knows of or has received a written notice of appearance. This means the lawyer may usually communicate directly with such a party. This Rule promotes filing a limited Notice of Appearance.

> **MPT Tip:** Opposing counsel must consent to communication with the opposing party. This absolute "no contact" rule applies even if the opposing party initiates the communication with the lawyer. Opposing parties themselves may directly communicate with each other.

3. Dealing with Unrepresented Person – MRPC 4.3: A lawyer shall not state or imply that the lawyer is disinterested to a person who is not represented by counsel.

a. Correct Any Misunderstanding: The lawyer shall make reasonable efforts to correct any misunderstanding the unrepresented person has of the lawyer's role in the matter. This rule suggests the lawyer must affirmatively state that (1) she is a lawyer, (2) who represents an identified opposing party, and (3) you should secure your own counsel.

b. Giving Legal Advice: A lawyer should avoid giving legal advice to an unrepresented party if that party is or may be adverse to a current client.

4. Respect for Rights of Third Person – MRPC 4.4: A lawyer shall treat people with civility and not use litigation tactics that have no substantial purpose other than to embarrass, delay, burden, or harass a third person who is not a party, such as a witness.

a. Depositions: Third parties may be compelled to give deposition testimony, but a lawyer should avoid subjects involving unwarranted intrusions. The lawyer may also not use methods to obtain evidence that are oppressive or violate the legal rights of third parties.

b. Receipt of Inadvertently Sent Documents: A lawyer may receive documents or e-mails that the lawyer knows were mistakenly sent to him by opposing parties or their lawyer. The lawyer must promptly notify the sender in order to permit him to consider initiating protective measures such as "claw back" procedures. The ABA comments suggest it is best to return such documents unread after a cursory review. The rule specifically excludes evidence provided by the client that the lawyer knows was wrongfully obtained. Using stolen information could become a complicit criminal offense by the lawyer.

V. LAW FIRMS, MARKETING, AND PROFESSIONAL INTEGRITY

A. Law Firms and Associations – TITLE 5

1. Responsibilities of Partners, Managers, and Supervisory Lawyer – MRPC 5.1: Law firms are not usually subject to professional discipline – only the involved lawyer(s).

a. Partner Responsibility: A partner or one with comparable managerial authority must ensure the organization has in place quality control policies and procedures that give reasonable assurance that all lawyers in the firm conform to the MRPCs.

b. Supervisory Lawyer Responsibility: A lawyer with direct supervisory authority over an associate lawyer must make reasonable efforts to ensure the associate conforms to the MRPCs. Whether a lawyer may be civilly vicariously liable for negligent supervision of another lawyer's conduct is not addressed in this ethical rule.

c. Responsibility for Associates' Acts: A supervisory lawyer is responsible if the lawyer directly orders improper conduct or, with knowledge of the specific improper conduct, ratifies the unethical conduct involved. If she knows of the conduct at a time when the consequences can be avoided or mitigated, she must take reasonable remedial action.

2. Responsibilities of a Subordinate Lawyer – MRPC 5.2:

a. General Rule: Even though a subordinate (associate) lawyer acts under the direction of another person, that associate lawyer is personally bound by the MRPCs.

b. Exception: A subordinate lawyer does not violate the MRPCs if she acts in accordance with a supervisory lawyer's ethical decision, and the question involved a reasonably arguable ethical issue. An example is whether the conflict provisions of MRPC 1.7(b) are put at risk by two different clients' interests that might foreseeably become adverse in the future. Another example is where an associate files a frivolous pleading at the direction of a partner, and reasonably relied on the supervisor's analysis of the relevant factual questions.

> **MPT Tip:** An associate's reliance on a supervising lawyer's decision is frequently tested.

3. Responsibilities Regarding Non-lawyer Assistants – MRPC 5.3:
Any lawyer with supervisory authority over non-lawyer employees (office managers, law school interns, paralegals, investigators, clerical, and accounting staff) must review their work, and the lawyer must always maintain a direct client relationship. If the non-lawyer was engaged in conduct that would be a violation of the MRPCs, the supervisory lawyer might be vicariously responsible. Liability applies if the lawyer orders or, with knowledge of the specific conduct, ratifies the conduct involved. The lawyer will be liable if he knows of the conduct at a time when its consequences can be avoided or mitigated, but fails to take reasonable remedial action.

> **MPT Tip:** ABA Opinion 1203 requires external reporting of clear ethical violations by lawyers in the firm. Simply "reporting up" within the law firm may be insufficient.

4. Professional Independence of a Lawyer – MRPC 5.4:

a. Improper to Share Fees with Non-Lawyer – MRPC 5.4(a): A lawyer or law firm shall not share legal fees with a non-lawyer. This is the principal deterrent to multi-disciplinary practice. Even splitting fees with a charity is disallowed. There are four **PEND** exceptions where fee sharing with non-lawyers is permitted.

(1) Purchase of Practice: Under a law firm purchase agreement, the ownership acquisition price may be paid to the seller, if alive. Similarly, payment to the estate of a deceased, disabled, or disappeared lawyer is authorized.

(2) Employee Payment Plans: A firm may include non-lawyer employees in a compensation or retirement plan. This exception is allowed even though the firm's compensation and retirement plan funding sources are ultimately derived from legal fees.

(3) Nonprofit Organization: Court-awarded legal fees may be shared with a nonprofit organization that employed, retained, or recommended the lawyer in the matter.

(4) Death or Disability of Lawyer: A firm or partner may pay the *pro-rata* law firm capital account benefits to a lawyer's estate or beneficiaries. Such death benefit payments may not extend beyond a reasonable period of time after the lawyer's death.

b. Non-Law Partnerships – MRPC 5.4(b): A lawyer shall not form a partnership with a non-lawyer if any of the activities of the partnership consist of the "practice of law." The "practice of law" is defined by the jurisdiction in question. The broadest definition is "the application of legal principles and judgments to resolve a problem or how to proceed under the law." This definition produces uncertainty as to whether the state could move against others, such as CPAs, financial planners, etc., for the unauthorized practice of law.

> **MPT Tip:** This is a common fact pattern on the Bar and easy to spot. To violate the rule, the business venture with the non-lawyer must be related to a legal matter.

c. Improper to Direct Lawyer's Professional Judgment – MRPC 5.4(c): A third party who employed, retained, or recommended a lawyer in a matter or pays the lawyer may not direct, regulate, or exercise influence over the lawyer's independent professional judgment. This issue arises on the exam if a third party "calls the shots." Examples include parents or insurance company that pay the lawyer's representation fee. There should not be any interference with the lawyer's independent professional judgment. The student should also review MRPC 1.8(f), No Fee Payment by Third Parties *supra* at 6-413.

> **MPT Tip:** This issue is likely to arise where a third party is paying the client's bills (such as a parent or insurance company) and the payer tries to interfere with the attorney's judgment.

d. No Non-Lawyer Owners or Corporate Officers – MRPC 5.4(d): A lawyer shall not practice law with a non-lawyer (or suspended lawyer). This applies if a non-lawyer owns any interest in the law firm or is a law firm corporate director or officer. A short-term exception allows a fiduciary representative of the estate of a deceased partner to own a nominal interest for a reasonable time during administration of the estate.

5. Unauthorized and Multi-jurisdictional Practice of Law – MRPC 5.5:

a. Unauthorized Practice: A lawyer may not assist a non-lawyer in the performance of any activity that constitutes the unauthorized practice of law, as defined by state law. Counseling with individual *pro se* parties is usually allowed but partnerships and corporations may not appear *pro se*. Delegation of legal work to non-lawyer assistants is allowed if the lawyer adequately supervises the details of the work and maintains a direct relationship with the client. Unauthorized practice usually includes engaging in the practice of law in a foreign state or while on inactive or suspended status. It also typically includes participating in the practice of law with an unadmitted, disbarred, or suspended lawyer.

b. Multi-jurisdiction Practice: A lawyer shall not practice law in a jurisdiction in which she is not admitted. This prohibition includes non-isolated transactions such as entering a formal court appearance, opening an office, holding out, or other systematic and continuous presence in the jurisdiction. Local admission may not be required for services provided on a temporary basis in a matter reasonably related to a controversy arising in the lawyer's home jurisdiction, or for mediation and arbitration proceedings in some states like California and New York. Most jurisdictions have *pro hac vice* (for a specific matter) admission in association with local counsel and permission of the tribunal. If the local rule is not met, the lawyer's home state licensing authority may also impose discipline for the unauthorized practice in another state.

6. Restrictions on Right to Practice – MRPC 5.6:

a. Non-compete Agreements: Entering into an employment agreement that restricts the rights of a lawyer to represent firm clients after leaving a law firm is improper. The client has the right to decide their own legal representation, and may switch lawyers or follow a lawyer to a new firm. A small exception is that a lawyer's non-compete agreement may be given in return for retirement benefits or the sale of a law practice.

b. No Further Representation Clause: A lawyer cannot make or sign an agreement not to represent her client or other persons or claims against the original adverse party in the future. A settlement agreement prohibiting the lawyer from bringing future suits against the same corporate defendant is contrary to the public interest. These pro-competitive restrictions apply even if the client urges the lawyer to agree to such a condition.

> **MPT Tip:** Two lawyers participating in an agreement prohibiting a lawyer from representing a client or bringing a different lawsuit against the opposing party are both acting improperly.

7. Responsibilities Regarding Law-related Services – MRPC 5.7:
A lawyer may engage in law-related ancillary services (such as accounting, tax preparation, title insurance, trust services, or financial planning), but all the MRPCs apply whether services are provided through the law firm or a separate entity. If the provider is a distinct separate entity, the customer must understand the services are not for legal representation. Disclosure must affirmatively be made that regular law firm protections, such as the attorney-client privilege and restrictions on conflicts of interest, do not apply and a waiver obtained. If the customer is also a law firm client, the conflict rules of MRPC 1.7 and transaction **TIC** rules of MRPC 1.8 may apply.

B. Public Service – TITLE 6

1. *Pro Bono Publico* Service – MRPC 6.1:
A lawyer should aspire to render *pro bono* public interest legal service and contribute to the community by serving people of limited means and charitable organizations at no charge or for a reduced fee. In most jurisdictions this is not mandatory, unlike accepting a court appointment; 50 hours per year is the ABA aspirational goal. *Pro Bono* representation may not violate the civil sanction provisions of Civil Rule 11 or any MRPCs, such as conflicts of interest with other clients.

> **MPT Tip:** *Pro bono* representation and public service is professionally aspirational, but it does not excuse a violation of the civil sanction of Civil Rule 11 or any MRPC, such as conflicts with the interests of other clients.

2. Accepting Appointments – MRPC 6.2:
A judge may appoint a lawyer to represent indigents and unpopular parties. The appointment should not be declined except for good cause. Good cause includes representation that would lead to likely violation of the MRPCs (including violation of MRPC 1.1 – competency requirements) or create an unreasonable financial burden on the lawyer. If the client or cause is so repugnant to the lawyer as to impair the client-lawyer relationship or the lawyer's ability to represent the client as an effective advocate, the appointment may also be declined. But mere unpopularity of the matter or disapproval by other clients is not usually considered good cause.

> **MPT Tip:** Financial burden must be extreme; just because a lawyer would not make as much money by taking the case, he/she is not excused from appointment. Likewise, repugnancy of the case must actually interfere with the attorney's ability to advocate for the client. Even the worst of offenders deserve some counsel.

3. Membership in Legal Services Organization – MRPC 6.3: Legal services organizations serve the public. A lawyer may serve as a director, officer, or member even if the organization serves persons whose interests are adverse to a client of the lawyer's firm. The lawyer must not knowingly participate in a decision or action of the organization if the decision or action would be incompatible with the conflict of interest rules.

4. Law Reform Activities Affecting Client Interests – MRPC 6.4: Participation in a law reform public-interest organization is acceptable even where reform measures may affect the interests of a client. If the lawyer learns that the interests of a client may be materially benefited by an organizational decision in which the lawyer participates, the lawyer must disclose that fact to the organization but need not identify the client. Note that there is no duty to disclose circumstances where a client may be hurt by the actions of the organization.

5. Nonprofit and Court-annexed Limited Representation – MRPC 6.5: This provision focuses on a lawyer sponsored by a nonprofit organization or appointed by a court to provide short-term legal services to a client without expectation of continuing representation. Examples are the completion of legal forms in a walk-in clinic or advice given on a hotline. The client must agree to the limited scope of representation and be informed if further assistance of counsel is desirable. The imputed firm-wide disqualification conflict of interest rules [MRPC 1.10] do not apply unless the lawyer has personal knowledge of a conflict.

C. Information About Legal Services – TITLE 7

1. Communications Concerning a Lawyer's Services – MRPC 7.1:

a. Includes: The Rule prohibits false and misleading communications or failure to disclose information that is necessary to make the statement not materially misleading.

b. Unjustified Expectations: The official ABA comments to MRPC 7.1 and 7.2 still require that advertising communications may not create unjustified expectations about results the lawyer can achieve. False achievement statistics, claims to experience, or statements of "influence with the tribunal" may create unjustified expectations and be a basis for discipline. Statements of prior law firm case dollar recoveries should include a disclaimer as to future awards and disclose that recovery depends on the merits of the individual case.

c. Comparisons: Any comparisons of the lawyer's services with other lawyers' services must be factually substantiated or otherwise verifiable. An example is, "We are the best tax lawyers in New York City"; such a marketing statement would be very difficult to verify factually. The burden is on the lawyer to show sufficient support for the statement.

> **MPT Tip:** False, misleading, or unverifiable marketing is improper. While advertising may not create unjustified expectations for potential clients, good taste is not directly required.

2. Advertising – MRPC 7.2: Commercial speech is usually protected by the 1st and 14th Amendments. (*Bates*) Still, narrowly drawn bar regulations such as a 30-day ban on mass-disaster blanket mailings are permitted.

a. Use of Public Media: A lawyer may advertise services through public media such as websites, radio, television, telephone directories, electronic search engines, blogs, yellow pages, legal directories, newspaper and other periodicals, and other electronic and written communications. Impersonation of a lawyer, client, celebrity spokesperson and/or depiction of accident scenes, injuries, or related are not allowed in many states.

b. Records of Advertisement Kept: Some jurisdictions require retention of a copy of an advertisement for two years after its last dissemination. This includes video, online, or television advertisements. The lawyer has the burden to show the basis of any factual claims advertised. Discussing the results of a past case requires that client's consent.

c. No Compensation for Recommendations or Referrals: A lawyer may not directly or indirectly compensate an individual or organization for recommending or referring a client, except a bar-approved, nonprofit referral service. A lawyer may pay to purchase a law practice or for reasonable costs of advertising. The payment of compensation to for-profit referral services, including paid online legal matching services, is not allowed in some states.

d. Name in Advertisement: In many jurisdictions, advertisements must include the name of at least one lawyer personally responsible for the advertising content. Client names and details of their cases may be advertised only with their prior express consent.

3. **Direct Solicitation of Prospective Clients – MRPC 7.3:** The concern is that the lawyer using in-person communications to solicit will overwhelm a potential client

a. Solicitation Breadth and ROFF Exceptions – MRPC 7.3(a): A lawyer may not directly solicit professional employment from a possible prospective client whether oral, in person face-to-face contact, live telephone, or real-time electronic communication. Such solicitation is permissible if directed to **ROFF** – **r**elatives, **o**ther lawyers, **f**ormer clients, or personal **f**riends with whom there was a prior personal or professional relationship.

(1) Examples: A lawyer may not solicit a stranger at a social event or use an agent, such as a "runner" or "capper," to pass out business cards at an accident scene or hospital emergency room. In comparison, setting up a booth at a street fair with signs stating "Legal questions answered" or answering phone or website inquires is not usually a violation since the lawyer waits for the potential client to approach and does not directly solicit.

> **MPT Tip:** Although direct, person-to-person solicitation is not allowed, blanket 'wide-net' mailings are permitted. Look for a lawyer – or their third-party agent – approaching a person who has just been injured at the accident scene, soliciting patients at hospital emergency rooms, or strangers at a social event.

(2) Referrals: A lawyer may agree to refer clients to another lawyer or non-lawyer professional in return for the undertaking of that person to refer back to the lawyer, as long as it is not exclusive and nothing of value is given. Reciprocal non-monetary referral agreements that are not exclusive (do not apply to any and all clients) and do not interfere with the lawyer's professional independent judgment are also usually permissible. The client must be informed of any allowable reciprocal referral agreement.

> **MPT Tip:** A lawyer giving reciprocal value as a *quid pro quo* for legal referrals is frequently tested. Is the relationship mutually exclusive?

b. Written Solicitation – MRPC 7.3(b) and (c): A lawyer's written offers to represent, such as sending solicitation letters to prospective clients who had a foreclosure action filed against them, are permissible (*Shapero*), but the envelope or email must state "advertising material." Targeting potential new clients who are in emotionally delicate circumstances is discouraged. a lawyer's response to information or internet inquiry requests are usually allowed.

4. Communication of Fields of Practice and Specialization – MRPC 7.4: A lawyer may communicate that she practices certain types of law and not others.

a. No "Specialists": A lawyer shall not state or imply that he is an approved specialist such as a "Tax Specialist Board Certified Attorney." Historical exceptions include "patent attorney" if the attorney is admitted to practice before the United States Patent and Trademark Office. A "Proctor in Admiralty" designation is also usually allowed.

b. Certification: A lawyer may refer to certifications, awards, or recognition she has been issued, as long as they are not misleading and identify the certifying organization. Included are a viable designation or earned award by a *bona fide* group that is authorized to issue such certifications. The ABA may also accredit the organization. An attorney-CPA may designate her dual credentials. (*Ibanez v. Florida*)

c. Additional Required Disclosure: Some jurisdictions require that the reference to acceptable credentials must state that the supreme court of the state does not recognize specialties in the practice of law or the credential. These disclaimers have been held unconstitutional. See *Hayes v. N.Y. Bar Grievance com.*, 672 F.3d 155 (2nd Cir., 2012)

> **MPT Tip:** The exam often combines advertising, solicitation, and specialization designation.

5. Firm Names and Letterheads – MRPC 7.5:

a. Trade Names: Trade names and web sites may be used in most jurisdictions by a law firm in private practice unless they are misleading, comparative, or imply a connection with a government related agency (*e.g.*, "New York City Legal Clinic" or "IRS Tax Law Firm") or charitable legal service organization (*e.g.*, "Community Legal Center").

(1) Misleading Prohibition: The law firm trade name and any web sites used by the law firm may not be misleading or communicate an unauthorized specialty designation. It is usually considered inherently misleading for a sole practitioner to use the term "and associates" in a firm's trade name if there are no associates in the firm.

(2) Former Partners: A law firm may use the names of deceased or retired partners in the firm name where there has been a continuing succession in the firm's identity.

b. Multiple Offices: A law firm with offices in multiple jurisdictions may use the same firm name on the individual offices' letterhead. If individual attorneys are listed on the letterhead, the jurisdictions in which they are admitted must be specified.

c. Holding Public Office: A lawyer holding a public office shall not use her name in the law firm trade name or in communications on its behalf during any substantial period when the lawyer is not actively and regularly practicing law with the firm.

d. Professional Organization v. Solo Practice: Lawyers practicing out of the same office who are not partners or shareholders of a professional corporation may not join their names together. Lawyers may state or imply that they practice in a partnership or other organization only when that is the fact. Solo separate letterheads, cards, pleading papers, etc. are required unless the lawyer is a partner, employee or "of counsel" to the firm.

> **MPT Tip:** The question of trade names or attorneys who share office space without having a formal partnership has appeared on the bar. The rule for sole practitioners is no joint holding out such as letterheads or business cards.

6. Improper Political Contributions – MRPC 7.6: Political contributions or solicitation of another's contributions by a lawyer is usually not improper. But if such contribution or solicitation is made for the purpose of obtaining assigned work or judicial appointment, it is not allowed. This rule prohibits only political contributions or solicitations that would not be made "but for" the consideration of an appointment or legal work.

D. Maintaining the Integrity of the Profession – TITLE 8

1. Bar Admission and Disciplinary Matters – MRPC 8.1: This communication rule addresses an applicant for admission to the bar or a lawyer in a disciplinary matter.

a. Admission Application: A lawyer's recommendation of an applicant for admission must be accurate and based on personal knowledge following a reasonable investigation as to the applicant's character, fitness, and qualifications. Any misstatements in an applicant's admission application must be corrected by a recommender because a lawyer must not assist an unfit or unqualified candidate in gaining admission.

b. Disciplinary Proceeding: All statements made by participants in any bar proceeding must be true and accurate, with full disclosure. Both an applicant and a lawyer must respond to all lawful state bar admission authority demands for information.

2. Judicial and Legal Officials – MRPC 8.2: The objective is to maintain public confidence in the legal system and the integrity of the involved jurists. A lawyer should defend judges and courts from unjust or uninformed criticism.

a. False or Reckless Statements: Lawyers must not make false or reckless statements about the qualifications, integrity, or record of a sitting judge, public legal officer, or candidate for election or appointment to a judicial or legal office.

b. Objectivity Required: A lawyer's candid opinions concerning a judge that are objective, factually accurate, and honest are allowed. A candidate for judicial office must comply with the Code of Judicial Conduct (CJC). A lawyer should defend judges and courts from unjust or uninformed criticism.

> **MPT Tip:** An attorney's outrageous untrue statements about the integrity of a judge are normally clear grounds for discipline.

3. Reporting Professional Misconduct – MRPC 8.3: Under the ABA Model Rules, a lawyer is required to ("shall" or "must") report serious ethical violations of another lawyer. Many jurisdictions reduce the required degree of reporting compliance (such as non-mandatory "should" or "may") to avoid personal antagonism between opposing counsels.

a. Knowledge of MRPC Violation: A lawyer with actual personal knowledge of a committed violation of the MRPCs by another attorney shall promptly inform the appropriate authority. The perceived violation must raise a substantial and clear question as to that individual's honesty, trustworthiness, or fitness as a lawyer. A failure to report a serious violation by another lawyer has led to discipline being imposed on the non-reporter. In addition, it is improper to threaten reporting as a bargaining chip in negotiating a settlement.

b. Knowledge of MCJC Violation: A lawyer with actual, personal knowledge of a judge's violation of the MCJC shall promptly inform the appropriate authority. Again, this is mandatory under the ABA Model Rules, not merely suggestive. The perceived violation must raise a substantial and clear question as to the judge's fitness for judicial office.

> **MPT Tip:** To raise the ethical violation reporting issue there must be at least two lawyers identified in the question's facts.

c. Appropriate Authority: If the matter is in litigation, the appropriate authority for a lawyer would usually be the trial judge. Otherwise it ordinarily would be the state lawyer disciplinary authority. For reporting a judge, it would be the Judicial Conduct Commission in the jurisdiction.

> **MPT Tip:** Some states also require self-reporting to the state bar under some circumstances.

d. CAD Exceptions: There are three **CAD** situations where reporting ethical misconduct by a lawyer or judge is not required. These exceptions include if the information to be reported is protected under the MRPC 1.6 duty of **c**onfidentiality to clients; if the information was received through an approved lawyers' or judges' **a**ssistance program; or if a lawyer is retained to **d**efend the attorney in question. Some states create another exception for a lawyer serving as a mediator in a fee dispute.

> **MPT Tip:** Judgment is required in applying the reporting obligation. The "substantial" requirement refers to questions about the lawyer's honesty, trustworthiness, or fitness. Knowledge of a clear violation by a lawyer goes beyond "mere suspicion."

4. Misconduct – MRPC 8.4: This catch-all category includes lawyers who:

a. Violate MRPCs: Violate or attempt to violate the MRPCs, knowingly assist or induce another to do the same, or do so through the acts of another, such as a legal assistant.

> **MPT Tip:** A lawyer may not use an agent to do indirectly that which a lawyer must not do.

b. Commit a Criminal Act: Commit a felonious criminal act or act of public moral turpitude and similar actions that reflects adversely on the lawyer's honesty, trustworthiness, or fitness as a lawyer to practice law.

(1) Included: Qualifying acts include violence (such as an unjustified assault and/or battery), "indifference to legal obligation," threatening witnesses, jurors, other lawyers, and judges, or other offenses relevant to the practice of law.

(2) Excluded: In comparison, matters of personal morality are usually insufficient standing alone. Examples could include a personal medical use of marijuana, act of marital infidelity, or similar offenses lacking a specific connection to fitness for the practice of law. Still, repeated occurrences of minor personal morality offenses may cumulate, thus elevating the level of misconduct and increasing the chances of professional discipline.

c. Engage in Dishonesty or Fraud: This includes engaging in conduct that clearly demonstrates intentional dishonesty, fraud, deceit, misrepresentation, breach of trust or fiduciary duty. This is not limited to the practice of law, and a criminal conviction is not necessary if the practice reflects adversely on the lawyer's fitness to practice law.

d. Conduct Prejudicial to Administration of Justice: This includes a significant expression of disrespect to or about a tribunal such as interrupting or arguing with a judge after a ruling. Rule Comment 3 makes it clear that conduct or statements in employment or while representing a client that manifest prejudice or bias on the basis of sex, race, age, creed, religion, color, national origin, disability, sexual orientation, or marital status are a potential violation if they are prejudicial to the administration of justice. Discriminatory peremptory juror challenges do not usually alone violate the rule.

e. Improperly Influence Government: A lawyer should not state or imply to a client or prospective client an ability to influence improperly a government agency, official, or tribunal. A statement promising to achieve results also is prohibited by the MRPCs.

f. Knowingly Assisting Judge in Violation: Knowingly assisting a judge or judicial officer in conduct that is a violation of applicable rules of judicial conduct or other law is prohibited.

g. Abuse of Public Position: Lawyers holding public office assume responsibilities beyond those of ordinary citizens. They may not use the public position to obtain special advantage for themselves or a client if such action is not in the public interest.

> **MPT Tip:** Many discrete MPRE offenses also qualify as MRPC 8.4 violations.

5. Disciplinary Authority – Choice of Law – MRPC 8.5: This rule addresses disciplinary power over lawyers in multi-jurisdiction practice.

a. Foreign Lawyer in State: This rule subjects a foreign lawyer admitted to appear under the *pro hac vice* rule to discipline by the local bar authority. *Pro hac vice* status usually requires the sponsorship of an attorney admitted in the jurisdiction. This temporary practice privilege usually is not available to persons who have failed the local bar exam.

b. Lawyer Outside State: Similarly, a state lawyer disciplinary authority may discipline a lawyer who is admitted even if the wrongful action occurred outside the licensing jurisdiction. If there are different rules between the licensing jurisdiction and the jurisdiction in which the violating effect of the conduct occurred, the latter jurisdiction's rules control.

c. Unlicensed Practice Practicality: Beyond the theoretical requirements, there is a practical problem for lawyers practicing in a jurisdiction where they are not admitted. *Birbrower v. Superior Ct. of Santa Clara County*, 17 Cal.4th 119, 70 Cal. Rptr.2d 304, 949 P.2d 1 (1998), held that a lawyer not admitted to the California state bar may be denied recovery of the legal fees charged a California client. This case involved a New York lawyer who made multiple visits to California to advise a California client on California law.

d. Federal Practice: In comparison, *Winterrowd v. American*, 556 F.3d 815, (9th Cir. 2009) allowed an Oregon lawyer to collect a fee from a California client when the Oregon lawyer was engaged by a California lawyer in a federal ERISA matter and there was never a state court appearance. At least on matters of federal law this opinion seems to approve a multi-jurisdictional partnership.

RIGOS PRIMER SERIES UBE REVIEW

MULTISTATE PERFORMANCE TEST REVIEW (MPT)

Index By Chapter

Chapter 1 – General MPT Information

Abbreviations in Answer 1-12
Admission Card 1-14
Approach to MPT 1-10
Answer Critiques 1-13
Cases 1-11
Citations 1-8
Combined Questions 1-9
Comfort in Exam 1-14
Confidence and Poise 1-15
Defensive Score 1-12
Effort Necessary 1-12
Ethics Issues 1-7, 1-9
Exam Concentration 1-14
Exam Details 1-4
File Contents 1-7, 1-11, 1-12
Grading System 1-6
Highlight Mark up in Analysis 1-10
Hotel Suggestion 1-14
Identification at Exam 1-14
Indexes 1-7
IRAC and CIRAC 1-12
Jurisdiction Setting 1-8
Library Contents 1-7, 1-11
Litigation Tasks 1-9
Mental Attitude 1-3
Mental Energy 1-14
Morning Performance 1-14
Myths and Facts 1-5
Objective Memoranda 1-9
Office Tasks 1-9
Organization Necessary 1-10
Outlining Answer 1-12
Persuasive Briefs 1-8
Persuasive Memoranda Trick 1-10
Pointer Memorandum 1-7
Practice Questions 1-12, 1-13
Precedent 1-8
Prior Questions 1-12, 1-13
Prior Exam Details 1-16
Professional Responsibility
    Issues 1-7, 1-9
Question Details 1-5
Question Source 1-6

Question Structure 1-7
Reading Tips 1-10
Red Herrings 1-10
Scoring 1-5
Seamless Process 1-3, 1-13
Skills Tested 1-6
Snacks in Exam 1-14
Spelling Error Correction 1-15
State Rules 1-6
Statutes 1-11
Study Tips 1-13
Task Memorandum 1-7, 1-10
Time Management 1-10, 1-11
Time Pressure 1-7
Transportation 1-14
Type or Handwrite 1-4
Type Size 1-4
Unusual Task 1-9
Working Questions 1-12
Writing Style and Format 1-12

Chapter 2 – Persuasive Briefs

Active Voice 2-21
Administrative Regulations 2-22
Analogizing Case Law 2-22
Analysis is Key 2-23
Answer Format 2-21
Approach 2-19
Case Law Application 2-22
Conflicting Case Law 2-22
Common Disguise 2-19
Distinguishing Case Law 2-22
Grading Structure 2-20
File Contents 2-19
Format Memorandum 2-20
Harmful Facts 2-21
Legislative Opinion Document 2-19
Library Contents 2-20
Older Authority 2-22
Opposing Counsel's Arguments ... 2-23
Other Sources of Law 2-23
Passive Voice 2-21
Point Headings 2-20, 2-21

Relevant Facts	2-21
Requirements	2-19, 2-20
Secondary Authority	2-23
Statement of Facts	2-21
Statutory Law Application	2-22
Structure of Question	2-19
Task Memorandum	2-19
Unfavorable Case Law	2-22
Viable Claim	2-20
Wording Opportunities	2-22
Working Practice Questions	2-32

Chapter 3 – Objective Memoranda

Answer Format	3-139
Balanced Analysis	3-138
Civil Case	3-137
Close Calls	3-140
Conclusion Necessary	3-140
Court Rules	3-139
Criminal Case	3-137
Differs from Persuasive Brief	3-138
Factual Differences	3-139
File Contents	3-137
IRAC Format	3-139
Library Contents	3-138
Memorandum Format	3-139
Modified CIRAC Approach	3-140
Objective of Task	3-137
Position of Neutrality	3-137
Precedential Value	3-139
Question Structure	3-137
Statutes	3-139
Task Memorandum	3-137
Unfavorable Case Law	3-139
Working Practice Questions	3-172

Chapter 4 – Office Tasks

Active Voice	4-242, 4-243
Actor Importance	4-243
Answer Format	4-241
Audience Focus	4-242
Author Signature	4-241
Clarity Importance	4-243
Client Letters	4-241
Conclusion Necessary	4-242
Drafting Explanation	4-243
Explaining Work Product	4-243
Facts	4-242
Law	4-242
Library Contents	4-221
Negative Facts	4-243
Objective Letters	4-242
Opinion Positions	4-242
Passive Voice	4-242
Persuasive Letters	4-242
Question Structure	4-241
Statute of Limitations Letter	4-242
Task Memorandum	4-251
Unfavorable Facts or Law	4-242
Wills	4-243
Wording Opportunities	4-243
Working Practice Questions	4-277

Chapter 5 – Litigation Tasks

Advocate Role	5-334
Answering the Question	5-334
Closing Argument	5-366
Dealing with Facts	5-334
Dealing with the Law	5-335
Facts	5-334
File Contents	5-333
Harmful Facts	5-334
Helpful Facts	5-334
Law Application	5-335, 5-336
Library Contents	5-334
Other Documents	5-334
Other Sources of Law	5-336
Pointer Memorandum	5-333
Pointer Memorandum Substitutes	5-333
Question Structure	5-333
Relevancy	5-334
Secondary Authority	5-334, 5-336
Statutes Analysis	5-336
Task Memorandum	5-333
Unfavorable Law	5-335
Wording Choices	5-335
Working Practice Questions	5-370

Chapter 6 – Professional Responsibility

See table	6-397

RIGOS PRIMER SERIES UBE REVIEW, MPT 2017 EDITION: COURSE EVALUATION FORM

Thank you for choosing Rigos Uniform Bar Review Series for your MPT review! We hope you feel that these materials have given you the tools and confidence to tackle the tasks tested on the Multistate Performance Test!

All members of our team – editors, instructors, graders, and students – are constantly striving to provide the best possible study materials to bar exam students. We want to hear from you! Please take a few minutes to fill out the form below and mail it back to us at 310 Sander Building, 4105 East Madison St., Seattle WA 98112, fax to 206-624-9320, or scan and email it to rigos@rigos.net. We will pay you $10.00 cash and your voice will be heard in the never-ending effort to improve this MPT Review. THANK YOU!

****

For each of the categories listed below, please rate **Rigos Bar Review Series MPT Review** on a scale of 1 to 5.

5 = Excellent   4 = Very Good   3 = Good   2 = Fair   1 = Poor

How do you rate the overall presentation of Rigos Bar Review Series?

Arrangement of Materials	5	4	3	2	1
Writing Style/Typography	5	4	3	2	1
Ease of Use	5	4	3	2	1
Professionalism	5	4	3	2	1

How do you rate the overall quality of the Rigos Bar Review Series materials?

Chapter Texts	5	4	3	2	1
MPT Tips	5	4	3	2	1
Practice Questions	5	4	3	2	1
Grading Guides	5	4	3	2	1
Sample Answers	5	4	3	2	1
Overall Accuracy	5	4	3	2	1

How do you rate the helpfulness of each component of Rigos Bar Review Series?

Chapter Texts	5	4	3	2	1
MPT Tips	5	4	3	2	1
Practice Questions	5	4	3	2	1
Grading Guides	5	4	3	2	1
Sample Answers	5	4	3	2	1

How well has Rigos Bar Review Series prepared you for each of the following aspects of the MPT?

MPT Skills Tested	5	4	3	2	1
Answer Format Suggestions	5	4	3	2	1
Time Management / Organization	5	4	3	2	1
Helpful Exam Tips	5	4	3	2	1
Common Exam Mistakes	5	4	3	2	1
Confidence Level	5	4	3	2	1

Continued on back of page

What is the likelihood that you would do each of the following?					
Recommend Rigos UBE Bar Review Series to others	5	4	3	2	1
Keep Rigos Bar Review Series for future reference	5	4	3	2	1
Use other Rigos products in the future	5	4	3	2	1

1. Did you read and study all of the text?
Yes _____ No _____

2. Did you work through all of the text's practice questions in this review book?
Yes _____ No _____

3. Did you enroll in the Rigos additional task grading and MPT improvement program?
Yes _____ No _____

If you felt that some chapters of the Rigos Bar Review Series MPT were better than others, rate them individually below:					
Introduction Information and Guidance	5	4	3	2	1
Persuasive Briefs Tasks	5	4	3	2	1
Objective Memoranda Tasks	5	4	3	2	1
General Office Tasks	5	4	3	2	1
Other Litigation Tasks	5	4	3	2	1

4. Did you work any additional practice questions (*e.g.*, those available from the NCBE or other vendor)?
Yes _____ No _____

5. Did you also take another review course for other parts of the bar exam? If so, which course?
Yes _____ No _____ Course _____ Portion _____

6. Did you pass the MPT?
Yes _____ No _____ Don't know yet _____

If you have any additional comments, critiques, praise, discussion of your experience and/or suggestions for improvements.

_____
_____

Please provide us the information below. It will allow us to send you $10.00, follow up on your suggestions for improvement, and thanks for your contributions.

NAME: _____ PHONE: _____ EMAIL: _____

LAW SCHOOL: _____ GRAD DATE: _____ ADDRESS: _____

Made in the USA
San Bernardino, CA
24 February 2018